Handel, Haydn,
and the
Viennese Classical Style

Studies in Musicology, No. 100

George J. Buelow, Series Editor

Professor of Music
Indiana University

Other Titles in This Series

Handel, Haydn, and the Viennese Classical Style

by
Jens Peter Larsen

translations by Ulrich Krämer

U·M·I Research Press

Ann Arbor / London

Produced and distributed by
UMI Research Press
an imprint of
University Microfilms Inc.
Ann Arbor, Michigan 48106

Library of Congress Cataloging in Publication Data

Larsen, Jens Peter, 1902-
   Handel, Haydn, and the Viennese classical style / by Jens Peter
Larsen.
   p. cm.—(Studies in musicology ; no. 100)
   Essays originally published 1935-1985; those originally in German
here published in English translations for the 1st time.
   Includes bibliographical references and index.
   ISBN 0-8357-1851-4 (alk. paper)
   1. Music—18th century—History and criticism.   2. Music—Austria—
Vienna—18th century—History and criticism.—3. Classicism in
music.   4. Handel, George Frideric, 1685-1759—Criticism and
interpretation.   5. Haydn, Joseph, 1732-1809—Criticism and
interpretation.   I. Title.   II. Series.
ML195.L13   1988
781.7436'13—dc19   88-1206
                                                                                        CIP

British Library CIP data is available.

Contents

Viennese Classical Style

Foreword

Jens Peter Larsen would perhaps enjoy a description of his career as toiling in the musical furrows of Baroque and Classic music, for he is himself an avid gardener. And just as he has had a lifelong passion for cultivating his two favorite flowers, roses and dahlias, so too much of his musicological achievement has been focused on two favorite composers, George Frideric Handel and Joseph Haydn, as well as on historical problems related to the concept of a Viennese classical style. And toil and cultivation it has been.

Larsen was among the earliest scholars to realize the importance of manuscript studies of various kinds to help determine accurate evidence for the dating of the compositional achievements of both Handel and Haydn. His studies began before the Second World War, before the conveniences of easy source study made possible through the now taken-for-granted processes of microfilming and photocopying. Through numerous travels to major libraries, before 1945 he had already achieved impressive results in his quest for greater and more detailed knowledge of manuscripts and manuscript traditions of the works of Haydn. Larsen's confrontation with Adolf Sandberger—who claimed to have discovered numerous previously unknown Haydn symphonies—brought Larsen fame as a Haydn scholar early in his career. This musicological disagreement also stimulated his own work, leading to the distinguished doctoral dissertation, *Die Haydn Überlieferung* (1939) and to a continuing study of Haydn source materials. Subsequently Larsen became general editor of the Haydn Society Edition (1949–51) and the Joseph-Haydn Institut, Cologne (1955–60). In 1975 he was the organizing chairman of the highly successful International Haydn Conference at the Kennedy Center in Washington, D.C.

Larsen's interests in Handel first became known through his major study of that composer's *Messiah* (1957), which focused on, among other aspects of the work, the first serious attempt to sort out and evaluate the numerous manuscript sources through an analysis of the handwriting of the copyists and other paleographical evidence. Here, as with his Haydn studies, Larsen laid the foundation for almost all future Handel research in the judging of the authenticity of Handel manuscripts. Numerous Handel studies followed, many of the important ones included in this volume. He became a member of the board of directors of the G.-F. Händel Gesellschaft (1955) and the council of the Göttingen Händel Gesellschaft (1972). Beyond his long cultivation of studies of these two composers, Larsen has also produced significant studies of Danish music and Mozart and a range of studies involving aspects of Viennese Classical music.

Larsen has been a frequent visitor to the United States, and a number of his articles have appeared in American music journals. But as one examines his enormously productive career (see, for example, the bibliography prepared in 1972 in *Festskrift Jens Peter Larsen* [Copenhagen, 1972]), it can be seen how little of his work is accessible to those unable to read German. Therefore it is especially important that the greater part of this volume is comprised of articles translated from German and published in English for the first time.

Jens Peter Larsen has celebrated four score and five years, and he remains a vigorous, productive scholar, currently preparing major studies of the origins of the Viennese symphonic tradition. His gentle ways and refined sense of humor, so much appreciated by his friends and colleagues, are balanced by a rock solid foundation of scholarship and a grasp of broad concepts of music history that have directed and nourished his entire career. And his career can serve as a model for all those who approach the study of music in history with his enthusiasm, scholarly exactitude, and reverence.

George J. Buelow
Indiana University

Preface

The present essays concentrate on three topics central to my scholarly work from my earliest years in musicology: Handel, Haydn, and the origin of the Viennese classical tradition. When, in 1928, I wrote my master's thesis (in Danish), "Haydn's Early Symphonies and Their Relationship to Previous Symphonic Art," the published music on which I had to base my work consisted of three primitively edited volumes of the old Haydn *Gesamt-Ausgabe,* and two volumes of the *Denkmäler der Tonkunst in Oesterreich,* which has an interesting, but rather limited and one-sided selection of works by Haydn's Austrian predecessors. A comprehensive search for sources, cataloging, collecting, and studying manuscript music scattered in numerous collections and archives, had to become central to all of my work. Certain developments in Haydn research in the 1930s forced me to give specific attention to the problem of authenticity in Haydn's music, resulting in my principal contribution to Haydn research: the *Haydn Überlieferung* (1939) and its companion, the edition of *Drei Haydn Kataloge* (1941). When World War II forced all traveling to a halt, I thought I could write a book about Handel's *Messiah* without any source investigation, using the well-established music text in Chrysander's collected edition, but I discovered I was wrong. After the war I had to make documentary manuscript studies an essential part of my work on Handel also.

Two other directions in my work need also to be emphasized. Being a former musician myself, and being privileged to have had close contacts with performers and performances, the many problems regarding performance practice became a special aspect of my interests and work. And through all of my work on eighteenth-century music there is a strong conviction, formed at a rather early stage: we can only hope to achieve insight into the problems of the music of former times if we are willing and able to forget our fixed (modern) textbook knowledge and to try to find our way to the spirit and expression, to the real traditions as revealed by the old music itself. I think some of my titles, such as "Changing Conceptions," and "Traditional Prejudices," may illustrate my goal. An examination and testing of the problems of "common knowledge" has been an essential feature of much of my work.

Permit me a few comments on the choice and relationships of the essays in each of the three parts of the present book.

Handel

The first essay, "Handel, the Great European," is a late (1985) survey of Handel's special position as one of the supreme artists of all times, one who appropriated several different styles for his personal use, making them part of *his* language. The second essay is completely different. Planned as an elaborate review of an important contribution to Handel research, it grew to become a brief general survey and evaluation of Handel sources and source problems. In the third essay a fundamental problem in our current approach to Handel is taken up: after a tradition of more than one hundred years of concentrating only on the oratorios, forgetting Handel's operas completely, the revival of his operas, beginning in 1920, has led to a completely unhistorical merger of opera and oratorio practice. The following essay (1986) is an extended and clarified statement of the problems surrounding this misinterpretation, not least in the way of performance practice. Next comes a short survey of the origin of Handel's English oratorio tradition, focusing on *Esther*. The last three essays are concerned with *Messiah* from three different points of view: the development leading to *Messiah,* the "changing conceptions" of this most famous oratorio in later times, and an examination—with bearing on performance practice—of the possibility of any real documentation of tempo variations in different periods.

Haydn

Like the Handel section, this one on Haydn is introduced by a late survey (Vienna Congress, 1982), partly regarding his works, partly regarding his personality. As opposed to some recent attempts to give Haydn status among Viennese literati, I found it necessary to stress his uncomplicated naturalness and pure musical genius. The next (early) essay takes up the question of "style periods" in Haydn's development. (I had already presented this concept of eight periods, in Swedish, in *Sohlman's Musik-Lexikon* [1950], and I used it later in similar articles in *MGG* and *The New Grove Dictionary.)* The following essay is one of my attempts to put a question mark to a statement repeated again and again without real evidence: that Haydn and Mozart really had a close contact like that of "Goethe and Schiller in Weimar." The essay on "Problems of Authenticity" compares authenticity problems in paintings and music. Special emphasis is placed on the need for authentic sources as evidence of authenticity in music, rather than stylistic evaluation—or even an evaluation of quality—which may give a strong conviction, but no decisive evidence. The next two essays (written for two quite different occasions) together outline a picture of the development of one of the most impressive genres in Haydn's work, with the peculiar contrast between the more casual tradition of Haydn's early and middle years, and the highly professional and self-conscious Mass tradition of his later years. The next essay deals with a problem common to much of Haydn's early music, the lack of dating, and sums up how various new findings in our time have brought an approximate dating of the early symphonies much closer. The last two essays—as a short flashback—give an impression of the development of Haydn research into a well-documented branch of musicology. The first one, "Haydn and *Das kleine Quartbuch*" (1935) was the first of a series of polemic articles (in *Acta musicologica,* 1935–37), starting out from a discussion of the source value of the *Quartbuch,* but above all, challenging alleged substantial findings of "unknown Haydn symphonies" (which never did turn up). The argument about these symphonies led to my comprehensive examination of the problems of authenticity concerning known and "unknown" Haydn works (*Die Haydn Überlieferung,* 1939). Since this book never has appeared in English, the essence of its principal achievements is found here in three selections: 1) part of the introduction, stating the principles for authenticity evaluation; 2) the chapter on the so-called *Entwurf Katalog* (draft catalog) that—as is indicated by its traditional designation—was supposed to have been made as a draft for the much quoted catalog of 1805. It can be shown, however, to be Haydn's personal catalog for his early years (in the main, ca. 1765–77), thereby gaining a unique importance for studies of his early works; 3) the conclusion, summing up the results of my examination of the authenticity question.

The Viennese Classical Tradition

After my early contact with the problem of the origins of the Viennese classical tradition, especially as manifest in Haydn's symphonies, it was not until the early and mid-1960s that I could pursue this, collecting an enlarged number of sources for this specific problem. My first attempt at a survey is the first essay in this section. Even if based on limited material, it did, I think, contribute a little to a more open view concerning the changeover from the Baroque to the Classical tradition. The next selection, my IMS Congress Lecture (Copenhagen, 1972), tries to elucidate the development of research on this problem, stressing again the need for broader resources for mid-century music. The next two focus on two basic problems in the search for the "roots" of the Viennese Classical tradition: the alleged importance of the so-called Mannheim School, and the problem of the so-called sonata form, in each case challenging traditional "common knowledge." The essay on traditional prejudices is still another example of the trend to a liberation from stereotyped concepts, discussing especially three problems: 1) the conception of the "Classical" style, 2) the problem of form in a work as a whole and in a single movement, and 3) some special features of period structure. The following short essay confronts the two conceptions of period style and generation style. In period style, as exemplified by Blume's well-known articles about Baroque, Classic, etc. in *MGG*, the point of departure is a general concept of a cultural epoch, which may or may not fit the musical development, whereas the generation style is a less specific but also less arbitrary conception. The last two essays are again, like the first one of this section, to be regarded as preliminary. The first one is a more general survey, whereas the second one focuses specifically on the development leading to the classical symphony. It may perhaps be a little difficult without relevant music examples to have a real impression of the development suggested through these short essays. But they must serve as preliminary representatives of rather comprehensive studies that I hope to be able to present in a finished form in due time.

I wish to thank Professor George J. Buelow warmly for suggesting this book, and for his help and advice in its preparation. Ulrich Krämer must also be thanked for his translations of my German essays.

Jens Peter Larsen
Charlottenlund, Denmark

Handel

1

Handel: The Great European

The question as to which nation may be credited with the honor of counting Handel among its countrymen may perhaps be considered of only secondary importance. Fortunately, Handel's art is at the disposal of all nations. However, with regard to the interpretation and the reception of his works, it is not unimportant which traditions contributed to and determined them. It is a fundamental precondition of his art that George Frideric Handel (1685–1759) candidly appropriated German, Italian, and English musical traditions and assimilated them into his own personal style.

Nevertheless, Handel's versatility was little perceived for a long time. Throughout the nineteenth century and even in the first decades of the twentieth but one facet of his creative genius was known and cultivated: the oratorios. Moreover, the way these were performed then was not based on Handel's own performance style, but rooted throughout in later continental, and especially German, traditions. The performing language was not the original English language, but German. The instrumentation was not the original, but furnished with many additional instruments. Most used was the "classical" Mozart arrangement, but other versions also appeared. In addition, the works were mostly performed by large choirs of "amateurs" rather than, as in Handel's performances, by small ones of professional singers from the church choirs. To be sure, nowadays there are still performances—even good ones—that are marked by the performing traditions briefly outlined above. But the development of Handel performances begun in the later nineteenth century has taken new directions.

The rediscovery of the operas was crucial for this development. In 1920 a young art historian from Göttingen, Oskar Hagen, had a vision of reviving Handel's operas, which for so long had been considered historical curiosities. In the summer of 1920 he brought about the "Göttingen Handel Renaissance" with a performance of the opera *Rodelinda*. And in a report about this performance,

Originally published in German in *Neue Zürcher Zeitung* no. 97 (27/28 April, 1985).

published in the *Zeitschrift für Musikwissenschaft* (September 1920), he introduced this Renaissance with almost prophetic words.

> If today of Michelangelo's works only the Medici's tomb sculptures, the dome of St. Peter, the *Last Judgment,* and the frescos of St. Paul's chapel, all creations from his last period, were accessible, whereas all the gifts to mankind from the most flowering and fertile years of this magnificent genius—first of all the ceiling paintings of the Sistine Chapel—had remained unknown and hidden from the eyes of the world by some kind of accident, should anybody in such a case have the right to prevent the prompt disclosure of the hidden treasures, maybe with the argument that Michelangelo was a sculptor by his profession and therefore his paintings were not entitled to further attention?
>
> One does not have to fantasize in order to imagine such an unheard of situation in music history: with regard to Handel it is a reality! The big crowd on the whole knows the artifacts of this powerful music dramatist only from his last twenty-five years: Those excellent works he had created between the ages of twenty-three and fifty-five, those, that is, by which he initially founded the international glory of German music for the first half of the eighteenth century, the creative productions of his most virile years—I mean that half a hundred operas—those works are entirely unknown. . . .

The impulses emanating from Göttingen stirred up a certain sensation and gave rise to further performances of Handel's operas. A real renaissance, however, did not come about during the years between the two world wars. Only after World War II did Handel's operas definitely break through, though they still did not find a place within the general repertory appropriate to their importance. For this the problems of performing baroque operas was too weighty, often quite prohibitive. But no longer are performances of Handel operas limited to the special centers of the Handel-cult, such as Göttingen, Halle, or London, but take place in many opera houses in Europe and in the United States. Moreover, many of his operas are now available on records.

The significance of the new era of Handel's operas for today's cultivation of his music in general is, however, not restricted to stage productions and recordings: the cultivation of his operas has also greatly influenced the performance of the oratorios. This is documented most obviously by the fact that many of the oratorios are presented in staged versions as operas. This practice is not, as is probably often assumed, a revival of old traditions, but rather a modern invention. Handel himself never performed his oratorios with scenery. Some of them may bear a staged production if one respects the fact that the scenic elements must be subordinate to the music. Unfortunately, all too often stage managers succeed in placing their contributions so much to the fore that the result is a strange hybrid having little in common with Handel's oratorios.

But the operatic style makes its influence felt even in oratorio performances in the concert hall. In the 1920s and 1930s the oratorio style from the beginning of the century had made way for an essentially altered performance tradition aiming primarily at a restoration of Handel's performing style. The instrumental additions were removed; the modern piano was replaced by a harpsichord; the choir more and more often was changed to a smaller choir with boys rather than women, and the massive effects, which were so characteristic for oratorio performances since the late eighteenth century, were reduced drastically. In many ways the style of performing the oratorios came close to the original performance style. Following the breakthrough of Handel's operas after 1950, however, a decisive change occurred, especially in one essential point: the vocal soloists have pursued and widely achieved an operalike function as "prima donnas." This becomes manifest most conspicuously in the interpolation of free ornamentation to the vocal melody similar to operatic practice, which for the oratorio can be justified neither historically nor musically.

Consequently, within a half-century the approach to Handel has turned from a one-sided commitment to the oratorio to a similarly one-sided commitment to the opera. Without any doubt, Hagen's pleading for a renaissance of Handel as a "powerful music dramatist" has been a success. It is deplorable, however, that the development has not led to a more comprehensive understanding, but only from one one-sided perception of Handel's music to another. The important rediscovery of Handel as dramatist has brought about a narrow conception of his music, especially of his oratorios, that has led astray the performance as well as the reception of this central group of works. An attempt will be made here to give an impression of Handel's multifariously changing course of development, which—although determined by his operatic activities to a large degree—cannot be comprehended and appreciated from this side of his creativity alone.

The striking difference between Handel's and Bach's activities often has been emphasized and is self-evident. Bach belonged to a family of which numerous members had for generations been active church musicians. They had been rooted in the long tradition of Protestant church music and had contributed greatly to carrying on this tradition. Handel, on the other hand, had no musical tradition as a point of departure. He had grown up in a home without music; and allegedly it was only the intervention of the Duke of Saxony-Weissenfels who induced Handel's father to give up his opposition to music lessons for his musically precocious son. Handel was given as teacher the excellent Halle organist Zachow, and thus was finally exposed to the tradition of church music. Very early, however, he became acquainted with another musical sphere of a peculiar attraction to him: the world of Italian opera. In some accounts published after his death are found references to early impressions of court music in Weissenfels and Berlin; they also mention his first encounters with the well-known Italian composers Bononcini and Attilio Ariosti, whom he would later meet again in London. These connections to Weissenfels and Berlin cannot be further documented; but even if they should in some details be imprecise, they probably conform to the main facts on the whole.

Handel was very young, certainly not older than eighteen, when he experienced this confrontation of two very different musical worlds. It is quite obvious that it was the world of opera that attracted him irresistibly. After one year as organist in Halle he left his hometown in order to enroll in this dream world in Hamburg, the only German city with a "free" opera (i.e., an opera not attached to a court). According to Mattheson, his friend of about the same age and also his rival in Hamburg, Handel was initially most at home in the church style when he got to the city. Hamburg was to him above all an intermediate station on his way to Italy, yet he learned a great deal there. Hamburg at that time, more than other German cities, was already an international city. In the sphere of opera there was in particular the especially gifted composer Reinhard Keiser, whose half-German, half-Italian melodic style could serve Handel as a model.

After about four years in Hamburg, Handel was able to set out for the promised land of Italy in order to complete his education as an opera composer. It might almost appear as if he had dedicated himself with body and soul to Italian music. This was not quite the case, although he benefited immensely from his encounter with the great Italian musical tradition and his close contact with composers such as Corelli and Scarlatti. Even though opera was his main concern, his adoption of Corelli's instrumental style was of no lesser significance. Choral works also belong to the first-rate achievements from his time in Italy. It is often believed that Handel became a great composer of choral music only in England, but this view cannot be upheld.

From Italy Handel went back to Germany, spending a short time in Hanover. But from 1711–12 until his death in 1759 with few interruptions he lived and composed in London. There, until about 1740, he composed mostly operas, but from 1740 on he wrote and performed almost exclusively oratorios, together with magnificent instrumental works and church compositions (Anthems, *Te Deum* settings and others). Very early Handel was acknowledged as the only truly great English composer of his time, and his work was still honored, so to speak, as a national relic almost throughout the nineteenth century. It must be noted in this regard, however, that only a small portion of his work was truly known, in particular, *one* work—*Messiah*.

Thus the traditional conception of Handel's style can be summarized as follows: The foundation of his musical development he owed to the German tradition of church music. This influence was pushed back so far during his years of apprenticeship in Italy that it was replaced by a new foundation: the Italian operatic style. This style prevailed for a long time in England as well. Only in his oratorios from about 1740 on did an English tradition come more to the fore.

From the beginning of our century, however, the English increasingly advanced a reevaluation of Handel's rank and significance as a national composer. Even though he adopted England as his country and became a citizen as early as 1727, he was refused acceptance as a true Englishman. Edward Dent, for example, writes in his essay "Englische Einflüsse bei Händel" (*Händel-Jahrbuch*

1929): "Handel never became a truly English composer. His ears remained insensitive to any inspiration that might have been drawn from the sound and rhythm of the English language."

From another aspect, Handel's moral integrity has been called in question. In 1906 appeared Sedley Taylor's book *The Indebtedness of Handel to Works by Other Composers*. With detailed documentation, Taylor pointed to extensive "borrowings" from the works of other composers in many compositions of Handel. At the end of his book he points a moralistic finger at Handel's practice: "As matters stand, the fact remains that he accepted, indeed practically claimed, merit for what he must have known was not his own work. That this was wrong can, it appears to me, be denied by those only who are prepared to estimate the morality of an act according to the amount of genius shown in performing it." The knowledge of Handel's "borrowings" was not new. Chrysander, the meritorious editor of Handel's works in the nineteenth century, supplemented his edition with six volumes of works by other composers Handel had "borrowed" from. New, however, was Taylor's Victorian approach, his tendency to consider Handel's practice primarily from a moralizing point of view. His verdict hardly attracted any followers, but a certain unease can still be sensed in Handel biographies as the authors dutifully devote some remarks to this problem.

Recent Handel research has again taken up the problem of the "borrowings," apparently devoting more attention to it. It is not the moral aspect, however, that now is of interest. Rather than Taylor, modern scholars prefer to cite Mattheson who said: "To borrow is a permissible matter. One only must repay one's debt with interest." (Handel certainly repaid a magnificent interest!) There are, however, other problems that need to be considered, three of which shall be outlined briefly here: the question of the origin and essence of the borrowings; the aiming at a complete recording of the cases; and—related to this—the discrimination of the different forms of utilizing the borrowed materials.

Handel's borrowing practice, his use of existing themes or parts of movements—from other composers, but also from his own earlier works—which are transformed or further developed, has many roots. The theater tradition may in Handel's case be considered the most prominent one. The inclusion of extraneous arias in an opera was a common practice, and also the so-called *pasticcios,* works pieced together from entirely unrelated compositions, enter Handel's operatic practice. We know of similar "borrowings" by other composers: Bach's adaptations of Vivaldi concertos are frequently cited counterparts. But Handel's case is unquestionably exceptional.

The recording of Handel's "borrowings" began already at the beginning of the nineteenth century: it was continued by Chrysander, Taylor, and others. In more recent Handel literature Winton Dean and Bernd Baselt have made essential additions to the list: most recently (1980/81) Bernd Baselt (Halle), Ellwood Derr (Ann Arbor, Michigan), and John H. Roberts (Berkeley, Calif.) presented independently three, by coincidence, simultaneously published essays, each of which dealt with Handel's extensive utilization of Telemann's *Harmonischer Gottesdienst*. In addition J. H. Roberts is preparing a new series of sources for Handel's borrowing practice.

Many listings of the "borrowings" make no attempt to distinguish between the different types of "borrowings," whether the incidental quotation of a few measures, the reworking of a longer period, or the rare instance of an unaltered adoption of an entire movement (parody). First steps toward a systematic description have been initiated, and a close study of the abundant materials is necessary. Whereas in earlier studies mostly negative reasons were put forward in order to explain Handel's borrowing practice—Taylor's moralistic criticism, disease, even lack of invention(!)—, future studies will presumably work out more positive reasons: his obvious delight in and his unique capacity for taking up and improving something already formed to make it something still superior.

Finally let us regard still a fourth aspect of Handel's "borrowings" that leads us back to the question of Handel's relation to the national musical styles. If one studies the available surveys of Handel's "borrowings," one finds many Italian, German, and even some Austrian, but no English composers whose music was used by Handel. It is quite natural that a direct line of relationships runs from the Hamburg operas to those composed in Italy, and from these to the Italian operas composed in England. Less easily explained is the fact that Handel repeatedly cites his Latin psalm settings from his years in Italy in his early English church music, but hardly any of his English predecessors. Moreover, most striking appears perhaps the fact that even the oratorios, which are commonly regarded as some sort of English national heritage, make use of all but English music. Handel's early English oratorios owe a great deal to his German Passion after Brockes; whereas the later ones borrow from Italian and German composers on a large scale, but apparently not from English composers. This does not, of course, imply that his work is completely devoid of any English influence, though it may perhaps seem to underscore Dent's disavowal.

Still, a striking and essential fact stands out: the "borrowings" in the oratorios come only exceptionally from operas, but mostly from church and instrumental compositions. The difference between the two traditions of opera and oratorios thus is confirmed by the "borrowings."

Handel spent almost fifty years in England, and of these more than thirty as an English citizen, and he was buried in Westminster Abbey. But his musical soul neither renounced his German origin nor the Italian way of expression that he had adopted in his youth in Italy. After half a century in England Handel still remained the great European.

2

Problems of the Handel Tradition

The object of these considerations was originally a review of the study *Händels Direktionspartituren ("Handexemplare")* by Hans Dieter Clausen, published in the series *Hamburger Beiträge zur Musikwissenschaft,* volume 7 (1972).[1] But for several reasons I found it desirable to go beyond a usual book review and to discuss the basic problems raised in the book in greater detail. The primary reason was the important and central topic of the book, combined with the consideration that the problems of the Handel tradition are very little known outside a small circle of Handel specialists. A second impulse came from the observation that the author tended a little too much to present his results as definitive in many cases in which a firm basis is lacking. The checking of details was only possible to a limited degree; nevertheless, it was largely responsible for the late appearance of my article.

All research dealing with the problem of Handel tradition has one important foundation in common: the very rich and still extant authentic source material of which, moreover, the majority is housed in a few libraries and collections, open to researchers. It is a remarkable fact that the works are handed down largely in the manner of great series, partly virtually complete, partly in selected collections. Two series are of primary importance: the extensive collection of Handel autographs, formerly in Buckingham Palace, now in the British Library, and the even more comprehensive set of so-called *"Handexemplare"* (conducting scores and harpsichord parts) in the Staats- und Universitätsbibliothek, Hamburg. (Some few volumes of each set have somehow been separated from the main body and are now parts of related collections.) Next to these there are some collections of secondary Handel sources that originate from Handel's copyist J. Chr. Smith (Schmidt), senior and a circle of co-workers, such as the two very comprehensive series in Cambridge (Barret-Lennard Collection, Fitzwilliam Museum) and Manchester (the main body of the former Aylesford Collection,

---

Originally published in German in *Die Musikforschung* 34 (1981), pp. 137–61.

formerly owned by Newman Flower, now in the Henry Watson Music Library), and two partial collections in the British Library (Granville Collection and the "Smith Collection").

A few remarks concerning the function and significance of the sources from one or the other of these collections may suffice here. After the completion of a work, Handel's autograph score was used by Smith (from the early 1720s on) to prepare a conducting score, in a few cases in collaboration with one of his assistants. In the course of time Handel entered corrections and alterations into this score that he used for all later performances as well. Thus this copy rather than the autograph score reflects the "last hand version" at all successive stages. With regard to a critical edition both manuscripts therefore have to be ranked as primary sources.

The other large sets of Handel manuscripts in London and Cambridge were not intended for use in performances, but for placement in private collections. In contrast to the smaller autograph and conducting scores (prevailingly in oblong *quarto* to fit the music stand on the harpsichord), they were mostly in larger or smaller folio size (to fit bookshelves). Only the manuscripts from the Aylesford Collection (at Manchester), originally made for Charles Jennens, are in oblong quarto size. Therefore one might conclude that they were made for performances as well, the more so since most of them are accompanied by instrumental parts. However, there is nothing about the scores and the parts that might hint at an actual use as performance material. We shall return to the significance of these many copies as authentic secondary sources after some general observations.

In most cases, investigations concerning the work tradition of a composer primarily have to deal with questions of authenticity and chronology in addition to questions of textual criticism. This is rarely the case with Handel. Questions of this kind may arise with regard to his early works, but we are so well informed about the works from his later years, especially the operas and oratorios, that questions of this kind will scarcely come up. However, there are two specific problems that more or less lead up to a study of the Handel tradition: the problem of the parody technique, periodically a very prominent impulse in his creative process (the "borrowings"), and the problem of alterations resulting from revivals of works in later seasons and under changed conditions.[2]

The questions arising from the parody or borrowing practice are concerned not only with the Handel tradition, but with the much more substantial tradition of all music that might serve as a model to Handel. A very characteristic example is the *Magnificat* allegedly composed by Erba, that Handel made use of extensively. The tradition of the work and the problems evolving from it was discussed in detail already by Chrysander. But in general the questions of tradition are not the main concern of studies devoted to the problems of this practice. Of basic importance is certainly the identification of the "models" used by Handel, but the decisive problems concern compositional and psychological questions: the manifold possibilities of reshaping preexisting material that obviously appealed quite specifically to Handel's creative genius.

The problem of changing versions—so-called *Mehrfassungen*—of Handel's works, on the other hand, is on both a large and small scale closely related to the specific Handel tradition. The revised forms of operas and oratorios may certainly to some extent be considered as revisions or improvements intended as such. By far the greatest part, however, were caused by changed performance conditions, in particular by the introduction of new vocal soloists. In some cases they may reflect Handel's reaction to a less favorable reception. The alterations occur in many different ways, such as cuts of entire recitatives and arias or parts of them; insertions of new arias, choruses, or instrumental movements; replacement of an aria by a different one; and, above all, in the alteration of an aria extending from a simple transposition to a thorough reshaping. How much the tradition of a major work is characterized by changing versions has to do with various circumstances, not least does it depend on the number of performances with a new cast. The changes were carried out in various ways. Generally they were entered into the conducting score *(Handexemplar);* here we find all kinds of alterations, such as crossings out, paste-overs, inserted arias, etc. The conducting score reflects the work in the version of the last performance for which it had been used, and furthermore to some extent gives us an idea of the preceding compositional developments. It must always be counted as a primary source, but one should not expect to obtain from it a complete picture of all stages of the work.

Through the confrontation of the two primary sources alone we are inevitably carried to the problem of changing versions in Handel's works. Reflected in the two manuscripts are two different stages of the work in question: its first conception and the version of the last performance that was based on this conducting score. Nevertheless we cannot simply speak of an original and final version. Apparently there was from the beginning a certain instability; it is scarcely possible to decide definitely how far the autograph reflects the version composed first or the version of the first performance. And similarly, we cannot state with absolute certainty whether the version handed down in the conducting score actually represents Handel's definitive version. Three uncertain factors are involved in our attempts at a clarification of the question of an authentic version of a given work: 1) the habitually changing form of a work in the case of successive revivals; 2) the uncertainty of assessing the documentary value of primary and secondary sources with regard to the question of changing versions; 3) the questionable relevancy of the methods of source appraisal that may serve an analysis of the sources in question. Our concluding question then must be how far it is possible to exceed mere hypotheses and assumptions and arrive at least at a clear distinction between knowledge and assumptions.

The Problem of Changing Versions

The conception of "changing versions of an artwork" is an ambiguous one. It can denote an evolutionary process, such as the development from the first version (draft) to the completed work and, at a later stage, to a revised final version. All these versions may be regarded as authentic, and it is actually a subjective decision of posterity to conceive one of them as the primary version. It may also occur—especially in the art of painting—that an artist, driven by a powerful creative urge, paints the same picture in ever-changing versions, again and again, as if he were obsessed by this specific motive. In this case we would scarcely speak of an evolution as in the first case, but rather of variations of a picture. Among Handel's changing versions both types occur: the new or final version resulting from a later reworking, and the variation characterized by the resumption of earlier material. The main type of Handel's changing versions, however, is determined not by the work itself, but by the performer. As mentioned above, the change of soloists at later performances was a main reason for alterations of the composition, such as transpositions, octave displacements of the entire vocal line, cuts, etc. These changes were common practice in Handel's time. They could sometimes amount to a reworking that stands out as an improvement, but often they just leave the impression of having essentially served practical purposes.

A major challenge to Handel research must be to identify the different stages of development within the substance of each work that exists in different versions. The aim is a purely objective one, even though the investigation itself and its results will not always remain quite objective. The purpose of the alterations can often be established quite objectively, especially if a manuscript indicates the singer for whom the new version had been made. The determination of the purposes of the different versions, however, is not indispensable in order to establish the different evolutionary stages of the composition. The extent to which changing versions occur within the tradition of a given work depends on various factors, such as the number of revivals and the changes of soloists. There are works that abound with altered versions, and others without any.

It must seem natural to ask whether it is possible to determine a "final version" of a work, a version that handel may have regarded, so to speak, as "definitive." But undoubtedly we shall have to reject this question quite generally. Everything we can deduce from Handel's practice seems to come down to the point that as a practitioner and pragmatist, he reserved for himself the right to include new versions, whenever he performed a composition anew after a certain period of time. To some degree it is possible to comprehend particular versions of an aria as concessions to a certain singer, occasional versions that he later gave up again. In many cases, however, we shall have to accept two different versions of an aria as equally valid, though perhaps respecting their different surroundings. In many cases, posterity established definite, unchangeable versions of Handel's works—especially of the oratorios—, whereas Handel's own performances were much less fixed, since he introduced new versions all the time. It is impossible to tell which version of a given work is the "best" or the "right" one. But which items can be determined as *authentic* versions must be considered a central question to Handel research.[3]

The Evaluation of Handel Sources

Since most of Handel's operas and oratorios are handed down in autograph as well as in the original conducting scores (CS), it might seem a rather easy task to bring about an absolutely convincing "original text" *(Urtext)*. However, as stressed above, this is not true with regard to many works, above all with respect to the problem of changing versions. That has to do with the function and the character of these two kinds of manuscripts.

A tradition of regarding an original manuscript as more or less identical with the work itself dates back to the age of Romanticism. Nevertheless, an autograph may have different functions and, correspondingly, a different character. To serve as a carrier of the creative message may well be regarded as its primary function, but it may also more or less directly suggest a function as a printer's copy. In Handel's case, however, its character is largely determined by its function as a basis not for a printed edition, but for an authorized fair copy, that took over the function to serve as the authentic version of the work in the practical performance. This influenced the character of both manuscripts. The autograph, which was frequently finished in an extremely short time, was not subject to later revisions, but left rather in the state of a self-contained first version; whereas the central position as primary source was taken over by the conducting score that had been copied from the autograph. This scarcely excludes that the autograph—besides the conducting score—may have been used sometimes as the direct source for further copies of the entire composition or, more likely, of separate sections. But since the changes in the works occasioned by later performances were normally entered into the CS, not into the autograph manuscript, it seems less likely that the autograph was used directly as the basis for copying at a later stage.

It is the merit of two of the foremost Handel scholars of the nineteenth century, Schoelcher and Chrysander, that the monumental series of conducting scores *(Hand-Exemplare)* was kept together almost completely for more than one hundred years, and is now in the *Staats- und Universitätsbibliothek Hamburg*. For Chrysander, this set served as primary source of his complete edition, even though, of course, he also extensively used (as far as possible) the Handel autographs, at that time deposited in Buckingham Palace. Unfortunately, he never accomplished a critical commentary or a critical catalog[4] that would have informed us about his use and evaluation of his sources. His unmistakable preference for the CS as a source has often been criticized, especially from English quarters, but Chrysander was right; an edition based entirely on the autographs would have left too many problems unsolved.

In my *Messiah* book[5] I have supplied a survey of the series of the *Hand-Exemplare* of Handel's works, with a short reference to size, watermark, and copyist of each CS. But Clausen's study (1972) is the first to present a detailed description and analysis of all CS's, serving as introduction to a catalog that in each case investigates the set-up of the score as to "original layers" and "insertions" and, by means of watermark registration, catalog the (often abundant) insertions; guided by a number of further criteria Clausen also attempts to establish the exact date of the changes within each work. We shall return to his methods and results later.

The CS's are the most important material for an investigation of the changing versions. For, as stressed already, in these scores new versions were entered which occasionally were made before the first performance, and otherwise in the course of the different performances. These alterations have been carried out in many different ways: in form of deletions or additions, in which case original and new version can continue to exist side by side; in form of paste-overs which often render difficult the identification of the alteration in question; or (even more radical) in form of an insertion of the new version and the removal of the earlier version, which makes an analysis of the development of the work impossible. The evaluation of a CS as a source for the analysis of the development of a work consequently leads to two essential questions: 1) to what degree can the intermediary stages of a composition still be recognized in the CS?, and 2) how likely does it seem that the final version within the respective CS can be regarded as actually definitive? The CS often supplies the means to help answer these questions: the indication of changing soloists as performers of a certain aria. (We shall return to this idea below.)

In addition to the conducting scores in the Hamburg collection there are—as suggested above—a great number of other copies that can be traced back to J.C. Smith and his assistants. Quite exceptionally—as in the case of the *Messiah* copy in Tenbury—we can meet an original performing score that somehow was separated from the other conducting scores. In most cases, however, we find copies made for amateurs, including the extensive series (Aylesford, Granville, Lennard, "Smith Collection"), and also many individual copies in the British Library and other libraries.[6] Compared to the autographs and CS's they must be considered secondary; with regard to the musical text they are generally of little importance. Concerning the question of changing versions, however, they certainly deserve greater attention. Occasionally the copies made for amateurs may contain, or corroborate a version that is either lacking completely, or only hinted at by a note of transposition in the CS. And even if they do not contain anything of that kind they may possibly help to answer questions about the changing versions in a work. At least this is the case with respect to *Messiah,* the only oratorio for which up to now an extensive compilation of the different versions in the primary and secondary authentic copies exists.[7] Notwithstanding small individual differences a distinct grouping of the sources can be made, reflecting in any case four different stages of performance (1742, 1743, 1745, 1749). The degree to which such a compilation might contribute a better understanding of the stages of development in other works still needs to be examined. Clausen himself stresses that such investigations are still lacking. Nevertheless, he ventures ("even though with some reservations") to advance several hypotheses disguised as facts which must be regarded as generalizations without sufficient basis. This is already true with respect to the introductory observation (made without reservation): "These collections only contain copies that were commissioned by the respective collectors, and therefore take into consideration the taste of the commissioners as to the selection of particular versions" (p. 3). There is hardly any foundation for this stressing of the "collector's wishes" (which are cited again several times in connection with the detailed description of such copies on pages 53–56). Nothing seems to suggest that the individual collector was able to order the version he wished, so to speak, from a menu. Watkins Shaw established a stemma of *Messiah,* in connection with an extensive comparison of the versions of the musical text. Based on a number of characteristic variants, he sorted out the copies dependent on and independent of the CS. This list has much to recommend it, especially that the continuation of the text variants proceeding from the CS irrefutably seems to establish their dependence upon it. But it may perhaps be questioned whether the connections between the manuscripts may have occurred a little less schematically.

To judge the Handel sources, both the CS and the mentioned secondary sources, it is absolutely essential to deal with the question of how we must imagine the origin of these many copies. There are, so to speak, three partners involved in this process: Handel, Smith, and a group of other copyists. Concerning their mutual relations within the process we only have indirect information and assumptions derived from the manuscripts themselves. It is, of course, a fact that Handel created the foundation of all subsequent copies, the autograph, often written in a very short time, almost as if in a single stroke. The autograph was delivered to Smith—perhaps in stages during the course of composition—who used them as the basis for the CS. In the great majority of cases Smith produced these alone, though in a few cases, especially in the early years, he worked with the help of an assistant. Many of the later alterations to the CS also stemmed from Smith himself. The secondary copies (notably the large series) were written by him and some few selected assistants (to whom we shall return): the Granville Collection by Smith and "S5," with only a few by "S1," the Lennard Collection chiefly by Smith, "S5," "S1," and "S9," the Aylesford Collection preponderantly by "S2," with the help of Smith and a few other copyists, and finally the "Smith Collection," prepared mainly by "S5" and "S10," with the help of Smith, "S11," and a few additional copyists. Of all these copies there are about fifty written by Smith, and approximately twenty by S1, fifty by S2, fifty by S5, and ten by S10. In addition, there are six copies by S9, and one to three each by S3, S4, S11, and S12.

No doubt, Smith, not Handel, must be regarded as the central figure of these extensive copying activities. He was responsible to Handel first of all for the making of the conducting score, for its revision by continuous entering of the later alterations, and, probably also for the making of performance material (although it is possible that this latter task—entirely or in part,—though certainly not including the harpsichord score—was performed by a group of copyists working for the orchestra or for the theater. Besides this activity, Smith also was treasurer of Handel's performances, as can be deduced from the still extant accounts of expenses on the occasion of the late *Messiah* performances in the Foundling Hospital Chapel.[8]

The manufacturing of secondary copies was carried out by Smith, probably not on behalf of Handel, but in agreement with him. During his early years in England he occasionally acted as publisher of Handel's works (Harpsichord Suites and *Radamisto,* 1720, and *Lotario,* 1730). As producer and retailer of Handel copies (written by himself and by others) his activities from the 1730s had some similarity with those of the approximately contemporary professional copying firms in Vienna, with the essential difference that the latter took pains to find as many clients as possible, whereas Smith appears to have been working for a very limited circle of connoisseurs.[9]

The following holds true for the copies managed by Smith: he could use the original authentic source material as his foundation; and he was informed about all the changes in the works better than anyone else. Due to the great variability of some performances, it frequently may have seemed questionable to him which form of the work he should pass on: Handel's original version, that of the first performance, the version from the latest performance, possibly with alterations that had been made with regard to certain soloists only, or perhaps a version without these purely opportunistic alterations, but which maintained the antici-pated remaining alterations. Perhaps we should follow this lead, and regard versions from the secondary copies in principle as versions edited by Smith in an attempt to eliminate the temporary concessions to the singers and to render the work in a version as purified as possible with regard to the time of the actual copy. As a working hypothesis serving a more extensive investigation of the source value of the secondary copies, this assumption might possibly contribute to a clarification of the problems of the changing versions. We must also visual-ize the copying process as making use not only of complete scores, but also (as needed) of separate aria manuscripts of variants that were present in Smith's stock of manuscripts. (In this case it will hardly make sense to try to establish a clear stemma.)

Printed editions also must be counted among the secondary sources. Here, too, we find occasional variants that can be conjectured as being authentic, though they are not found in the primary sources. But for several reasons the printed versions must generally be viewed with greater reservation than the secondary manuscript copies. They are not complete, and probably they were not revised or controlled by Handel or Smith, even though they (presumably) were produced from a source supplied by one of them. In new editions they are sometimes supplemented by some "additional songs" and thereby inform us of the introduction of new versions. However, they cannot be regarded as a primary source of information.

An important, though not unproblematic kind of sources are the librettos that accompanied Handel's performances. Winton Dean gives an extensive account of the libretto activities.[10] He stresses the care that was spent on the continued revisions of the text. "As a rule the most scrupulous care was taken to keep the librettos of Handel's London performances accurate and up to date. This applies particularly to insertions and deletions, less so to changes of setting; for instance, if an air were reset as a recitative the fact might not be indicated since the words were already in the text." Dean[11] gives a very characteristic example of such misleading information from the libretto of *Samson:* "Hamilton headed the last six lines of the oratorio ('Let the bright Seraphims . . . endless blaze of light') Grand Chorus, and Handel sketched 'Let the bright Seraphims' as a chorus. But when he composed the air, he forgot to alter the libretto. Tonson accordingly printed it as a chorus, and it appeared as such in all librettos until 1752." This example may suffice to demonstrate that librettos may not be considered first-rate sources with regard to the clarification of questions concerning changing versions. And we must always take into account the danger of an adherence to a version already abandoned in a libretto still in stock from previous performances. An extensive examination of the information that can be derived from the librettos must be counted among the urgent tasks of Handel research.

Methods and Tools for the Source Investigation

Various methods and forms of inquiry have been employed for the investigation of sources, aiming to establish, as objectively as possible, the changing stages of a work. Three areas of such investigations shall be discussed here, particularly: the paper qualities, the handwritings of the copyists, and the indications of soloists. In my book, *Handel's Messiah* (1957), I gave the first systematic analysis of the value of all three as means of Handel documentation. During the following years a number of studies devoted to a confirmation of these investigations appeared; the most recent and most extensive is the book by Clausen (1972) that especially expanded the study of paper qualities, and also made some contribution to the problem of the copyists.

Of these three special questions the one concerned with the paper qualities has gone through a particularly striking development. I made my listing of the Handel manuscripts in the British Museum (British Library), Fitzwilliam Museum (Lennard Collection), and in Hamburg chiefly in the years 1946–50, unfortunately just before the breakthrough of the modern research of watermarks in the studies of Heawood, Stevenson, and others (from 1950 on). Jan LaRue as early as in the report of the 1956 Viennese Mozart Congress (1958), and in the issue of *Acta musicologica* published for the New York Congress of the IMS[12] (1961) called attention to the effects of this research in the area of music. And Frederick Hudson demonstrated new methods with regard to Handel research in a paper in the 1959 Halle Congress report (1961).[13] With respect to one particular question James Hall contributed an essential piece of evidence. But only in his book could Clausen reap entirely the fruits of this development in his extensive description of the Hamburg collection. It is a strange fact, however, that—besides one reference to James Hall—this is done without any mention of the developments that had taken place in this area after 1950, only referring to the *Handbuch der Wasserzeichenkunde* by Karl Theodor Weiss (ed. by Wisso Weiss, 1962). In stating that my classification of the watermarks from before 1950 "is too broadly outlined for exact datings" and that it is "not suitable for a more exact dating of the papers" it might well have been appropriate to point out that the mentioned "broadness" is related to the simple fact that the more refined methods of watermark research only emerged after my study was finished, and thus were not available to me. That my classification of the watermarks nevertheless remains a pioneering work of complete validity and was even used by Clausen himself as a basis of his own classification is not to be seen anywhere in his discussion. Of course, the research by Heawood et al. means an invaluable enrichment of the possibilities of watermark research; and that Clausen made use of these achievements very skillfully, deserves full acknowledgment. Two discoveries of the modern watermark research (after about 1950) in particular contributed to the development of methods of paper investigation: the statement of the frequent change of the chain lines (taking place in short intervals, two to three years or so) used for the manufacturing of the paper, which may lead to a series of variants of the same basic mark; and the realization that two different marks belong together forming a fixed pair of watermarks. Without this refinement of methods, Clausen's chronological determinations simply would have been impossible.

The value of the information supplied by watermarks is limited by the fact that leftover sheets may well have been used later than the bulk of that particular paper. The possible use of leftover stocks of music paper is especially significant with regard to short insertions—precisely what we are most concerned with here. Therefore new datings, "based on the watermark,"[14] but contradicting other criteria calls for caution. A *terminus post quem,* but not a *terminus ante quem,* can often be established with some certainty through the evidence of watermarks.

Besides the registration of watermarks, Clausen's book successfully employs another kind of paper documentation: the establishment of the arrangement of sheets in the manuscripts,[15] the original manuscript's composition of "bifolios" (*"Binionen"* are folios folded twice into four leaves) and "folios" (*"Unios"* are folios folded once into two leaves), and the alterations caused by "insertions" (resulting in "gaps") or from deletion of leaves. In his catalog of the scores from the Hamburg collection Clausen supplies a survey of the arrangement of sheets for each work. For each act he lists the composition, the original layering ("U" stands for *Urbestand*) and the insertions ("E" stands for *Einfügungen*), followed by a list of watermarks that can be found in the U or E parts. A very extensive source investigation has been performed here, that undoubtedly will contribute to a separation of the insertions on an objective basis. However, I cannot quite free myself from the impression that this examination has to some extent been performed for its own sake. Its results may well be able to confirm findings gained by other means, but they can scarcely be regarded as the definitive solution they seemingly pretend to be, according to the arrangement of the catalog. To the questionable points may well be counted the length of the mentioned gaps; it is not to be seen how the precise indications of the length of the gaps have been determined.

In turning from the questions of paper qualities to the second of those cited problem areas, to the question of the copyists' handwritings, we shall be on less solid ground. We do not find here an entirely objective, systematic method of investigation, as in the case of watermarks, but we may well find a way to develop our power of distinction through a comparison of characteristic details. Based on a thoroughgoing familiarity with the handwritings in question—including extensive material for comparison—one frequently can establish the writer of a copy with approximate certainty. However, some interpretation will always be involved, even though the specialist will many times be able to make nearly infallible decisions. A pronounced expertise and a long and extensive familiarity with the material and its problems are needed if one is to be able to handle these questions with reasonable safety.

The problems of the Handel copies are related first of all to two circumstances: to the above-mentioned abundance of manuscripts from Handel's closest surroundings; and to the position and activities of Handel's leading collaborator in this area, John Christoph Smith (Johann Christoph Schmidt), senior.

The conception of Smith's role as manufacturer and distributor of copies went through a series of different stages. The basis of the information on Smith in the Handel literature is found in a short passage from the *Anecdotes of George*

Frederick Handel and John Christopher Smith:[16] "When Handel arrived at Ansbach in 1716, he [J. C. Smith] renewed an acquaintance which had commenced at Halle, and soon became so captivated with the great master's powers, that he left his wife and children in Germany, and accompanied Handel to England, where he regulated the expense of his public performance, and filled the office of treasurer with great exactness and fidelity." There is no mention of Smith's activities as copyist here, only of his function as Handel's "manager." The date of 1716, or of early 1717—if Smith "accompanied Handel to England"—has been taken up by most later biographers; Chrysander,[17] however, has him travel to England with Handel only "in the year of 1719," and this date is also given by James Hall in his article "Schmidt" in *MGG*,[18] in both cases without indication of source. Handel's travels to Germany in 1716/17 and 1719 make both dates appear as possible. The remark concerning the "renewed acquaintance" would fit a first meeting in 1716 and the joint travel of Schmidt and Handel after the second visit in 1719 very well, since the reference to an earlier meeting in Halle (as "university friends," according to Sasse's documentary evidence)[19]—by Chrysander and others—must be considered untenable. It would also seem much more likely that Handel, in connection with his preparations for grandiose new operatic enterprise, needed an assistant in 1719, rather than in 1716/17, when it seems difficult to see any reason for such an engagement. Real evidence of Smith's activities in London is found only in the editions of the harpsichord suites and *Radamisto* (1720) where he is cited as co-publisher.[20] Sasse's examination of the Ansbach sources, on the other hand, where Smith is registered as taxpayer until 1715 only, might point to the earlier date of 1716. We may therefore have to conclude with W. C. Smith that the time of his arrival in London is uncertain, "somewhere between 1716 and 1719."[21] It seems to be a fact, however, that he was invited by Handel as "manager" or "treasurer," and not as copyist.

The earlier Handel research accepted Smith's function as copyist as one part of his work as Handel's "amanuensis," but apparently did not really form an idea of the scope of the work, or of the possible distribution of the many copies among several hands. Chrysander in his preface to the first volume of his Handel edition, *Susannah* (dated "October 16th, 1858"), mentions as possessions of the Royal English family besides the autographs "the beautiful copies of the oratorios taken by Handel's amanuensis, John Christopher Smith"; it can be derived from the context that he refers to the so-called Smith Collection that was once in Smith's possession, only a small part of which, however, was written by him. Further, Chrysander refers to "the Handelian manuscripts, which, by some now-forgotten circumstance, came into the hands of Lord Fitzwilliam," that is: to the fragments in the Fitzwilliam Collection, not to the Lennard Collection. Finally, he reports of the collection of the *"Hand-Exemplare,"* that had just emerged at that time. They are referred to as conducting scores, and are traced back to Smith's descendants, but the question of copyists is not touched upon. Unfortunately Chrysander did not publish further critical reports of any importance in the later volumes. However, in the preface to the last volume of the Handel edition, *Messiah* (1902), there is a survey of sources by Seiffert who had finished the volume after Chrysander's death. Referring to Chrysander, he correctly states that the copy given to the Foundling Hospital after Handel's death was not written by Smith; on the other hand, he counts the so-called Goldschmidt copy—besides the two conducting scores—among the Smith copies, although it was made by two other prominent Handel copyists (S1 and S5). In the catalog of the music manuscripts in the British Museum, published a little later,[22] a number of manuscripts again appear that incorrectly—with or without reservation—are ascribed to Smith. As late as in the well-known Handel biography by Newman Flower[23] one can find a rather general summary, such as the following:[24] "The Smiths, father and son, appear to have made three copies of all Handel's music. A portion of one set is divided between the British Museum and the Fitzwilliam Museum at Cambridge; a number of copies of the second set, containing Handel's pencilled corrections, are at the Hamburg Museum. The third set, the most complete, was given to the first Earl of Aylesford by Jennens. . . . " The first of the three groups mentioned probably must be regarded as a combination of the "Smith Collection" and the "Lennard Collection," which together with the two other collections comprise more than 350 scores (conducting and harpsichord scores) in addition to a great number of parts. It is perhaps understandable that Newman Flower associated the senior Smith—maybe in order to facilitate his job?—with Smith junior as an assistant. However, there is no basis whatsoever for this assumption.

This account appears to be negated when Barclay Squire, in a short and sober summary in the preface to his catalog of the Royal Music Collection,[25] states:

It will probably be noticed that, in describing the various copies, no attempt has been made to ascribe them to either the elder or the younger Smith, as has been done somewhat arbitrarily in most catalogues of Handel manuscripts. It is impossible that the elder Smith can have written the enormous mass of copies with which he is usually credited, and a careful examination of the manuscripts in the Royal Music Library, and of the watermarks of the paper on which they are written, proves without doubt that they are the work of a number of copyists. As to the younger Smith, though it has been repeatedly stated that he acted as Handel's amanuensis, the matter seems very uncertain. The only accessible autograph of his—a score of his opera *Issipile* (Ad. MS. 31,700)—though the handwriting has some resemblance to a few MSS. in the Royal Collection, cannot be said to prove decisively that any of them is in the younger Smith's handwriting. In the absence of definite evidence it has therefore been thought best to omit any attempted identification.

When, during my studies of the problems of *Messiah*, the question of the changing versions became more pressing, the question of the copyists, too, became prominent; and I found it indispensable to attempt a classification of the many copies in order to help solve my problems. To begin with, I was mostly interested in sorting out the copies of Smith senior, and in checking the question of the activity or non-activity as a copyist by Smith junior. Little by little the appearance of a number of copyists assisting Smith—partly, it seems, for longer periods—became a primary question too. With regard to Smith junior I was able to confirm Barclay Squire's assumption quite definitely; occasionally he inserted a transposed aria or so, but he does not belong to the series of Handel copyists.[26]

A great number of copies by Smith himself could be proven to be "authentic," in Hamburg, in London, in Cambridge, and elsewhere. His activities covered a very long period, from his early years in England until after Handel's death.

> Surviving scores show his hand to be undoubtedly the dominating one, found in a very great number of copies and particularly in those used by Handel. That Smith is *the* Handel copyist is beyond dispute. The earliest of Smith's copies (from the period around 1720) reveal a slightly different picture from those made later. The handwriting is rather stiff and stylized, more "copyist-like" than the majority of his manuscripts, and the title-pages at the beginnings and ends of acts are often furnished with ornaments in the baroque manner (*Rinaldo* and *Pastor Fido* [R.M. 19.d.5 and e.4] and *Amadis* [Hamburg 191]). A number of manuscripts, apparently from the early 1720s (*Acis*, Chandos Anthems 2 and 4–11, and *Amadigi* [Tenbury MS. 885, 881–83 and 884], *Acis*, *Radamisto* and *Floridante* [Hamb. 185, 231 and 209] and *Muzio Scevola* [R.M. 19.c.8]), show Smith's hand to be on its way towards the form known from so many of his copies, as found in the working from about 1722 onwards (*Ottone, Flavio, Giul. Cesare* [Hamb. 225, 208 and 210] etc.).[27]

Three stages of Smith's handwriting are counted on here: an early style, marked by a certain stiffness, a second (transitional) style, and a third, definite style (with certain, but less conspicuous modifications through about forty years). The first two stages are found only until about 1721; from about 1722 on the style of Smith's handwriting is rather consistent, as can be seen in an abundance of manuscripts, manifesting itself in a number of characteristic details (shape of the clefs, of the notes, rests, etc.). We shall return to this question.

A still more comprehensive and difficult task was the tracking down and identification of the handwriting of Smith's assistants. Barclay Squire had stated that it was impossible that Smith could have produced all the copies generally ascribed to him, and that the manuscripts from the Royal collection must have originated from a number of different copyists. But there was no information concerning a collaborating group or assistants of Smith. Little by little, however, I was able to sort out from an immense mass of individual handwritings a more limited group. Two features characterized the copyists of this group: first, they wrote quite a number of copies, some of them so many that they must have been active as Handel copyists for a long time; and second, they worked closely with Smith, and to varying degrees can be proven to have collaborated with him directly. This is evidenced in various ways. For example there are copies that were divided up among Smith and certain copyists, either so that each wrote a separate part, or so that they alternated in writing several times during the process; there are a number of copies the musical text of which has been written by another copyist, and the words (entirely or in part) by Smith.

Of the sixty to seventy copyists that I had registered, I sorted out (after many deliberations) a group of thirteen copyists that I called the "Smith circle." I did not call them the "Handel circle," not only because this designation would not be sufficiently precise, but above all because they must undoubtedly be regarded as a circle of collaborators of Smith, and not of Handel. James Hall, who shed new light on the Smiths' circumstances of life, stressed that "the Smiths, as becomes evident from the wording of the testament that we found a short time ago, by no means were employees of the composer, but rather business friends who had employed copyists themselves in order to supplement their own work, as has been added by Sir Newman.[28] Undoubtedly, we must regard Smith as their principal, who also copied himself, but of whom the other copyists were employees. Smith was the one to whom Handel handed over his manuscripts for further treatment; the composer probably had little direct contact with the other copyists.

Among the copyists of the Smith circle were a few principal assistants who must have had a continuous connection with Smith for many years, especially those I have called S1, S2, and S5. Whereas Smith himself actually wrote about 130 volumes (and cooperated in many others to a smaller or larger extent), S5 copied more than sixty, S2 in any case fifty-five (plus many parts), and S1 at least twenty-five and, in addition, like Smith, cooperated in many others). As secondary copyists must be regarded: S3, S4, S9, S10, and S13, who copied five to ten volumes each, whereas S6, S8, S11, and S12 executed only one to three volumes each, and S7 wrote two sections (alternating with Smith), but (as the only one of the circle) not one complete volume alone. That other copyists, too, copied for Smith, but only more occasionally, is pointed out in the following statement: "In addition to these copyists we have defined as belonging to the Smith circle, the Handel copies in the collections examined reveal a large number of other copyists, who only on occasion copied for Handel, for Smith or for themselves."[29]

The time of activity of these co-workers as Handel copyists I specified as follows:[30] Smith ca. 1720 (?)–ca. 1760; S1 the 1730s and later; S2 the 1730s,[31] S3 and S4 approximately like S1 and S2; S5 the 1740s until well into the 1760s; S9 and S13 ca. 1760, and S10 1766–70; the other copyists (S6, S7, S8, S11, and S12) wrote so few copies that a dating doesn't say much; but in any case S11 seems to belong to the late copyists of the 1760s as well. It may perhaps surprise that some composers from the 1760s (not the primary copyists) are included here. This has to do with the fact that they must be considered not as Handel's, but as Smith's employees. After Handel's death (1759), there could, of course, not originate new authentic "changing versions" by Handel, but only changes in the Smith conducting scores. However, the copies made by the copyists' circle around Smith and, after his death in 1763, around his son John Christoph Smith junior must be placed before other copies or prints from the same time for two reasons: they still could dispose of Handel's own collection and, as in Handel's lifetime, of the experience of the best connoisseurs of Handel's performance traditions, the two J. C. Smiths.

The present classification and identification of the copyists of the Smith circle has been generally adopted by later Handel research as basis of the description of Handel manuscripts.[32] However, Clausen apparently wanted to appear as a reformer here, too. Unfortunately, his statements are rather misleading in several respects. He did not understand my basic classification or, at least, he misrepresented it: "Nevertheless, Larsen's classification of the copyists into those who worked by order of John Christopher Smith senior (sigla S1 to S12) and copyists of secondary importance (sigla according to the collections in which they have turned up) is inaccurate: for also Larsen's Hb 1 and Hb 2 collaborated closely with Smith, whereas this cannot be proven for S6, S8, and S13, and whereas it is unlikely for S10 and S12."[33]

My discussion of the individual copyists[34] clearly reveals that—as stressed above—only three copyists actually "collaborated closely with Smith" (S1, S2, and S5) whereas the others by order and under the direction of Smith—and even several years after his death under the direction of Smith junior—made copies to a varying extent on the basis of the conducting scores and the autographs. Clausen wants to consider Hb 2 as an example of a copyist who "collaborated closely with Smith." However, his collaboration with Smith according to our present knowledge is limited to the writing of the first seven pages of the harpsichord score of *Partenope* (ca. 1730); then he obviously was definitively dismissed! The difference between the copyists with the sigla S1–S13 and the others is in my presentation not an absolute one, as Clausen postulates; as stated above I used sigla according to libraries for those copyists "who only on occasion copied for Handel, for Smith or for themselves." To the Smith circle I counted only those copyists who copied to some greater extent and who, in most cases, carried out the copying of a number of volumes, but not those who—such as Hb 2 and other "Clausen copyists"—only occasionally wrote a few pages.

A number of such "emergency copyists," who occasionally contributed some few pages to be inserted into a copy written by others, serve as a basis to Clausen's setting up a new inventory of copyists: "A new investigation required by the present study revealed that further copyists beyond those established by Larsen cooperated in the writing of the *Hand-Exemplare* and their insertions. For these copyists, the designations H1 to H12 are introduced; for the others Larsen's sigla are adopted."[35] A survey of the cited copyists follows as appendix 2,[36] which reveals that there is only very limited evidence of the activities of these copyists; exact information is not given, and even in the main catalog of the conducting scores (pp. 91–248) it often can be found only by hard work or not at all. In addition it must be stated that their activities to a large degree had to do with the making of pasticcios or of harpsichord scores, and not of true Handel scores. A short survey will clarify this matter.

Quite on the outer edge are the following copyists: H2 (two pages in *Acis*); H4 (two pages in *Rodelinda* and one page in *Tamerlano;* in addition a few pages in *Elpidia*, a pasticcio with six or seven different writers); H5 (six pages in *Alessandro;* active in *Elpidia*, too); H7 (only pasticcio work in *Ormisda*); H10 (two pages in *Hercules*). To this list of "emergency copyists" could further be added a number of copyists who are not specified by sigla but only by a reference such as "a further writer" or something similar *(Belshazzar, Elpidia, Occasional Oratorio, Samson, Sosarme, Tolomeo).*

The following copyists deserve a little more attention (although they also must be regarded as emergency copyists): H6, identical with H9 (six pages in *Scipione*, one page in *Tolomeo*, four pages of the harpsichord score of *Ezio*, but in addition to that almost the entire harpsichord score of *Il parnasso in Festa*); H8 (102 pages of the harpsichord score of *Sosarme*); H11, identical with H12 (later insertions to *Solomon* [four pages], *Joseph* [two pages], *Saul* [two pages], *Theodora* [eleven pages], but especially eight insertions in the *Occasional Oratorio*, approximately sixty pages altogether).

Even stronger represented is Hb 1. He copied the third act of the CS of *Lotario* and essential parts of the harpsichord score of *Rinaldo;* in addition there are small supplements in his hand in *Tolomeo* (six pages) and in the harpsichord score of *Poro* (sixteen pages), and moreover he participated in the copying of pasticcios *(Lucio Papirio, Ormisda, Venceslao).* In some cases it might appear as if he had adopted the function of a "filler," that he carried out a complementary retouching, to make the musical text more readable in performance. This, however, still needs further examination.

The two remaining copyists, H1 and H3, take us back to a question mentioned before: how early did Smith begin to work as a copyist himself? As stated above, I had assumed three stages of Smith's handwriting in the early copies: a rather "baroque-like" one, a transitional stage, and the "mature" Smith from about 1722 on. As an example of the transitional style I showed a facsimile from *Radamisto*,[37] and altogether I regarded the parts written by the two copyists H1 and H3 (H1: *Radamisto, Muzio Scevola*, six pages of *Floridante*, and forty pages of *Tamerlano;* H3: *Acis* fol. 26–61 and fol. 81–228, forty pages of *Flavio*, and one page of *Floridante*) as evidence of the transitional style of Smith. Especially the hand of H1 is very similar to the one of Smith in many respects; peculiar to him is only the tendency toward an oblique direction of his writing, a sort of "italics," whereas H3 is more different from (the later) Smith. But I must now agree with Clausen that we are probably facing two secondary copyists here rather than early stages of Smith's handwriting. As for H3, this becomes evident in the alternation of the handwritings of Smith and of H3 in *Acis* (MA 996); with respect to H1, the last forty pages of *Tamerlano* in his hand are confronted by the preceding parts of the copy in Smith's hand. However, if the copies of *Radamisto* (1719/20) and *Muzio Scevola* (1720/21) stem from H1, and not from Smith, then the question must arise: when did Smith actually start to copy? And here one must be warned against Clausen's statements that tend to pretend a knowledge that we do not really have.

Clausen made up a new designation for some copies allegedly made by Smith of works from the time before he had come to England: *"Archiv-Partituren"* ("archive scores") *(Rinaldo, Amadigi, Il Pastor Fido, Acis);* concerning the copy of *Il Pastor Fido,* for example, Clausen states:[38] "Handel had this score written about 1717, shortly after J. C. Smith's arrival in England. The plans of the performance in 1733/34 reveal that at least until then he had kept it as his archive score." Here we are dealing with a dangerous tendency of Clausen's book. The reader will probably conclude from a statement such as this, that there is documentary evidence for the assumption that the copy in question was written by Smith in or about 1717 in England. As stated above, however, we do not even know whether Smith came to England as early as 1717 or only in 1719. Clausen's formulation is typical of the argumentation of his book: in very many cases a similar formulation is used, which seems to be a factual report, but actually is an *ad hoc* conclusion by the author, or, put in other words, in which a "thus was it" actually must be read as a "thus must it have occurred (in the author's opinion)." In spite of the exact information supplied by Clausen, we do not know when these copies (RM 19 d5, *Rinaldo;* RM 19 e4, *Il Pastor Fido;* and MA 1003, *Amadigi)* were written, and it may also be regarded as questionable by whom they were written. My earlier explanation—adopted by Clausen—that here we are facing an early stage of Smith, now seems to me to be barely tenable. It seems more likely that we are dealing with scores that actually were made before Smith appeared in London.

I should like here to refer to some information by Terence Best that he kindly made available to me some years ago. The collection of the Earl of Malmesbury among other things contains some early Handel copies from the possession of an Elizabeth Legh, and these copies also cite the names of copyists. Into a score of *Il Pastor Fido* is entered by her: "Elizabeth Legh 1716," and "Transcribed by Mr Newman, Febr 1715"; and in a score of *Teseo* is similarly stated: "Elizabeth Legh her book 1717," and "Transcribed by Mr Linike June 1717." In the Newman manuscript the same angular C clef is met with as in the "archive score" discussed above. I quote from the commentary of Mr. Best: "If Larsen and Clausen are correct in attributing to Smith these early MS copies with their various distinctive clefs and rests, then the Legh keyboard MS, pages 1–109, and the *Teseo* score are by Smith, whatever part Linike may have had in the latter. If these authorities are not right, then the 'early Smith' could be Linike." I believe this information makes it plausible to no longer regard these copies as early stages of Smith's copying work, but as the work of

English copyists; whether other copyists, in addition to those cited by Best, come into question, needs further investigation. We will probably end up with the conclusion that Smith, who first (presumably from 1719 on) was employed as "treasurer" and, occasionally, as publisher, started his activity as a copyist and eventually as principal of a circle of copyists, as late as 1721/22 (*Floridante*, second CS of *Radamisto*).

Let me briefly summarize. Unlike Clausen's painstaking and exact examination of paper qualities, his arrangement of twelve "new" copyists (and his remarks concerning the question of copyists altogether) seems to be somewhat misleading. In two instances he lists copies that clearly belong together as stemming from two different copyists. He only arrived at the number of twelve (ten) copyists allegedly "collaborating closely" with Smith by placing emergency copyists with a few pages of copy work side by side with the permanent copyists of Handel's (Smith's) with thousands of pages, and in accepting the work on the inferior pasticcio copies as of full value. It is strange, too, that whereas Clausen supplies exact information with regard to the arrangement of sheets of paper and the description of the watermarks, he prefers surprisingly imprecise formulations with respect to the specification of copyists, such as the following: "Sm, S1, and Hb1 in close collaboration," even in cases where Hb1's role is entirely subordinate if compared to Sm and S1, and easily could have been specified exactly (*Lucio Papirio, Venceslao*). A positive contribution to the question of the copyists, however, is the perception of the "italics" in some few copies from the time around 1720 as being the handwriting of an individual copyist (H1) rather than an early stage of Smith's handwriting. In connection with the information of Terence Best, cited above, this seems to suggest a changed conception of Smith's early activities, and to postpone the beginning of his copying activities until 1721/22.

As a third tool of the Handel documentation I mentioned the indications of soloists that can be found in many of Handel's conducting scores of oratorios and similar works. Similar indications may also be found in some autographs, although in a much more limited scope. These indications are often valuable as independent information or as verification of information from other sources. Nevertheless, certain limitations of their source value are quite evident: 1) If Handel himself places the name of a singer for a certain aria, then this indication alone will scarcely suffice to tell whether the singer in question actually sang the aria, or whether he was only taken into consideration for this job by Handel; 2) If a singer is mentioned who belonged to Handel's ensemble for many years, then it can be difficult to determine exactly when within this period the variant intended for him was performed; and 3) The indications of soloists were not entered by Handel alone, but also by Smith and by other copyists or users of the score. In that case it can be difficult to determine whether the entry stems from a performance from Handel's time, from the time of his blindness when he hardly was able to enter names himself, or from the time after his death. However, most problems of this kind have probably been solved.

In spite of these limitations an analysis of the indications of soloists may frequently supply valuable information. This is especially true of a work such as *Messiah* where arias are not bound to persons, but may be freely interchanged. We are dealing here with several soloists' ensembles that clearly stand out against each other, such as the ensemble of the first performance in Dublin in 1742, or the first London ensemble of 1743, and the ensemble of 1749 (except for a few singers who participated only temporarily). Thus it was possible to exactly fix the chronology of changes of different pieces by names of soloists alone.[39]

For a long time Handel research has been pursued only to a limited degree in the Federal Republic of Germany, all the more reason why Clausen's book must be welcomed as a comprehensive contribution to Handel documentation. That it has been accomplished with painstaking effort cannot be mistaken. Whereas his predecessors in as many pages discussed only a *single* work by Handel *(Messiah)*, Clausen in his catalog gives a documentary analysis of almost all of Handel's greater works. This certainly is a great achievement; and whoever entirely acquaints himself with the subtle system of Clausen's description will be able to gain a wealth of information from his catalog. But the longer one works with it, the more often the question comes up: how far can one rely on this information? Has it really been possible to scrutinize this wealth of details? Have they been derived from the relevant sources, and has a fundamental evaluation of the sources taken place?

As a primary problem of the investigation of the Handel tradition we pointed to the question of changing versions, meaning first the establishment of the changes of a composition in relation to the alternating performances, and second—based on this establishment—the (perhaps unsolvable) problem of a "definitive" version. For such an examination we do not turn to the autographs in the first place, but just to the conducting scores, Clausen's primary concern. However, it is his goal not simply to establish the information in the conducting scores. He actually wants to state the changing states of each work, and to achieve this he makes use of a number of other sources. The information gained by the examination of the arrangement of papers, of watermarks, of the handwritings of copyists, and of the indications of soloists in the CS, is supplemented by further indications, which—as far as the chronology of changing versions is concerned—are taken mostly from the librettos or from Winton Dean. In this connection, the librettos are generally considered as primary sources, in spite of their mostly rather unclear source value. Winton Dean is mostly accepted without reservation; yet occasionally Clausen opposes his statements.

No particular importance is attached to the secondary copies that played an essential role in the source investigations regarding the *Messiah* versions (Larsen, Shaw), Two entirely different characterizations of their special qualities are given. On the one hand, Clausen supposes that they were characterized by the taste of those who commissioned them,[40] and on the other hand he suggests that they were to some extent related to each other[41] and, otherwise determined by the "copyists' rule of thumb," allegedly always to copy the oldest of two or more versions.[42] As stressed above, neither the supposed influence of the orderer on the specific plan of a copy, nor the postulated "copyists' rule of thumb" seems to hold true. Clausen further states: "If a work were revised frequently, then hardly two of its copies correspond to each other. It seems impossible to ascertain whose directions the copyists followed in this case." However, this is certainly not true, either. As far as we are dealing with copies of Smith and his circle, it can scarcely be doubted that Smith gave the directions that were authoritative for the other copyists. Within the Handel tradition Smith must be regarded besides Handel—in some way even more than Handel—as a central figure. He did not need any rule of thumb, but he probably on principle considered those versions less important that were introduced as concessions to certain soloists, and this in many cases undoubtedly leads to an older version. The copies supervised by him—that is at least all (or most of) the copies of the large series (Aylesford, Granville, Lennard)—on the one hand must presumably be regarded as indirect reflections of the changing stages of a performance tradition, but on the other hand also as versions purified by Smith from "accidental" changes. As with the librettos, so also the secondary (authentic) copies must be critically scrutinized with regard to their source value, but their dating back to Smith and his collaborators undoubtedly makes them count among the essential sources.

In conclusion, let me once again caution against a dangerous tendency within Clausen's argumentation (to some extent perhaps a rather modish manifestation): against the obliteration of the borderline between fully evidenced knowledge and hypothetical conjecture. Many formulations must give the impression that established facts are presented here rather than suppositions and hypotheses. A few examples will suffice.

Besides the designation "archive score," mentioned above, Clausen invented yet another, similar expression: *"Ur-Handexemplar"* ("Pre-Conducting Score," or "PCS"). This term, too, cannot be recommended; on the one hand because CS normally refers to a copy that has been used for performance, and frequently can supply some information concerning the circumstances of the performance, whereas here we meet "first versions" that dropped out before the performance, and on the other hand because the term "conducting score" suggests a complete score, whereas the "pre-conducting score" only in one case *(Rinaldo)* refers to a complete score, while in the few other cases *(Ariodante, Floridante)* it refers only to a portion of the first act. Besides these three "pre-conducting scores" once more we are confronted by an alleged "pre-conducting score" *(Giulio Cesare)*. Based on two leaves in the CS, Clausen constructs a lost (complete?) CS:[43] "The CS was written on the basis of a PCS which, except two leaves (today bound as fol. 85 and 86 into the autograph of the opera), seems to be lost." He continues by speaking about a mixing up of the sheets in the PCS.

A most characteristic example of hasty and far-reaching conclusions from an insufficient amount of material is found in a description of Handel's working procedure derived from the autograph of *Samson*.[44]

> In this respect it is often useful to know that Handel arranged the composition of larger works as follows: At first he wrote only the text of the recitatives, and from the arias, duets, and choruses he wrote the bass and a vocal or instrumental melodic line; he then supplied the missing inner voices on the staves left out for this purpose, and finally he composed the recitatives. This order, of course, can only be perceived when unforeseen circumstances disturbed the normal progression of the work, such as, for example, in the autograph of *Samson*. For here Handel interrupted the composition because he had found out that he would not be able to perform the oratorio in the following season [Clausen's footnote: The invitation to Dublin must have reached him while he worked on *Samson* in September or October 1741]. When Handel, a year later, continued the composition. . . .

Here Clausen talks about a (seemingly) general Handelian working procedure involving the larger works. As the only piece of evidence *Samson* is cited. Allegedly, Handel should have interrupted the composition, because he obtained the invitation to Dublin while he was still working on it. But Handel had actually finished his work, noting at the end: *"Fine dell' oratorio. London. G. F. Handel. Octobr 29.1741."* When a year later he prepared its first performance, he introduced a number of alterations and expanded the concluding section. That is a typical Handel procedure, and it is misrepresented by Clausen's interpretation. Also the statement that he received the invitation to Dublin as late as then can hardly be true and is pure *ad hoc* conjecture ("the invitation must have reached him"). Since Horatio Townsend's account[45] the Irish have established that *Messiah* not only was first performed in Dublin, but also was composed for the respective charitable institutions in the town, as was stated first in an announcement in *Faulkner's Journal*, 1742. For these and other reasons, the negotiations between Handel and Dublin must date back to a earlier time, not as late as September/October 1741. That would certainly not have left him enough time to prepare the trip to Dublin that he set out for in early November. It may well be that the procedure of composition as described by Clausen is characteristic of Handel—to a larger or smaller extent—but neither does the one example, the special case of *Samson*, give a sufficient foundation, nor may the argumentation put forward be regarded as conclusive evidence.

Clausen's book is a remarkable contribution to the study of the Handel tradition. He worked through very extensive material and gathered a surprising wealth of information; and by this he certainly made a valuable contribution to the clarification of the changes of Handel's works. Yet it remains a fundamental weakness of his study that his hypotheses and conjectures are not marked as such clearly enough, but frequently create the impression of an unproblematic clarity, even though a secure foundation for them is lacking. This is primarily a book for Handel specialists, on the one hand because presumably they alone will take the pains to appropriate the subtle system of the catalog (and altogether to feel enthusiastic about the wealth of information), and on the other because a critical approach is needed for being able to discriminate between fact and conjecture. It can hardly be recommended as a handbook for nonspecialists.

Notes

1. (Hamburg: Karl Dieter Wagner, 1972).

2. Cf. S. Taylor, *The Indebtedness of Handel to Works by Other Composers* (1906; repr. New York: Da Capo Press, 1979, with preface by J.P. Larsen, "Reflections on Handel's Borrowing Practices").

3. Clausen completely misunderstood my intention in stating (p.38) that I undertook my *Messiah* studies "in order to ascertain the best of the versions that served as performing versions of the oratorio." My task primarily was a clarification of the development of the changing versions, as objectively as possible, and not an evaluation.

4. Clausen, p. 35.

5. J.P. Larsen, *Handel's Messiah* (1957), pp. 285–303.

6. Larsen, pp. 207–13, 285–303, 325; Clausen, pp. 54–56.

7. Larsen, pp. 246–47; W. Shaw, *A Textual and Historical Companion to Handel's "Messiah"* (1965), schedule A, p. 96.

8. Cf. facsimile, Larsen, pp. 260–61.

9. Cf. W. Shaw, p. 73.

10. W. Dean, *Handel's Dramatic Oratorios and Masques* (1959), pp. 95–101; cf. also M. Knapp, "Probleme der Edition von Händel's Opern," *Händel-Jahrbuch* (1967/68): 113–23.

11. Dean, pp. 347–48.

12. *Bericht über den internationalen musikwissenschaftlichen Kongress Wien, Mozartjahr 1956* (1958), pp. 318–23; *Acta musicologica* 33 (1961), pp. 120–46.

13. *Händel-Ehrung der Deutschen Demokratischen Republik, Konferenzbericht 1959* (1961), pp. 193–46.

14. Clausen, p. 173. Also his remarks concerning the chronology of the Lennard-Granville collection seem to be based too one-sidedly on the information of certain watermarks. If "almost all operas composed by Handel until then [1735] contained in it [the Lennard-Granville collection] are written on the same paper" (Clausen, p. 55), this may clearly point to the fact that the purchase of a larger stock of paper does not involve the simultaneous origination of all these copies; otherwise Smith and S1, beyond their additional duties, must have written at least twenty-four complete scores in a very short time only for this collection.

15. Clausen, pp. 40ff.

16. *Anecdotes of George Frederick Handel and John Christopher Smith* (1799; repr., New York: Da Capo Press, 1979), p. 37.

17. Chrysander, *G.F. Händel* 1 (1858), p. 455.

18. *MGG* 12 (1965), cols. 796–97.

19. K. Sasse, "Neue Daten zu Johann Christoph Schmidt," *Händel-Jahrbuch* (1957), pp. 115–25.

20. James Hall's record of his London apartments ("John Christopher Smith: His Residence in London," *Händel-Jahrbuch* [1957], pp. 133–37) is based on protocols that start as late as in 1722, and accordingly fail in our case.

21. W.C. Smith, *A Handelian Notebook* (1965), p. 32.

22. A. Hughes-Hughes, *A Catalogue of Manuscript Music in the British Museum* 1 (1906).

23. N. Flower, *George Frideric Handel. His Personality and His Times* (1923).

24. See p. 122, footnote.

25. British Museum, *Catalogue of the King's Music Library,* by W. Barclay Squire, Part 1: *The Handel Manuscripts* (1927).

26. The same, of course, is true with regard to Charles Jennens, the compiler of the *Messiah* text, although a fragment of a vocal score of *Messiah* could be attributed to him.

27. Larsen, pp. 262–63.

28. *Händel-Jahrbuch* (1957), p. 127.

29. Larsen, p. 273.

30. Larsen, p. 286.

31. Based on the Aylesford manuscripts that were not available to me then: at least until 1748.

32. Such as, for example, by W. Shaw, p. 54: "This classification deserves to become standard and I adopt it in Chapter III below with full acknowledgement."

33. Clausen, p. 47.

34. Larsen, pp. 262ff.

35. Clausen, p. 47.

36. Clausen, pp. 269–70.

37. Larsen, p. 308.

38. Clausen, p. 196.

39. Cf. Larsen, pp. 216–59; Shaw, pp. 109–21. Rather surprisingly, Clausen writes in this regard (p. 39): "Shaw's keys to the history of *Messiah* are the changes within the ensemble of the performances under the direction of the composer. It is based first of all on the names of the singers in the Conducting Score. His method could be adopted in the present study in similar cases." In contrast to this, I must point out that not only this "method," but also all the possible results of its employment with regard to the conducting score of *Messiah* in Tenbury can already be found in my *Messiah* book of 1957, not first in Shaw 1965. If Clausen read my book—and this probably must be assumed—he must have read it superficially.

40. Clausen, pp. 3, 54.

41. Clausen, p. 55.

42. Clausen, p. 56.

43. Clausen, p. 151.

44. Clausen, p. 68.

45. H. Townsend, *An Account of the Visit of Handel to Dublin* (1852), p. 29ff.

3

Oratorio versus Opera

With the last opera performances of the season 1740–41 Handel's long career as an opera composer came to a close and he may have been undecided as to where to turn from there. It is entirely possible that he thought of leaving London. He went to Dublin for the following season 1741–42, which included as a major event the first performance of *Messiah*. But by late summer he was back in London and remained there for the rest of his life. Instead of operas, he now produced oratorios. After a preamble in about 1720, he had started to experiment in 1732 by alternating between opera and oratorio performances. Now, however, oratorio performances no longer served as an alternate possibility; they took the place of opera completely although they were given in concert form, not staged.

After Handel's death, the original manner of performance was faithfully continued under John Christopher Smith, the younger, who had assisted Handel in presenting the oratorios during his last years when he was totally blind. But towards the end of the eighteenth century we encounter the rise of new Handelian performance traditions—radically different but of decisive influence throughout the nineteenth century and still in evidence in the twentieth. Finally, the overthrow of numerous old traditions after World War I led to a fresh evaluation of Handel's work, most importantly and prominently, a rediscovery of Handel's operas—the so-called Göttingen Handel Renaissance that began in 1920.

Even though the early performances in the "Göttingen Handel Renaissance," made possible through the enthusiasm of Oscar Hagen, were influenced to a great extent by Romantic music traditions, they succeeded in revealing a hitherto unknown Handel. The strong impression left by convincing performances of Handel's operas did not only lead to a revision of the widely held opinion that these works were hopelessly outdated antiques, it also led to a questioning of the foundations of traditional oratorio performance. From time to time during the 1920s, staged performances of oratorios were attempted, mostly in Germany *(Saul, Hercules, Theodora, Alexander Balus, Belshazzar);* and in

Reprinted from *American Choral Review* 14 (1972), pp. 42–48.

the 1930s this trend shifted to England *(Samson, Saul, Jephtha, Susanna, Athalia, Belshazzar, Hercules)*. Compared with the number of traditional oratorio performances, however, these staged performances remained exceptions; they were regarded as interesting experiments, but scarcely as a serious challenge to the established oratorio tradition.

Since World War II, performances of Handel oratorios in staged versions have increased considerably and there has been a general tendency towards obliterating the borderline between oratorio and opera. To quote just one example: in the summer of 1969 the oratorio *Susanna* was performed by the London Handel Opera Society in the course of the Göttingen Handel Festival in a staged version and presented without any reservation as an "Opera (sacred drama)." The roles of the two judges were presented almost as types from comic opera and there were many other surprising details. There is no reason to doubt that a good performance of this kind may bring the work in question closer to some people, just as a modernized Shakespeare performance or a Shakespeare film may convey to some of its viewers a new impression of *Hamlet*. But since a certain reservation towards the nineteenth-century oratorio tradition is bound to influence modern judgment, the staged performance might be accepted as a new norm—or even as a historically founded oratorio performance.

Some clarification is needed here. The oratorio performances of the past were in the main stamped by post-Handelian traditions, as we have pointed out. Does a modern operatic oratorio performance, therefore, bring us closer to the true Handelian spirit? Is the tendency towards identifying oratorio with opera founded on facts? Are we faced with something that comes close to historical truth or are we dealing with a misinterpretation of history? And one more question: How much does the interpretation of oratorio as disguised opera influence the actual musical performance? I would like to comment briefly on these questions.

The trend towards merging oratorio and opera and towards disregarding the differences between these two genres has appeared most noticeably in England in recent years. The bequest of the Victorian Age, by which *Messiah* is presented in the manner of devotional music, met with strong opposition, which in turn created a polemic attitude apt to obscure rather than to resolve the issues at hand. What is presented as fact is stamped by opposition to traditional views rather than by impartiality. I might quote one example: on the first page of Winton Dean's book, *Handel's Dramatic Oratorios and Masques*—undoubtedly one of the most brilliant contributions to Handel research in our time—the author makes the following statement: "At all periods—except perhaps the nineteenth century—some oratorios have been staged and others not." It is not made clear what should be regarded as the normal case and what as an exception. The reader will have to believe that either of these possibilities would be quite normal. Nevertheless, it would, in fact, be most difficult to find any staged oratorio performance at all until after Handel's time. The older liturgical drama was based on different traditions. The oratorio, as shown by its name, originated and developed in the prayer hall; it had no connection with the stage from its very beginning. "We now know that not a single oratorio in Italy before 1750 was acted. The only thing sometimes to be seen on a 'stage' was an altarpiece or a decoration, and, of course, the performers," says Ursula Kirkendale in her penetrating analysis of the Ruspoli Documents on Handel.[1]

Handel's own oratorio performances were never staged, even though they took place in the theater, serving as a concert hall. We are often told that Handel's first performances of *Acis and Galatea* and *Esther* around 1720 were staged, but this cannot, in fact, be true.[2] When he received the two works in 1732, the public announcement contained the specific statement: "There will be no action on the stage." Nevertheless, there is a certain difference in the text for the announcement of the two works. The announcement for *Esther*—billed as "The Sacred Story of Esther: an oratorio in English"—continues as follows: "but the house will be fitted up in a decent manner for the audience. The music to be disposed after the manner of the Coronation Service." In the announcement for *Acis and Galatea*—presented as a "Serenata"—the corresponding sentences read: "but the scene will represent, in a picturesque manner, a rural prospect, with rocks, groves, fountains and grottos; amongst which will be disposed a chorus of nymphs and shepherds, habits and every other decoration suited to the subject." Obviously neither of these two performances was staged, but the serenata *Acis and Galatea* did call for some scenic decoration and nymphs' and shepherds' choruses, whereas the oratorio *Esther* was presented strictly in concert performance, as we know from other sources, too. This became the tradition of Handel's own oratorio performance style for the rest of his life. Only in the case of *Messiah* were there some church performances aside from those given in the theater—those given in the Foundling Hospital Chapel for charity purposes. But these were also in concert style, without any suggestion of a liturgical function.

The difference between oratorio and opera as performed by Handel is, therefore, clearly expressed: an oratorio was always performed in the manner of a concert, but an opera performance involved a complete display of theatrical means and effects. That oratorio and opera were regarded as two separate categories was also underlined by the fact that oratorio performances were normally given on Wednesdays and Fridays in Lent when theatrical performances were traditionally prohibited.

The opinion that oratorio and opera should be regarded as equals is, of course, primarily based upon the premise that these two forms, after all, present dramatic action in a rather similar manner. But do they really? Undeniably, they have something in common, but if one compares the artificial intrigues of treacherous kings, jealous queens, sly villains, and spiteful rivals in the operas with the tragic fates of protagonists like Saul or Jephtha in the oratorios, one cannot possibly overlook the difference. Very soon after the establishment of Handel's oratorio performances in London, objections were raised against the use of the theater even though the performances were in concert form. This was scarcely mere prudishness but rather an expression of a clear understanding, even in Handel's time, of the essential distinction between the two art forms.

The difference was, of course, further stressed through the choice of language and the character of the text. Instead of Italian libretti, in which the text of individual arias had to establish above all a definite "affection" to which both composer and performer would be committed, English texts were now introduced, some of them taken directly from the Bible, others founded on stories from the Old Testament, or, in general, upon a "moral" idea. One might have some reservations about the "moral" interpretation of oratorio texts today, but one could not ignore it as an original tendency in oratorio. It has been suggested that Handel favored such tendencies to meet the taste of the growing English middle-class public. Whether or not this is true has to do with the history of English taste rather than with an appreciation of Handel's music.

The affinity of oratorio and opera rests mainly upon their fundamental construction—their predominant use of arias with connecting recitatives. But this affinity is not quite as unproblematic as we are usually told. A close comparison of the style of arias from oratorios and operas will reveal important differences. This has to do with the change of text and subject matter but it is also connected with the change of singers that took place in the course of the 1730s. This change has been described in a rather matter-of-fact manner by Sir John Hawkins in his *A General History of the Science and Practice of Music* (1776):

> Instead of airs that required the delicacy of Cuzzoni, or the volubility of Faustina to execute, he [Handel] hoped to please by songs, the beauties whereof were within the comprehension of less fastidious hearers than in general frequent the opera, namely, such as were adapted to a tenor voice, from the natural firmness and inflexibility whereof little more is ever expected than an articulate utterance of the words, and a just expression of the melody. . . . To such a performance the talents of a second-rate singer, and persons used to choir service was adequate.

Finally, a very clear distinction between Handel's oratorios and operas can be seen when we turn to the question of the use of the chorus. In the operas there are no choruses in the real sense but at most some ensembles that might suggest a choral texture. In the oratorios, however, the chorus plays a fundamental role. It might seem, therefore, that this feature alone would establish the difference between the two art forms. Yet in English opera before Handel's time, as in French opera of the same period, arias and choruses customarily stood side by side. This may account for the tendency among English scholars to relate

Handel's oratorio choruses to a specifically English tradition of dramatic music. The English scholar Edward J. Dent wrote in his essay on English influence in Handel's music (*Händel-Jahrbuch,* 1929): "Handel's treatment of the chorus was the most valuable thing he learned in England; its dramatic use did not derive from the English church but rather from the English theater."

No doubt there are some works, such as *Acis and Galatea* or *L'Allegro, il Penseroso ed il Moderato* in which traces of a specific English choral tradition can be found, but the richness and diversity of Handel's choral style cannot be explained as a result of his supposed contact with English dramatic practice alone. There are other influences—above all influences coming from church music, though not necessarily from English church music. Handel wrote magnificent church music even in the early years he spent in Italy and some of these works served as models for works he later wrote in England. One example is his fine psalm setting, *Laudate pueri* (1707), which he used in his *Utrecht Jubilate* (1713) and again in his anthem *O be joyful in the Lord* written a few years later. Another important source for his choral style was the German church music with which he grew up. His German heritage is still obvious in his Brockes-Passion (1716–17), from which he drew much material for his early English oratorios.

A comparison of choruses from Purcell's dramatic compositions—e.g., *King Arthur* or *The Fairy Queen*—with choruses from Handel's oratorios shows a basic difference in character. Purcell's choruses serve a purely dramatic purpose: they are relatively short, often rhythmically accentuated and dancelike, and in most cases homophonic or containing only slight suggestions of polyphony. They form a natural counterpart to the arias, most of them also short and, in fact, represent a continuation of an aria more often than a contrast to it.

Such connection of aria and chorus will also occasionally be found in Handel's works, e.g., in *L'Allegro,* but Handel's large, typical oratorio choruses are different. They are often written as fugues or in the manner of concerted movements and at times show a cantus firmus structure. Many of these choruses can be identified with the choral traditions of church music, with such models as the introductory cantus firmus setting for the psalm *Dixit Dominus* or the chorus "Tu es sacerdos in aeternum" from the same work, used again in revised form thirty years later in the famous chorus "He led them through the deep" from *Israel in Egypt.* Handel's *Coronation Anthems* of 1727 were used without any essential changes in *Esther* and *Deborah,* and his profound *Funeral Anthem* became, as we have noted, the first part of *Israel in Egypt,* the words being adapted, with slight changes, to a lament on the death of Joseph. But even many outstanding oratorio choruses that cannot be traced to specific anthems are unmistakably related to their style, whereas they have very little in common with the choruses in Purcell's operas. Such choruses serve neither as continuation nor as counterpart to the arias; they are entities in their own right—dramatic statements in themselves rather than mere accents of a dramatic continuity.

In summary, the Handelian oratorio cannot be made to fit into the world of opera; its individuality must be respected. oratorio was distinguished from opera from the outset and throughout Handel's career as a nonstaged genre performed only on certain days in Lent. The different character of its texts is reflected in a certain limitation of musical expression, as compared with opera, and a reduction of the amount of technical skill demanded of the singers. The latter fact is obviously connected with a new choice of soloists in Handel's oratorio performances.

The very important role of the chorus in Handel's oratorios marks another clear distinction between oratorio and opera. I have stressed the fact that Handel's extensive use of the chorus cannot be directly related to English opera traditions. These may have contributed towards an easier acceptance of the combination of arias and choruses in the oratorios, but we cannot speak of an actual influence. Not only do we lack any information as to how much Handel knew of these traditions—or if he was acquainted with them at all—but seventeenth-century music drama shows no affinity to the Handelian oratorio to begin with, least of all with regard to the use of the chorus.

Having arrived at the conclusion that staged performances of Handel's oratorios have nothing to do with Handel's own performance practice, we must regard them as experimental modernization—a "new look." If the question of staging had no bearing on the purely musical character of the performance, then we could stop here. The consequences of approaching oratorio as opera, however, are more far-reaching, especially because many conductors tend to deal with eighteenth-century opera from the point of view of nineteenth- or twentieth-century opera. They are apt to ignore the fundamental differences in pacing, sonority, orchestral volume, and other matters. The determining structural factor in Baroque opera—and in Baroque music in general—is the contrast of major units (e.g., arias and choruses), each founded in one particular expression—in Baroque terminology, the "affection"—which, in turn, is reflected in one specific sonority and one rhythmic motion. But a "modern" interpretation is apt to alter the basic character of Baroque music by a dynamically varied and accentuated performance in which everything—tempo, rhythmic motion, sonority, and volume—becomes a means of expression at the discretion of the conductor, as it would in the performance of a Romantic opera or a tone poem. This has to do with the fact that the performance of an oratorio is often no longer in the hands of the person who has carried out the task of preparing the work with the chorus from the beginning. Rather, it is turned over at the last moment to a harassed orchestral conductor who deals with it between rehearsals and performances of works by Beethoven, Wagner, Stravinsky, Schönberg, and Stockhausen. Thus, not only the borderline between oratorio and opera, but also between oratorio and modern orchestral repertoire, is vanishing.

Oratorio performance in our time is, therefore, continually confronted with new problems. The nineteenth-century tradition, with its semidevotional approach, vast choruses, and unavoidable "additional accompaniments," must be regarded as outdated. At the same time, the recent tendency to change oratorio into opera by dramatizing it, tampering with the steady quality of its rhythmic Baroque texture, and dissolving its melodies in modern pseudo-improvisation, must be regarded as equally invalid.

The true spirit of oratorio demands a performance that is sensitive but natural and direct, using a limited number of performers, preferably with boys' choir, and using soloists without prima donna attitudes (though, if possible, of prima donna qualifications!). Above all, it demands a quality of pacing devoid of "modern drive" and ambitious interpretative distortions but governed rather by an even rhythmic flow (almost comparable to that which one finds in a good jazz ensemble). Handel's music must be allowed to unfold on its own terms: simple in its greatness, great in its simplicity.

Notes

1. *Journal of the American Musicological Society*, Vol. XX (1967), p. 235.

2. Cf. p. 7.

4

G. F. Handel's Operas and Oratorios:
Form, Typology, and Performance Practice

Performing practice is related to traditions. Nowadays it is possible to preserve a performance tradition by means of tape or record. However, with regard to the performance of music from former times we face many problems that would be nonexistent for a contemporary of the music in question. We lack the immediate approach to this music, rooted in its foundations. We must attempt to enter into the spirit of the music and into the style of its performance as far as possible. Nevertheless, there are enough obstacles. A general difficulty, of course, is to free ourselves from the traditions of today, for example with regard to tempo conceptions. A similar difficulty is the unbiased interpretation of contemporary sources of performance practice from a certain period. An obvious danger is not the tendency toward an often far-reaching generalization, for example, of instructions or interpretations of an isolated text passage. All too often one neglects to ask, where, when, by and for whom this opinion or instruction has been recorded on paper.

This tendency toward generalization becomes immediately apparent in the frequently used term "baroque music." Again and again one can hear that "the baroque music" must be performed in this way or another, as if there were but *one* tradition of baroque performance practice. Everybody who has participated in a discussion of these questions will recall such assertions. The present discussion, too, will have to focus on the question of generalization. Since World War II an approximation, almost an assimilation, of the performance practice of Handel's oratorios and of his operas has occurred. Does such a far-reaching approximation actually make sense with respect to the relation of these two genres among Handel's oeuvre?

In order to compare the two main genres among Handel's oeuvre, opera and oratorio, and their performance traditions, I should first like to summarize the problems that must be discussed into three main questions: 1) Is the marked tendency of our time toward approximation, or even assimilation of operas and oratorios, and toward standardization of their performance practice, motivated by Handel's own traditions? 2) To what degree may the performances of operas and oratorios that we witness today be considered as relevant renditions in Handel's sense? 3) Must the character and original performance style of a composition be largely taken into account with regard to the performance of works of an earlier time—such as in our case of Handel's operas and oratorios? Or must a new arrangement of the composition—with respect to music, text, scenery—be regarded as equivalent or even superior to a traditional interpretation?

In these questions—and their answers—appear both objective and subjective aspects. Objective statements enable a clear answer to the first and, in part, to the second, but not to the third question; here only a subjective answer is possible.

As a starting point to our discussion, a short survey of the changing phases of Handel's activities as a composer of operas and oratorios must be given. I shall attempt not to simply review a historical development that is known to all of us, but primarily to outline the different types of operas and oratorios as they emerge in the course of this development, even if we must confine ourselves to suggestions. Throughout his life Handel was a great pragmatist. All too general conceptions of fixed types of *the* Handel opera and of *the* Handel oratorio must be opposed, even though there is not enough time to enter further into such discussion.

Handel familiarized himself with opera in Hamburg. Unlike other German operatic enterprises of the time, the Hamburg opera was not linked to a court. It was a free, public opera similar to the Venetian opera, and of a rather popular character. Musically, it was much different from the style of Handel's later operas. In Handel's first opera *Almira,* for example, there is only a harpsichord accompaniment to almost half of the arias. Fundamental to the style of the Hamburg opera around 1700, which in particular was determined by Reinhard Keiser, was the middle baroque Italian operatic style with Steffani as immediate model. In the instrumental pieces a French influence—transmitted already by Johann Sigmund Kusser—is prominent, thus this is true in the overture which also in Handel's operas largely remains the classical French overture. But also the refined tradition of the German solo song seems to assert itself in Keiser's operas, and similarly in Handel's *Almira,* in arias of great simplicity and immediacy.

Here a singular feature must be stressed that became very significant for Handel's oeuvre: his frequent reuse or recreation of a preexistent musical material, taken either from his own compositions, or—very frequently—from the works of another composer. As a "principle of parody" a similar way of composing was common practice long before Handel, and there are examples by other composers of his time as well. Bach's concertos after Vivaldi (and others) often have been cited as counterparts. Nevertheless, such a systematic and extensive practice of reworking can presumably be found only in Handel. Proceeding from moralistic ideas and from conceptions of originality rooted in the nineteenth century, one later tried to explain Handel's so-called borrowings as indications of a moral weakness or even as morbid symptoms. Today, however, we have freed ourselves from such Victorian views. Already Mattheson clearly expressed the conception of his own and Handel's time in saying: "To borrow is a permissible matter. One only must repay one's debt with interest."

The more we enter into the world of Handel's "borrowings," the more his unique talent for such kinds of "new versions" comes to light—and also his obvious pleasure in them, almost such as in a private hobby. There is an abundance of fine examples of such new versions, and just in these years the problem of the "borrowings" and reworkings has become very prominent. Nevertheless, I should like to stress two less noticed consequences of Handel's reworking practice: 1) Occasionally, it might appear as if Handel had chosen his "models" rather arbitrarily, and certainly chance is involved to some degree, too. However, hardly can it be accidental that in his later oratorios he seems never to have made use of materials from his operas composed in London, whereas he utilizes quite a number of different models from church music of his own and of other composers. We shall return to this later. 2) The adoption and rearrangement of Keiser's music in his Italian works not only is interesting because of the new versions, but also for quite a different reason: thus the adherence to the Hamburg traditions is emphasized on a large scale.

When, in late 1706, Handel travelled to Italy, he certainly aimed at his further education as primarily an operatic composer. In Italy, however, other musical genres, such as cantatas and oratorios, serenades and church music, occupied him to a similar degree as did opera. He was so impressed by the style and rhetoric of Italian baroque music, that it became a never-ending source of inspiration for him. The melodies of the arias partly were characterized by a heightened, instrumentally conceived melodic deployment, and the orchestral accompaniment became more prominent. But even though his Italian operas were composed for singers of a higher class than his Hamburg operas, the difference of melodic expression is not as striking as one might assume. As late as in his *Agrippina,* his last, very successful opera from the Italian time, Handel extensively appropriated melodic impulses from the Hamburg opera, from his own *Almira,* and from Keiser's operas including *Octavia.*

After a short time in Hanover—after a first visit in 1711—from 1712 on Handel found a permanent place of activity in London. Italianate operatic experiments had begun right before Handel's move, and thus the time was ripe for a fully Italian opera. The time until about 1720, however, must rather be considered as a time of preparation, but with the foundation of a Royal opera academy ("Royal Academy of Music") in 1719 came the great time of the Handel opera in

London. In the domain of the Royal Academy until 1728, and later as a free enterprise, it lasted until about 1740, when Handel definitively ceased to continue with opera.

Handel's operas from these approximately twenty years had another basis than his early operas in Hamburg and Italy. Right at this time, so to speak, the situation was changed by the presence of Italian vocal virtuosos who had established profitable international careers from extraordinary professional skills (as did movie stars earlier in our century, and as do rock stars or soccer and tennis players today). During Handel's London period, opera became not so much a dramatic art form, but rather a musical "show," an ordered display of (often) outstanding vocal achievements of the expensive foreign (Italian) soloists. Opera itself—text and music—was destined to create situations in which the prominent soloist could express his or her feelings in an aria determined by a particular affect. In the first place the soloists were castratos, and besides them some important female singers, prima donnas. They were expected to sing beautifully and to act properly and, besides this, as something special, to more or less elaborate the vocal line with free ornaments or, so to speak, to paint it over with "graffiti." The composer had to put up with this ornamentation mania, although one can hardly assume that Handel thought the singers to be better qualified to determine the vocal line than was the composer. But the sportlike professionalism of the singers placed this abuse much in the fore. P.F. Tosi, a castrato himself who lived in London during this time, was the author of a famous tutor of the vocal art, entitled *Opinioni de cantori antichi e moderni* (*Observations on the florid song*, translated by J.E. Galliard) emphasizing the significance of this practice thus: "Without varying the *Airs*, the Knowledge of the Singers could never be discovered; but from the Nature and Quality of the Variations, it will be easily discerned in two of the greatest Singers which is the best." One could scarcely state more clearly that this was considered a matter of sporting ambition, and not a musical affair.

The operas of these years mostly display a rather stereotyped sequence of different da capo arias, held together by a similarly stereotyped plot. Added to these are instrumental pieces or ballet insertions in some operas. Choruses, however, only occur as a final ensemble or something similar. In Handel's time, the success of an opera was determined more by the performance of the singers than by the music itself. For this reason the competition which took place during the 1730s with a second operatic enterprise that managed to engage the best singers was decisive for Handel's operatic activity. From 1738–39 on, Heidegger, Handel's partner as manager, ceased to engage the expensive Italian soloists. Handel immediately drew conclusions from this development; and rather than writing two operas for the coming season as usual, he composed two new oratorios. After two seasons mixed with operas and oratorios, he turned entirely to oratorio after 1741.

Handel had come to know the oratorio in Italy, but not in its modest form as a popular devotional piece in the oratory of a monastery. For the concerts of Prince Ruspoli in Rome he had performed—in addition to a number of cantatas—his oratorio *La resurrezione* (on Easter 1708, of course without scenery) not as a drama, but as an "elegant entertainment." In England he had, around 1720, composed and performed two works of a similar kind for a private, noble circle as well: *Acis and Galatea* and *Esther* or *Haman and Mordecai. Acis and Galatea* continues the tradition of the English masques; *Esther,* on the other hand, is directly entitled "oratorio." Up to then there was no oratorio tradition in England, as Burney clearly states in his music history: "Oratorios though common in Italy during the last century, were never attempted in England, either in public or private until the year 1720, when Handel set the sacred drama of *Esther.*" As in the case of *La resurrezione,* it was a private entertainment for a noble circle, but this is about the only similarity between the two works. Another kind of stimulus probably came from the famous biblical dramas of Racine, *Esther* and *Athalie;* an English version of Racine's *Esther* was published a few years earlier in London.

Already this first oratorio that Handel composed in England presents a number of essential features that are also characteristic of the later oratorios on a large scale. 1) The text is English, not Italian; 2) the soloists were not Italian opera singers, but English singers who were chiefly involved in church music; 3) here, as in many later oratorios, Handel modelled his characteristic reworkings after church compositions: eight pieces go back to prototypes from the Passion music on the text by Brockes, composed a few years earlier; and 4) another quite decisive element of Handel's oratorios goes back primarily to the tradition of church music too: the introduction of choral movements as essential parts of the work. The use of the choir serves several functions. Some of the choruses are directly involved in the action, as collective expression of a group as opposed to the individual expression in the arias; other choruses are more contemplative in adding a commentary to the action (such as the famous chorus of envy from *Saul*). Finally, there are the essential and significant "framing choruses that are often large-scale introductory or concluding choruses that very clearly point to church music, such as the frequent concluding choruses of praise which Handel himself occasionally calls "anthems." All these choral types can already be found in the early composition *Esther,* either foreshadowed or fully developed. But this second attempt of Handel in the realm of oratorio was not immediately continued either.

Only in 1732 did the problem of the oratorio come up again. A performance of *Esther* with the boys of the Royal Chapel—in a private circle, as a kind of school comedy—was so successful that it was decided to arrange a staged performance. The Bishop of London, however, did not permit choir boys to participate in such a public performance. As a compromise the plan was changed so that the work could now be given in the theater in a concert performance without costumes and decorations and without stage action.

It has often been maintained that the Bishop hereby created a new tradition in that the usual practice of scenic performances of oratorios arbitrarily was altered to a concert performance. This, however, is not true! Neither *before* nor *by* Handel was the oratorio performed with scenery and action. The private performance of *Esther* by the boys in the hall of a tavern neither was initiated by Handel, nor was it a real theater performance. The concert performances of *Esther* and of Handel's later oratorios continued the old performance traditions of the oratorio even when they were transferred from the private houses of aristocracy to the commercial theater. Nevertheless, in one respect the performances of the oratorios during the years 1732 to 1738 were different from all others: they were produced predominantly with Italian operatic soloists, not with English singers. That caused a fundamental difficulty: they had much trouble coming to grips with the English language, as is revealed by contemporary reports. This circumstance certainly contributed to the fact that the oratorio, after the first small sensation was over, quickly retreated in obscurity again. In the subsequent year, 1733, two further oratorios *(Deborah* and *Athalia)* followed, but then Handel again gave up the composition of oratorios. Until 1738, a few annual performances of the existing oratorios took place, but no new ones were composed.

With the abandonment of the engagements of the Italian vocal virtuosos, however, things changed immediately. At the end of July 1738, Heidegger, in the *London Daily Post,* announced that he was not going to hire foreign soloists for the winter season; and at exactly the same time Handel started to compose *Saul,* and after *Saul, Israel* for the following season. Both were performed in the early months of 1739. The soloists were local, mostly English singers of quite a different sort and much less professional than the Italian opera virtuosos. For these soloists, and for the singers of the church choirs of St. Paul's and Westminster Abbey, Handel regularly composed and performed new English oratorios until 1751, until the decline of his eyesight. Only during the first two seasons did oratorios alternate with some opera performances.

In almost every respect Handel's oratorios are compositions of a sort quite different from his operas. Already the textual basis, such as the story of Saul or Samson, is extremely different from an intrigue comedy on Julius Caesar or a magic comedy on Alcina. Rather than the stereotyped series of *da capo* arias, the oratorio employs a number of different aria types; and, most important, the arias alternate with choral movements in a variety of ways.

The change of soloists, however, remains the core of the renewal. The oratorio soloists were certainly less skilled than the Italian operatic soloists. But after twenty years Handel had at his disposal a group of soloists who wanted to serve his music, and not to rule over it. With regard to the impact of the oratorio as a whole the change of soloists was a clear advantage—despite the decline of the level of vocal performance. Only with the ending of professional egoism of the star soloists did it become possible to realize the permanent interaction of individual and collective expression in the soloistic and choral sections, which is so essential to the oratorio. Every in-depth comparison of Handel's opera and oratorio traditions may reveal new aspects of the contrasting characters of these two types. Therefore we can give a clear answer to our first question—whether the tendency of our time toward an assimilation of opera and oratorio and toward an equalization of their performance practice can be derived from Handel's own traditions. This tendency has nothing to do with Handel's traditions. Opera and oratorio were so different in almost every respect that on no account can such an approximation be justified by referring to Handel's practice.

Our second question is not concerned primarily with Handel's practice, but with the performance of his works in later times. For almost two centuries the development of the Handel tradition was limited to the practice of the oratorio. Here, as early as in the late eighteenth century, an essential change of the performance traditions had occurred. Three characteristic aspects of this change stand out in particular: 1) the enlargement of choir and orchestra related to the performance of oratorios in large cathedrals leads to a preference for massive effects, surpassing by far Handel's own performing forces; 2) the development of the orchestral sound about 1800 leads to a new instrumentation, an "additional accompaniment" by which Handel's oratorios, especially *Messiah,* come closer to classical and romantic conceptions; and 3) the rise of the large amateur choirs and musical societies in the nineteenth century increasingly leads to an undertaking of the oratorio performances by such choral associations that replaced Handel's modest church choirs.

This Handel oratorio tradition—with as large as possible forces, with additional instrumentation, and with large amateur choirs as main bearers of the performance—prevailed well into the twentieth century. After the revival of the Handel opera from 1920 on, however, a question concerning the performance tradition of the opera inevitably had to come up with regard to the tradition of both music and scenery. And almost simultaneously a reaction against the old Handel tradition made itself felt: the call for a restoration of Handel's original world of sound. Here we cannot pursue the development of these two new impulses within today's performance tradition of Handel's works any further, but must confine ourselves to a few remarks.

The struggle for a restoration of the original performance style brought with it much that was positive. A first, rather obvious effect was the abandonment of the added instrumentation. Furthermore, one could aim at a reduction of the orchestral and choral masses, maybe even at the reestablishment of the boy's choir, as in Handel's own tradition. A reestablishment of the older types of instruments was initiated with the replacement of the modern piano by the harpsichord. Only after World War II was there a return to the baroque types of string and wind instruments on a large scale.

Thus one may well speak of two degrees of a revival of Handel's sound conceptions: 1) a reestablishment of the performing forces of the original score without additions, but played on modern instruments besides the harpsichord and, occasionally, special incidental instruments; 2) a possibly complete reconstruction of the sound by means of original (or rebuilt) baroque instruments. This latter performance practice will for now (and probably on the whole) be limited to some special ensembles that specialize in such performing—though of course it must be remarked that even the specialists who want to play in a manner that is "historically correct" have not always found the ultimate truth concerning the "historically correct." It is certainly very valuable to have concerts and recordings of such ensembles, but it would be wrong to consider only such performances as relevant. Performances with modern instruments and with amateur choirs that try to avoid all "improvements" of Handel's music, and that aim at the "true" Handel, even without the possibility of specialization, should certainly be regarded as relevant as well. It could scarcely be considered progress if only the specialized performances, and not the amateur performances, survive.

The revival of Handel operas in Göttingen in 1920 inevitably led to new problems. Whereas the oratorio still had a performance tradition—however changed—a new tradition had to be established for the operas, since Handel's operas had not been performed for almost 200 years. Textually, dramatically, and musically, new ways had to be found and, more than that,—as opposed to the oratorio—largely by perhaps highly qualified theater people to whom Handel and his operas had so far scarcely meant anything concrete. It cannot surprise that the results of their efforts could turn out very differently.

I should like to mention three characteristic attitudes toward the fundamental problem of shaping Handel's operas: 1) the vision of a revival of baroque opera in its total originality; 2) the aiming at a representation of the Handel opera in a "timeless" shape, placing to the fore as a lode-star the spirit of the work and the music, rather than the baroque fashion; and 3) the—nowadays widespread—renunciation of all traditions in order to create a freely shaped version, adjusted to the so-called modern man, for example, by emphasizing social or psychological aspects.

The first of these attitudes, the "museumlike" approach, came up to some extent during the early stages, probably because the attempt to develop a new tradition from the original performance style suggested itself. Nevertheless, it is as natural to see the Count in *The Marriage of Figaro* in costumes of the eighteenth century—costumes of his own time—as it is unnatural to look at Julius Caesar in a baroque costume. For him it is also more suitable to appear in costumes of his own time—or at least in something suggesting an "antique" tradition. With stage design and costumes of an "antique" character many Handel operas were given a relevant representation from a contemporary point of view.

The last-named performance tradition, the "free" staging that today is very prominent, has become particularly fashionable during the past ten to twenty years. A number of different motives and tendencies are included in this new performance tradition. To some degree we certainly have to face a reaction against the "antique" stagings because they allow only little creativity to the director, and easily give rise to a rather stereotyped performance tradition. To a large degree, however, the reaction seems to have originated in a general attitude of protest: a protest against the world of an old "bourgeois" operatic tradition, an often rather forced search of unexpected effects, an overloading of stage action, frequently without any regard for the music which hardly can come to its own right because of these stage effects. During the past years I have witnessed many performances of Handel operas that made clear that the stage manager had only one goal: to create a performance that by virtue of his own inventiveness would become a great dramatic success. That the music was the main thing and that his work should serve the music could not be perceived. Handel's score almost becomes a kind of accompaniment, and one may often be tempted to ask whether the responsible stage manager should not instead find other accompanying music that might serve his stage work better!

Let me cite only one typical example of the conflict between the original work and a modern staging. A victorious king returns from war. As an elementary illustration of his victory and his power, he is joined by a number of captives who shall glorify his entrance. The modern producer, however, takes a different view. Captives expelled from their country are refugees, and they come with their incidental belongings, one with a bicycle, another with a typewriter, etc. One can discuss the director's intent, but one thing is clear: only a distortion of the ideas intended by the text and the music can come about, something that produces a countereffect rather than a cooperation of work and the staged version. A relevant performance of Handel's opera cannot be achieved that way.

In addition to stage problems, the revival of Handel's operas brought with it even musical problems. As far as the scoring is concerned, the problems are similar to those of the oratorios, and the development took a similar course even though the operatic orchestra occasionally has allowed a freer shaping. (In the world of theater alterations of the original appearance of a work are more frequent than in the concert hall.) Instead, there are problems of essential significance with regard to the singers, especially the problem of the castrato parts. I must content myself here with a few remarks on this problem.

In surveying the *dramatis personae* of *Giulio Cesare,* one will find six male and two female roles. Of the six male roles, however, four are performed by castratos. For this reason the list looks much different if it is ordered according to vocal categories: two sopranos, three male altos, one female alto, and two basses. On occasion of the revival of Handel opera (1920) all castrato parts were cast with male voices. Thereby, the visual illusion was supported much better, but musically it was an incisive alteration of the sound when rather than six voices in high and two in low tessitura, two had to sing in high and six in low tessitura. Eventually, though slowly, one arrived at a performance of the castrato roles by women or by countertenors. Musically this is certainly an advantage. A further discussion here of the problems, however, must be left aside.

Finally, the emergence of a new tradition of Handel's operas has had some influence on the tradition of the oratorio as well. In many cases oratorios have been staged with scenery as a kind of opera performance; and even when they were performed in a concert setting the singers took up the tradition of Italian opera soloists rather than that of the English oratorio singers (i.e., they added operatic ornamentation and cadences). I have stated already that both the staged performance and the transfer of vocal manners of the opera singers to oratorio performances did not have roots in Handel's time but must be considered as fashionable conceptions of today. Nevertheless, there are major differences between such performances. There are, so to speak, "half-scenic" performances that—with a limited scenery and action—aim at an illustration of the drama within the oratorio; and there are others where the stage manager seems to have so little confidence in the appeal of the musical power of the oratorio that he regards it necessary to go his own way. This, however, leads directly to our third question: whether a new arrangement of the work—with respect to music, text, and scenery—must be regarded as equivalent or even superior to a traditional interpretation. This question does not deal with objective information, but with value judgments, and with the motivation for such judgments.

In my discussion I have proceeded from the conception that it must be our goal to realize Handel's work in performances that allow his music to be the absolutely central concern. That must certainly be the natural point of view of a music scholar and the lover of Handel's music. But, of course, I am aware that there are other views as well. When, several years ago, I had the fine experience of helping to organize a large Haydn festival in Washington, I collaborated with an excellent artistic director, and I still remember him saying, with a smile, but seriously: "my point of view is the box office." The great violinist also comes to mind who on the same occasion expressed his view of eighteenth-century performance problems succinctly: "my point of view is: it must be convincing." Of course, I am also aware that a stage manager must think in terms of effectiveness on the stage, and probably would argue that the performance must be *dramatically* effective. And the singer must think of his or her personal career, hoping that the performance will be successful for him.

All these views are quite natural and more or less justified. However, it will be decisive whether a person involved is able to place the overall success of the performance above or at least on the same level as his personal success. Without any doubt the greatest danger of a derailment of the performance emerges from those who are responsible for the staging. If the basic character of a performance is arbitrarily determined by an idea that can be related to the nature and the whole concept of the opera only quite speculatively or not at all, then the danger of such a derailment is almost inevitable. And here I should like to stress our specific situation. Of course the works of Shakespeare or Mozart are also performed with stage concepts that are far removed from the wonted traditions. However, these traditions are still extant, and one can use them as a means of comparison. But with regard to Handel there is no similar tradition. The arbitrary stage concepts that we witness today certainly do not contribute to the establishment of a natural Handel opera tradition.

5

Esther and the Origin of the
Handelian Oratorio Tradition

Presentations of the history of past epochs are bound to include elements of a purely accidental nature; this may apply to matters of general or specific cultural significance. Whatever is deemed worthy of a record for posterity depends upon subjective judgment, and whatever is slighted by the eyewitnesses may be forever lost. It is an old truth that history is written by the winning party. This applies directly to the account of situations, to the distribution of light and shadow, and to the inclusion or omission of personages, happenings, or developments.

A similar adjustment of historical material for posterity, however, takes place to a certain extent during the very course of events. Those who won the first round, the conspicuous participants, command the attention. The spotlight rests on them, and on their acts—often, of course, rightly so. But it can happen, too, that later analysis will register a quick decline of works that were initially accorded the greatest interest, and overwhelming recognition of works that were hardly noticed at first.

The most striking example of such reevaluation and posthumous understanding of unrecognized quality is probably Bach's *St. Matthew Passion.* The first performance of this great work roused such little interest that it is impossible to ascertain its date. (This fact may give some consolation to neglected composers, or it may serve as a sobering reminder for successful ones—depending upon situations and temperaments.) Though especially poignant, this case is not to be considered unusual. The music historian will often find himself faced with material for hundreds of works that seem quite unimportant today, whereas the sources are silent on the one work that does seem important.

The work with which we are concerned at present, the first version of Handel's *Esther*—probably performed originally in the fall of 1720—cannot be compared with Bach's *St. Matthew Passion* on artistic grounds, but from the

Reprinted from *American Choral Review* 14 (1972), pp. 7–14.

point of view of Handel's development and of the development of the modern oratorio tradition in general, it assumes a decisive role. Yet what we can say about its origin and its first performance is inversely proportionate to its importance. *Esther,* or, as the work in its original form was also called, *Haman and Mordecai,* was written, according to traditional biographic information, in 1720, at a time when Handel was said to be chapelmaster to the Duke of Chandos at Cannons, his residence near London. Recent scholarship has raised some questions about this traditional account. There is no doubt that Handel composed a number of works for the Duke, but he could not have been his chapelmaster—this post was held by Pepusch, the compiler of the music for the famous *Beggar's Opera.* Handel probably lived in London at that time, coming to Cannons only for certain performances, such as *Esther* and *Acis and Galatea* which was composed at about the same time.

With regard to the performance of *Esther* the situation is even less clear. A contemporaneous account of the performance has not turned up so far, and it is therefore not clear whether it took place in the court chapel at Cannons as has been stated by the English music historian Charles Burney, among others, or in the large hall of the castle itself. It remains to be investigated whether a theatrical performance with scenery and action was involved, or whether the presentation contained limited dramatic action or was merely sung. English scholars are inclined to assume a genuine theatrical production, though without any documentation for such an opinion. In fact, a contrary opinion is supported by a newspaper notice of a somewhat later date.

In 1732 both *Esther* and *Acis and Galatea* were revived, and from these new performances the great English oratorio tradition has taken its point of departure. On May 2, 1732, a performance of *Acis and Galatea* was announced in *The Daily Post* with the following comment: [*Acis and Galatea* will be presented] "with all the Grand Chorus's and other Decorations, as it was perform'd before his Grace the Duke of Chandos at Cannons." This seems like a clear confirmation of the thesis of a dramatic presentation at Cannons. But now something surprising happens. The notice, which had been repeated on May 3, was revised from May 6 on as follows: [*Acis and Galatea* will be presented] "with all the Grand Chorus's, Scenes, Machines, and other Decorations; being the first Time it ever was performed in a Theatrical Way." This change, which must be considered a correction of the first announcement, proves only a non-theatrical performance for *Acis and Galatea* at Cannons, but in my opinion it implies beyond any doubt a nontheatrical production for *Esther* as well.

Not the least part of the uncertainty to which we are committed results from the fact that the production of *Esther* must decidedly be considered to have been an experiment. There was no English oratorio tradition. Burney states this as follows: "Oratorios, though common in Italy during the last century, were never attempted in England, either in public or private, till the year 1720, when Handel set the sacred drama of Esther for the chapel of the Duke of Chandos at Cannons!"[1]

Surely there was no intention of establishing an oratorio tradition implicit in the *Esther* performance at Cannons. It would be difficult to say why such an intention should exist, and it might suffice to point out that during the twelve years before the revival of *Esther* in 1732 not the slightest suggestion of a continuation of such a trend appeared. Probably the first public presentations of Racine's *Esther and Athalia,* which were given in Paris, served as an impetus for this experiment. These works, however, cannot be regarded as direct models which guided Handel, for their musical content was confined to the great choruses. The strong emphasis on the chorus, the biblical subject, and the "classic," monumental character are probably the three principal qualities that link Handel's work to that of Racine. The musical components for the oratorio *Esther* from which the entire Handelian oratorio tradition was to evolve, must be found elsewhere. There was *one* definite line of development in Handel's work up to this point: that of the opera composer. Yet aside from this definite line we can recognize a number of subsidiary lines—various influences which do not seem to lead to a clearcut individual goal but which nevertheless suggest another principal line of development to those who are aware of the later aspects of Handel's work. This line, which marks a less obvious and less conscious road towards the oratorio, will be sketched briefly here.

Like Mozart, Handel belongs to a group of composers who are not tied to one country whose traditions they essentially continue, but who are influenced by changing traditions early in their careers. In the case of Handel there are three national traditions which determined the course of his work: the German environment of his early period, the Italian environment of his ensuing years, and the English environment of his mature and late years. In each of these he gathered elements that helped to build his oratorio style.

Even in the very first phase of Handel's career—his apprenticeship under the excellent Halle church musician Zachow—style elements appear which point towards the oratorio. What Zachow taught him was well founded and sound, German church music tradition at its best—choral writing and contrapuntal art, not the fashionable, melodic style of opera. Yet the merging of church music and opera, from which in time the specific form of the Handelian oratorio was to take its origins, seems to have made its appearance early. A somewhat unclarified account has it that the young Handel became acquainted with the world of court opera in Berlin in his youth. It is, however, certain that at eighteen he moved from Halle to Hamburg, the only city in Germany in which he could enter upon an operatic career without court connections. Here opera occupied a central position, but in addition there were influences that widened his musical horizon still further. It was in these very years that there arose in Hamburg the new form of the "oratorical" or "theatrical" Passion without which Bach's Passion works could hardly have come about. Among the works formerly attributed to Handel is the shorter setting of the *Passion according to St. John.* A later setting—the so-called "Brockes Passion," probably composed during a trip to Germany—leads us directly to one of the chief sources for the music of *Esther,* the first English oratorio. We will return to this point shortly.

After about three years in Hamburg, Handel had saved enough money to go to Italy. There is no doubt that Italian opera attracted him. Italy was the promised land of opera. From there the influence of Italian operatic traditions spread through all of Europe. The three or four years that Handel spent in Italy gave him the opportunity to become steeped in this tradition. He was closely associated with Italy's leading opera composer, Alessandro Scarlatti, and other outstanding composers. In the course of these years, Handel himself became one of the foremost opera composers of his time. His opera *Agrippina* (Venice, 1709) in particular established his fame.

In this phase of Handel's development his attention was still mainly directed towards opera. In addition, however, there were influences upon his work, the effects of which were to become fully apparent only later. The style of Corelli became decisive for his instrumental music, as his concertos and violin sonatas unmistakably show. But the impulse for the oratorio tradition, which was to arise much later, can also be traced largely to Handel's Italian period. This refers to the genre of oratorio in general as well as to the monumental choral style that is such a distinguished characteristic of the Handelian oratorio.

Handel's work became associated with the form of the oratorio in Rome in the spring of 1708. Opera performances were ruled out in the Holy City at this time and oratorio performances served as a substitute. Handel wrote his first two oratorios there: *La Resurrezione* and *Il Trionfo del Tempo e del Disinganno.*

These works have little in common with his later oratorio style. Above all, they are written almost entirely as solo works without the choral effects that are so essential to the later oratorios. But superb choral writing by Handel appeared during these years in his Latin Psalms, especially *Dixit Dominus* and *Laudate Pueri.* As these works show, he had fully absorbed the grand choral style of the Baroque that had originated in Venice around 1600. This needs to be emphasized; it has often been overlooked that Handel had proven his strength as a choral composer even before his English period, although he received new impulses in England that were to contribute decisively towards the development of a highly varied and unparalleled choral style.

From Italy, Handel—now a musician of international reputation—went to Hanover as court chapelmaster; but, as is well known, his Hanoverian period was to become merely an episode between Italy and England. Only a few months after his appointment in Hanover, towards the end of the year 1710, he made his first journey to England, where, after a renewed short stay in Hanover, he settled permanently in 1712. His chief occupation in England remained opera for many years to come—with an interruption during the period between 1715 and 1720. This may be the least explored portion of his life. As has been mentioned, we are not sure of the places where he stayed during these years, what works he composed, and under what circumstances they were performed. Only one thing is certain: this span of time is marked by the smallest operatic output of the entire active period of his middle years. Instead, Handel cultivated a number of other musical forms. In the field of instrumental music, with which we are less concerned in this connection, he was highly active writing clavier suites, chamber sonatas, and concertos. Much more important from our point of view is his growing interest in such vocal forms as were rooted in English musical traditions.

At the very beginning of his English period, still during Queen Anne's reign, Handel had been commissioned to write two major works which were bound to place before him the problem of taking a stand in following such traditions. This applies especially to the *Ode for the Birthday of Queen Anne* of 1713. There were models by Purcell, Handel's great predecessor, from which he could take a point of departure—or we might say, could have taken a point of departure. The situation is this: If we compare the *Birthday Ode* with earlier choral works by Handel, certain differences clearly emerge; but if we make a comparison with Purcell's writing, the differences are certainly no less clear. This might best be explained as follows: Handel probably had the opportunity of seeing compositions of this kind by Purcell. If this is so, they may have had an influence on the planning of the general outline of his works, but we can in no way speak of a direct imitation. There are certain isolated traits that reflect Purcell's style—or may reflect Purcell's style—such as the typical combination of solo introduction and choral refrain sharing the same musical material. Also obviously deviating from the choral style of Handel's Italian works, is the growing tendency towards simple rhythmic effects, often veritable dance patterns, as opposed to the essentially sonorous choral effects of the Italian works that appear here in only two numbers.

In the case of the other early example of a Handelian setting of an English text, the *Utrecht Te Deum* and *Jubilate,* composed about the same time, a connection between Handel's and Purcell's work has often been strongly argued. But I do not believe that the conjecture of such a correlation touches upon the basic issue. The corresponding arrangement of the text in small sections and similar features have been quoted as evidence of Handel's indebtedness to Purcell. But even if we were to assume that Handel might not have arrived at such an arrangement without the model of Purcell, we would merely acknowledge proof of Handel's acquaintance with Purcell's work though not his musical dependence upon Purcell. For in the *Utrecht Te Deum* and *Jubilate* the influence of Handel's Italian choral style from the Latin Psalms is convincing. This is especially clear in the *Jubilate,* for its beginning is based upon the magnificent concertato opening of his Psalm *Laudate Pueri.* The direct connection is manifest. It seems plausible that Handel went through appropriate models in Purcell's work before composing both the *Birthday Ode* and the *Utrecht Te Deum,* but these seem to have merely guided him in a general conception of the form without affecting the essence of his musical style.

Among the compositions that are traditionally known to have been dedicated to the Duke of Chandos, the eleven or twelve *Chandos Anthems* occupy the first place. Again we are dealing with a specifically English tradition, and again it seems justified to state that Handel created a novel form which could not easily be identified with the tradition of the English Anthem—granted that without the existing English tradition he would not have composed works of this genre. In the anthems we find reminiscences of the Latin Psalms and of the *Birthday Ode,* and, by no means least important, we find conspicuous quotations from German Protestant chorales. These might be traced, of course, to impressions from his childhood and youth, but it is more plausible to relate them to the renewed impression of the religious service with which he had grown up. He had been in Germany in 1716 or 1717 (or in both years), and apparently he had become acquainted with the new trends of sacred music. Important among them was the new form of the church cantata, traces of which we can recognize in the *Chandos Anthems.* Particularly important, however, was the Passion on the text by Brockes which we have mentioned. What prompted him to set this text to music is one of the questions from these years for which we cannot supply an answer for the time being.

We encounter a closer contact with English traditions in three works which probably all date from the end of this period in Handel's work: the so-called Chandos *Te Deum* in B-flat major and the two oratorios *Acis and Galatea* and *Esther.* In the B-flat major *Te Deum* Handel departed somewhat from Italian traditions. The choruses often suggest more the melodic style of the aria than the monumental choral style—a tendency which points to the future.

With the two oratorios Handel shows that he is guided by an impulse, the entire development of which we cannot trace, although we find it documented in the renewed interest in the genre, especially through the revival of the two works in 1732. From the English tradition of the so-called *masque* a line of development leads through Purcell's *Dido and Aeneas* to Handel's *Acis and Galatea.* The *masques,* originally derived from allegorical plays, during the sixteenth and seventeenth centuries assumed a manner of *Gesamtkunstwerk*—a combination of ceremonial presentations, dances, and elaborate stage effects, all of them supported by music. At first a self-contained work, the *masque* became in some of the great examples of Purcell's incidental stage music a set piece within a larger work. From the little that we know about Handel's performance at Cannons, it does not seem safe to conclude that conditions for the elaborate apparatus needed for this genre existed. If we find both the designations *masque* and *oratorio* for *Esther* (or *Haman and Mordecai*), we are led to the conclusion that there was no readily suitable term, since an experiment, so to speak, of an improvisatory nature, was being made. The argument for the term *masque* is founded upon purely musical grounds—the combination of arias and choruses forms the basis of the musical structure, and it has remained the basis of the Handelian oratorio. It is not justified, however, to interpret the term *masque* in the sense of a scenic performance, or conversely to interpret the term *oratorio* in the sense of a nondramatic performance.

The question as to what Handel knew of such works and performance traditions is even more important here than it is in connection with the works we mentioned earlier and which were related to a then existing English tradition; for this type of *Gesamtkunstwerk* may be assumed to have died with the passing of the Purcellian era. Thus we are bound to arrive at the realization that the original version of *Esther*—or, to use the designation the work was given by the Handel biographer Friedrich Chrysander, *Esther I*—was a highly unusual work. On the one hand, it was tied to the tradition of many models or antecedents; on the other, it could obviously not be placed in direct comparison with any of these antecedents. The suggestion may come from Racine's *Esther,* but this was a drama with no musical elaboration other than choruses. From the point of view of musical concepts Handel might have classed *Esther* as an oratorio even if the type of oratorio with which Handel had become acquainted in Italy and which he himself had briefly cultivated was a solo oratorio to which the central element of alternation between solo and chorus was foreign. *Esther I* had many musical characteristics which related the work to the *masque* tradition, but the typical *Gesamtkunstwerk* tendencies of *masque* performances were probably absent in this case.

If we turn from conceptual considerations—from considerations of the essentially dramatic nature of the work—to purely musical considerations, the picture becomes even more complex. We have touched briefly upon the question of Handel's use of already existing material. This is an aspect of artistic activity that stands in contrast to the stereotyped search for originality which we find in later periods. The composers of the eighteenth century, like their predecessors, aimed above all at *excellence,* not necessarily at *novelty.* To a large extent they quoted or utilized not only their own works but also works by other composers in order to create valid new material. In particular, they followed the practice of the so-called *contrafactum*—they gave new texts to works they had written for special occasions and which they considered outdated with those occasions; they remodeled them according to new needs and adapted them to new contexts. This practice can be documented with many examples in the works of both Bach and Handel.

The practice of *contrafactum* leads us finally to an important source for *Esther I* and for the rising Handelian oratorio tradition: sacred music. No fewer than eight numbers from *Esther* were taken from Handel's setting of the Brockes Passion. The fact points out again that we face a synthesis of a number of latent antecedents in the case of *Esther*. The connection with forms of sacred music is clearly expressed in the choruses, especially in the monumental choral conclusion. In turn, if the initiative of a young friend and follower of Handel's had not resulted in a revival and a subsequent revision of *Esther* (1732), which caused the rise of a new tradition of nonstaged oratorio performances in the theater, *Esther I* would have remained an interesting experiment from Handel's early period. Through the course of events, however, this experiment prepared the ground for the oratorio tradition that was to come. It did not present a definitive form of the Handelian oratorio. (Fortunately, there are no definitive forms.) Rather the work paved the way for a genre that represents the successful synthesis of sacred and secular, dramatic and contemplative, English, German, and Italian prototypes. The revision of 1732 stood for a certain assimilation of opera, and opera soloists became the principal performers in oratorio presentations for a number of years. This does not mean a greater emphasis upon the dramatic aspect of oratorio—in fact, it does not touch on the question as to whether or not a staged dramatic presentation was involved. But with the greater emphasis upon the soloistic element, a balance between the two cardinal lines of development in Handel's creative career was brought about: that of opera, which Handel took up consciously and which was founded upon the tradition of Italian solo singing, and that of oratorio, which Handel took up involuntarily and which slowly rose to a dominant position marked by the reconciliation of soloistic and choral elements. This decisive reconciliation originated in *Esther I*.

Notes

1. *A General History of Music* (1789), new edition by Frank Mercer (New York: Dover, 1957), II: 775.

6

The Development of
Handelian Oratorio and *Messiah*

In the history of European music certain outstanding names and genres are so closely connected that they are almost invariably mentioned together. Mozart and the opera, Wagner and the music drama, Beethoven and the symphony may serve as examples for such pairing of composer and form. No doubt the combination of Handel and the oratorio belongs in this series.

If we are not content, however, with the mere idea that such connections exist but probe more deeply into their nature, distinguishing features characteristic of each of the associations begin to emerge.

To single out some obvious situations: Mozart's role as opera composer or Beethoven's role as symphonist would never be considered the roles of initiators. Here we are not dealing with the origin but with the decisive reinterpretation of musical forms. Mozart was in no way consciously concerned with a reform of opera, and Beethoven based his work clearly upon the mature phases of Haydn's and Mozart's symphonic writing. Nevertheless, both Mozart and Beethoven arrived at new approaches of entirely original quality.

In Wagner's case the circumstances are different in spite of seeming similarities. Though taking his point of departure from existing opera, Wagner's whole interest guided him towards new territory. He wished to free himself of the conventions of opera, and this wish was fulfilled to a large extent. Establishing a new theoretical basis and experimenting with new musical concepts, Wagner arrived at a totally novel form of art. Music drama is a phenomenon rooted in Wagner's work in a manner quite different from that in which the phenomenon of opera is connected with Mozart's or the phenomenon of the symphony is connected with Beethoven's work.

In the light of these considerations, how are we to judge Handel's position with regard to oratorio? Are we concerned with a creative impulse directed towards a new genre as in the case of Wagner and the music drama, or did

Reprinted from *American Choral Review* 14 (1972), pp. 15–22.

Handel merely reawaken a traditional form without radically changing it? In some measure this question is easily answered. There is no doubt that Handel brought about a radical change. The concept of the Handelian oratorio is so unparalleled that it must be considered an original creation in the strictest sense. Nor was there an established tradition upon which Handel could build. On the contrary: Burney has expressly stated that no attempt at producing oratorios had been made in England prior to Handel. It is true that Handel had become acquainted with the form of the oratorio during his early years in Italy and that he tried his hand at it. But his mature works—those truly representative of the Handelian oratorio—are in no way a continuation of his early oratorio writing; they must be considered in terms of a new individual genre. This was doubtless also the impression these works gave to Handel's contemporaries and direct followers.

Yet, at the same time, our comparison points out a complete divergence of Wagner's and Handel's approaches to a new form. Wagner's fight for the music drama is conscious and manifest. Handel enters his career as oratorio composer accidentally and without any firm resolve. Wagner's music drama is the result of eminent intellectual will power. Handel's oratorio is the result of the steady growth of a musical instinct forever directed towards dramatic expression, but not a result systematically planned to become the form of oratorio. One might rather say that the form of oratorio systematically captured Handel. The student of cultural history who is also interested in the psychology of the creative artist will find Handel's road towards this genre one of the most fascinating episodes in eighteenth-century art. With the present discussion, I would like to trace Handel's development as oratorio composer and to describe the role of *Messiah*, his best known oratorio, within this development.

As we have mentioned, Handel encountered the oratorio in Italy, where he stayed between the years 1707 and 1710 and where he received the impressions that were to become decisive for him, above all through Scarlatti's operas and Corelli's instrumental music.

Originally intended to serve devotional purposes, the form of the oratorio had taken on most of the musical conventions of opera during the second half of the seventeenth century. Its function had changed. Rather than devotion, its purpose—in the circles where Handel met with the form—had become entertainment. Opera being ruled out during Lent, and in Rome at this time in general, nobility had turned its musical patronage to oratorio, opera's legitimate and closely related counterpart. The oratorio plot had to be chosen from the Bible or from the lives of the Saints or similar subject matter, but the character of the oratorio was akin to that of opera, the primary object of both being the soloists' vocal display. Handel's two oratorios from those years, *La Resurrezione* and *Il Trionfo del Tempo e del Disinganno,* are actually of this kind.

After the two precursors of his later work, Handel seems to have given no further thought to the composition of oratorios for about a dozen years. In the two new works written about 1720 for the Duke of Chandos (*Acis and Galatea* and *Esther*) we can recognize links with Handel's later work that suggest the origin of the Handelian oratorio proper, but our knowledge about these works and their performance is sparse, and Handel's renewed concern with the genre seems to have been a matter of chance rather than plan.

After these two works, produced for a small, private audience, approximately another dozen years passed before Handel returned to the form of the oratorio. This time the spark ignited, although it took Handel a few more years to complete the transition from opera to oratorio. The occasion for this return to the form again seems accidental. One of the members in the original *Esther* cast of 1720, Bernard Gates, had meanwhile been appointed to the office of Master of Children of the Chapel Royal. For Handel's birthday, February 23, 1732, Gates planned a performance of *Esther* with his group of boys and with the assistance of other choristers from the Chapel Royal and Westminster Abbey. While this performance was again privately held, it stirred up so much general interest that several repeat performances took place. Handel was even prompted to schedule a public performance. Thus oratorio emerged from its earlier seclusion into the bright light always shed on public theater. The Handelian oratorio became, like opera, a public entertainment and renounced its original intimate and devotional character.

Connected with the absorption of oratorio into the London stage repertoire is the establishment of special performance traditions which grew in part from the circumstances of the moment.

There is, first of all, the manner of presentation. It seems to have been Handel's intention to give scenic performances, as in opera, with stage sets, costumes, and action. Here he met with unexpected resistance. The Bishop of London simply forbade the chapel boys to appear in the common environment of theater life. As a compromise, one arrived at a concert performance—a non-scenic presentation without costumes or action, as has remained the general custom until today.

A second, equally important departure from Handel's earlier practice was the change from Italian to English texts. It might seem relatively inconsequential whether one or the other language was used, but this is not so. The shift of language had a decisive effect in several respects. For one thing it made it possible to reach a much wider audience—the exclusive character of the earlier oratorio began to disappear. For another, it was possible to abandon the stereotyped character of libretto that formed the basis of Italian opera and oratorio and give oratorio texts an aura of the great English dramatic traditions. The text of oratorios became more alive and natural than the conventional opera libretto. It enhanced Handel's capacity for achieving great results with simple means.

A third consequence of the use of a new performance language might have seemed a serious drawback initially but eventually proved a favorable factor: the elimination of Italian opera stars—so far the only possible source of performers—as interpreters of Handel's work. From the point of view of purely vocal performance, the conversion of Handel's staff of soloists that took place in the following years was doubtless a loss. Handel's soloists were now English singers of average quality or Italian singers without the European reputation of Handel's former operatic stars. But these singers were not encumbered with the prima donna attitudes of a Cuzzoni or a Farinelli. Their approach to musical work was not conditioned by the demand that it must serve merely as a basis for vocal virtuosity, even at the cost of the dramatic sense. With these singers Handel found opportunities for attaining a dramatic and musical unity that he could never have attempted with his Italian forces. (We might be reminded here that Gluck's reform of opera, thirty years later, was accompanied by a similar change of singers.)

To these characteristics of the newly arising English type of oratorio a very important one must be added which—though not quite unknown in the Italian oratorio—assumed such a prominent role in Handel's writing that it led to totally new consequences: the use of the chorus.

What caused Handel to develop oratorio as strongly in this direction is a question to which perhaps no complete answer can be given. To some extent he may be indebted to English seventeenth-century forms of dramatic music. But Handel's acquaintance with the larger forms of church music doubtless exercised a particularly strong influence upon the new character of oratorio. We cannot consider it mere coincidence that *Esther* in its original version of 1720—Handel's first English oratorio—followed the *Chandos Anthems,* a series of veritable church cantatas. Nor can it be ascribed to coincidence that the second *Esther* version of 1732, rearranged for the London stage, contained large choral portions from the *Coronation Anthems* of 1727, and that the complete *Funeral Anthem,* composed on the death of Queen Caroline in 1737, was incorporated (with changed text) a year later into *Israel in Egypt.* Sacred music was the most important factor in Handel's choral interpretation of the oratorio form.

It would be tempting to trace detailed aspects of the role of the chorus in the development of the Handelian oratorio, but this would lead beyond the scope of the present essay. We will have to limit our discussion to the general principles involved. And here we must single out above all the observation that while the monumental chorus derived from models of church music dominates Handel's first English oratorios, many other choral forms were soon added. Not the least important among them is the smaller, agile choral episode which is easily integrated in the dramatic continuity and which, unlike the somber anthem chorus, does not claim the preferred position at the beginning or end of an oratorio act. The universal wealth of Handelian choruses is one of the musical miracles of the classical European age. Their choral multiformity, depth, originality, simplicity, and grandeur are appreciated in our time by only a small segment of the audiences that attend the all too rare performances of Handel oratorios.

With the revival and revision of *Esther* in 1732, the Handelian type of oratorio was more or less established. Yet this type remained merely a point of departure. In the ensuing years, Handel continued to discover new possibilities, always arriving at greater variety. He never ceased to cast new light on the dramatic and musical content of the form. After the new *Esther* version, Handel wrote two further oratorios dealing with biblical heroines: *Deborah* and *Athalia* (1733). But after this first phase, it seemed that both Handel and his audience required some interval of time in order to absorb the new genre. During the next few years Handel revived the existing oratorios but did not add any new ones. *Alexander's Feast,* composed in 1736, as well as the *Ode for St. Cecilia's Day* that followed three years later, were works that suggested the connection with English traditions in the domain of the secular cantata. Above all, they offered new examples of the flexibility in choral writing and of a closer integration of choral and soloistic elements than can be found in the earlier works.

A high point in Handel's choral work is the *Funeral Anthem* of 1737, which we have already mentioned—a superb piece consisting of choral movements only. At this point in his career Handel must have realized that his operatic activity was doomed. Encouraged, we may assume, by the artistic success of such works as the two previous ones listed in our survey, he turned his efforts fully towards the oratorio in 1738 and broke off his operatic endeavors two to three years later.

The oratorios of Handel's most mature years, i.e., essentially from 1738 to the beginning of the loss of his eyesight in 1751, number approximately twenty works of rather diversified nature. Considered particularly characteristic of the form—probably rightly so—are those oratorios in which Handel presents the fate of one of the major Old Testament figures: *Saul, Samson, Judas Maccabaeus,* to mention only three of the best known. These works, which are all of a strongly dramatic, heroic, and lofty quality, and which deal more or less with the general subject of Israel's suppression and liberation, stand in contrast to another series of works, also drawn from the Old Testament but not equally monumental in character. Among these we might mention *Joseph, Solomon,* and *Susanna*—works generally viewed as less representative of Handel's oratorio art than the "heroic" oratorios.

Completely detached from the biblical sphere are two other groups of oratorios. One includes two works written in 1743–44 on subjects from classical antiquity: *Semele* and *Hercules.* These oratorios almost give the impression that Handel tried, in a roundabout way, to revive opera. Rather than operatic oratorios, one might consider them operas written in the oratorio manner, and it is quite natural that modern attempts to place oratorios on the theater stage have been especially inspired by these two works. The other group of nonbiblical oratorios from Handel's later years includes *L'Allegro* (1740) and the third version of *Il Trionfo* (1757), which is Handel's last oratorio. In these two works Handel again took up the type of allegorical oratorio he had written in his youth.

There is one group, not mentioned so far, that is closest to sacred music. Aside from the *Occasional oratorio* (1746), whose chance nature is indicated in its title, this group contains two of Handel's most prominent oratorios: *Israel in Egypt* (1738) and *Messiah* (1741).

These two oratorios are distinguished in several ways from all others. They are rightly counted among Handel's greatest works. Yet they are not typical representatives of the Handelian oratorio, though they cannot be separated from the development of the form that led to them. We would like to turn our attention primarily to three characteristic features which these two works have in common and which can help to explain their special quality: 1) Both works are based on purely biblical texts (except for some minor additions in *Israel*), i.e., they are not merely based on biblical subjects, but arias and choruses are set to the scriptural words themselves, rather than to the usual paraphrased libretto; 2) The action is not carried by individual personages as is otherwise the case in oratorios. This does not mean that there is no action, no dramatic development—it is merely of a kind different from that of the oratorios regarded as "typical"; 3) In both oratorios the connection with the anthem—the sacred choral work—is particularly tangible. As we have mentioned, Handel incorporated the complete *Funeral Anthem* on the death of Queen Caroline into *Israel in Egypt,* altering the text to make it suitable as a lament for Joseph. The last part of this oratorio is based on the Song of Moses, thus again of distinctive anthem character. Similarly, the last part of *Messiah* is a large anthem of praise extolling the Redemption.

These three points are essential to the character of the two works. There are, of course, further characteristics of their unusual quality. In the case of *Israel in Egypt* in particular, we might mention two: the use of directly expressive means in the epic description of the Egyptian plagues, and the overwhelming role of the chorus as main protagonist. *Israel in Egypt* is almost entirely choral, and in this respect without parallel among Handel's oratorios. It is tempting to conjecture that the *Funeral Anthem,* written one year earlier and subsequently absorbed in the plan for *Israel in Egypt,* inspired in Handel the thought of writing an entirely choral oratorio. The perfection that he achieved in the music for the *Funeral Anthem* may have had such an effect upon the composer that he may have given serious thought to the plan of developing the form of the oratorio in this direction. But he overlooked the fact that a choral work three times as long as the *Funeral Anthem* and lacking the variety created by the combination of soloistic and choral elements would prove too formidable a challenge for his audience.

Israel in Egypt met with no success, and even the insertion of several Italian arias and various cuts in the choruses failed to save the work.

After this overemphasis upon the choral element, Handel was apparently somewhat apprehensive about the use of the chorus. In the *Ode for St. Cecilia's Day* (1739) he placed choral sections only at the beginning and at the end and in a small episode in the middle of the work. The major musical interest is given rather to the soloistic use of instruments. In *L'Allegro* (1740) there are only three larger independent choral portions, otherwise merely choral refrains for arias whose melodic fabric they continue. These choruses are all very lively and bright, totally different from the ponderous choral weight of *Israel in Egypt*.

In *Messiah*, Handel's most celebrated work, written in the fall of 1741 and first performed in Dublin in 1742, the choral and soloistic elements are conspicuously balanced, especially when considered against the background of the oratorios that precede this work.

Handel's *Messiah* has given rise to many—more or less well-founded—arguments and will continue to do so for a long time to come. As we have stated, its text is entirely biblical, but in contrast to the *Israel* text, we are not dealing here with a connected passage from the Scriptures. The words for *Messiah* represent a sensitive composition of Bible verses for which Charles Jennens, a friend of Handel's, was probably responsible. What prompted the idea of an oratorio of this kind may remain an open question. It is possible that Handel had his earlier oratorio *La Resurrezione* in mind. This work, however, differs from *Messiah* in nearly every respect, except that the central idea in both cases is the Redemption of Mankind.

Messiah is not, as has often been assumed, a representation of the life of Christ—a combination of Nativity, Passion, and Resurrection plays. The work is guided by the single idea of presenting the drama of Redemption, the struggle between light and dark, between God and mankind. In a certain sense the work is akin to Handel's allegorical oratorios. As in *Il Trionfo*, the first two parts of the work are entirely rooted in the contest of good and evil. But the scope is broader, the forces brought into play are incomparably stronger, and the total conception expresses an unmatched magnificence.

The musical structure of *Messiah* shows Handel's manifold creative powers most strongly. This is apparent both in the whole plan and in every single phase of the work. A most convincing example of Handel's innate sense of drama is given in the sequence of scenes that form the first part. It is devoted to the theme of Redemption through the advent of Christ: the prophecy and the appearance of the Messiah. In six scenes, this theme is treated in ever-changing expression of light and dark. It is represented by the basic musical means of contrasting tonalities and elaborated upon in endless fine musical detail. After the somber darkness of the overture, which suggests no ray of hope, the first scene, made up of *accompagnato,* aria, and chorus, spells gentle radiance: "Comfort ye my people, saith your God." The following scene introduces, in genuine dramatic contrast, the fear of the Lord and the messenger of his covenant: "But who may abide the day of his coming." Two more scenes contrasting Darkness and Light follow before the actual introduction of the Christmas message.

In the second part the contrasts mount and a final balance of forces is achieved. The scenes are bigger and less readily distinguished from one another, but here, too, Handel's dramatic genius is revealed at its height.

The third part, a concluding anthem of praise, proclaims the end of the struggle and the victory of light. But even here there remains a reflection of lightning contrasts. The Last Judgment scene with its mighty aria, "The trumpet shall sound," follows after the sublime credo of the aria "I know that my Redeemer liveth." As in the second part, the dramatic continuity leads to overwhelming choral compositions.

Messiah represents a unique achievement within Handel's oratorio oeuvre. Its stature is to some measure founded in the conception of its text and its challenge to Handel's creative powers. Handel's music discloses his greatest dramatic force and his ability to blend simplicity with grandeur. The unity of its conception and the diversity of its execution impart to this work a quality of perfection that will endure beyond all changes, shortcomings, and vicissitudes in interpretation.

7

Changing Conceptions of Handel's *Messiah*

Performances of Handel's *Messiah* are a deeply rooted, old tradition in Germany, its bordering countries, the United States, and—above all—in England. The more such a tradition is held onto, the less likely it is that problems in the conception of this great work (which may still exist today) will be acknowledged. A tradition can, however, become so antiquated that a reaction must occur. This has been the case in Britain more than elsewhere. The history of the Handel reception in Britain in many ways presents a different picture from the Handel reception in Germany. To a certain degree this is related to the character of *Messiah,* but even more to changing musical traditions and also—more generally—to national traditions. In England tendencies toward a change of the Handel traditions inherited from the nineteenth century came about already at the end of the past century, whereas in Germany and bordering countries they occurred no sooner than about 1920/30, in the years after World War I.

For the sake of clarity it is perhaps necessary to stress that the expression "changing conceptions" can be comprehended in a double sense. Decisive changes in the style of musical performance, as for example in our times the rendering of an aria from an oratorio in a manner based on operatic traditions, doubtlessly can be regarded as changes of the conception, the *musical* conception, of a work. However, it will be more to the point to call them changing traditions of *performance* rather than of *conception*. Strictly speaking, a tradition of conception denotes the changing stages within the conception of the essence and the individuality of Handel's oratorios in general and of *Messiah* in particular. There is a certain reciprocity between the traditions of performance and of conception, but no parallel development. Here I should like to focus on the traditions of *conception* in the strict sense of the word. However, this will not be possible without an investigation of the changing traditions of *performance* as well.

Originally published in German in *Göttinger Handel-Beiträge* 1 (Kassel, 1984), pp. 7–20.

First let us ask how Handel was brought to compose a work such as *Messiah*. What was his intention? How did he himself conceive it? But just as we are unable to establish a systematic progression in the development of Handel's oratorio tradition in general, we also cannot establish that line within this tradition that leads to a work like *Messiah*. Handel was above all a man of practice, not a theorist, and he would hardly have entered into a discussion about the concept of the oratorio. The fact that his late works were called oratorios does not mean that they were a continuation of the older tradition of the oratorio. Since there had been no oratorios in England before Handel, the name was not encumbered with any musical or theoretical conceptions. Therefore he could use it for works the general character of which incorporated not only the traditions of the Italian oratorio, but also those of German church music, English masque and choral music and, inevitably, the traditions of opera that he had cultivated for such a long time. In the intermediary position of the oratorio lies the possibility of its great changeability, and at the same time this position opens up the possibility of divergent conceptions of the nature of the oratorio. This has been true from the inception of the oratorio to the present and not just in relation to the question of a primary affinity of the oratorio to church music or opera. The church character of the oratorios was overly stressed for a long time, whereas today a tendency toward overemphasis of the operatic elements prevails. We shall return to this aspect later.

When Handel composed *Messiah* in the fall of 1741, he had definitively given up performing operas only half a year earlier. After early experiments in Italy (1708) and in England (about 1720), he had taken up the oratorio again in 1732 only incidentally; it was not a principal concern of his musical activities until 1738. His earliest English oratorios (*Esther, Deborah, Athalia*) were dedicated to representing biblical women. (Perhaps he was inspired by Racine's dramas on similar subjects.) Particularly operatic elements in these works were the great number of arias, largely sung by Italian opera singers. Not operatic, however, was the performance in the concert hall rather than on the operatic stage (although this had not been chosen by Handel himself) and, above all, the employment of the chorus, recruited from the church choirs of St. Paul's and Westminster. For the choruses and other pieces Handel made use of material from the coronation anthems and from his setting of the so-called *Brockes-Passion,* which is pure church music!

After this first encounter with the oratorio, Handel composed no new oratorios for four to five years, but performed only revivals of the earlier ones. But when in summer 1738 impresario Heidegger announced that the low number of subscriptions for the following season forced him to refrain from hiring Italian opera singers, Handel immediately accommodated himself to the new situation. For the spring season 1739, instead of operas he composed two new oratorios: *Saul* and *Israel in Egypt.* In both works the operatic elements are greatly reduced. For a soloist ensemble consisting mainly of English singers (or singers acclimatized to England), Handel composed arias aiming more at expressiveness than at vocal virtuosity. Here, there are only a small number of the da capo arias that had dominated the operas composed for Italian singers and that had also occurred in the early oratorios. The chorus, on the other hand, is more prominent, in particular in *Israel,* which is almost a choral oratorio. With these two oratorios Handel had not established one or two types of the oratorio. Especially *Israel* had little success, demonstrating that it was a mistake to create such a long composition almost entirely out of choruses. In the following two works, the *Ode for St. Cecilia's Day* and the oratorio *L'Allegro, il Penseroso ed il Moderato,* he substantially reduced the number of choral sections, and diminished altogether the character of church music. They are also not operatic in character, but rather cantatalike, pointing back to English traditions.

In 1741 two new oratorios followed: *Messiah* and *Samson,* which took up biblical subjects again, and which were almost parallel to *Israel* and *Saul.* But, again, one cannot speak of an established type of the oratorio. During the next years two oratorios, *Semele* and *Hercules,* were written which were both far removed from the biblical oratorios and came closer to opera than any other earlier or later oratorios. The subject matter is taken from the world of antiquity, not from the Bible; and the typical form of the operatic aria, the da capo aria, again becomes more prominent. But once more the picture changes. The later oratorios have mostly biblical (or Christian) subjects, but a certain balance between the elements from the church music and those from the operatic tradition is brought to bear. In most cases a biblical figure stands at the center of the action, as the liberator or leader of the Israelite people, but the dramatic development, on the other hand, may be rather different. In the course of time, however, the conception of Handel's oratorio came to be defined by the type of action that places a heroic element—especially the liberation of the Israelite people—in the fore, as in *Judas Maccabaeus* and *Joshua.* Yet among the long series of changing oratorios, *Messiah* is an exception, even though it is related to the other works by the exclusive use of a biblical text. Nevertheless, it is a work without conceptual counterpart.

It may be appropriate to ask who had the idea to write this kind of oratorio. The compiler of the text was Charles Jennens, who had already shaped the texts of *Saul* and *L'Allegro,* and who later would furnish the libretto of *Belshazzar.* It has often been presumed that Handel himself had contributed to the arrangement of the text. However, a recently discovered letter from Jennens seems rather to suggest that Handel obtained the completed text from Jennens. On July 10, 1741, six weeks before Handel started the composition, Jennens wrote to a friend: "Handel says he will do nothing next winter, but I hope I shall persuade him to set another Scripture Collection I have made for him, & perform it for his own Benefit in Passion Week. I hope he will lay out his whole Genius & Skill upon it, that the Composition may excell all his former Compositions, as the Subject excells every other Subject. The Subject is Messiah."[1] According to this letter the idea and composition of the text would appear to have originated solely with Jennens, and this may be true. Yet as is revealed by other letters (to be quoted below), Jennens was a vain person who did not tend to underestimate his own share in the effort. However, Handel in a letter from Dublin did acknowledge Jennen's full responsibility for the text, writing: "Sir, it was with the greatest Pleasure I saw the Continuation of Your Kindness by the Lines You was pleased to send me, in Order to be Prefix'd to Your oratorio Messiah, which I set to Musick before I left England."[2]

Another question concerning the origin of *Messiah* is whether the work actually was intended for Dublin, or whether it was only made use of there on that one occasion. Another letter by Jennens clearly reveals that, indeed, he had thought of London and not of Dublin: "I heard with great pleasure at my arrival in Town, that Handel had set the oratorio of Messiah; but it was some mortification to me to hear that instead of performing it here he was gone into Ireland with it. However, I hope we shall hear it when he comes back."[3]

Presumably, Handel quickly realized that Dublin would be a favorable choice when he became acquainted with Jennens's text. He was in a situation in which he had to perform a new work for an unknown audience and partly with local soloists whose qualifications he also did not know. With regard to *Messiah,* however, the audience would be familiar with the subject matter—undoubtedly a very favorable circumstance. And since this oratorio was without individual characters, the arias were much more freely interchangeable among the soloists than if they were allotted to particular persons, as is documented by the subsequent performing tradition of *Messiah.* An aria that was too difficult for a local singer could be performed by another man or woman singer without difficulty. From a number of changes that can be traced back to the first performance in Dublin we know that such problems actually occurred.

Even though certain performance problems occurred, they did not affect the reception of the work after the first performance. The newspapers were unanimous and positive in their praise of the work. There were enthusiastic press reports even after the public rehearsal. *Faulkner's Dublin Journal,* for example, reports that "Mr. Handel's new grand Sacred oratorio called *The Messiah* was performed so well, that it gave universal Satisfaction to all present. It was allowed by the greatest Judges to be the finest Composition of Musick that ever was heard, and the Sacred Words as properly adapted for the Occasion."[4] *Dublin News-Letter* writes that "Mr. Handel's new biblical oratorio . . . in the Opinion of the best Judges, far surpasses anything of that Nature, which has been performed in this or any other Kingdom. The elegant Entertainment was conducted in the most regular Manner, and to the entire Satisfaction of the most crowded and polite Assembly." After the first performance, on April 13, *Faulkner's*

Dublin Journal again comments: "The best Judges allowed it to be the most finished Piece of Musick. Words are wanting to express the exquisite Delight it afforded to the admiring crowded Audience."

It becomes evident from these accounts that at this stage of the performance history of *Messiah* there were no problems of conception. The new oratorio—"Mr. Handel's Sacred oratorio"—simply was characterized as the most perfect of its kind or even as the finest musical composition altogether. The report continues: "The Sublime, the Grand, and the Tender, adapted to the most elevated, majestick and moving Words, conspired to transport and charm the ravished Heart and Ear." The uniqueness of both the musical quality and the accurate adaptation of the music to the compilation of the biblical verses are praised as unique.

After his great success in Ireland, Handel returned to London in late summer of 1742, where, after some delay, his *Messiah* was heard in March of the following year. Here the reception was not quite as unproblematic, as unqualifiedly positive as in Dublin. It is remarkable that in 1743 only three performances took place, and two more in 1745. Only after 1749 were yearly performances of *Messiah* to become an established tradition. It is also striking that the work's title—*Messiah, an Oratorio,* as introduced in Dublin—had been dropped in favor of the neutral title *A (New) Sacred Oratorio.* In 1743 and 1745 the work was performed under this title, and only from 1749 on was it again entitled *Messiah, an Oratorio,* as at the first performance in Dublin.

Behind the suppression of the oratorio's original name was an attempt to prevent anticipated opposition. Many people found it distasteful that a work such as *Messiah* should be performed in a theater, even though the theater actually served as a concert hall without any scenic effects. It was a reaction similar to that of the Bishop of London, who in 1732 would allow the boys' choir from Westminster and St. Paul's in the performance of *Esther* only if there would be no action or stage decoration. A reaction to a performance of a work such as *Messiah* in a theater stands out in many letters and documents from that time. There might have been other motives involved as well, but the world of the theater was regarded as a morally inferior one, and the soloists who performed the vocal parts in the oratorios were singers from the theater. The attitude of the public—or at least of certain dominant circles—is illustrated by a little episode that occurred to one of these singers.

One of the foremost singers of Handel's oratorios was the tenor John Beard. He was educated as a singer in the Chapel Royal, and he had very early gained a reputation as a soloist. Except for a few interruptions he was Handel's favorite tenor soloist from the time of his appearance in *Alexander's Feast* in 1736 until Handel's death. He seems to have been a very fine artist and a more cultured person than most of his colleagues. However, when he went so far as to marry Lady Henrietta Herbert, the daughter of an Earl, this was considered completely unacceptable. We have an amusing account of the situation in a letter of Lady Mary Wortley Montagu, who wrote that Lady Henrietta Herbert had asked a priest "to marry her the next day to Beard, who sings in the farces at Drury Lane. He refused her that good office, and immediately told Lady Gage, who . . . asked my advice. I told her honestly, that since the lady was capable of such amours, I did not doubt, if this was broke off, she would bestow her person and fortune on some hackney-coachman or chairman; and that I really saw no method of saving her from ruin, and her family from dishonour, but by poisoning her; and offered to be at the expense of the arsenic, and even to administer it with my own hands, if she would invite her to drink tea with her that evening."[5] (To comfort the reader I should add that Lady Henrietta was *not* poisoned and that she supposedly lived happily with Beard for many years.)

A letter of Jennens confirms that there actually was an opposition to *Messiah*. Jennens writes (March 24, 1743): "Messiah was perform'd last night, & will be again to morrow, notwithstanding the clamour rais'd against it, which has only occasion'd it's being advertis'd without its Name."[6] Personally, however, Jennens was not completely satisfied with Handel's composition of the text he had prepared for him. For he continues: "Tis after all, in the main, a fine Composition, notwithstanding some weak parts, which he was too idle & too obstinate to retouch, tho' I us'd great importunity to perswade him to it." Even two years later Jennens refers to this criticism, saying in a letter of August, 30, 1745: "He has made a fine Entertainment of it, tho' not near so good as he might & ought to have done. I have with great difficulty made him correct some of the grossest faults in the composition, but he retain'd his Overture obstinately, in which there are some passages far unworthy of Handel, but much more unworthy of the Messiah."[7] It is difficult to see what the "grossest faults" of the composition were. We do not know of any changes by Handel that could be related to this criticism.

In March 1749, after a four-year hiatus, and again in 1750, *Messiah* was finally performed again as *"Messiah, an oratorio,"* both times in the Covent Garden theater. But in 1750 a new performance tradition began that finally achieved the breakthrough of the work in the English concert world. In 1742 Handel had performed *Messiah* in Dublin for the benefit of several charitable institutions. In 1749, he had become member of the board of the London Foundling Hospital—an orphanage—for which he had given the first of a long series of *Messiah* performances on May 1, 1750 in the chapel of that institution. These performances in a chapel—though still as a concert, a "fine entertainment," and not as part of the service—created a new, entirely positive reception for the work. That performances in the Covent Garden theater went on unchanged did nothing to alter this reputation. Handel performed *Messiah* in the Foundling Hospital with very few musicians, as can be deduced from the still extant receipts of expenses.[8] The performances in the theater made use of a somewhat larger number of musicians, but the character of the performance was the same as those in the chapel of the Foundling Hospital. During the first twenty-five years after Handel's death *Messiah* achieved the rank of the most popular oratorio even outside of London.

In the history of Handel's reception, the year 1784 marks a decisive turning point. In London a splendid celebration was planned for both the twenty-fifth anniversary of Handel's death and the hundredth anniversary of his birth (though set a year too early). Some of his major works were to be performed in a grandiose style, "which could not be done like this in any part of the world." The Handel commemoration took place during the last days of May and the first days of June 1784 under the auspices of the crown and before crowds crammed into Westminster Abbey.[9] In contrast to the performances at the Foundling Hospital with 50 to 60 musicians, here more than 500 singers and instrumentalists were involved: 60 sopranos (47 boys, twelve women, and one man), 48 altos (exclusively male singers in accordance with the English tradition), 83 tenors and 84 basses, an orchestra of 48 first violins, 47 second violins, 26 violas, 21 cellos, 15 double basses, 6 flutes, 26 oboes, 26 bassoons plus 1 double bassoon, 12 horns, 12 trumpets, 6 trombones, 3 pairs of timpani, and organ. The performances were enthusiastically received by the press. The attitude of the listeners, on the other hand, made clear that ultimately the event had to be regarded as a concert, or "fine entertainment," and not as a church celebration. This again provoked an objection from conservative church circles. The most extensive document of its kind is a collection of as many as fifty sermons by the minister John Newton on the texts used as the basis for the *Messiah*.[10] However, the success of the Handel commemoration was incontestable. As all too often, the great number of performers alone had assured a sensation.

The London Handel commemoration of 1784 became the starting point of Handel performance tradition in the following century. In England it initiated a series of similar celebrations, and in Germany and its neighboring countries it gave the impetus for a Handel tradition in the proper sense of the word. In his discussion of *Messiah* (1824) Rochlitz writes: "In Germany the work for a long time was known only to a few connoisseurs. Only the newspaper reports in the newspapers of its splendid and most successful performances in the societies that organized the Handel commemoration in London drew the general attention to this work. Father Hiller was the first to follow up this attention."[11] Nevertheless, in the 1770s there had been several smaller scale performances of *Messiah,* or parts of it. Zelter gave an almost romantic account of a concert for the crown prince in Potsdam in 1783: "Never before I have had a similar feeling when I listened to music. Since from my youth my mother has kept me reading the Bible, I immediately recognized the text, and Handel's music was an exhaustive paraphrase of every word to me. Words and music together so suited my innermost perception of the Lutheran Christianity, so merged together with it, that my joy erupted in loud, even painful exclamations and attracted attention. I was thought to be indisposed, and the crown prince inquired what was wrong with me. At nine o'clock, after the music was over, I bashfully creeped away, walking back to Berlin at night, dampening the lonesome road with tears of emotion."[12]

The performance Rochlitz referred to was the great performance organized by Johann Adam Hiller in the Berlin cathedral in May 1786. It called wider attention to Handel's *Messiah* for the first time. Although on a slightly smaller scale Hiller aimed at mass effects in the manner of the performances in Westminster Abbey. He had at his disposal 118 singers and 184 instrumentalists, altogether over 300 musicians. Three aspects of the London commemoration had an effect here: the idea of a music festival, the choice of a cathedral as the place of performance and, related to this, the mass effects. All the three were characteristic of the commemoration, but not of Handel's own performances. Therefore, it can be asserted that the continental *Messiah* tradition emerged not from the original but from a posthumous performance tradition. And this changed tradition of performance more or less went hand in hand with a changed tradition of conception. Lutheran North Germany knew little or nothing of an oratorio tradition. In London, *Messiah* became known as a link in a long chain of Handel performances, leading from operas via cantatalike compositions—such as *Alexander's Feast* and *Ode for St. Cecilia's Day*—and the biblical oratorios—such as *Saul* and *Israel in Egypt*—to *Messiah*. The changes within this tradition were determined entirely by Handel's creative development. There was no tight link to church or operatic traditions; the uniting force appears to have been the character of the performances as "fine entertainments." Yet when the cultivation of the oratorio—and especially of *Messiah*—was transferred from the London commemoratory performance in 1784 to Hiller's performance in the Berlin cathedral in 1786, the three aspects mentioned above of the *monumental, festival* performance in the *cathedral* started to dominate the momentum of the "fine entertainment." *Messiah* came more or less to be regarded as a great work of church music. Zelter's words about the merging of Handel's music and his own perception of Lutheran Christianity probably expressed the conception of many of his contemporaries. Even though the continental *Messiah* tradition was carried on mainly in the concert hall and less in the church—and even here not as part of the service—the conception of *Messiah* as a work closely connected with church music continued steadfast.

About the same time, however, another tradition of performance and perception emerged in the Catholic south, in Vienna. In connection with a series of Handel performances arranged by van Swieten, *Messiah* became famous in a Mozart arrangement. An imitation of the London performances was out of the question in Vienna. Here, there was an independent oratorio tradition. From 1740 to the death of Karl VI, an old tradition of oratorio performances existed at the court in the imperial chapel. In the 1770s a new oratorio tradition was established in the concerts of the *Tonkünstlersozietät*. In 1775 Haydn composed his *Il Ritorno di Tobia* for these concerts. These oratorios of Italianate character were somewhat different from Handel's oratorios. However, with such performances there was a clear tradition regarding the size of the orchestra and the chorus, and in contrast to North Germany, here the understanding of the oratorio corresponded much closer to Handel's own conception of "fine entertainment"—a conception that also originated in Italy.

Mozart's *Messiah* arrangement was performed not in a church but in the State Hall of the Imperial court library. The essence of the arrangement lies in the changed instrumentation. As is known, it had been motivated by the absence of an organ in the hall: the added wind parts were intended as a substitute for the organ accompaniment. But actually, the new instrumentation was first of all a stylistic adaptation, a "translation" of the language of instrumental sound from the baroque to the classical expressive idiom. Even before Mozart, Hiller had provided a similarly altered instrumentation, and in principle he had spoken out for this kind of updating. He said in this regard: "By the employment of wind instruments in accordance with the principles of modern composition one could add much beauty to Handel's compositions. In the entire *Messiah*, Handel seems not to have thought of oboes, flutes, or horns, which are so characteristic of our modern orchestras."[13] Hiller describes the purpose of his arrangement as the desire "to enhance and to heighten the effect of the whole," and he formulates the naive conviction (often stated in later times as well) that it was possible by this means to bring about a version of the composition that was "similar to the way Handel would have composed it today."

Mozart's arrangement of *Messiah* (in the version that Breitkopf & Härtel had published as early as 1803) was quickly disseminated. In his *Messiah* essay Rochlitz writes: "With regard to the music, Handel's original, as it is, has not found wide distribution in Germany, as has Mozart's arrangement, which was published some twenty years ago, and which as far as we know has been used since then in all public performances."[14]

It might be said that the consequences of Mozart's *Messiah* arrangement were both positive and negative. In any case, one positive effect must be stressed: by the "modernizing" of its sound the work moved into the repertory of the great choral works representing the classic-romantic concert tradition. Without the added instruments *Messiah* probably would never have become such a central work. But naturally, this "modernizing" must be considered an unjustifiable alteration of Handel's original work. To a large degree the rapid success of Mozart's edition depended first of all on the fact that it included incomparably fine moments—even if these were foreign to Handel's style, as for example the added wind instruments in the bass aria "The People That Walked in Darkness." The success of Mozart's arrangement, however, inspired lesser minds to supplement his instrumentation or to substitute arrangements of an inferior quality. With regard to *Messiah*, the nineteenth century was the century of the "additional accompaniments" in both English-American and continental performances.

The nineteenth century's performances also were widely influenced by other tendencies of a changed conception of *Messiah* emerging around 1800. The tendency toward festive mass-performances was exaggerated to almost the absurd at the London performances in the Crystal Palace; and the tendency toward massive effects was a preponderant characteristic in continental performances as well. Undoubtedly, such performances gave pleasure to the many enthusiastic choral singers and to listeners as well. But on the other hand they were very different from the original performances under Handel's own direction. In England, where for so long Handel's music served, so to speak, as a national symbol, they functioned as a kind of national or religious confession.

In addition there developed a special kind of *Messiah* performances in England that is still carried on widely today: the performances of excerpts from the *Messiah*—especially its first part—in a church as a half-liturgical event at Christmas time. This is far removed from Handel's own approach and performance style of *Messiah*. But again one must concede that this specifically English—or Anglo-American—*Messiah* tradition has become an indispensible annual experience for many people, that no doubt it will continue to expose coming generations to a *Messiah* presentation rooted in the nineteenth, and not in the eighteenth century.

In our century an increasing reaction against the traditional ways of performing *Messiah* has emerged. England was the first country to revise extensively its traditional Handel conception already at the end of the previous century. The English reaction was a complex development that can be only sketched here. It brought together in part a reaction against the Victorian era and, related to this, a reaction against the age-old canonization of Handel's music as a national symbol. (The simultaneous emphasis on Bach's music can be regarded as a related process.) There was a reaction, too, against *Messiah* performances in churches at Christmas time. The first reaction was an entire rejection of this particular tradition, but later one referred to the many compositions by Handel that never were heard because of the constant repetitions of *Messiah*. Finally a reorientation of the conception of the oratorio took place which, even if not caused by the *Messiah* situation, came to influence the *Messiah* conception as well. But before we proceed, we must consider briefly the continental, and especially the German, development of the Handel tradition.

In our century the development of the Handel traditions in Germany has been set in motion first of all by two phenomena: the "Göttingen Handel Renaissance" from 1920, and the rising interest in and growing comprehension of the specific performance problems of baroque music (primarily Bach's music) in the early postwar years (1920–30). Initially the "Göttingen Handel Renaissance" was not very historically oriented. It was the great merit of its founder Oskar Hagen that as the first to envisage a revival of Handel's operas and with modest resources available to him, he was able to initiate a movement that continues today.

The far-reaching consequences of this movement came later, and fully only after World War II. About 1930 the new perception of the nature and the uniqueness of baroque music started to determine the development of the Handel tradition on a larger scale. The replacing of the modern piano by the harpsichord and the employment of a new "baroque organ" were the basis for discontinuing further performances of the Mozart arrangement of *Messiah*. During the 1930s and 1940s the original version of *Messiah* was increasingly used, though not without opposition from Mozart lovers. Inevitably, the question of the scoring, of the size of choir and orchestra, had to come into discussion, and this made untenable mass performances. But as was mentioned above, this aspect revealed that a change of the performance tradition did not necessarily go hand in hand with a change of the tradition of conception. For these alterations were considered first of all as musical changes, and the question of whether they should indicate a new conception of the work hardly arose.

A much closer connection between the tradition of performance and the tradition of conception occurred when, after World War II, the consequences of the "Göttingen Handel Renaissance" became clearer. More than before the war, the performance of Handel's operas became a musical reality. Three centers of cultivation emerged: Göttingen, Halle, and London, and at many other places Handel operas were also performed. This was of great importance for the oratorio, too. The oratorio was in a way more or less in a kind of vacuum. The abandonment of the Mozart instrumentation had loosened its long-standing contact with the classic-romantic concert tradition without reevaluating its position in principle. There was ample space for a new interpretation. To some extent the oratorio was regarded as a kind of offspring of opera, and this strongly influenced both the tradition of performance and the tradition of reception. Nobody, of course, has maintained that a work such as *Messiah* could pass for a disguised opera. *Messiah* and several other oratorios, such as *Israel in Egypt,* were considered as a separate group of works; but the majority of the oratorios were regarded as "dramatic oratorios" which at times were staged and on the whole approached an operatic interpretation. Most clearly this becomes evident in the tendency to ornament the vocal parts. This was a specialty of the Italian stars from Handel's time as opera composer. The soloists of the oratorio performances, on the other hand, had been trained in England, and seldom (or only exceptionally) did they show off with such vocal ornamentation. That performances to a large degree were determined by the conception of the oratorio as a kind of variant of opera is also seen in questions of tempo, articulation, and expression. And now we come to the point: for performances of *Messiah* these operatically conceived interpretations remain largely characteristic, as can be demonstrated easily by certain recordings. This is in itself consistent to a certain degree, since in Handel's time there was hardly a difference between the performance style of *Messiah* and that of the other oratorios. However, also with regard to the other oratorios, the operatic interpretation is undoubtedly a fashionable prediliction of our time, a fashion that cannot be regarded as a revival of Handel's own practice.

I should like to summarize some of the main streams of the development of the *Messiah* tradition:

1.   When, from 1738/39 on, Handel was forced to cease hiring internationally renowned Italian singers, he quickly changed over to the oratorio. The oratorio, however, was not merely an opera on a biblical subject and without scenery and stage action. Three essential characteristics differentiate it musically from the opera: the extensive participation of the chorus, the considerably different types of arias (such as the reduction of the number of da capo arias) and, last but not least, the use of local singers trained in English rather than Italian vocal traditions.

2.   *Messiah* is firmly rooted in this tradition. It is neither a composition for the church of the type of Bach's Passions, nor is it connected to opera in any way. It is in its own way a drama with utmost tensions, presenting the struggle between Light and Darkness, between Good and Evil, between God and Man in a masterly construction of text and music. But it does not employ acting roles, as do the so-called dramatic oratorios. More than with these, it shares certain characteristics with the "allegorical" oratorios, such as *The Triumph of Time and Truth*. However, *Messiah* is more profound: it is not ideological in an abstract sense, but existential in the truest meaning of the word.

3.   After 1784 Handel's concert music, composed as a "fine entertainment," was converted to elevated church music in the grand style. This tradition was carried on in the nineteenth century, especially in England, where both mammoth performances in concert manner, and half-liturgical Christmas performances were introduced into churches. In Germany, on the other hand, most took place in concert performances, in Mozart's arrangement and as a pendant to Haydn's *Creation*.

4.   The changes that occurred in our century are twofold: the arrangements of *Messiah* and other oratorios by Handel were abandoned, and the original performance practice was restored as far as possible. On the other hand, however, there was construed a relationship between opera and oratorio that is reflected by many aspects of the modern performances of Handel's oratorios including *Messiah,* even though it is accepted that there is no connection whatsoever between this work and opera.

5.   Doubtlessly, there will still be a wide range of rather different performances and conceptions of Handel's *Messiah* in years to come. On the whole this

is the fate of all great works. However, we must consider all the different possibilities in the attempt to perform the work in Handel's manner, and not according to our own conception and performance practice. In this regard it is generally established today that mammoth performances and performances with additional accompaniment are a closed chapter. The basis of any performance must be a not-too-large ensemble with boys' choir and original instruments, if possible, and a concert setting. But within this framework there are still problems to be resolved: the characteristics of sound, tempo, etc. borrowed from the church tradition—in Germany this was related to the all too massive sound of the choir—on the one hand, and the tendency to overemphasize the operatic elements, especially of the solo parts, on the other. The more we are prepared to conceive the work itself in its elementary simplicity and unattainable greatness, the more joy *Messiah* will give to us through generations as the "fine entertainment" compiled by Jennens and composed by Handel.

Notes

1. Charles Jennens to Edward Holdsworth, July 10, 1741, Collection Gerald Coke; see *Händel-Handbuch 4: Dokumente zu Leben und Schaffen. Auf der Grundlage von Otto Erich Deutsch:* Handel: A Documentary Biography *herausgegeben von der Editionsleitung der Hallischen Händel-Ausgabe* (Kassel, 1985), p. 334.

2. Handel to Jennens, December 19, 1741; see Otto Erich Deutsch, *Handel: A Documentary Biography* (London, 1955), p. 530.

3. Jennens to Holdsworth, December 2, 1741, Collection Gerald Coke; see *Händel-Handbuch* 4: 339.

4. For this and the following newspaper quotes see Deutsch, *Handel*, pp. 544 ff.

5. Victor Schoelcher, *The Life of Handel* (London, 1857); see Deutsch, *Handel*, p. 472.

6. Jennens to Holdsworth, March 24, 1743, Collection Gerald Coke; see *Händel-Handbuch* 4:360–61.

7. See Deutsch, *Handel*, p. 622.

8. Jens Peter Larsen, *Handel's* Messiah: *Origin, Composition, Sources* (New York, London, Copenhagen, 1957), p. 262.

9. Charles Burney, *An Account of the Musical Performances . . . 1784 in Commemoration of Handel* (London, 1785).

10. John Newton, *Messiah: Fifty Expository Discourses . . .* (n.p., 1786).

11. Friedrich Rochlitz, *Für Freunde der Tonkunst* 1 (Leipzig, 1824), p. 234.

12. *Schriften der Goethe-Gesellschaft* 44: *Carl Friedrich Zelters Darstellungen seines Lebens*, ed. Johann Wolfgang Schottländer (1931): 255.

13. Johann Adam Hiller, *Nachrichten von der Aufführung des Händelschen Messias in der Domkirche zu Berlin den 19. May 1786* (Berlin, 1786), p. 14.

14. Rochlitz, *Für Freunde der Tonkunst* 1: 278.

8

Handelian Tempo Problems and *Messiah*

Handel's music—and Baroque music in general—poses problems to the performer that one can scarcely hope to solve completely. Even though it may be agreed among all concerned that a modern performance ought to be guided as far as possible by the artistic effect intended by the composer, we have to face the fact that a modern performance cannot be an exact reproduction of a performance in Handel's time. Too much has changed in the intervening two centuries. Considering some of the major issues—choral sound, orchestral sound, soloistic vocal art, size of vocal and instrumental groups, auditorium size, and especially the changing musical attitudes of performers and audiences—it becomes obvious that an "ideal" performance, satisfying all demands of authenticity, is, in fact, unattainable. Every performance must in some way represent a compromise.

In view of this fact, one might raise the question whether there is any justification for a historical approach to performance at all. Due to a fairly widespread misunderstanding, such a "historical approach" has become categorically distinguished from the "artistic approach": there is a tendency to associate any historical investigation with the concept of a passive replica diametrically opposed to artistically intuitive reinterpretation. Fortunately, such a distinction does not in reality exist. The purely historical performance is only a phantom created by polemic imagination. Nor is there such a thing as a purely intuitive performance free of all influences of tradition. It is important to bear in mind that the composer conceived of his work in actual sound. Good performances and satisfying artistic experiences can doubtless be accomplished with means of sound different from those at the composer's disposal. But without a conscious exploration of the work's own world of sound, the performer will never be in a position to bring the work truly to life again.

Nevertheless, one might still question the validity of discussing Handelian norms of tempo. Handel's tempi seem to be something too elusive—tempo, in general, might be something too elusive and too variable—to be dealt with on any terms other than the performing artist's free reign. For this reason Handelian

Reprinted from *American Choral Review* 14 (1972), pp. 31–41.

tempo problems have not found much detailed consideration in the past. Editors of *Messiah* editions have made individual tempo suggestions in the form of metronome indications for single pieces, but I think William Cusins, the distinguished nineteenth-century English conductor, was the only one who tried to investigate the problem of whether the conception of tempo had changed since Handel's day and whether it would be possible to find some foundation for evaluating the original tempi. We shall return to his study later, but first it will be necessary to say a few words about the measurement of tempo in general.

Until about 1700 we find very little, and little of importance, in the way of actual indications of time in music. One may refer to something like Johannes Buchner's *Fundamentbuch* from about 1550, in which we are told that one *tactus* should fill out the time between two steps of a man walking moderately. Michael Praetorius says in his *Syntagma musicum* that in the case of a moderate tempo, 160 *tempora* would last a quarter of an hour. This would lead to a metronome indication of 80 or 90 for a quarter-note.

References to the pulsebeat as a time unit are to be found as early as in the writings of the Renaissance theorist Gafurius, who fixes the time of a whole note as follows: "It should take as long as the pulsebeat of a man breathing quietly," which suggests about 70 as metronome indication. In the eighteenth century, the idea of using the pulse as a unit for time values was especially propagated by Bach's contemporary, Johann Joachim Quantz. He arrived at modifications of tempo in a fairly simple way, through a doubling of the duration of note values. Thus in an *Allegro assai* (in $\frac{4}{4}$ time), a half-note is fixed at 80, in an *Allegretto* it is the quarter-note, and in an *Adagio cantabile* it is the eighth-note that will have 80, whereas in an *Adagio assai* the eighth note should have 40 as metronome indication, according to the system of Quantz. One quite understands that he himself tries to modify these rough indications, telling us that it would be unreasonable and impossible to measure the time for each and every piece of music according to the pulse. On the whole it would seem as if Quantz's rules were meant mainly as a guide for beginners. I do not think we should attach too much significance to his system.

The idea of using a clockwork as a basis for fixing musical time values had been put forth occasionally in earlier times, but it was not until the turn of the eighteenth century that a way was found to construct an apparatus in which the pendulum principle was used for measuring time values in music. Various French scholars have contributed to such constructions and others have left us results of their experiments with them dating back to Handel's early years of oratorio writing. Their indications of time values are, quite naturally, based mostly on arias and dance movements from the operas of Lully and his followers. We cannot discuss these indications here. It may suffice to point out that they seem to indicate pronouncedly lively tempi throughout.

It would be extremely welcome if contemporary measurements of time values for Handel's music could be found, but to the best of my knowledge, so far we have nothing of the kind. The only, and unfortunately not very exact, indications of this sort that I remember having seen are a few original annotations by Handel in the autograph score of *Solomon*. At the end of the first part he writes "50 minutes"; at the end of the second and third parts he puts "40 minutes." These are certainly not to be taken as measured time values in a strict sense, but we must regard them as authentic estimated values for each part of the oratorio. As they probably represent the only authentic indications of their kind, they seem very important, despite their rather casual character. We might even try to use them as basis for an evaluation of time values in connection with other oratorios.

If we want to learn what these figures can tell us about Handel's tempi, our first step should be to compare them with similar figures from later times, which we are able to check. I have used the metronome indications in Novello's edition as the basis for a comparison. Counting no time for pauses between the single numbers, nor for traditional final ritardandi, etc., and leaving out the aria "Sacred raptures," which is not in Handel's manuscript, I arrive at the following figures for each of the three parts: about 61 minutes, 59 minutes, and 57 minutes. In addition, I have tried to play through the score of the entire oratorio, deliberately aiming at lively tempi throughout, according to my own conception of time values. This led me to the following figures: a little less than 60 minutes for the first part, and about 50 minutes for each of the two following parts.

When we compare these figures with Handel's own (50 minutes, 40 minutes, and 40 minutes), we must arrive at the conclusion that he wanted to have his music performed in what we would call very quick tempi. Of course, this is not simply a question of tempo, but of the whole style of performance, especially of the singing of soloists and chorus. No doubt the English manner of singing is more suited for a free flowing style of performance than the heavier German one. May I answer an argument here which might be advanced against the value of our comparison. It might be suggested that the surprisingly short time indications given by Handel himself could be explained by the fact that a number of arias were shortened or left out in his own performances. But this is not the case. Of course, Handel did rearrange his oratorios at times and substituted new versions of arias for old ones, but the ruthless abridgment of oratorios so familiar in our time is, as I have mentioned before, an invention of a later period, not Handel's.

When we add up the time of performance for the whole of *Solomon,* according to Handel's own indications, the result would be 2 hours and 10 minutes. This is, of course, without any regard to pauses between the three parts or to the possible introduction of organ concertos played as interludes. Taking these two factors into consideration, we may suppose that a total duration of from 2½ to 3 hours would be a reasonable time for an oratorio performance in Handel's own day. Further evidence for this conclusion follows.

One of the first to comment on Handel's oratorio performances was the old Oxonian Thomas Hearne, who left some rather unkind remarks in his journals about the Handel performances at Oxford in the summer of 1733. He reports that the *Esther* performance on the 18th of July lasted from 5:30 p.m. to around 8:00 p.m. That would mean 2½ hours, and it fits well into the picture at which we have just arrived. Of course, we must ask whether the two works in question are of roughly the same dimensions. They certainly do not differ very much in length even if *Esther* may be a little shorter than *Solomon*. This might indicate a slight reservation with regard to the very quick tempi suggested by Handel's annotations in *Solomon*.

A second piece of evidence—though only indirect—for our suggestion regarding the normal duration of an oratorio performance in Handel's time may be found in the correspondence between Handel and his librettist, Charles Jennens, concerning the composition of *Belshazzar*.[1] Jennens was inclined to let his text outgrow its natural limits, and Handel found it necessary to oppose this tendency in a letter of October 2, 1744, in which he writes: "Dear Sir/I received the 3rd act with a great deal of pleasure as you can imagine, and you may believe that I think it a very fine and sublime oratorio, only it is really too long, if I should extend the musick, it would last 4 hours and more." It is quite obvious that Handel regards 4 hours as a monstrosity, quite unacceptably exceeding the normal duration of an oratorio. Actually, the first part of *Belshazzar* is so long that in a complete performance it would last about 20 minutes longer than the first part of *Solomon* or of *Messiah*. Thus there was ample reason for Handel's protest. The third part was shortened, but nevertheless the performance time approaches 3 hours, or rather 3½ hours, if we count on some time for an organ concerto or a pause between the various parts.

We have reviewed all the references from Handel's own times that I have so far been able to discover. Very likely some further evidence may be found in other letters and memoirs from the eighteenth century. I should like to add only a few references from the late eighteenth century, after Handel's death, which seem to throw some light on later development in performance traditions. Manson Myers quotes one or two pieces of evidence for a slowing down of tempi from about the year 1785, when the monumental festival performances in Westminister Abbey began.[2] In the journal of one Miss Hamilton we hear about a performance on the 5th of June, 1784, which lasted from 12:00 noon to 4:00 p.m., i.e., the very 4 hours that Handel himself found intolerable. A letter from Horace Walpole dated May 29, 1786, confirms this, once again giving 4 hours as the duration. How much external circumstances, such as long intermissions, may have been responsible for this development cannot be said, but it seems reasonable to assume that the actual performance, even without a break, was of longer duration than in Handel's day.

Finally, exact information occurs in some very remarkable annotations in a few orchestral parts to *Messiah* from the British Museum (class mark: g 74 v 52). Here we are dealing with 3 parts, presumably dating from about 1800: 1 violin I, 1 violin II, and 1 bass part. In the part for the second violin the exact time of duration is noted at the end of each of the 3 acts, namely, "1 h. 18 min.," "1 h. 15 min.," and "39 min." In the part for the first violin the following indications occur: "1 h. 20 min." at the end of the first act, and "3 h. 25 min." at the end of the third act. If we combine these indications, we arrive at the duration of each act, and, through addition, obtain a playing time for the entire oratorio of 3 hours and 12 minutes, and a duration for the whole performance, including intermissions, of 3 hours and 25 minutes. It should be noted that a few cuts have been made in the performance in question.

Now we arrive at the period where the development of tempi can be checked through a vast number of editions that have metronome indications for the single numbers. A list of such metronome indications in various *Messiah* editions (table 1) may serve as a basis for the observations given below. My list comprises eleven different editions, the first from the beginning of the nineteenth century, the later ones from about 1900—Prout (Novello), Chrysander/Seiffert (Breitkopf & Härtel))—up to about 1940—Coopersmith (Carl Fischer).

The two editions listed at the beginning by Smart and Horsley are the ones whose importance had already been stressed by Cusins in an article about *Messiah* that appeared in 1874. Cusins wanted to find a basis for evaluating the tempi of his own time and he used the two sets of metronome indications given by Smart and Horsley for his comparison between old and new performance traditions. He refers to the fact that, as a boy, Sir George Smart had turned pages for Joah Bates, who conducted the great Handel performances in 1784, whereas Dr. Horsley's indications probably date back to Wilhelm Cramer, one of the section leaders in the same performances. It may be questioned whether traditions of tempi from 1784 could be preserved in this manner, and it must be kept in mind that there is evidence for the fact that the performances of 1784 lasted a good deal longer than those of Handel's time. Nevertheless, we might follow Cusins in assuming that these two lists reflect the performance style from about 1784. As already noted by Cusins, the tempi found in these are rather quicker than the tempi from the middle of the nineteenth century. Smart's tempi in particular are, as Cusins puts it, "the quickest of all." According to Grove's *Dictionary* they might command authority reaching even farther back. Grove tells us that Smart was much sought after by singers who wanted to acquire the proper style of performing Handel's songs, which he had learned from his father, who, in turn, had seen Handel conducting his oratorios.

The figures in the third column, though published earlier than those just mentioned, must definitely be taken as reflections of a later performance tradition. They come from a vocal score by Dr. Crotch, comprising only the choruses

Table 1. Tempo Indications in *Messiah*

	Smart	Horsley	Crotch	Rimbault	H. Bishop	Novello	Elvey	Prout	R. Franz	Chrysander/ Seiffert	Coopersmith
Overture I	60	60	50	42	42	60	50	60	54	58	60
— II	116	126	112	126	112	116	108 (216?)	116	112	—	116
Accomp. recit. ♪	80	80	—	60	69	80	58	72	80	120	80
Aria	76	88	—	72	76	66	92	80	80	84	88
Chorus	116	116	96	116	116	116	108	100	120	116	116
Accomp. recit.	76	—	—	60	60	72	{ ad lib./ 72/ ad lib.	76	76	—	—
Aria I ♪	96	88	—	76	76	100	72	88	88	—	88
— II	138	120	—	144	144	138	176 (88?)	138	120	—	138
Chorus ♪ (Recit.)	144	132	126	120	138	116	144	144	144	— (♩=84)	168
Aria/Chorus ♪	138	126	120	120	138	120	150	138	120	120	126
Accomp. recit. ♪	80	60	—	76	66	80	72	72	80	76	80
Aria	72	72	—	66	66	63	84	72	72	69	72
Chorus	76	80	66	66	69	69	92	76	76	72	80
Sinf. ♪	—	92	88	104	104	104	80	132	168	162 (♪=56)	104 (♪=54)
Accomp. recit. I ♪	104	72	—	92	76	88	88	112	112	138	138
Accomp. recit. II ♪	—	72	—	108	96	80	100	144	112	168	168
Chorus	88	76	63	—	72	80	84	80	88	84	88
Aria (Recit.)	104	96	—	96	104	96	—	88	92	100	96
Aria ♪	112	150	—	104	80	126	80	112	112	174 (♪=58)	120
Chorus ♪	144	132	126	132	152	120	176	138	138	168 (♩=84)	160 (♩=80)
Chorus	44	56	37	42	40	40	40	40	44	54	44
Aria ♪	72	63	—	60	63	72	56	72	84	120 (♩=60)	88
Chorus ♪	88	72	74	—	69	72	92	72	84	80	80
Chorus ♩	96	88	84	80	96	88	100	80	80	69	88
Chorus I	100	66	76	88	100	76	100	92	92	92	92
— II	80	66	76	(88)	60	60	58	60	(92)	88	66
Accomp. recit. ♪	80	60	84	63	72	80	88	80	76	—	80
Chorus	88	72	82	69	69	88	88	80	80	88	88

Table 1. Continued

	Smart	Horsley	Crotch	Rimbault	H. Bishop	Novello	Elvey	Prout	R. Franz	Chrysander/Seiffert	Coopersmith
Accomp. recit. ♪	—	—	—	56	—	—	—	—	—	58	—
Arioso ♪	69	60	—	56	60	66	100 (50?)	66	76	100 (♩=50)	66
Accomp. recit.	—	—	—	—	—	—	—	—	—	56	—
Aria ♪	108	104	—	92	104	88	84	108	120 (♩=60)	132 (♩=66)	108
Chorus (Recit.)	88	76	74	76	76	88	92	76	80	84	80
Chorus	92	80	—	80	88	72 (♪=144)	92	72	88	—	88
Aria	96	96	—	100	100	84	108	84	92	—	84
Chorus	72	66	66	58	72	80	76	80	72	92	80
Aria ♪	108	96	92	96	96	120	80	104	104	174 (♩=58)	108
Chorus	88	80	66	88	96	72 (♪=144)	76	88	88	88 (NB) (Vers.B)	88
Aria	120	108	—	120	120	112	132	112	116	116	126
Chorus (Recit.)	104	88	72	92	104	80 (♪=160)	104	76	92	—	88
Aria	108	88	—	108	108	80 (♪=160)	92	84	100	—	84
Chorus	72 (♪=144)	66	72	—	76	66 (♪=132)	76	72	88	88	92
Aria	72	66	—	60	69	72	54	72	72	63	76
Chorus I	60	52	36 (♪=72)	50	54	60	80	60	58	63	60
—	92	92	88	84	104	84/80	96	84	92	96	92
Accomp. recit.	—	—	—	—	—	—	—	—	—	69	—
Aria (Recit.)	100	92	—	104	104	80	92	80	100	92	84
Duet ♪	104	92	108	100	60	88	66	138 (♩=69)	108	—	69
Chorus ♪	152	112	120	72	80	112	88(?) (♩=88)	138 (♩=69)	144 (♩=72)	—	69
Aria	98	88	—	104	120	88	92	88	100	—	88
Chorus I	60	54	30 (♪=60)	50	33(?) (♪=66)	60	60(?) (♪=60)	60	60	66	60
— II ♪	116	132	100	84	92	100	100	120	72	76	168(?) (♩=84!)
— III	80	69	60 (♪=120)	72	76	60 (♪=120)	80(?) (♪=80)	72	80	84	76
Chorus	92	84	76	84	92	84(?) (♪=84!)	92	84	96	112	92

and the two orchestral pieces.[3] This edition must date from about 1820 and shows the year 1817 as part of the watermark. The metronome indications refer to the early period of such markings; they are not given in normal metronome figures but in terms of pendulum lengths, which I have transcribed here to ordinary metronome indications. It will be seen that the figures given by Crotch indicate a pronounced slowing down of tempo compared to Smart and even to Horsley. If we calculate the duration of the pieces given by Crotch, excluding all recitatives and arias, we will arrive at the following figures: Smart, about 1 hour, 8 minutes; Horsley, 1 hour, 13 minutes; and Crotch 1 hour, 22 minutes.

The next four editions belong to the middle of the nineteenth century. No clear pattern of development emerges from these. They have been listed merely to show the arbitrary nature of the metronome indications in a number of editions published almost at the same time. In some of these editions we find especially strange indications that aim at an increased effect, either in the form of slowing down or of quickening the tempo, or combining both to create a pronounced contrast: for instance, in the aria "But who may abide" or the chorus "All we like sheep." On the whole, these editions seem to indicate a certain quickening of tempo as against Crotch's edition. If we take Novello's edition—for so many years a standard edition of the work—as a comparison, the total time for the pieces given by Crotch will give us 1 hour, 17 minutes, i.e., 5 minutes less than Crotch, but still 8 or 9 minutes more than Smart. With the Prout edition of 1902 we get still closer to the tempi of the two editions first mentioned. Prout takes the duration of the Crotch selection back to 1 hour, 13 minutes, as does Horsley, but his timing exceeds Smart's by 5 minutes. Even shorter performance times are given in the three last editions. The once very popular German edition by Robert Franz, dating from about 1875, carries us to 1 hour, 11 minutes, and the two others—the edition by Chrysander and Seiffert of 1902 and that edited by Coopersmith in about 1940—bring us back to 1 hour, 8 minutes, exactly the duration of these pieces according to Smart.

In this brief summary I have concentrated on the choruses and orchestral pieces; first, because this was the only possibility of bringing Crotch into the picture, since he includes only these numbers, and secondly because the choruses are rarely subjected to completely arbitrary changes in tempo. Thus a general tendency in the development of performance traditions emerges more clearly. Before I try to sum up the conclusions of our investigation regarding such a tendency in general, I should like to add a few remarks about the modifications of tempo in some specific pieces, among them some of the arias.

If we go through the single pieces, comparing the metronome indications in the various editions, we find that some of them show only a rather limited variation of tempo. This applies, for instance, to the second part of the overture, to the first chorus, "And the glory, the glory of the Lord," to the arias "O thou that tellest good tidings to Zion" and "The people that walked in darkness," and to the chorus "For unto us a child is born." Considering the variation in these pieces "rather limited" is certainly to be understood in a relative sense. Obviously a change of metronome indication from 66 to 92 or from 96 to 120 is more than a small nuance. However, compared to the radical changes found in other numbers, a certain moderation still remains here.

A slightly more pronounced variation of tempo occurs in a number of other pieces not listed separately here. But particularly interesting is a group of pieces showing quite extraordinary variations of tempo in the different editions. This group includes the following numbers: the *accompagnato* "Comfort ye, my people" (58–120), the sinfonia (80–168), the *accompagnati* "And lo! the angel of the Lord" (72–138) and "And suddenly there was with the angel" (72–168), the aria "He shall feed his flock" (80–174), the aria "He was despised" (56–120), the aria "How beautiful are the feet" (80–174), the chorus "Since by man" (36–80/84–104), the duet "O death, where is thy sting" (60–138), and the first half of the chorus "Worthy is the lamb" (30–66/72–168).

In the case of nearly all these pieces, the slowest performance takes more than double the time of the fastest. The reader will find an actual performance in the differing extreme tempi highly instructive. In the present context we can only offer a few general observations on the nature of the pieces involved.

It is to be expected that arias of a markedly emotional character would be particularly liable to an exaggeration of the expressive element through a pronounced slowing down, and indeed this fate has overtaken both the aria "He was despised" and the arioso "Comfort ye, my people." A second category of pieces is likewise predestined to suffer from exaggerations of tempo, namely, those that contain contrasting tempi. This category includes the Christmas recitative and the two choruses "Since by man came death" and "Worthy is the lamb." But tempo variations are particularly pronounced in yet a third category of pieces where it was perhaps less to be expected, namely, that determined by a typical "flowing" Baroque tempo. This applies above all to the Sicilianos or similar sections, namely, the pastoral *Pifa,* the arias "He shall feed His flock," "How beautiful are the feet," and finally, the duet "O death," so strongly characterized by a consistently moving bass.

In most editions, these pieces have—in accordance with nineteenth-century conceptions—been assigned tempi that are undoubtedly too slow because editors failed to recognize their essential character.

Only the tempi of Chrysander/Seiffert seem to have caught the essence of these pieces; it must be noted, however, that the tempi of this edition are based, so far as the Sicilianos are concerned, on a pattern of two, not six stresses, because the dotted quarter-note, not the eighth-note, is the unit employed. Our table might give rise to several other observations, but we must limit ourselves to the following final conclusions.

From the source material available—admittedly scanty—several stages of development in the conception of tempo determining the performance of Handel's music seem to emerge. First, the tempi of the original Handel performances up to the 1760s, which may strike us as surprisingly lively. Second, the tempi from the period of the first great Handel celebrations in 1784–85, which, as a consequence of the change in musical approach and the transference of oratorio performances from the theater to the cathedral, had slowed down perceptibly. Third, the tempi from the early nineteenth century, which, following the general tendency of the time towards a slow performance of church music—and that is what oratorios were generally considered to be—represent a maximum of tardiness. Fourth, the tempi from the mid-nineteenth century, which, although quickening somewhat, still show a tendency towards exaggeration of contrasts combined with some obvious uncertainty. Fifth, the tempi of the period around 1900, which may to some degree—particularly in Chrysander/ Seiffert—claim recognition as a revival of eighteenth-century traditions. Broadcasts and recordings suggest that this tempo interpretation has, to a certain extent, been accepted in our time.

Everything points to the fact that excessive slowness has been the besetting sin of most Handel performances. If, however, we must consider a lively tempo a fundamental requirement, it should once again be stressed that such a tempo is not created merely by speeding up a performance in terms of mechanical metronome markings; it should rather be the result of a fully pulsating motion in which Handel's music may truly live and breathe.

Notes

1. See Otto Erich Deutsch, *Handel; A Documentary Biography* (London/New York: 1955), p. 595.

2. Robert Manson Myers, *Handel's* Messiah (New York: 1948).

3. London, printed for Robert Birchall. A copy is preserved in the British Museum, class mark h 435 n 5. Cf. also the discussion of Crotch's tempo measurements by Barry Brook in *Fontes Artis Musicae* XII, 1965/2–3: 196–201.

Haydn

9

The Challenge of Joseph Haydn

At the beginning of this century, before World War I had put an end to the old cultural traditions—there still was a generally accepted conception of Haydn. The formation and staying power of this Haydn image, the well-known "Papa Haydn"-concept, was made possible not least through the fact that the knowledge of Haydn in many respects was very limited. Two functions of Haydn were especially emphasized: "Haydn as pioneer" and "Haydn as classic." On the one hand he was honored as "father of the symphony," as "father of the quartet," and on the whole, without reservation, as father of Viennese Classicism. On the other hand, only a small portion of his works—a small selection of his late symphonies and quartets, maybe a few of the keyboard sonatas and keyboard trios and, of course, the two late oratorios—were counted as part of the classical repertory. For the most part, this sufficed to represent Haydn as a classic composer. In our time, slowly a change has come about. Beginning with publications connected to the Haydn anniversary years of 1909 and 1932, and even more so through the Haydn research of the past fifty years, new foundations were established for the expansion and reshaping of the Haydn conception. The Haydn research of these decades was certainly not directly engaged in changing the Haydn image, but was involved primarily in basic research. Its first and foremost task was to bring together as completely as possible the works handed down to us under Haydn's name, and to make clear which of them might be counted as authentic, as dubious, and as spurious works. Then, above all, the half-completed Cologne edition of Haydn's works has created a new basis for further research. Moreover, a large number of valuable contributions to Haydn documentation in monographs, congress reports, and various periodicals have appeared. Many new results came to light in this way, both new facts that can be regarded as complementary detail information and also others that suggest more or less actual revisions of the customary conceptions.

The latest research has been widely considered in the Haydn biographies of

Originally published in German in *Proceedings of the International Joseph Haydn Congress,* Vienna, September 5-12, 1982 (Munich, 1986), pp. 9–20.

this half century—from Geiringer's first biography (1932) to Landon's monumental biography (completed in 1980) and my short biography in *The New Grove* (also 1980). Nevertheless, in many respects the basis of the account is still to some extent stamped with traditional conceptions that can hardly pass for unchangeable axioms. I should like to refer to some elements of uncertainty and thus add some question marks, so to speak, to the current Haydn conception. Yet it may be an exaggeration to speak of a "contemporary Haydn conception." Regarded dispassionately, our situation is, rather, the following: we have abandoned the untenable "Papa Haydn" image, but we have not as yet succeeded in creating a new conception devoid of old prejudices.

I should like to discuss the problems of a new Haydn conception in three aspects: 1) How do we regard Haydn's position today as a pioneer, as founder of Viennese Classicism? 2) To what extent is our conception of Haydn's personal and artistic character invaded by old (or also new) prejudices that may lead to false interpretations? and 3) To what degree is Haydn's music *alive* today? How does the Haydn reception of our time manifest itself as compared to the traditional Haydn reception of the nineteenth and early twentieth centuries?

The first question regarding Haydn's position as founder of Viennese Classicism entails immediately several further questions: to what degree must we recognize Haydn as an inventor or discoverer of new forms, such as string quartet and symphony, or rather as the first classic master in these areas? Where shall we seek his point of departure? What determines his exceptional position: formal achievements, the development of a compositional technique, the creation of a new musical language, or altogether a new stylistic concept, a new musical approach?

Gerber's dictionary of 1790, I believe, gives a clear account of how the problem of Haydn's alleged discovery of new forms was regarded in his own time: "He gave our instrumental pieces, especially the quartets and symphonies, a perfection that was unknown before him," (I, col. 610). This means: he did not create these forms, but he decidedly left his stamp on them. Only in the nineteenth century, when the prehistory of these forms had been completely forgotten, did Haydn come to be regarded as the "father of the symphony," and the "father of the quartet." In a time, however, that was entirely determined by evolutionary thought, it appeared unacceptable that they had come out of the blue. At first C. P. E. Bach, whom Haydn himself had referred to, was praised as forerunner to Haydn. Later, Riemann "discovered" the little known Johann Stamitz, whom he made out to be "Haydn's predecessor who had been sought for so long a time." Riemann's proclamation then induced Guido Adler to bring forward the early Viennese composers, especially Wagenseil and Monn. The two volumes of the *DTÖ*, edited (1908 and 1915) by Adler and his associates initiated the publications of music by Haydn's Viennese precursors, a continuation of which would be much welcomed.

Today, we have a different approach toward these problems. No longer is it characterized by questions of priority as at the beginning of this century, when the dispute among the followers of Riemann and of Adler resembled a sporting contest. However, if we want to uncover Haydn's development, his course toward a "perfection that was unknown before him," we must first consider two questions: 1) From what kinds of premises did he proceed? and 2) How well are we informed about his early development, and in particular, how can we gain a more accurate idea of the time of origin of his early works?

In this connection, it is natural to think especially of the beginnings of the symphonies. More than any other genre, the symphonies are marked by an unbroken development through many decades. The symphony appears to have adopted the new function of concert music, not simply as an introduction to opera, in the 1750s when Haydn lived and studied in Vienna. From 1760 on this can be documented with the help of catalogs of music collections and publishers' catalogs (such as the famous Breitkopf catalogs), but unfortunately we have only little knowledge about what happened in the 1750s. Even today it would be a difficult task to sort out even a limited number of symphonies by Haydn's predecessors or his older contemporaries, about which one can say Haydn *must* have known these works. We must be content to say: symphonies of this type could be among those that may have served as a starting point for Haydn.

As for Haydn's own early symphonies, however, we are on firmer ground, even though definite knowledge is limited. The catalogs of the symphonies compiled by Mandyczewski, that appeared together with the first volume of the Breitkopf & Härtel Complete Edition in 1908, became the foundation for new research. This catalog discriminates between authentic, doubtful, and spurious works. The numbering of the 104 authentic symphonies that is still used today was placed in an approximate, chronological order. Of course, since the compilation of this list much new material has appeared, and has made possible many corrections. Many additional symphonies of doubtful attribution have turned up, and from them as well as from Mandyczewski's symphonies of doubtful authorship again a large number have been eliminated as spurious works. However, this does not diminish the merits of Mandyczewski.

Also the chronological order of the symphonies may be improved. This results in part from the increase in material, in part also from the special ordering principle of Mandyczewski: "In particular, it has been avoided to date a work too early." Based on manuscripts discovered at a later time, symphonies No. 40 and 49, for example, should be placed somewhat earlier in the order. In two cases, newly discovered source material has helped to determine a new order of a whole group of symphonies. Haydn's own entries in the so-called *Entwurf-Katalog* reveal rather clearly the chronological order of the symphonies composed between 1765 and 1772. And when in 1959, with the publication of the catalog of Haydn's works at the Széchényi library in Budapest, the Fürnberg copies in

Keszthély became known, this had an even more striking effect on the chronological reordering of the early works. The provenance of the manuscripts from
the Fürnberg family immediately suggests an early date of origin of the works in
question. And beyond that, the collection of works itself unmistakably points
toward an early time of composition. Besides some early quartets, it includes
eleven or twelve symphonies, none of which can be shown—or is likely—to
have originated from the Esterházy years (from 1761 on). It is likely that all these
symphonies stem from the earliest years, and it seems a reasonable assumption
that Baron Fürnberg, Haydn's first patron, ordered copies of the works by the
young Haydn. Recently, it has been suggested by Landon as another possibility
that this group of works was actually a Morzin collection, or a Fürnberg-Morzin
collection. This interesting hypothesis cannot be discussed here. However, it
seems certainly questionable whether Haydn's activities for Count Morzin continued so long that all these symphonies may be considered Morzin symphonies.
In any case, it seems justified to trace the symphonies in question back to his last
years in Vienna preceding his appointment at Eisenstadt (1757/8 to 1761).

The question of the time of origin of the early symphonies is not raised here
simply for the sake of creating order, or striving to correct the chronological
order (however laudable that may be), but it has to do, above all, with the Haydn
image, with the question of Haydn's way towards Viennese Classicism. Many
years ago when I worked on a small academic essay on Haydn's early symphonies, Mandyczewski's then relatively new edition was, of course, my point of
departure. I still remember the trouble I was caused by the joining of symphonies
of greatly varied character. The symphonies No. 28 to 31 composed in 1765
preceded symphonies such as Nos. 32, 33, and 37, which now are ranked among
the works composed before or about 1760. Haydn's consistent efforts to come to
terms with the problems of the symphony seemed difficult to recognize.

Today, things have changed. Three groups of symphonies can be distinguished: 1) approximately twelve symphonies that originated in Vienna before
Haydn's employment as Esterházy Kapellmeister (1761); 2) about twenty symphonies composed in Haydn's early Esterházy years (ca. 1761 to 1765); and 3)
the fifteen to twenty symphonies composed about 1767/8 to 1772. Experimenting with the new form comes to the fore in the symphonies of the first group from
Haydn's late Viennese years. Haydn does not follow any given model, but tries a
number of possibilities. A strong, individual stamp is hardly recognizable. In the
symphonies of the early Esterházy years, formal experiments are reduced. Haydn
favors certain types of movements, and even though there is still a quite great
distance to the late symphonies, the connoisseur of the young Haydn will feel
increasingly at home. The symphonies of the years about 1770, including the
so-called Storm and Stress symphonies, finally carry the symphony to a first high
point. Haydn's words are made intelligible: "Thus I had to become original." In

regard to form, musical language, and means of expression, this is Haydn! The symphonies composed about 1770 are distinguished by such novelty and individuality that we can speak, with Gerber, of a "perfection that was unknown before him."

When the symphonies of these years, in particular, some of the expressive symphonies in the minor mode, came into the limelight at the beginning of our century—after a long sleep—they almost evoked a shock. As compared to the already familiar later symphonies, they must have appeared as the expression of an entirely different personality. It is understandable that they were thought to be manifestations of a crisis, for only a crisis would have compelled the then-imagined Haydn to compose in such a manner. And, of course, it was natural for the spirit of the age to suggest such a crisis not only as a musical affair, but as a "Romantic crisis."

I do not believe it necessary today to resort to this way of interpreting Haydn's development during those years. In my opinion, this development primarily marks Haydn's musical breakthrough, which at the same time was also an essential breakthrough for Viennese Classicism. An adequate, extensive account of this breakthrough remains, as I see it, one of the major challenges to Haydn research. However, here we must let this substantial question rest and turn to our second main question regarding Haydn's human and artistic personality.

It may be obvious to question how these two aspects of Haydn's personality are related to each other. Haydn was a man of the eighteenth, not of the nineteenth century. No one would resort to an investigation of Handel's personal character in order to throw light on the musical character of his oratorios—which originated only twenty-five years before Haydn's "Romantic crisis." With regard to Haydn, however, things seem different. The grouping together of Haydn, Mozart, and Beethoven as a self-contained group of the three great classic masters had the effect, initially only for Beethoven but later also for Haydn and Mozart, that one was inclined to interject between the listener or spectator and the music the image of the artist's personality. This image was determined at least as much by the listener's personal conception of the human qualities of the composer as by the music itself. This might be possible with regard to Mozart, since the family correspondence gives a deep insight into Mozart's performances and feelings. Yet even this correspondence could not prevent the great variation in the conception of his personality, which at times has shifted from one extreme to the other.

With regard to Haydn, the situation is quite different. The openness of Mozart's letters has no equivalent in Haydn's correspondence, hardly even in the letters to Frau von Genzinger. In more than one respect this is probably caused by Haydn's isolated position. A conception of his personality can be extracted only more or less directly from his letters and from reports (in most cases, of his last years). As a matter of fact, the "Papa Haydn" image largely replaced a realistic conception of his personality. Here is another central problem of Haydn research that must call for new attempts at a solution of the problem.

In order to arrive at a new or an expanded conception of Haydn, attempts in later years were made to gain new ideas of Haydn's cultural background, especially in regard to his literary background. Such attempts are worthy of attention, indeed, although less convincing than might appear. Proceeding from a survey of a (rather limited) collection of books from the Haydn estate, an attempt was made to establish essential literary interests of Haydn. Supposedly, these interests had been stimulated by Haydn's contacts with the salon of Herr von Greiner, who was a member of the same Freemasons' lodge as was Haydn.

Yet a number of objections must be raised against these findings. I cannot see that this collection of books—made up, for the most part, in his later years, probably from gifts by visitors—legitimately can be taken for the expression of a "profound literary comprehension." Pohl says occasionally (without citation of sources): "Haydn had a strong dislike for aesthetic contemplation, and whoever heard him talk about his art would never suspect the great artist behind his words" (II, 30). And regarding his contact with von Greiner, there is only little evidence that Haydn actually was—or could have been—influenced by his literary salon. A close contact cannot have been established at the lodge since Haydn, after the day of his admission, never took part in the meetings. Von Greiner's name is only mentioned in two letters to Artaria of May 27 and June 23, 1781, with regard to the publication of Haydn's first song collection. Haydn had asked for his "opinion with respect to the printing," but in both letters he deplores the lack of an answer from von Greiner. Moreover, it is very questionable how Haydn could have managed to visit von Greiner's salon before his move to Vienna in the fall of 1790, definitively at the latest in 1795, after his journey to London—only one year before von Greiner's death. During the opera season at Esterháza—continuing almost throughout the year in the 1780s—Haydn could travel to Vienna only on very special occasions. The assumption that "he mostly spent the winters in Vienna" belongs to the traditional statements for which there is still no documentation. There are documented stays in Vienna for the years 1785 and 1789, but for the time in between we have no concrete evidence. Here, again, is an open question that can be regarded as a challenge to Haydn scholars, or perhaps rather to the experts of Viennese history in the Josephine period.

In recent times, the following (much later) remarks of Caroline Pichler, von Greiner's daughter, have been quoted frequently: "Mozart and Haydn, whom I knew well, were men whose personal manners were devoid of any other power of the mind and who showed almost no type of intellectual culture, of scholarship, or higher aims. Commonplace character, insipid jokes, and with the former, a frivolous way of life was all they manifested to acquaintances. And yet, what a depth, what a universe of fantasy, harmony, melody, and emotion was concealed in these ordinary wrappings!"

It seems obvious that this description (especially the words about the "commonplace character" and the "insipid jokes") reflect a rather superficial impression. And yet it seems just as clear that the central element of Caroline Pichler's experience was the feeling of a distinct contrast between the spiritual greatness of both in the realm of music and their rather unobtrusive, "commonplace" appearance. It is difficult to bring this statement into harmony with the assumption of a "profound literary comprehension" in the manner of von Greiner's salon. I believe there is in several recent descriptions of Haydn a tendency to upgrade his "social status." Actually Haydn himself protested against such attempts in advance, saying: "I associated with emperors, kings, and many *grand Seigneurs,* and was told many flatteries by them; but I do not want to be on too familiar terms with such persons, and I rather keep to people of my [social] class."

What was Haydn's social class? In the first place, of course, he had the status of a musician, of a Kapellmeister. However, I believe that he always remained loyal to his roots in village life and in the class of peasants and craftsmen. In his substantial article, *"Joseph Haydn als Mensch und Musiker,"* Georg Feder opposes an emphasis on the peasant aspects of Haydn's personality with an almost irritated statement:

> Besides Papa Haydn, the philistine, the business man, the narrow-minded, and the princely servant as well as other clichés, we encounter in the literature the peasant bound by blood and native soil. Yet actually Haydn lived in a village only for the first five or six years of his life; then he lived in the country town of Hainburg for a couple of years, and afterwards for almost two decades in the capital city of Vienna. The next thirty years he spent at the brilliant court of one of the wealthiest princes of Europe. In London he was the celebrated maestro, who associated with artists, rich townsmen, and court circles. In his old age in Vienna he was the patriarch of music, respected by both superior and inferior social classes. What, then, are the peasant or even boorish sides of his character?

One cannot help having the impression that here—once again—a city dweller is taken in by his rather condescending conception of peasantry as being on a lower level. This is particularly evident from the introductory words mentioning the peasant in the same breath with the "philistine, . . . the narrow-minded, and the princely servant." Yet with respect to Haydn, it is not a question of "peasant or even boorish" manners, but of a fundamental attitude toward life. At no time did Haydn identify with the way of life found at the splendid court. He contributed to the splendor of festivals on the highest professional level, but he did not participate in person except in his later years, when he had become an official showpiece. As a young man in Vienna he doubtlessly encountered the popular sides of the capital rather than the salons, and he did not want to stay in London in spite of the attempts by the royal family to keep him there. During the many years in Eisenstadt and at the remote Esterháza he was in the country rather than in town, and his last domicile in Vienna was not in the city, but in rural Gumpendorf.

Many aspects of Haydn's way of living recall peasant traditions. Very characteristic is the connection of an immediate friendliness and an apparent openness that, however, seldom passes over the borderline to an insight into deeper currents. This may lead to an interpretation of his reserve as a lack of personality, as documented by Caroline Pichler. A peaceful sojourn in good traditions with proper variations, as in the yearly cycle of the farmer, appears to characterize Haydn too. Abert's pertinent description of the difference between Haydn's and Mozart's reactions to artistic impressions may point in the same direction: "Haydn's genius was not as pliable as Mozart's. It took him longer to react to artistic impressions, and he approached them above all in a more critical way than the young Mozart" (*Zeitschrift für Musikwissenschaft*, 2 [1919/20]: 557).

There was *one* particular side to his parental traditions that Haydn was never able to realize: the harmony of a happy family life. The reason for this lack of domestic happiness cannot be reduced solely to the fact that his wife had no understanding of his art and was altogether unworthy of his partnership, as it had also much to do with the fact that he could not have children. This again was behind his relations to other women, as he stated. It is well known that he took care of the sons of Luigia Polzelli almost like a father. We may well see also his own use of the "Papa Haydn" epithet as a suggestion of this unsatisfied desire. The finest expression of Haydn's desire for a happy family circle may perhaps be found in his famous letter of thanks to Frau von Genzinger. In recollecting the beautiful days in Vienna after his return to Esterháza in winter, he writes: "Well—here I sit in my desolation—lonely—like a poor orphan—almost without any human company—sad—full of remembrance of the past noble days—yes, past, alas!—and who knows when these pleasant days will return? these fine parties? where the entire circle is one heart and one soul—all these beautiful musical evenings—that can be remembered but not described—where is all the enthusiasm?—all is gone—and gone for a long time. . . ." In this company of a music-loving family and its friends Haydn felt quite at home—in contrast to von Greiner's circle; here *his* language was spoken.

To these few hints, I should like to add the evidence of some Haydn portraits. When in 1799 Breitkopf & Härtel were looking for a good portrait to be included in their edition of the *Oeuvres complettes* their mediator, Griesinger, negotiated the question of the portraits with Haydn. Haydn characterized three English engravings as unsatisfactory, and called attention to the well-known drawing by Dance as the best portrait. Griesinger furthermore did recommend a portrait bust by Grassi, which in Haydn's circle, was regarded as fine and of good likeness. If one compares these two very lively and natural depictions with the famous, often reproduced "official" paintings by Hoppner and Hardy, one can feel the contrast: these paintings certainly deserve our admiration, but Haydn recognized himself less clearly in these noble pictures than in the plain and true-to-life portraits by Dance and Grassi. Despite the simplicity, Dance and Grassi depicted a marked personality, and not an insignificant "Papa Haydn" figure.

To what degree does Haydn's personal character, as I have tried to sketch it here, conform to his musical personality? As mentioned above, the demand of an "artistic personality" that fuses both life and work together, is the product of a later time. Of course, we may expect to find even in Haydn certain personal characteristics, such as the sense of simplicity and unaffectedness, in his works as well. First of all, however, Haydn's musical personality is determined by his ingenious talents as a musician.

The persistent one-sided and narrow conceptions of Haydn's musical personality were brought about primarily by two factors: the small number of well-known and frequently performed compositions, mostly late instrumental works, and the perfection of these works from the perspective of Beethoven's music and the musical development of the entire nineteenth century. The motivic work, peculiar not least to the quartet style, on the one hand, and the impressive songlike themes, such as the famous theme from the slow movement of the Surprise Symphony, on the other, were stressed as Haydn's specific features. Frequently Haydn's sense of humor was also emphasized, with reference partly to selected examples from his oratorios, partly to some purely instrumental effects, such as the sudden *forte* chord within the just cited theme from the Surprise Symphony. Another example is the subtle but perhaps somewhat over-rated effect of the so-called pseudo-recapitulation. All the time the "Papa Haydn" image continued to serve as a foil for the general conception of Haydn's music as a lovely, friendly, and always unproblematic music without depth.

In an attempt to sketch Haydn's musical personality today, we are faced with much more serious problems, because the basis of our conception has expanded enormously. Two developments contributed most to this fundamental extension: 1) the Cologne Complete Edition and other publications—in particular many of Landon's editions for Doblinger—as well as the great number of recordings,—make possible a more intimate knowledge of not only the late, but also the middle and early Haydn works; and 2) whereas in earlier times (except for the two late oratorios) a small number of his instrumental compositions almost exclusively determined our conception of Haydn's style, we are now faced with the problem of taking into consideration Haydn the vocal composer as well, especially with regard to the masses and the operas. The masses as "functional" music had certainly been reestablished in the liturgical service of Vienna for a long time after they had become a *terra incognita* in the course of the nineteenth century due to certain liturgical-musical prejudices (and for a long time had remained thus outside of Austria and southern Germany). Only the new editions and the great number of recordings since about 1950 paved the way for a far-reaching renaissance of the Haydn masses. Haydn's operas, too, were almost entirely unknown; only one or two had at times been performed, mostly in badly arranged versions. A Haydn opera tradition did not exist. During the past twenty to thirty years a number of operas have been performed, although in arranged versions. However, most operas have been published in exemplary editions within the Cologne *Joseph Haydn Werke* edition. Also a comprehensive series of recordings of the operas has been initiated. The problem of reestablishing a Haydn opera tradition has given rise to many scholarly discussions, not least as far as the question of stage production is concerned. This problem is one of the principal challenges to Haydn scholars and opera producers. We shall return shortly to this question.

Today, of course, one cannot conceive of a concise formula similar to the antiquated "Papa Haydn" image. This is not possible any more and, on the whole, such images would primarily create new prejudices. Any attempt to characterize Haydn's musical style must avoid proceeding only from a limited number of works, such as the late instrumental works. Starting out from them alone one may be able to establish a typical side of Haydn's stylistic idiom and form of expression, but not the typical Haydn. Haydn's musical universe is much more complicated and much more plentiful than is mostly assumed. For the shaping of changing stages in Haydn's music, however, certain main impulses stand out as determining factors.

1.   Which genres dominated a certain stage in the first place depended on the duties of each of Haydn's employments. Respect for this fact by eighteenth-century composers goes without saying. The difference between Bach's works from his Cöthen years and from his Leipzig years may serve as elementary examples. Strange to say, however, that one does not regard the Cöthen Bach as a "servant of princes."

2.   Next to the large number of compositions that go back to such obligations—the symphonies, operas, and other works—there are others that were either occasional works, or that were composed on commission of foreigners (mostly publishers). In addition, there are some works whose origin and function have not been clarified as yet, as for example some string quartets and keyboard sonatas. With regard to the genres that were constantly requested (such as symphonies), a tradition, a coherent development can be determined, whereas other groups of works rather astonish by the contrasts and unexpected breaks within the development. One need only consider the following three stages of the quartets: the early quartets of the late 1750s, with their five-movement divertimento structure; the three series of six quartets each, op. 9, op. 17, and op. 20 (composed some ten years later from about 1769 to 1772) which realize the

classical quartet style; and the series of op. 33, following after about another ten years (1781), which is renowned especially for the motivic work.

3.   Haydn's stylistic development was determined by the generation in which he was born. The preceding group of composers, Reutter, Wagenseil, and others, successors to the great baroque masters Fux and Caldara, had to cope with the rather thankless task of setting up against the impressive style of the baroque a new, contrasting style that should aim at being easily accessible, easy to perform, and "agreeable." This "mid-century" or "galant" style can be found in numerous divertimenti for keyboard as well as for strings or wind instruments.

Haydn grew up with this "agreeable" style. For him the problem of finding a style of his own was not to overcome the baroque, but the "galant" style. And this may have been exactly the effect that C. P. E. Bach's sonatas had on him; behind the modern style he could recognize a powerful old tradition. Works carrying on the baroque traditions could also still be found in Vienna, especially in the sphere of chamber music (for example, a great number of string quartets by Gassmann). Warren Kirkendale has given a full report about this.

4.   The crucial period of Haydn's development was, without argument, the years from about 1765 to 1772. It is the time of the so-called Romantic crisis or the Storm-and-Stress years. Rather than applying these nonmusical terms to Haydn's musical development, it seems more appropriate to assume a primarily musical process. In short, this process perhaps can be described as follows: in the works of this period Haydn overcame the "galant" style. He was inspired by the fundamental attitude of baroque music, and he adopted also some essential features of baroque structure, such as fugal construction and the concerto form. But he developed his musical language in a decisively new way. He substituted the short sentences and periods of "galant" melodies by longer periods made possible by a widely extended harmonic phrasing. A new intensity of expression was made possible by enhanced rhythmic tension and by the frequent use of minor keys, up until then rarely used in instrumental works. And Haydn tried this new style out in just a few years in all leading instrumental forms: symphony, string quartet, and keyboard sonata. A series of remarkable major works dates back to just these few years.

5.   The conception of those years from ca. 1765 to 1772 as a kind of crisis is not only derived from the character of the works, but has just as much to do with the fact that this striking stylistic development, so to speak, comes to an end without any forewarning. What initiated this period should result in reflection, but the reason for its sudden end seems to be still more mysterious. It is probably most easily conjectured that the prince, not Haydn, wished the change.

Prince Nikolaus unmistakably seems to have had a taste for less difficult pieces. In just these important years Haydn had composed so many easy baryton trios for the prince, that apparently he could for a long time proceed undisturbed in his own way with other types of music. Around 1772, however, a change seems to have occurred. The prince's interest in the baryton trios seems to have diminished, and that perhaps finally made him quite aware of Haydn's changed style. This can be deduced from an entry in the autograph of the Symphony No. 42 (1771), where Haydn cut some measures and remarked: "this was for all too learned ears." That sounds like the echo of a discussion between composer and his privileged listener. Even more weighty and more to the point is the report in Framery's *Notice sur Joseph Haydn* (1810) concerning the origin of the *Farewell* symphony in 1772, as newly referred to by Landon. This report certainly completely deviates from the familiar account of the origin of this symphony and may on the whole sound somewhat improbable. Yet it gains some credibility since it probably goes back to a report by Pleyel who then (or a little later) studied with Haydn and lived in his house.

According to Framery's report the prince suffered from depressions. During one of his attacks Haydn had composed a new symphony and usually that would have had a good effect on the prince. At the performance, however, he appeared entirely uninterested. Haydn became quite beside himself, and after a sleepless night, the next day he asked for his dismissal, as did almost all his musicians. The *Farewell* symphony in this version not only was to pave the way for an early end of the season, but it became the instrument averting a catastrophic development. The exactness of the details remains questionable. Yet other sources also say something about the prince's plan to dissolve or reduce the orchestra.

Haydn seems to have faced a difficult decision in those days. He had found the way to a new musical style that revealed many new possibilities, and of whose novelty and originality he was aware. But if he were to continue on this way, would he possibly jeopardize his own position as well as that of his musicians? He had run too fast and anticipated the taste and perceptive faculty of his audience, and especially of his most powerful listener. He had been too much concerned with the "Kenner" and too little with the "Liebhaber."

6. The dualism of two certainly related, yet characteristically and in other ways contrasting musical forms, is a well-known phenomenon. Clear examples of such opposing forms in the seventeenth and eighteenth centuries are church and chamber sonata as well as *opera seria* and *opera buffa*. In several respects, a similar dualism is typical for the young Haydn. This has been documented at length by Georg Feder in his Graz lecture, *"Die beiden Pole im Instrumentalschaffen des jungen Haydn"* (1970), stating, however, that rather than "two poles" one should perhaps speak of "the different tendencies or, maybe even more neutral, the different genres."

Initially, serious and light music had coexisted in Haydn's works without problem. In the years before the period described above, the baryton trios had continued the lighter style of music in clear opposition to the symphonies, quartets, and keyboard sonatas. But then Haydn had to face the problem of being forced to make his serious music less serious. The problem of dualism was transferred from the opposite genres into the single work. It would not be possible to clearly distinguish between compositions for the connoisseur and pieces for the amateur. It seems that from then on he was urged to remember that all of his works (or most of them) were intended for an audience of amateurs. As has been pointed out, we cannot document in detail how all this occurred. However, if we compare the works dedicated to the prince shortly after this event—the *Nicolai Mass* of 1772 and the six keyboard sonatas published in 1774—to the immediately preceding works, we cannot fail to recognize the development.

The effects of the prince's supposed intervention may be summarized as follows: for a time, Haydn ceased to compose string quartets altogether. He continued with the composition of symphonies, some of them important, some of them with a less personal character, but none of them of the same expressive potential as the most important symphonies from the time before the change. A few collections of keyboard sonatas mostly follow the trend of compositions for amateurs. A mass, the *Little Organ Mass,* relates itself to the light and pleasant compositions.

In 1779 the prince made a new contract with Haydn that no longer required him exclusively to compose music for the prince's use, and in the same year Haydn established contact with the publisher Artaria. In 1781 he resumed composing string quartets, and in 1782 he composed a mass in the grand style. In the 1780s came further quartets, and works such as the Paris symphonies, the *Seven Last Words of the Redeemer,* and other large-scale compositions. In many works, however, dualistic features can still be sensed, more strongly in works like the piano trios, less obviously in the symphonies. And again, it is one of the challenges for us to clear up these problems of Haydn's creative genius.

There is another side to Haydn's musical achievement in the 1770s and 1780s that indirectly might be related to this development: the operatic production. During the time in which the composition of symphonies, quartets, and keyboard sonatas was less prominent, the composition of operas increased. This wave came to an end with *Armida* (1783), and the instrumental music again came to the fore.

A lucky coincidence allowed Haydn, in his final active years, to achieve a reconciliation between his own aspirations and the tasks set before him. In the six great masses and the two late oratorios we meet with Haydn's finest expressive creations.

I should like to conclude with a few remarks concerning the Haydn reception. After World War II we witnessed an amazing increase in performances of Haydn's music. I think I must mention one name here in particular: Robbins Landon, who has contributed quite uniquely to this increase, through books, editions, performances, and recordings. One of the reasons for this Haydn-wave was certainly the demand of the broadcasting and recording companies. However, these may not always belong to the most faithful friends, since they will always cry out for new and unknown music. In spite of the great demand of the past decades, we still have to ask: When the present Haydn-wave declines—and this is perhaps not far away—what will be the future of the Haydn tradition, and what will be the demands on us as Haydn specialists, if we would help make the many hidden treasures in Haydn's music available?

The easiest (and at the same time, the hardest) burden may go to the specialists in Haydn operas: the easiest because here almost everything is new and unknown, the hardest because the revival of operas depends so much on the contribution of stage managers. Unfortunately, there seem to be many stage managers who meet eighteenth-century operas with too little confidence. They regard them only as being realizable if they are filled up with numerous extramusical jokes and gags. One hopes that the possibility of creating a staging tradition that primarily serves Haydn's work will develop. The masses have asserted themselves more and more from 1950 on, and they will certainly retain their position.

The main problem is probably related to the famous old instrumental genres, the symphony, string quartet, and keyboard sonata. Many believe that they know these works quite well. Yet in most cases they know only a small number of them. One major difficulty remains that only a "dogged specialist" is able to survey approximately all the works. It is our responsibility to find among the great number of unjustly forgotten works those pieces that can make it evident how much musical nourishment may be found in entirely unknown symphonies. How valuable it would be to point out to pianists and piano teachers that there are many sonatas among Haydn's never or rarely performed works that may be less suited to exercise the fingers but at the same time may exceed musically some often-performed sonatas. These should perhaps rather be compared to J.S. Bach's preludes and to C. P. E. Bach's sonatas, than to the traditional image of the Viennese Classics.

Above all, it is necessary to do away completely with the worn-out image of "Papa Haydn." The Haydn conception that I have sketched here is no more than an interpretation of accounts and assumptions that are difficult to verify. This is necessarily so, due to the present state of research. Yet I have tried to give a picture of Haydn's character and of the development of his music from his own perspective, without external finery. This might appear easy, yet one is mistaken in so believing. The challenge of "Haydn" will remain for a long time to come.

10

On Haydn's Artistic Development

Descriptions of the development of great composers tend to focus sometimes more on their internal development, and other times more on the external circumstances of their careers. The establishment of Beethoven's *trois styles* can be regarded as an early example of the first; the division of Bach's development into a Weimar, a Cöthen, and a Leipzig period as an example of the second approach. More recently, Wyczewa and Saint-Foix, in their famous Mozart biography, rendered a striking example of a more complex arrangement, based on a combination of both approaches.

An attempt to survey Haydn's development will undoubtedly meet with considerable difficulties. This is due partly to the lack of a finished complete edition and partly to the incomplete chronological ordering of his works, to mention only two fundamental questions. At the present stage of research it is hardly possible to achieve more than an outline of his development, and even this must be presented with strong reservation. Therefore, the following observations should be regarded as no more than such an outline, as a guide to further research and verification.

Haydn's career as a composer comprises the years between about 1750 and 1803. Owing to the external circumstances of his life this length of time can be subdivided into three periods: 1) the early Viennese years from ca. 1750 to ca. 1760, which preceded his employment as Kapellmeister; 2) his years as Kapellmeister for Prince Esterházy ca. 1760 to 1790 at Eisenstadt and Esterháza; and 3) the late years which again can be subdivided into two periods: the London period from 1791 to 1795, and the concluding Viennese years from 1795 on. The year 1766, when the new castle at Esterháza was complete, represents a further external landmark within the second period. Musical activities at the prince's court were extended considerably, in particular by the opening of the court opera.

This sketch of the external circumstances of Haydn's career as composer,

Originally published in German in *Festschrift Wilhelm Fischer zum 70. Geburtstag überreicht im Mozartjahr—1956* (Innsbruck, 1956), pp. 123–29.

however, does not tell much about his internal development. It is evident that the works of the Viennese years up to ca. 1760 have a juvenile character and also that the years after ca. 1790 represent a late period which, however, appears amazingly little affected by old age. The long period from ca. 1760 to 1790 cannot, on the other hand, be characterized by such general attributes. A subdivision according to decades which is occasionally attempted may perhaps serve a certain clarity of description, but it does not effect an insight into the internal development.

The division of Haydn's works according to primarily musical criteria was initiated by Sandberger's classic essay of 1899 on Haydn's string quartets. In this essay he called attention to a new quartet style said to assert itself in the quartets op. 33, the so-called Russian Quartets of 1781. According to Haydn's own words in a letter to the prince of Oettingen-Wallerstein, he had composed these works "in a quite new and special manner." Sandberger's essay left such a strong impression that it subsequently became customary to use the expression "new and special manner" almost like a slogan, and to regard the year 1781 as the decisive landmark in the development of the Viennese classical style in general. The question of how much truth there is behind this assertion can be disregarded here with respect to the Viennese classical style in general. The question, however, of whether it is justified to consider the year 1781 as a decisive turning point within Haydn's development calls for an answer. I do not think it is justified, and I shall return to this question later.

A few years later Wyczewa made a new and significant contribution to the discussion of Haydn's internal development in his essay "A propos du centenaire de la mort de Joseph Haydn" (1909). He calls the time about 1772 a *"crise romantique,"* a "storm and stress period" in Haydn's life. This idea has been taken up in later years as well. It may appear questionable whether the designation "Romantic crisis" or "storm and stress" appropriately states the facts. In any case this alleged "crisis" took much longer than Wyczewa assumed. But there can be no doubt that we face here a decisive turning point within Haydn's development.

During the past twenty to thirty years, comprehensive and valuable studies of Haydn's art have appeared. I need only to refer to studies by Abert (keyboard sonatas), Marion Scott and Blume (string quartets), Brand (masses), Wirth (operas), and Therstappen (London symphonies). These studies pave the way for a general discussion of Haydn's internal development which, however, is hardly yet in reach. Geiringer's Haydn biography (1932/1946) may well be regarded as the most successful survey, although it relies on the arrangement according to those decades mentioned above.

Various circumstances induced me to outline a picture of Haydn's internal development that differs from the usual one in several ways. First, the results of my chronological determinations published earlier[1] necessitated more than a few revisions: not only a new dating of isolated works, but even changes in the total Haydn conception were required. Second, the principal preparatory work for the complete edition of Haydn's works has made a comprehensive clarification of the problems of chronology an urgent task. Finally, a major article for an encyclopedia was the compelling reason for my attempt at a complete survey of Haydn's development.[2] I should like to stress that I tried as much as possible to avoid characterizing a particular period on the grounds of a single genre alone. Rather, I tried to consider all genres favored by Haydn at any given time.

In Haydn's artistic development it is possible, as far as I can see, to distinguish at least eight major periods. These periods are not all equally well-defined. In some of them Haydn develops strikingly new features, whereas in others he mainly exploits these innovations in various ways, trying out all possibilities inherent in the material.

The first major period of Haydn's development will for the time being—and perhaps forever—remain largely *terra incognita*. From the years ca. 1750 to ca. 1760, up to Haydn's appointment as Kapellmeister for Count Morzin in Lukavec (Bohemia) and later for Prince Esterházy, we have so few definite criteria for dating his works that a general chronological survey must seem out of reach. Still more extensive research is needed to establish a somewhat solid basis. Only two works from this decade, a *Salve Regina* and a keyboard concerto in C, both from 1756, can be dated by their autographs. Some further information can be derived from the memories of Haydn as told to Griesinger, Dies, and Carpani fifty years later. With regard to the early years these memories have served as the basis for all Haydn biographies up to now, although a critical revision of the somewhat corrupted account might often be desirable. To the early 1750s we can presumably date the first Mass in F, the (lost) *Singspiel* "Der krumme Teufel," some divertimenti for various ensembles as well as for keyboard solo, a number of string trios and, certainly some dance music. In the later 1750s these works are joined by the first string quartets, some more keyboard concertos, divertimenti, and church music. But it is impossible, even approximately, to establish the chronological order of compositions from this time. Quite generally we may state that during the 1750s Haydn experimented with all genres with which he had real contact. In the works of this period, baroque traditions and the Austrian spirit of the divertimento stand next to each other undisturbed. For the works for instrumental ensembles he makes use of a fixed form, a five-movement form with two minuets. This form not only prevails among the early string quartets, but also among the divertimenti for mixed ensemble and among the works for wind ensemble (the so-called *Feldparthien*). It may well be that it even survived in a number of compositions from the next period.

The second period I should like to set from ca. 1760, to the mid-1760s. Here we are in a more favorable position, since at least one genre, the symphony, is represented by a sufficient number of dated works in order to fix a line of a development. Haydn proceeded from a mixture of operatic symphony, *concerto grosso* tradition, and offshoots of *sonata da chiesa*. During the short span of approximately five years he arrived at a standard form, the four-movement scheme that was to become the classical form of the symphony. Haydn had not invented this cycle, but he raised it to classic perfection. A number of concertos do presumably stem from the beginning of this period. The quartets called "Op. 3" may date back to the first half of the 1760s as well. Like the symphonies they typically adopted the four-movement cycle. The four-movement symphonies of 1765 (complete edition Nos. 28, 29) had established the frame of the following development of the instrumental genres. The next step was to be the content.

The years from about 1765 to 1772 are a period unparalleled in Haydn's life. If I had to specify a short period that can be regarded as the essential breakthrough of the Viennese classical style, I would not hesitate to refer to this period. In the works of these years we see the essential characteristics of the transition from the baroque to the classical style: the merging of a number of formal and expressive traditions that were rather separated before, the quickly realized synthesis which becomes manifest with an impressive clarity. Everyone who is used to regarding Haydn as the harmless personification of a traditional classicism should study the works of this period to get to know him as a revolutionary.

So many threads of tradition are intertwined in this process that it is not possible to give more than a few comments. From these years on Haydn's activities as an opera composer are of a considerable influence on his further development, although initially they did not absorb too much of his compositional power. As opera composer, to begin with, he skillfully continued along the lines of the current *opera buffa* traditions. Also the baryton trios, composed by the dozens in these years for princely entertainment, predominantly exhibit an elegant conversational tone. But in what came to be the three most characteristic genres of Viennese classicism—keyboard sonata, string quartet, and symphony—Haydn presents a new image.

The early, divertimentolike sonatas are superseded by entirely different works. Similar to Bach's Italian Concerto and to C.P.E. Bach's Württemberg sonatas, these new sonatas palpably demonstrate the transformation of the concerto into a composition for keyboard solo. The sonatas, No. 45 in E-flat (1766), No. 19 in D (1767), and No. 46 in A-flat (ca. 1768?), are the still-extant instances of this development. But eight other sonatas, which must be regarded as lost, though their themes are preserved in the *Entwurf-Katalog*, would certainly have given further proof of this development. With his three sets of string quartets, op. 9, 17, and 20 (1768/69?, 1771, and 1772), Haydn made a giant stride towards the classical quartet style. Already here we encounter technical skill and artistic originality which truly bear witness to a "quite new and special manner."

The most striking changes, however, occur within the development of the symphonies of these years. This development is characterized by an intensification of the rhythmic drive, the exploitation of harmonic and tonal tension, and a stunning increase of general expression. Already in symphonies from the time about 1768 (Nos. 39 in g, 49 in f, 59 in A) this intensification of the expression stands out. Even more powerfully it asserts itself in the symphonies composed in 1771 and 1772 (Nos. 42 in D, 43 in E-flat, 44 in e, 45 in f-sharp, 46 in B, 47 in G, 48 in C). It is quite understandable that the strong increase of expression in these symphonies could bring about the notion of a "Romantic crisis." But all things considered it seems to me more likely that this is not a matter of a personal crisis, but rather of a consistent realization of a purely artistic development, the culmination of a long-lasting struggle to obtain complete mastery of form and expression.

I should like to set the next period from 1773 to about 1777/78. It appears as if the immense exertion of power was followed by a certain relaxation. That is primarily true for the instrumental works, and most clearly is seen in the keyboard sonatas, in which a certain taste of divertimento is once again discernible. The composition of string quartets stopped. Among the symphonies a work such as No. 55 in E-flat (*The Schoolmaster*) may be mentioned because of its almost *buffo*-like features. In return, the vocal compositions came to the fore. Works such as the *Missa Cellensis* ("Cäcilienmesse"), the *Stabat mater*, and *Il Ritorno di Tobia* may seem characteristic of this period. Within the operas at the same time an increased insight and a growing penetration into the central problems of opera can be perceived. The classical "character opera," culminating in Mozart's operas ten to fifteen years later, is on its way. On the whole it may seem as if opera during this period in Haydn's conception almost outdoes instrumental music.

As the fifth period, I would indicate the years from 1779 to about 1783/84. This period appears to me, more than of any other time (apart from the period from ca. 1765 to 1772), to have an imprint of experimentation, at times so markedly that Haydn's image seems changed almost beyond recognition. The cello concerto and various symphonies of this time (1783/84) are characteristic examples. In this connection mention must also be made of the "new and special manner" of the "thematic working out" [*thematische Arbeit*] which asserts itself not only in the quartets op. 33, but even in symphonies of a somewhat earlier date. I certainly would not dispute the fact that Haydn clearly realized this principle that became so important for the development of the classical style and especially for Beethoven, and that in the cited series he successfully implanted it to the quartet style. In relation to Haydn's general development, however, this feature must be given a less decisive character than is generally assumed. The experimental tendency is manifested in opera as well. After his long-lasting occupation with the *opera buffa*, Haydn turns to *opera seria* with works such as *L'isola disabiata* and *Armida*.

In his last years as active Kapellmeister (ca. 1784 to 1790) Haydn was less concerned with compositions for performances at the princely court than with compositions commissioned by outside clients. During these years he did not compose new operas. And although they were certainly utilized for the court orchestra as well, all the symphonies of this period were intended for foreign publishers, concert agents, or private *Liebhaber*. To these must be counted the six *Paris* symphonies Nos. 82 to 87, the two *Tost* symphonies Nos. 88 and 89, and the three *d'Ogny* or *Wallerstein* symphonies Nos. 90 to 92. This development is seen very clearly in the piano trios as well, a genre composed regularly by Haydn from ca. 1784 to ca. 1795. They were created first of all for English publishers, initially Forster, then Longman and Broderip, and others. In some of these works the experimental tendency can still be perceived to some extent. Doubts have been raised concerning the authenticity of the first set from this time. But the problems might be caused by the adaptation of a new genre. Another tendency appears, often rather strongly marked, in the works composed for Paris and London. They reveal a more "representative" character which can be sensed in works from the previous period, too, and which appears in later ones as well. Obviously, it is certain that in his works from ca. 1785 on, Haydn had gained complete maturity of style. The stylistic unsteadiness of the preceding period has been generally overcome. Haydn has adopted some traits of Mozart's style, as he did even in later years, but his stylistic balance is not at stake. The individuality of his style remains unaffected even when it becomes tinged with foreign traits or when he directly seeks inspiration in the art of another great composer, as in the case of the late oratorios.

The works of the seventh period from the first half of the 1790s are almost entirely determined by Haydn's two stays in London. The traditions of the previous period with regard to the prevalence of commissioned compositions continues, and on the whole, the main stylistic features remain the same. A strengthening of the trend towards a direct, elementary impression seems to be rather general. It is almost tempting to speak of a "tendency towards popularization," which manifests itself in the use of songlike themes, in some instances probably of actual folk melodies, or specific instances such as the famous surprise effect in the Symphony No. 94. Since our impression of Haydn's art has up to our time rested almost exclusively on the compositions of these years, it is easy to understand that this tendency quite unduly has been considered a characteristic aspect of Haydn's music in general. Needless to say, many subtleties of his London compositions have remained undiscerned.

Haydn's return from London marks the beginning of the last period of his development. This was a turning point which, in several respects, is unique. First of all, the instrumental works which had dominated his music for such a long time recede markedly. The composition of symphonies ceases completely after thirty-five years of continuous development. In turn, large-scale vocal compositions of a churchly or half-religious character start to prevail: the six late masses, the greatness of which has slowly begun to dawn on the musical world only in our time, and the two late oratorios in which Haydn singularly, happily spans a bridge between baroque and classicism.

As stated above, the only pretension of this short survey was to furnish an outline and an impulse to further investigations. It will take much more assiduous research until we can undertake a delineation of a somewhat complete picture of the development. But above all it seems essential to me to lay the foundation for an account of Haydn's development that is free of the traditional tendency to value Haydn more or less as "precursor" and "pathfinder," as Beethoven's predecessor and as initiator of an ultimately not too well-defined "Viennese classicism."

Only if we bear in mind this goal shall we be able to appreciate Haydn's genius on its own terms. And only such an appreciation of Haydn's importance will enable us to unfold the under-utilized, stimulating ideas that we owe to Wilhelm Fischer's pioneering studies of the development of the Viennese classical style.

Notes

1. *Die Haydn-Überlieferung* (1939); *Drei Haydn-Kataloge* (1941).

2. Sohlmans *Musiklexikon,* vol. 2 (1950).

11

Haydn and Mozart

The names of Haydn and Mozart have been mentioned in the same breath so often that it has become customary to take for granted a close relation between these two great classicists. Of course, we do have ample evidence of their mutual esteem. Yet if one gets down to an unbiased investigation of the question of what the extent of their personal and artistic relations actually were, one may experience a certain surprise.

If one begins by asking how long both simultaneously lived in Vienna, one discovers that only for the short time between Haydn's move to Vienna from Eisenstadt and his departure for London—two to three months in the fall of 1790—did both have their domiciles in this city. Haydn's youth in Vienna had ended before Mozart came there for the first time. And Haydn's late years there came only after Mozart's death. During Mozart's Viennese years, from 1781–91, Haydn was often there, but only for short stays, before he finally settled in Vienna in the fall of 1790.[1] Furthermore, if one tries to establish by means of the available biographical literature (including the letters of the Mozart family and other contemporary documents) how often Mozart and Haydn personally met, one will be surprised by the scarcity of references to a meeting of both. When on December 24, 1781 Mozart had to go through with the famous contest with Clementi in the presence of the emperor and his Russian guests, Haydn was in Vienna, but apparently he had no connection with Mozart. On the following day there was a concert at court of music mostly by Haydn, performed by "the most excellent Viennese artists of both sexes then in Vienna," as a report states. During her stay in Vienna the Russian Grand Duchess took some lessons with Haydn, suggesting that he must have been there for some time. Yet neither Mozart's letters, nor other documents thus far known, mention a meeting.

Apparently, the first mention of their friendly relations is to be found in Leopold Mozart's letter to Nannerl of January 22, 1785, in which he reports the contents of a (lost) letter by Wolfgang.[2] Leopold writes Wolfgang "had his

Originally published in German in *Oesterreichischer Musikzeitschrift* 14 (1959), pp. 32–39.

quartets which he had sold to Artaria for 100 *Ducaten* played for his dear friend
Haydn and other good friends." Shortly after, Leopold himself was in Vienna,
where he met Haydn. In the often-cited letter to Nannerl of February 14, 1785[3] is
found Haydn's fine statement about the younger friend. Leopold writes:

> Saturday night Herr Joseph Haydn and the two Barons Tindi were with us; the new quartets
> were played, but only the three new ones which he added to the three others that we already
> have—they are a little easier but are excellently composed. Herr Haydn said to me: "Before the
> eyes of God, as an honest man I tell you that your son is the greatest composer I know by
> person and by name, he has taste and, moreover, the greatest science of composition."

Michael Kelly, the Irish singer to whom we owe also the famous and very
realistic portrayal of the dress rehearsal of *The Marriage of Figaro,* reports a
similar, maybe slightly earlier quartet evening. In his memoirs he recorded his
impression of an evening of quartets at the home of his friend, the English
composer Storace. He writes: "The players were modest in ability; none excelled
on this instrument. Nevertheless there was among them a certain expertise as one
will certainly acknowledge when I mention them: First violin . . . Haydn/second
violin . . . Baron Dittersdorf/violoncello . . . Vanhal/viola . . . Mozart."[4] Provided his statements are correct, this quartet evening should probably have taken
place in summer 1784,[5] but it seems perhaps questionable whether Haydn was in
Vienna at this time.

All these references to meetings of Haydn and Mozart are related to quartet
playing, and it seems rather likely that the composition and performances of
string quartets were what initially brought them together and formed the close
bond between them. The finest expression of their association in this domain is
given in Mozart's famous dedication to Haydn in the first edition of his six great
quartets.

Haydn expressed his friendship and his deep understanding of Mozart's
genius just as beautifully in his letter to the Prague *Verpflegsoberverwalter* Roth,
written two years later, in which he refuses a commission for an opera and refers
to Mozart. Every Mozart lover will be familiar with his extremely cordial and
impelling words.

There is no evidence whether they met in the years between 1785 and 1789.
Only from the last days of this year and from January 1790 do two letters exist by
Mozart to his faithful friend Puchberg, in which Mozart invites him to rehearsals
of *Così fan tutte,* both times together with Haydn.[6] In the first letter he expressly
states: "I am inviting only you and Haydn." These are the last known authentic
references to their being together. It seems likely that they met several times in
the fall of 1790, but as much as one should like to know more about this, we have
no information about it.

In summarizing these remarks about the personal relations between Haydn
and Mozart, we may state that their friendship apparently did not lead to frequent

meetings and sociableness. It may even appear that they met rarely and only at longer intervals. But on the other hand there is no doubt that their friendship was determined by a deep sympathy, personal and artistic, and by a mutual high esteem. Each was aware of his friend's greatness, and, free from envy, they openly expressed their admiration. An essential, mutual influence, however, in the form of an exchange of ideas, the discussion of new compositions and of artistic objectives, etc., scarcely came about, for they had too little opportunity for personal contact.

The mutual artistic influence of Haydn and Mozart developed largely independently from their personal relationship. But even in this regard a revision of wonted assumptions might be appropriate. Their artistic orbits were so different that they did not often come close to each other. Although there are some decisive interconnections, these are restricted mainly to a few specific periods and genres.

Haydn grew up in a transitional period that was determined by two contrasting currents, a conservative one rooted in baroque traditions, and its counterpart which was opposed to the baroque traditions. The musical expression of the latter, however, was rather uniform, so that the musical style itself soon was regarded as rather traditional.

Haydn's latent opposition to this fashionable style was awakened when he became acquainted with C. P. E. Bach's keyboard music. Here he found an original synthesis of old and new, of the music of Johann Sebastian Bach—which Haydn probably did not know—and the music of his own time. We do not know exactly when this exposure to C. P. E. Bach's music, an experience that he emphasized later on many occasions, took place. It is evident, however, that from the mid-1760s he started to challenge the shallowness of the fashionable music of his time. An in-depth study of the works from about 1765 to 1772 may help to recapture Haydn's creation of a new style of expression. In these works more than in any others, one can sense the truth of Haydn's famous declaration: "I was isolated from the world. There was nobody about me who could raise my doubts concerning my doings and torture me, and thus I had to become original." It is hardly an exaggeration to designate these years as the hour of birth of Viennese classical music.

The decisive aspect of Haydn's development during these years was, undoubtedly, the creation of a new style of expression. At the same time, however, a realization of classical forms took place which were of specific importance for future developments. In this regard three forms became established in these years, a position that they were to retain for many generations: the symphony, the string quartet, and the keyboard sonata. None of these genres was entirely new; none of them had been "invented" by Haydn. But Haydn had reshaped them so convincingly and so originally, that it seems quite appropriate to conceive of these years as the starting point of their classical careers.

The symphonies of these years, works such as nos. 39 in G, 49 in F, 44 in E, and 45 in F-sharp, reveal many strikingly new features: the use of minor keys in many works, which was very unusual for this time; the powerful rhythmic drive; and the increase of harmonic tension, which asserts itself both in the formation of themes and (especially) in expanded developmental passages.

In the realm of the string quartet Haydn achieves a synthesis of the divertimento tradition and the style of the *sonata da chiesa*. In the three sets of six quartets each, op. 9, 17, and 20, dating from about 1769 to 1772, Haydn had worked through problems of quartet style and established the foundation of the classical quartet style.

Less known, but also of decisive importance was finally the development of the keyboard sonata within Haydn's oeuvre of these years. From the earlier divertimento serving as musical entertainment Haydn turned to an art of sonata influenced by the keyboard concerto and the symphony, and culminating in the c-minor sonata of 1771. If this sonata is approached with the traditional image of the harmless old "Papa Haydn," it may be hard to accept the fact that already about the time of Beethoven's birth Haydn had achieved such an individual style and such a power of expression.

Up to the early 1770s Mozart could scarcely have been much aware of Haydn's achievements in the out-of-the-way residence of Prince Esterházy. Of the eleven years between 1762 and 1773, from the age of six to seventeen, Mozart spent so much time traveling that he was absent from Salzburg for approximately seven years. His musical stimulations came from the ever-changing impressions received in London, Paris, Munich, and Italy. He had not as yet found his way to a strongly personal style. He followed the trends, imitated different models, and created the many early works, which do not point to a new direction, but which, in charming little details, foreshadow Mozart's later magic power.

In fall 1773, however, he must have become aware of Haydn's importance. He spent some time in Vienna with his father, just before he unwillingly became tied to Salzburg for a long time. On this occasion he must have heard Haydn's latest symphonies, quartets, and keyboard sonatas. Although we do not have any account of a possible meeting of the two, Mozart's music of the following period clearly reveals that he knew Haydn's works and was inspired by them.

We find this development evidenced in those three genres of classical instrumental music which Haydn had just brought to perfection. Already during his stay in Vienna Mozart composed six quartets (K. 168–73). It is not quite easy to say whether it was actually Haydn who had inspired Mozart in these early quartets, because at that time the string quartet was a popular genre in Vienna. Whereas we can only conjecture the connection with regard to the quartets, it is impossible to mistake Haydn's influence in Mozart's symphonies of late 1773 and early 1774, especially in the G-minor and the A-major symphonies (K. 183

and 201). In particular the G-minor symphony, with its powerful rhythmic drive, would scarcely have been possible without Haydn's work.

Whereas these symphonies with their intensified expressiveness point to Haydn's "revolutionary" period, the piano sonatas K. 279–83, composed in summer and fall 1774, reflect the impression of Haydn's sonatas dedicated to Prince Nikolaus, composed in 1773, which mark the end of his period of breakthrough.

After this short period of contact, Haydn's and Mozart's development again proceeded on different courses for a long time. During Mozart's Salzburg years symphony, quartet, and sonata recede into the background, superseded by the serenades and violin concertos, genres which played no role in Haydn's oeuvre during those years when he was mainly acting as opera composer and Kapellmeister. Neither did his tour to Mannheim and Paris 1777 to 1778 bring Mozart any closer to Haydn's music.

During his Viennese years (1781 to 1791) Mozart was primarily devoted to the composition of piano concertos and operas, genres which could not possibly have been influenced by Haydn. The significance of Haydn with regard to Mozart's mature quartet style, on the other hand, cannot be questioned. The question of whether there are any connections between Haydn's and Mozart's late symphonies, and of what kind they may be has not been answered as yet. However, there seems to be a direct line from Haydn's Paris symphonies of 1785 and 1786 to Mozart's three great symphonies of 1788, and another one from the latter to Haydn's London symphonies of 1791 to 1795.

Between Mozart's and Haydn's late works there is only one direct connection, which I should like to stress here: the connection between *The Magic Flute* and Haydn's two classical oratorios. It might seem questionable whether Haydn would have arrived at the wonderful expression of noble popularity in his two late masterworks, *The Creation* and *The Four Seasons,* without Mozart's *Magic Flute.* It is quite evident that Haydn's late oratorios are much indebted to Handel's oratorios and to Haydn's own masses. But Mozart's influence asserts itself, too. It is less specific, less clearly emphatic, but of no lesser importance with respect to Haydn's melody. In these works Haydn became Mozart's heir, adopting and continuing his heritage. These works transform the friendship of Haydn and Mozart into a musical symbol.

Notes

1. According to Griesinger in his *Biographische Notizen über Joseph Haydn,* p. 23, Haydn used to visit Vienna "in winter for two to three months," but it is rather questionable whether this statement also applies to the later time of his employment at Eisenstadt.

2. *Die Briefe Mozarts und seiner Familie,* ed. Schiedermair, vol. 4, p. 297.

3. Ibid., p. 299.

4. *Reminiscences of Michael Kelly,* 2nd ed., 1826, vol. 1, p. 237.

5. Kelly reports that it took place shortly before the first performance of Paesiello's *Il re Teodoro* (August 23, 1784).

6. *Die Briefe Mozarts und seiner Familie,* vol. 2, pp. 309–10.

12

Problems of Authenticity in
Music from the Time of Haydn to Mozart

Problems of authenticity with regard to art works have been known for generations, especially in connection with paintings. How often has the press reported
the sensational discovery of a masterpiece by this or that great painter, which
later turns out to be a work of a less gifted contemporary. The problems related to
such occurrences can be manifold. Before entering into specific musical problems of authenticity, I should like to discuss two cases from the realm of painting
that seem to me an appropriate way to introduce musical problems.

Anybody interested in problems of authenticity will not have forgotten the
Vermeer–Van Meegeren affair, one of the most amazing trials following the
Second World War. Around 1940 there emerged several previously unknown
paintings by the Dutch painter Vermeer van Delft. His paintings, rated among
the world's rarest and most valuable, almost never are offered for sale. One of
the newly discovered works, an Emmaus painting, was especially praised as one
of Vermeer's finest paintings. After the war the little-known painter van
Meegeren was arrested, accused of having passed paintings by Vermeer, regarded as national monuments, to the occupying enemy forces. Most surprisingly, he
defended himself against the accusation by stating that the paintings were not by
Vermeer, even though art critics had confirmed their authenticity, but by van
Meegeren. The whole affair was a matter of forgery, and it turned out that a
painter who had not had very much success with his own work had earned great
recognition through his imitation of the style of an old master!

It is hardly necessary to mention the numerous instances of trivial forgeries
of a similar kind. They are purely commercial affairs without any artistic significance. One takes advantage of the snobbishness and the willingness to invest of
credulous clients by conscious fraud. A forgery may be a new painting made to
look old or an old painting given a counterfeit signature so as to yield more

---

Originally published in German in *Mozart-Jahrbuch 1971/72*, pp. 7–18.

profit. The deceptive intention remains the same, but it is obvious that the substance of the respective paintings is entirely different; for testing authenticity, this leads to entirely different problems of examination, which cannot be discussed further here.

My second example introduces a different kind of authenticity problem, placing in the foreground the discernment of artistic originality rather than the commercial side. From my early youth on, I have had a passion for the paintings of Bruegel, i.e., of the great Bruegel, the father, not the much less important sons. Whenever I was in Vienna I visited the unique Bruegel collection in the Kunsthistorisches Museum. One day in the early 1930s I also visited the gallery in the Liechtenstein Palace in Vienna. Here I found a painting unknown to me up until then, the "Census in Bethlehem." I found striking in this picture certain details that pointed definitely to the father, and others rather to one of the sons. The picture was ascribed in the catalog to Peter Bruegel the Elder, but with the comment: "clever, but for Peter Bruegel the Elder a little too broadly treated. One justifiably can make a strong case for the son, Peter Brueghel the Younger." A year later I visited the Antwerp art museum, where I found the same painting, again with the same stylistic details pointing partly to the father, partly to the son. Shortly thereafter I visited the Brussels art museum, and there I found the solution to the riddle in a particularly striking way: beside each other were placed the original painting, "Le Dénombrement de Bethlehem," signed by Bruegel (the father) and dated 1566, and a copy of this work signed by P. Brueghel the Younger and dated 1610. This copy had the same mixture of stylistic details I had noted in the two other copies I had seen earlier. The catalog referred to still two other copies in French collections.

The contrast to the first example becomes quite obvious: in the second case there is no question of a modern commercial forgery which attempts to render each detail as "original" as possible, since the entire picture is spurious. We are dealing here with old copies of a popular painting where certain stylistic details are changed because a forged "authenticity" was not attempted.

I have chosen these two examples because the facts in both cases are quite clear. However, as is well known, there is an enormous number of pictures that were first attributed to a great master and then later proven to be by an artist from the master's circle, and for which one cannot arrive at a definite solution as in the case of the Bruegel painting. On many pictures one sees inscriptions such as "attributed to Rembrandt," "Rubens' workshop," "Raphael's school," etc. It may be that the great master had contributed a little to a particular painting, but in most cases the citation of his name points to no more than the influence of his style. Usually this does not involve a problem of a forgery, but a difficulty in determining who was the artist. One has to deal with three causes in particular: 1) the history of the particular painting, its progress from the artist's workshop down to its present owner, which is not adequately documented; 2) the style of the painting, its character, and its technique, which are not so unmistakable that it can be attributed to only one particular artist; and 3) the fact that even the best expert today cannot bridge several centuries without biases. The individual style of an artist and the period style come together in the specific art work, and it is difficult to ascertain where one ends and the other begins.

What then are the problems of authenticity that we meet in music, and especially in the music of the mid- to the late eighteenth century? It is self-evident that real forgeries—supposedly "old" works that are fabricated today—are of almost no importance. This, of course, has to do with the difference between painting and music. The original painting is unique; it can be copied or reproduced, but it cannot be repeated; whereas the musical work, once published, can be repeated at one's convenience. The success of each performance depends exclusively on the talent of the performing artist, not on whether the original manuscript or a good printed edition was used. Therefore, there is little reason to fabricate forgeries when the original works are generally accessible. For the sake of completeness, it should be mentioned that from time to time one does encounter forgeries of supposedly old musical works. There are two different kinds: sometimes in public libraries one can find faked "masters' manuscripts" that were made for less-well-informed collectors of autographs. A different case exists with certain works that appear in concert halls as "unknown masterpieces," and after closer examination turn out to be free pasticcios. "Handel's viola concerto" comes to mind, or the supposed arrangements by Kreisler of classical compositions which were actually skillful stylistic imitations by Kreisler himself. Such pieces should be regarded as harmless entertainment music, and they have little to do with serious musical research.

The problems of authenticity in eighteenth-century music that give us such difficult and substantial tasks are not caused by actual forgeries, but are rather related to the wrong indications of the authors, which in most cases presumably are inadvertent mistakes. As early as 1762 the music publisher Johann Gottlob Immanuel Breitkopf deplored such difficulties in recalling in his first volume of his thematic sales catalogue:[1] "How many quarrels and how many secret fights one has to carry out if one wants to give each author what is his, and to attribute the pieces that are found under *different names* to their true masters? And if in such dubious cases that I have met many times one does not find out much by inquiry, how easily then is one just as often misled by one's own judgment as one is guided safely."

That the focus on the problems of determining a composer is a general problem with regard to the period around 1760 is quite understandable. It is open to question whether there is another period within modern European music history when this difficulty is so pronounced. Partially this is connected to the rise of publishing houses. In Paris, London, and Amsterdam, music publishers disseminated music by Italian, German, Austrian, and Bohemian composers without much opportunity to verify the authenticity of the copies from which they made their editions. Presumably, most of their supply came from copyists' firms in Vienna, Italy, and elsewhere, who sent copies into the market without placing much value on controlling or giving correct names of composers.

With the growing decentralization of the publishing houses in Vienna after about 1780, local publishers increasingly undertook the publication of works by local composers. This led to a reduction of copyists' activities and to a lessening demand for editions from Paris, London, etc. Control of the authenticity of sources for these local editions was achieved by customers who in part had associations with the composers. Thus the problem of author determination receded into the background.

In addition, in the nineteenth century the composers themselves, not the publishers, gave opus numbers, and the increasing esteem for creative achievements contributed to fixing the art work in its identity. Problems of authenticity of the kind described by Breitkopf no longer occurred. Even when in the mid-nineteenth century the rediscovery of eighteenth century music took place, these problems did not emerge on a larger scale. One could point to works such as the pseudo-Bach St. Luke's Passion, or the so-called *Jena* Symphony, supposedly by Beethoven. These works, however, are exceptions. Even the so-called Romantic violin sonatas by Mozart could be cited, but the problem of their authenticity was recognized generally only later. It is significant that the second edition of Köchel's Mozart catalog (1905) gave its entries in the original order and with only about thirty new works added.

The new discovery or new recognition of the problems of authenticity not as a speciality for exceptional cases but as a principal problem with far-reaching consequences came up at the beginning of this century with the growing revival of Haydn's symphonies. This is quite logical since there is hardly another group of works in which the problem exists so clearly. Against the little more than 100 authentic Haydn symphonies we know of at least 150 symphonies that appear in one or another collection under Haydn's name. But scarcely one of them can be regarded as authentic.

For the first three volumes of a projected Haydn complete edition published by Breitkopf & Härtel in 1907, Mandyczewski compiled a list of 104 authentic symphonies, 16 overtures, 38 spurious, and 36 doubtful symphonies.[2] This list, based on the preparatory work by Pohl, is still in general usage today—the numbering of the symphonies in Hoboken's catalog for the authentic works was simply taken over from Mandyczewski's list. Mandyczewski had based his decisions regarding the authentic and spurious works on the catalog of 1805 that was compiled by his copyist, the young Elssler, under Haydn's supervision. It bore the title: "A list of all those compositions that I remembered composing from my 18th to my 73rd year." In order to distinguish the spurious from the doubtful works Mandyczewski made almost exclusive use of the Breitkopf catalogs from the years 1762 to 1787, and Perger's catalog of Michael Haydn's instrumental works, published in the *Denkmäler der Tonkunst in Oesterreich* (1907).

In many respects later research succeeded in establishing a broader basis for a catalog of Haydn's symphonies. However, with respect to the time this list with its clear distinction of authentic, doubtful, and spurious works was a great improvement, and for many years it came to be regarded as untouchable in its field.

Therefore, it came as a shock when a short notice appeared in the international press late in 1932 announcing that the famous German musicologist, Sandberger in Munich, had discovered 78 hitherto unknown Haydn symphonies.[3] In a lecture Sandberger severely criticized Mandyczewski's list of symphonies, stating that dozens of symphonies missing from his list of authentic symphonies had to be added. Since Sandberger—justifiably—had the reputation as one of the foremost musicologists of his time, no one dared to reject this highly improbably assertion immediately. And even though most Haydn specialists probably regarded the story of the alleged seventy-eight newly found symphonies as rather a gross exaggeration, it was commonly believed that at least a certain number of symphonies had been discovered. I remember the late Arnold Schering's remark to me: "Shouldn't it rather be seven, eight symphonies?"

At that time I had already worked some years on Haydn's symphonies, and I was one of the few who were privileged to have access to the archive of Prince Esterházy, by far the most important collection of Haydn manuscripts. For this reason I was forced to take up the problem of known and unknown symphonies for the sake of my own work. But at the same time I felt obliged to oppose publicly Sandberger's allegations.

There is no need to repeat here the long discussions between Sandberger and me in *Acta musicologica* in the years 1935–37.[4] Nevertheless, it came to influence greatly my research and to change the course of my studies. Instead of continuing with problems of style in the symphonies I felt it necessary to try to throw more light on fundamental questions concerning authenticity and evidence in musical research, above all on the determination of authenticity based on source-critical investigations. The results were published in *Die Haydn Überlieferung* (1939). The general problems involved were briefly outlined in the introduction, but above all it was an attempt to figure out how much each of the different sources of information about authenticity—autograph manuscripts, copies, prints, and in Haydn's case especially some important catalogs of works—might contribute to a real knowledge of the problems of authenticity. Today it is not necessary to stress the importance of these kinds of investigations, but at that time I would often meet those who expressed surprise, even pity, that I had found it worthwhile to spend so much time on such "unmusical" work.

After the war source-critical investigations have played an important role in musicological research. It is not possible for me to quote the many important works of this kind. It is widely known the change within Bach research resulting from the source-critical works by Dürr and Dadelsen. The Swedish scholar, Ingmar Bengtsson's major book on the eighteenth-century composer Roman is one of the most brilliant contributions in this field and deserves to be named too. In the field of Haydn research there is a wealth of valuable studies to be noted that have brought considerable advances, such as Robbins Landon's book on the Haydn symphonies, Dénes Bartha's and Laszlo Somfai's book *Haydn als Opernkapellmeister,* and in the *Haydn Studies* edited by the *Joseph-Haydn-Institut* in Cologne, in particular by its director Georg Feder.[5] And it is self-evident that the preparation of the new complete editions of Mozart, Bach, Haydn, and others, make use of source-critical and on the whole "philological" methods as well.

At the Salzburg Congress 1964 a symposium was held on "The Present State of Mozart Research." Wolfgang Plath presented a paper, which served as the basis for subsequent discussion, in which he expressly emphasized the need to renew the source-critical basis of Mozart research.[6] He stated: "Basic research means methodical-systematic source investigation. This is the only way to make progress in the handling of fundamental questions of Mozart research." Plath's statement may perhaps be said to take its point of departure a little too much from specific problems of the New Mozart Edition. Nevertheless, the insecurity that the editors of the New Mozart Edition felt is a basic one, and it would seem that Mozart research only slowly has been able to free itself from the many traditional suppositions, or as Plath expressed it, because Mozart research "still possesses no secure foundations and up to now its assuredness is based on a deception."

Unfortunately this somewhat sharp wording by Plath led to a certain derailment of the discussion. Rather than dealing with the problems themselves, it was preferred to discuss the rather idle question whether other problems, such as aesthetic and analytical ones, were not just as important as the source-critical problems stressed by Plath. The discussion dissolved into a great number of questions of detail, and Plath's concluding question seems to be entirely understandable: "Does Mozart research exist as a whole? We should ask ourselves seriously whether we are able to work with the so frequently and carelessly cited *scholarly methods.*"

In the *Mozart Jahrbuch 1964* (1965) Anna Amalie Abert presented her nicely relevant essay, "Methoden der Mozart-Forschung."[7] In it she put up against Plath's remarks the classic article by her father, Hermann Abert, "Über Stand und Aufgaben der heutigen Mozart-Forschung" (1923)[8] and tried to establish a synthesis of the two tendencies that Plath had characterized as "artistic" and "scholarly". In her defense of the necessity for an "artistic" approach, also in a case when the source situation seems secure, she pointed to the so-called *Lambach* Symphony, published by Wilhelm Fischer in 1923.[9] In her opinion, this symphony has been mistaken for another Lambach symphony which exists in a copy bearing the name of Leopold, not Wolfgang, and which had been recorded as a new acquisition of the Stift on the same day as the first one. I do not believe that Abert's reasoning can be regarded as extensive enough in order to come to a definite decision in this case. This she expresses herself in her final remark where she talks of a "hypothesis based on an exact and clear methodology." Even though a musical evaluation might support her hypothesis, the case seems to be too specific to draw any possible conclusions from it with regard to questions of methodology.

In his lecture at the Ljubljana Congress (1967), Friedrich Blume opposed Plath's statements much more sharply.[10] This might seem a little surprising since Blume himself has played such an important role in the publication of critical, complete editions. Moreover, he said he would like his lecture to be regarded "not as criticism, but as a balanced statement." Nevertheless, he fired off a broadside of warnings at source and text criticism as a branch of modern musicology. Of course, there have been certain instances of onesidedness and limitations—as in all other branches of musicology—which might give cause for critical warnings. But a statement such as "the so-called Neo-Positivism will only be useful in a quite limited number of specific cases" is not only an exaggeration, as Blume himself admits, but also a disregard of the entire basis of not only complete editions, but also of stylistic studies of the music from these editions which, among other things, could never gain a firm footing without strictly philological work on chronological questions.

An example of the new tendency to emphasize strongly purely musical criteria as evidence of authenticity is found in Georg Feder's essay, "Haydns frühe Klaviertrios—Eine Untersuchung zur Echtheit und Chronologie"[11] (1971). It is self-evident that source-critical methods are to a great extent taken into consideration, but the final determination of the authenticity of a given composition is based largely on the intuitive, little-documented evaluations of musical style and the quality of the pieces in question. A few examples might suffice: "Due to its convincing style and its highly expressive and compositional qualities there can be no doubt about the authenticity of this work" (p. 292). "The music itself—especially the sprightly Allegro Molto—speaks clearly for its author, and even though there is no external evidence of its authenticity, there can scarcely be any doubt about it" (p. 298). "This beautiful composition has already been published in new editions. For internal reasons there is no doubt about its authenticity" (p. 298). "Quality and style of all movements do not allow the slightest doubt about Haydn's authorship" (p. 302). Most extreme appears the recognition of a work's authenticity solely on the basis of opening themes, as when he says: "According to style and quality of the opening themes, the work is undoubtedly authentic" (p. 294). Even the following statement seems rather daring: "Even if it were handed down to us only as an anonymous composition, its style would have suggested the young Haydn" (p. 295).

Besides the consistent appeal to the arguments of "style and quality," one notices in these statements the stressing of an absolute certainty. Every attempt to prove the authenticity of a work must proceed in two stages that correspond to these two questions: *could* this be a work by a given composer, and *must* it be a work by a given composer? The first question may be answered perhaps on the basis of an investigation limited to the works of the composer in question. However, the the second question—which could also be stated, *can* no other composer come into question—it seems impossible to arrive at a definite conclusion without a comparison with works of other (contemporary) composers. This would imply that either the style of the composer in question is unmistakably individual or that the quality of all of his works is so unexcelled that no mistake would be conceivable. However, we are dealing with a period in which, for several reasons, misjudgments cannot be excluded, as is suggested by Breitkopf's remarks previously cited. We all know that such misjudgments cannot be excluded, and even in the case of great masters such as Haydn and Mozart, we know such misjudgments are possible.

We face here the fundamental question of a clear distinction between facts and assumptions. I have stressed this in the very first sentence of my *Haydn Überlieferung*:[12] "It should be recognized as an elementary claim to every scholarly work, that it must be possible to make a clear distinction between the certainties on which it is based and the uncertain questions which it wishes to solve." Plath expressed similar thoughts much more strongly:[13] "The scholarly discussion became impure because the strict distinction between certain unquestioned knowledge and only conditional hypothesis was visibly disregarded. Especially in relation to questions of authenticity and dating the art of logical reasoning degenerated more and more into the mere exchange of at best plausibly motivated opinions."

Where is the borderline between knowledge and supposition? Is it possible in every case to determine which works are authentic and which are not? Can we obtain such results on testimony of the source information or on the character of the music itself? Are there research methods that are so well-tuned to these problems of authenticity that we are able to speak of a "systematic" investigation of authenticity? To what degree is it possible to distinguish between objectivity and subjectivity within the different methods of source criticism, style analysis, and asthetic judgment? These are some of the questions that emerge when we attempt finally to determine the possibilities and limitations of the scholarly examination of authenticity.

How does one start in order to test the authenticity of a musical composition, i.e., the reliability of its attribution to a certain composer? In most cases one will try to gain a first impression by a quick survey of the composition. This serves to satisfy immediately one's curiosity about the quality of the piece. One wants to know if it is worth a closer examination. This quick survey, however, should be regarded only as a prelude to the real investigation. And in some respects this may include a certain danger of veiling the objectivity through a hasty decision. One must take care not to attach real importance to this first impression.

After having satisfied one's first curiosity, the first question must be: "Where does the piece come from?" The real examination of authenticity starts with the question of a work's tradition. There are several reasons for this procedure. May I once more quote from my *Haydn Überlieferung:*[14] "Every examination of authenticity must proceed from a basis secured by undisputed authentic sources. Style analysis alone provides no basis for judgment, but only style comparison. Such a comparison cannot be initiated before there is a basis of verified source material, and this can only be obtained through the evidence of the sources. The broader the basis of authentic sources the more trustworthy are the results of a style comparison." The great importance of the source investigation first of all rests on the fact that in many cases it yields complete certainty, and when it does not, one can obtain some evidence of authenticity by means of simple and obvious criteria. Sources of primary importance comprise signed autographs, authentic editions, autograph entries in thematic catalogs, and authentic documentation in letters.. In many instances we may be able to establish an unbroken author tradition from the time of the composition, which alone would suffice to confirm authenticity.

Each investigation of authenticity rests on sources and documents of this kind. One should not forget that works such as *The Marriage of Figaro* or *Don Giovanni* have not shown their authenticity by means of stylistic investigation, but vice versa: they can be used as a basis for an investigation of Mozart's style—even more precisely of his mature operatic style—because their authenticity has been established by tradition, by authentic sources.

Opposed to the great advantage of source investigation are certain limitations. In this connection one thinks of the many instances when the source investigation does not yield certainty, not even evidence of assumed authenticity, or when even two or three composers are given as the author of the same composition in different sources, and one of the sources does not seem to be more trustworthy than the others. If one does not come across better sources it will be impossible to progress in this way. Later, perhaps, an uncertain source will turn out to be authentic, if new information is found, but this cannot be forced. We must remain with clear and simple decisions whether a work is authentic on the evidence of the source, whether presumably it is authentic, probably authentic, uncertain, etc., but these classifications yield a high degree of objectivity and should be regarded as of fundamental importance.

When source study does not promise further information then one must employ stylistic examination. It, too, has certain advantages and limitations that are different from those of source analysis. A fundamental difference lies in the fact that here the musical composition itself, and not the documents of its tradition, serve as the point of departure. It is evident that such a "musical" approach has its special attraction, but it cannot be taken for granted that it will give a more solid foundation for solving the questions of authenticity, though this is certainly assumed by many.

Besides the advantage of the satisfaction just mentioned gained from a study of the music itself, there are several other advantages of style analysis as well: The art work itself stands in the center of one's efforts, and one can make use of more extensive and varied methods of analysis. Formal structure, thematic invention and construction, texture, harmony, instrumentation, and much more can serve as starting points for such an analysis. After having finished one examination one can proceed to the next immediately. Style analysis has a much broader basis than source examination.

But this widened basis of authenticity study also increases the danger of possible derailment of the investigation and a lessening of its objectivity. This, of course, has to do not least with the fact as previously said, that the examination of authenticity must proceed from style *comparison* and not from style analysis. Even in dealing with the simple question, *could* this be by Mozart, not *must* this be by Mozart, we will have to compare the work in question with similar works by Mozart in order to conclude and to document whether the alleged authorship is likely or whether it is improbable. At this point several basic questions—questions of method—arise. We cannot deal with them here at length, and therefore we limit ourselves to a few suggestions.

Style comparison presupposes a foundation built on works as a *comparison* basis. But this basis is often made up of an insufficient number for comparison. Here, I have to add a few remarks to the quotations of Feder's unreserved authenticity declarations concerning a number of early piano trios said to be by Haydn. The most problematic aspect of these works is that there seems to be no absolutely secure source basis in favor of their authenticity, although they *could* be authentic, but perhaps not necessarily originating as piano trios. In discussions about Mozart's early symphonies we must acknowledge also here a problem of the basis of comparison, perhaps not related so much to their authenticity as to an established dating. And if we approach the lesser masters such as Vanhal, Dittersdorf, Asplmayer, Ordoñez, Schlöger, it is even less possible to proceed from a satisfactory basis of comparison.

If a style comparison is to arrive at substantial results, then it must depend on a *relevant* and *unequivocal* terminology. The use of the term "secondary theme" is an obvious example. How often does one read that a movement of a symphony or a sonata does "not yet" employ a real secondary theme. Clearly this is meant to say this is a primitive or archaic feature. Nevertheless, one only needs to trace back the formal traditions in Haydn's works in order to realize that the position and function of the secondary theme in the respective movements depends on historic form traditions and on Haydn's own originality, rather than on primitive and archaic procedures. The term "secondary theme" probably is the most abused of all the distorted terms from the sonata form tradition, and it is suited best to mislead an analysis.

These remarks on the "secondary theme" can be expanded to a more general observation: a successful style analysis of works from the time of Haydn and Mozart must be based on a historically founded rather than purely systematical or didactic concept of style. The textbooks of music theory have set up patterns of musical forms derived from formal traditions of the early nineteenth century, and these were intended for the teaching of composition. For an analysis of a composition from about 1770/80 and to compare it with works by Haydn, Mozart, or other composers from the same time, it is meaningless to determine whether these style and form concepts from a much later time are or are not still valid.

In order to determine the stylistic individuality of a composer from a number of his works put together for the sake of comparison, it is an important task to distinguish between the common style of the period and the personal style of the composer. If a stylistic feature was used by all contemporaries it no longer has a value for investigations of personal style. In her essay on the two *Lambach* symphonies, A. A. Abert wants to show that a symphony edited by Wilhelm Fischer in 1923 as a symphony by Wolfgang is really by Leopold Mozart. To demonstrate this she stresses the predominant use of two-bar groupings. She speaks of a "lame addition of two-measure groups" in the two closing movements, and calls this "lame succession which is so characteristic of the Lambach symphony" a principal feature of Leopold Mozart's symphonies and an argument for his authorship.

I think one must raise some doubts concerning this argument. First of all, because the use of two-bar groups must be considered a common feature of the period that can be found in the contemporary (other) symphonies by Wolfgang as well. Secondly, the disparaging expression of the "lame" effect of these two-bar groups must be seen as more a subjective judgment. I find the Andante with its lovely accompaniment in parallel thirds and other nice details quite charming and not at all "lame." I have listened to the recording several times in order to control my judgment. And still I find it lovely—which, of course, is as subjective a judgment as is Abert's.

To what degree must the *similarity* to or the *dissimilarity* from the works to be compared be regarded as the decisive criterion? Again we shall have to admit that one must be cautious with regard to conclusions if the similarity is not really significant, but rather part of the stylistic tradition—as in the comparison of individual stylistic features mentioned previously. And conversely, it is very problematic to call a composition spurious on grounds that there are no direct parallels with the authentic works by the alleged composer, even though its style is in accord with the style of the period. It would not be difficult to find authentic works by Haydn or Mozart whose authenticity might be doubted, if one relied only on an evaluation of style, not on a first-rate source. It belongs to the royal prerogatives of genius that he must be able to create unbounded by traditions, even his own.

Let us ask, having made these tentative remarks on the uncertainties contained in stylistic comparison, how much certainty can we gain from style analysis. The answer seems to me not difficult. We will not arrive at the same clear-cut results with similar implications as in the case of the study of authentic sources. However, we will often gain valuable clues that may give a subjective certainty. And this will be very useful in the many cases lacking source traditions.

To some extent, these statements anticipate the answer to our other, comprehensive question, i.e., whether a composition *must* necessarily be a work of a certain composer (e.g., Haydn, Mozart)? Can *no* other composer be considered possible? It is quite evident that this question can be answered even less securely on grounds of style analysis. An answer to this question is already impossible because of the mass of unexplored, even inaccessible music from the second half of the eighteenth century.

There is still another question that we have not attempted to answer: the question of the possibility of deciding about the authenticity of a composition on the basis of an evaluation of its quality. The answer to this question is difficult and at the same time easy. Difficult, because we must admit that the judgment of a doubtful work's quality is a subjective one, determined to a large degree by a first impression. Easy, because there are no objective criteria for measuring quality. We only have to think of the prejudiced judgment of, say, Haydn's masses that were for generations regarded as rather unimportant or even bad music, and which are now counted among the finest music of the Classic period. If we acknowledge that terms such as originality, gift of variation, power of expression, etc., are bound up with the nature of the creative personality, then we can conceive of the uniqueness of the works of the great composers. However, even less gifted composers at times are endowed with original, strongly expressive, and significant creative faculties. The borderline between the genius and the foremost of his contemporaries is not always sharply defined as one might assume. To attempt to establish authenticity of a composition on grounds of an evaluation of quality means to abandon entirely objectivity.

I hope to have been successful to some degree in defining the roles of source study and style analysis within the area of an examination of authenticity. Both are indispensable, complementary, rather than competitive. In most cases, source criticism gives us utmost certainty, in others none at all. Style analysis never gives us complete certainty, but it never leaves us completely in the dark—provided we rise to our task.

We will not get far in our study of music history if we limit ourselves to taking into consideration only certified facts. We must draw on conjecture as well. Nevertheless, we need to make a clear distinction between fact and conjecture. Haydn research has largely followed this principle. With respect to Mozart research it seems, despite admirable achievements from Köchel to Abert and Einstein, that it has need in this regard to catch up. If one wants to designate this clear distinction between evidence and conjecture as Neo-Positivism, then I say we need Neo-Positivism.

Notes

1. New edition (Barry Brook), p. 29.

2. *Joseph Haydn Werke. Erste kritische durchgesehene Gesamtausgabe.* Series 1, *Symphonien,* vol. 1 (1907).

3. W. Krienitz, "78 neue Haydn-Symphonien," in *Allgemeine Musikzeitung* (1932/33), p. 153.

4. "Haydn und das kleine Quartbuch," etc., in *Acta musicologica* (1935–37).

5. See G. Feder, "Die Überlieferung und Verbreitung der handschriftlichen Quellen zu Haydns Werken, 1. Folge," in *Haydn-Studien* I, 1(1965): 3–42.

6. International Musicological Society, *Bericht über den neunten internationalen Kongress, Salzburg 1964* I (1964): 47–55.

7. *Mozart-Jahrbuch 1964* (1965): 22–27.

8. *Mozart-Jahrbuch, erster Jahrgang* (1923): 7–22.

9. Ibid., pp. 35–68.

10. F. Blume, "Historische Musikforschung in der Gegenwart," in *Acta musicologica* (1968): 8–21. See also *I.M.S. Report of the Tenth Congress, Ljubljana 1967* (1970): 13–25.

11. *Haydn-Studien* II, 4(1970): 289–316.

12. Op. cit., p. 9.

13. Op. cit., p. 50.

14. Op. cit., p. 15.

13

Haydn's Early Masses: Evolution of a Genre

Haydn's Masses were black-listed for a long time. This had nothing to do with their musical value; the argument was of a different nature. It was currents in church music, or perhaps rather in church music ideology, that caused leading authorities to condemn them. In the famous papal rescript "Motu proprio" (1903) a general statement says: "A piece of music that is meant to serve in the Church is the more sacred and liturgical the more it comes close to Gregorian chant in its nature, spirit and taste; it is conversely the less worthy to serve in the House of God the more it strays from this model." Haydn's Masses were obviously not close to Gregorian chant and there were serious objections to their use in the church service, but a strong Austrian tradition carried them through the crisis. It was above all the historian Alfred Schnerich who in the early part of this century fought for the continuation of a specific Austrian Mass tradition. But outside of Austria and its neighboring regions, Haydn's Masses were scarcely known and performed, and critical evaluations—or devaluations—such as those found in Hermann Kretzschmar's influential *Führer durch den Konzertsaal* (A Guide to the Music of the Concert Hall), contributed to keeping them out of the choral repertoire, though it might have seemed reasonable to ask for their use as a concert music—as in the cases of Mozart's *Requiem* or Bach's *Mass in B Minor*—even if they were not to be used in the church service.

   An important step towards a new approach to these works was made by Carl Maria Brand, who presented a substantial examination of them in his book *Die Messen von Joseph Haydn*, unfortunately published at a most ill-fated time, 1941. (I still remember with gratitude how meeting Brand in the 1930s helped me towards a better understanding of the Masses early in my career.) It fell to the Haydn Society, initiated by H. C. Robbins Landon in 1949, to make a pioneering contribution to a revival of the Haydn Masses; and this happened in two ways:

Reprinted from *From Schütz to Schubert, Essays on Choral Music*, a special issue of *American Choral Review* 24 (2/3 1982), pp. 48–60.

through undertaking a critical edition of all the Masses, begun by the Haydn Society and completed by the *Joseph-Haydn-Institut* in Cologne, and through recording a number of the Masses, taking advantage of the new possibilities of the long-playing record, which had come to life just about that time.

It may seem strange to a young generation that Haydn's Masses, now easily available in any reasonably well-equipped record library, were virtually unknown outside a small area of Europe until about thirty years ago. This is not merely a historical fact; it means rather that there was not—as in the cases of Bach's Passions or Haydn's own late oratorios—a long general performance tradition from which to take a point of departure, or, perhaps, of opposition. The first recordings of Haydn Masses, issued by the Haydn Society, were made in Vienna and clearly show a performance style emanating from the traditions of Austrian church music; but a considerable number of later recordings had scarcely any connection with tradition at all, so that the same Mass may be heard in rather different performing styles with regard to sound quality, character of vocal and instrumental forces, tempo, pacing, etc. On the other hand, Haydn's Masses do not form a stylistically unified group. We need only remember that his first Mass was composed about 1750, at the time of Bach's *Art of Fugue,* and his last in 1802, at the time of Beethoven's *Eroica.* Not only do they cover a longer span of time than any other group of Haydn's compositions, but they were also created under rather varying conditions and in varying intervals, only in Haydn's late years forming a regular series.

From Haydn's early years in Vienna dates his first Mass, the *Missa Brevis in F,* composed about 1750; we have only references from later years to this work, pointing to either 1749 or perhaps 1753 as the year of composition. A second Mass from the early years, *Missa Sunt bonae mixta malis,* seems to be lost. A third one, *Missa Rorate coeli,* was entered by Haydn in his so-called *Entwurf-Katalog*[1] very late (just before 1800) and, since the Mass is found in a number of sources under the name of Johann Georg Reutter, and only in one case under Haydn's name, it is most likely not by him. When Haydn was made Kapellmeister for Prince Esterházy in 1761, he had no church music duties for the first five years, i.e., until the death of the nominal First Kapellmeister Gregor Joseph Werner in 1766. In the same year he wrote a most extended and elaborate Mass, the *Cäcilienmesse,* which, as it might seem, was a composition meant to demonstrate his proficiency as a church music composer, after this field had been opened up to him again. It was followed by an impressive *Stabat Mater* in 1767, and a second Mass, composed 1768–70, the *Great Organ Mass.* Two minor Masses from the 1770s, the *Missa Sancti Nicolai* and the *Little Organ Mass,* and one in a grander style, the *Mariazellermesse* from 1782—a total of three in the course of fifteen years—make it evident that the Mass did not occupy the center of Haydn's activities. In 1782 Emperor Joseph II ordered a curtailing of traditional church music; thus the *Mariazeller Mass* marked the beginning of a long period in which Haydn wrote no Masses at all. Only after his return from London did Haydn again take up the composition of Masses, now spurred by the interest that the young Prince Nicolaus showed in church music. In the years 1796–1802 he composed the wonderful series of six great Masses: *Heiligmesse, Paukenmesse, Nelsonmesse, Theresienmesse, Schöpfungsmesse,* and *Harmoniemesse.* Here we can speak of a specific style of Haydn's Masses for which the earlier works prepared the way in varying degrees. It is all the more interesting to consider the development of these early Masses and the individual chapter they constitute in Haydn's creative career.

Haydn came to Vienna as a choirboy at St. Stephan's in 1740, just at the time when, within a few years, two important Viennese composers—Fux and Caldara—died, and when the death of Emperor Karl VI suddenly put an end to a long period of church music of a high level of quality. Haydn probably heard some of the Masses by Fux and Caldara, but the music he grew up with was that of their much less important successor, Georg Reutter the younger. Reutter's compositions are not easily available, and the Mass published in *Denkmäler der Tonkunst in Oesterreich,* Vol. 88 (1952), could scarcely be regarded as typical. Far from the contrapuntal mastery shown by Fux and Caldara, Reutter's Masses seem to be marked largely by a rather simple style and a limited range of variety, with a prominent tendency towards a vocal-instrumental dualism: the chorus sings in a chordal texture containing many tone repetitions in the individual parts, and the instrumental accompaniment is dominated by a violin melody of often stereotyped figurations, referred to by Reutter's contemporaries as his *"rauschende Violinen"* (rustling violins). The *Rorate Mass* mentioned above suggests this style; if it were to be credited to Haydn, not Reutter after all, it would certainly have to be taken as the young composer's endeavor to imitate the style of his master, not as the harbinger of new promise.

If the *Missa Brevis in F,* the earliest undoubtedly authentic Haydn Mass, was composed as early as 1749, it would date back to his last year as a choirboy at St. Stephan's. But it may well have been written a little later. In any case, compared to the *Rorate Mass,* it stands out much more as a first brilliant achievement. There is a more direct contact between voices and instruments. A leading structural principle is the constant exchange between full chorus and two solo voices, more or less in the way of the *ritornello* structure so typical of the Baroque concerto, and also known from Reutter's Masses. But what distinguishes Haydn's early Mass from these is above all its natural melodic flow. The very beginning of the Mass is a typical passage. The setting is quite homophonic though it is not characterized by neutral repeated chords; the manner in which the melody unfolds—in a rather simple style in the sopranos, and in a lightly embellished version in the violins—inevitably attracts our attention (see example 1). There are no genuinely polyphonic sections, only occasional imitation ("et resurrexit," etc.). The *Sanctus* is very short, the *Benedictus*—using only the two solo sopranos—is, as so often in Haydn's Masses, more elaborate (55 measures against 17 in the *Sanctus*). The *Agnus Dei* consists of two sections, the first more clearly in the style of chord declamation than any other portion of his Mass, and the second following the tradition of resuming the music of the *Kyrie*.

In a way it is strange that there are apparently no more Masses by Haydn from the approximately ten years he spent in Vienna after leaving the St. Stephan's choir because we know that he had much contact with church music performance. There exists a *Salve Regina* (from 1756) and at least one organ concerto from these years (there are probably several), but there are no Masses. Indeed, a great number of Masses have circulated under Haydn's name, some of which might perhaps go back to this time, though not a single one—other than the Masses named before—can reasonably be claimed as an authentic work by Haydn. And since he had to leave the composition of church music to Werner during his first years as Esterházy Kapellmeister, it was not until 1766 that he again tried his hand at writing a Mass.

It is not surprising that the new Mass is entirely different from the earlier one. Not only does it express in every respect Haydn's growth as a composer through about fifteen years—from promising youth to the beginning of maturity—it is also quite clearly a very ambitious work—by far his most complex Mass. Apparently he had to lessen his ambition somewhat in the course of writing the work, as can be gathered from the length of the various sections of the Mass. After a *Kyrie* of 236 measures, the *Gloria* follows with no less than 821 measures, the *Credo* numbers 386, but the *Sanctus* is quite short (21 measures), the *Benedictus* again longer (129 measures), and the *Agnus Dei* rounds off the total work with 151 measures. The extraordinary length of this Mass, especially of the *Gloria*, has to do with the overall form: the work belongs (as the only one among Haydn's Masses) to the category of "Cantata Mass." This means that the principal parts of the Mass, especially the *Gloria* and *Credo*, are divided up into a number of self-contained arias, choruses, or ensembles in the manner of the Italian oratorio or similar forms. Haydn may have encountered this type of Mass in Vienna; the Mass by Reutter published in the Austrian *Denkmäler* is a Cantata Mass. But more likely the church music of Johann Adolf Hasse had furnished the model.

One thing above all characterizes the difference between the early *F-Major Mass* and the *St. Cecilia Mass* of 1766. The early Mass, expressly called a "Missa Brevis," is quite obviously chamber-music-like in its nature, whereas the new Mass of 1766 is just as obviously symphonic. Instead of the ensemble of the "Viennese Church Trio" (2 violins and bass with organ) that we find in the first Mass, the score of the second one shows an orchestra with a full string complement with organ, 2 oboes (apparently also 2 bassoons), 2 clarini, and timpani. And from the very beginning it is clear that this is a composition in which the tutti character dominates.

Example 1

In this large structure there is obviously room—and need—for a much more varied choral style than in the early *Missa Brevis*. We can single out here only a few characteristic textures. There are variants of a homophonic style as, for instance, in a short introductory phrase with suspensions (*Kyrie*, introduction), in the typical combination of an instrumentally conceived melody in the violins and a corresponding choral setting with reduced melodic figuration ("Kyrie," *Allegro*; "Qui tollis"), in a choral recitative ("Cum sancto Spiritu"), or in choral phrases alternating with solo *ritornellos* (*Credo*, beginning). But above all there are extended fugues or fuguelike sections, mostly in fixed, traditional places such as the end of the *Gloria* ("In gloria Dei Patris, Amen"), of the *Credo* ("Et vitam venturi saeculi, Amen), or of the *Agnus Dei* ("Dona nobis pacem")—as well as at other points ("Kyrie II," "Gratias"). And to these varied choral settings we have to add the combinations of choral and soloistic phrases, the arias, and the ensembles of from two to four solo voices. Altogether this is a very impressive demonstration of the younger Haydn's abilities as a composer of vocal music in the grand style and on a high level of quality. On the other hand, though it does not actually suggest foreign models, the work seems less characteristic of Haydn than the early *Missa Brevis* with its rather unsophisticated style of writing. Yet there is no doubt that Haydn took an important and very conscious step ahead here towards his full mastery as a composer of choral music.

Haydn's next Mass is the so-called *Grosse Orgelmesse* in E-flat. We do not know exactly when it was composed, but to judge from the place of its listing in the *Entwurf-Katalog*, it seems to date from about 1768–70. Thus it leads us to the highly interesting period in Haydn's work characterized by an unparalleled growth and expansion and often misleadingly named his *Sturm und Drang* period—a description that applies only to one aspect of a highly complex development. It is the time in which the Classical instrumental forms—symphony, string quartet, and piano sonata—make decisive gains; Haydn's three series of string quartets from these years, known as Op. 9, Op. 17, and Op. 20, determined the course of the Classical string quartet. And when we approach the Mass he composed most likely at about the same time as the six quartets of Op. 9, there can be no doubt that we must consider it a vocal counterpart to the new achievements in chamber music from these years. The *Great Organ Mass* is not in the symphonic style of the *St. Cecilia Mass,* either in regard to instrumental scoring or to overall structure. In the place of clarini and timpani there are two other outstanding instrumental features: the use of English horns, replacing oboes not only in one specific section but in the whole Mass, and the use of an *organo concertato* also in all sections of the Mass and most particularly in the *Benedictus.* It is obvious that these singular qualities of sound—especially as compared to the effect of trumpets and kettledrums in the previous Mass—signify a much more intimate character in general.

In this shorter Mass—kept more within the confines of chamber music—the choral style is rather different from that of the *St. Cecilia Mass;* it is less varied and less extrovert. There is a fine consistency, an intimate character about it, whether it is basically homophonic or more or less polyphonic in nature. Rather long passages are in reality chord progressions, e.g., the first part of the *Credo,* which, however, is shaped by a similarly prominent melody joining the vocal and instrumental parts as found in the early *Missa Brevis.* An increased intensity of harmonic approach is sensed very strongly, above all perhaps in the *Adagio* section of the *Agnus Dei,* which suggests an instrumental "slow movement" (see example 2). Fugues proper are reserved in this Mass for the traditional endings of the *Gloria* and *Credo,* but there are fine imitative textures, less strict in character, at the beginning of the *Kyrie,* the *Sanctus,* and the second section of the *Agnus Dei* (the "Dona nobis pacem") with its contrast of an almost chantlike theme—conveying the old cantus firmus tradition—and a livelier countermotif stressing the $\frac{6}{8}$ meter established by the instrumental component.

The significance of one further particular feature must here be stressed, even though it is of only indirect concern to the choral style: the use of a quartet of soloists—no longer merely a single soloist or a duet singled out from the chorus. In the *Benedictus* a soprano-tenor duet phrase marks the entrance of the voices after an instrumental introduction (measure 14), and it is answered by an alto-bass duet phrase (measure 16). This is followed by a long four-part section (measure 18) which only towards the end (measure 31) is indicated as "Tutti" (3 measures); the same sequence (duets, four-part solo, four-part tutti) is carried out once more before the return to the "Osanna."

The general impression of this Mass—like its name—is customarily determined by the use of the organ as a concerted instrument. But in the evolution of Haydn's individual style as a composer of church music it is not this specific feature that counts. At a crucial moment in Haydn's development, characterized by both a major synthesis and expansion of instrumental forms, the *Great Organ*

Example 2

Mass stands out as a gesture of a new approach, a breakthrough of Haydn's personal style. In the series of Haydn's early Masses it is perhaps less conspicuous than the *St. Cecilia Mass,* but it is certainly no less important.

The *Missa Sancti Nicolai* was composed in 1772 as indicated by Haydn in the autograph manuscript. There is a considerable change in Haydn's music at that time. In the years immediately preceding this time, Haydn had been a forceful innovator of musical style and expression. The standstill in Austrian music following the period of Fux and Caldara had finally been overcome. New trends had arisen, especially in the central instrumental forms: symphony, quartet, and keyboard sonata. But from about 1772 on Haydn clearly slows down his pace. He stops composing quartets for a long time, and his symphonies and sonatas become less powerful and, while still full of fine craftsmanship, less impressive. We have no real information about the reasons for this change, but there seem to be indications of a certain influence from his princely patron, a possible recommendation to Haydn for placing more stress on entertaining values in his music than on creating a new and original style. We may remember the kind of music specially composed for the prince in the previous years: the baryton trios, which are indeed elegant entertainment, quite different from the revolutionary quartets from the same period. And we may point to some works carrying the name of the prince: the six keyboard sonatas, composed in 1773 and printed in 1774, dedicated to Prince Nicolaus, and this Mass, carrying his name and probably composed for his name day in 1772.

The *St. Nicolai Mass* is a beautiful piece of music, but compared to the two previous Masses it is obviously more traditional and simpler, less venturesome. One highly characteristic feature may be singled out: the preponderance of homophony, leaving very little room for genuine contrapuntal development. A concluding fugue is found only at the end of the *Gloria*—and only a short one—but not at the end of the *Credo* or *Agnus Dei,* as in many (or most) cases. It is neither a Mass for typical tutti forces nor a Mass in a pronounced chamber music style; it merges both tendencies.

The *Kyrie* is a remarkable piece in itself: a cantabile movement in a rather unusual meter, $\frac{6}{4}$ time—actually so rare that the Mass has been named the *"Sechs-Viertel-Messe."* The initial melody is almost lied-like, more in the manner of the early *F-Major Mass* than any of Haydn's Mass settings that lie between these two works. The construction is very close to the one found in the *Benedictus* from the *Great Organ Mass:* two introductory duet phrases followed by a more developed quartet section with changes only towards its end to tutti, and, after a cadence on the dominant, a similar construction leading back to the tonic.

Both the *Gloria* and *Credo* are kept mainly in a full vocal-orchestral texture, though with contrasting sections. In the *Gloria* there are thirty-seven measures of writing in what might be called an "aria" style ("Gratias agimus"), followed by weighty chord declamation ("Qui tollis") and leading to the final *Allegro* ("Quoniam") which consists of a chordal introduction and the mentioned short fugue. In the *Credo* a contrasting *Adagio* section sets in (as usually) at the words "Et incarnatus est"; it contains a solo *arioso* of eight measures and a quartet in a rather free texture, and eventually returns to the opening *Allegro* ("Et resurrexit") and the initial musical motifs, which now lead in free development to "Et vitam venturi saeculi, Amen," avoiding the usual polyphonic conclusion.

The *Sanctus* setting is given a uniform instrumental background through a continuous sixteenth-note motion, against which a single exposition of a motif of one-and-a-half measures is carried; it is framed by introductory and concluding cadential phrases and is followed by a contrasting "Pleni sunt coeli" and "Osanna" in a rhythmically intense *Allegro* in $\frac{3}{4}$ time. The *Benedictus* is a chamber-music-like quartet with two slightly contrasting phrases placed one against the other, and it is followed again by the rhythmically pointed "Osanna." The *Agnus Dei* is, like the *Sanctus,* marked by a rather consistent accompanimental motion, which serves as a foundation for a compact chordal declamation; the second "Agnus Dei" takes up the traditional repetition of the *Kyrie* music, with slight changes for the 'Dona nobis pacem" that concludes the Mass (we saw a similar formal arrangement in the early *F-Major Mass*).

The *Missa Brevis Sancti Joannis de Deo* or *Little Organ Mass* cannot be dated exactly. Haydn's autographed manuscript is extant, but, in distinction to his normal practice, he did not add the year of composition. A copy in the Austrian convent Göttweig was entered in the catalog of music of the convent in 1778, and the Mass was probably composed not long before that time. The name

Sancti Joannis de Deo refers to the Patron Saint of the Brothers of Mercy (with whom Haydn had been in contact from his early youth), and the work was supposedly written for their church in Eisenstadt. It is quite obviously written with a small body of performers in mind. Apart from the indications "Soprano Solo" and "Organo Solo" at the *Benedictus*—a pronouncedly concerted piece—there are no annotations for solo or changes of solo and tutti as appear in the other Masses, doubtless because the group of singers was so small that there was no basis for a contrast of that kind. The instrumental body is small too: the "Viennese church trio," as in the early *Missa Brevis*. And one additional feature of a different kind stresses the work's rather "private" character: the compression of the text, achieved in the *Gloria* and *Credo* through having different sections of the text sung in individual parts simultaneously.

The *Missa Brevis Sancti Joannis de Deo* is unquestionably one of Haydn's most popular and most often heard Masses. To some extent this may be attributed to the fact that it is so easy and graceful to perform, while at the same time the work gives charming proof of Haydn's originality and inventiveness even under rather limited conditions. All movements in the Mass with the exception of the *Benedictus* are short, most strikingly so the terse *Gloria* (31 measures, as against the 821 measures of the *Gloria* in the *St. Cecilia Mass*). There is obviously no room for fugal development or long drawn-out phrases. Most of the music is based on homophonic declamation, but varied in so many ways that a constant change of texture is sensed. In some cases a characteristic instrumental motif determines the impression of a section, but often the harmonically conceived vocal melody merges with the instrumental line, serving as an ornamented, yet always closely related escort. Above all, the vocal writing impresses the listener as a melodic, not just a choral gesture.

The *Kyrie* is a model of blending a harmonically conceived vocal and instrumental texture that anticipates the formal design of the sonata structure. In the short *Gloria,* chordal declamation is placed against the instrumental elaboration of a clear-cut motif used in constant exchange between violins and basses; it is rounded off with a short "Amen" episode which contains a suggestion of imitative writing. The *Credo* starts out with a homophonic vocal-instrumental *Allegro* section followed by a rhythmically poignant *Adagio* section ("Et incarnatus") and leading to a second part with solemn vocal declamation and arpeggiated instrumental accompaniment; in a concluding *Allegro* section the *Gloria* setting is taken up again and developed, the end being formed once more by the short "Amen" episode. The *Sanctus* combines within a rather homogeneous $\frac{6}{8}$ *Allegro* a first episode with initial imitation ("Sanctus"), a second episode with rhythmic-chordal declamation ("Pleni sunt coeli") and a third episode with another imitative opening ("Osanna"). The *Benedictus* that follows is clearly set off against the preceding sections. A broadly conceived movement with two soloistic parts and elaborate orchestral *ritornellos,* it is patently the principal piece of the Mass. (The name *Orgel-Solo-Messe* is more strongly borne out in this case.) The following episode is a repeat of the earlier "Osanna" section. The *Agnus Dei* is a small wonder. It is a $\frac{3}{4}$ *Adagio*, both highly unified and yet made up of a number of individual motifs which constitute a very impressive melodic development and which are enhanced by repeated dynamic changes (from *ff* to *pp*)—rather unusual in Haydn—leading to the extraordinary *pianissimo* closing phrase. Haydn apparently wrote this Mass for a group with limited means of performance, but not with a limited understanding of music.

In 1782 Haydn composed his last Mass before the interval caused by the Josephinian reforms. It is once again a Mass in the grand style, such as the *St. Cecilia Mass,* and, like the latter, it was meant to be performed in Mariazell, the famous place of pilgrimage; it is therefore called the *Mariazeller Mass.* It was commissioned by a Viennese patron, "Signor Liebe de Kreutzner," as stated in the autograph manuscript. Yet, unlike the first Mass for Mariazell, it is not a Cantata Mass. Only the rather long "Gratias agimus" section stands as an aria in its own right, giving an impression of the Cantata Mass structure. A further movement, the *Benedictus,* is modeled on an aria, a piece originally belonging to the opera *Il mondo della luna.* In the eighteenth century such fact did not give rise to any objections; actually the *Benedictus* is so far from an operatic nature that it fits perfectly into the Mass, and it would scarcely be perceived as a parody composition by anyone not knowing its background. But in the nineteenth century, when a separation of church music from opera traditions came to be regarded as much more important, this transfer of a piece of operatic music into the Mass was considered an unforgiveable sin, causing the banishing of Haydn's church music mentioned above.

There are some features of a traditional nature in this Mass and some more progressive ones. The rather compact chord declamation in tutti episodes plays a greater role here than in the preceding works. Introducing it—as is done in the beginning of the *Kyrie*—by a solo phrase is in a way an old tradition, yet at the same time it points to similar examples in the late Masses. Haydn's symphonic style, which became stabilized in the years just preceding as well as in the time of the composition of the Mass, determines the instrumental idiom, but also the formal structure; there is a trend towards a formal organization more or less modeled after the individual movements of the symphony and mostly approaching the "sonata form" as found in this stage of Haydn's music. This is obvious already in the *Kyrie,* which—as in the *St. Cecilia Mass* and in most of the later Masses—opens with a short introduction, leading to a *fermata* chord on the dominant as in many of Haydn's later symphonies. This introduction is succeeded by a *Vivace* in a veritable sonata form with primary theme group, transition section, secondary theme group, modulation or development section ("Christe eleison") and slightly changed recapitulation section (again "Kyrie eleison").

The *Gloria* opens with a similar tutti section, followed by a softer "Gratias" aria and succeeded by a "Qui tollis" section in chordal declamation with instrumental accompaniment in sixteenth notes and occasional imitation ("Suscipe"). In a final *Allegro con brio,* the sound of the clarini and timpani from the first section returns, and a compact "Quoniam" section leads to a concluding "Amen" fugue. The *Credo* is a very consciously structured movement. It consists of a main section with rhythmically stressed chordal declamation in a well-constructed modulatory design, followed by an "Et incarnatus" section that presents contrasts in almost every respect and contains an arialike interpolation (with an unusual tonal contrast: a–c); this leads directly into a short imitative "Crucifixus." The "Et resurrexit" resumes the music of the first section, somewhat shortened, and the "Et vitam venturi" section rounds the movement out with a regular fugue.

The *Sanctus* is again strictly chordal and so is the "Pleni" section, but the "Osanna" compensates for this in a freely imitative style. The *Benedictus*—the piece modeled upon an opera aria—presents the most original and impressive choral setting in this Mass, alternating between a mainly homophonic tutti section in g and a solo section (quartet) with typical duet imitations—the first time in B-flat, and the second time in G; the movement is concluded by a short "Osanna." The *Agnus Dei* is made up of an *Adagio* section, which twice presents the text "Agnus Dei" in chordal declamation and the text "Miserere nobis" in a short imitative answer, and a further section on the words "Agnus Dei" which introduces a long and elaborate fugue.

When the Josephinian reforms interrupted the development of Austrian Mass composition for a considerable period of time, Haydn had indubitably established a type of Mass setting that could serve as a basis for a tradition that was taken up again and carried further during his last years in Vienna in the six great Masses written in 1796–1802. But it is obvious that his development towards this established type of Mass was not, as in his symphonies, based on regular elaboration of its inherent possibilities.

After his charming early *Missa Brevis in F,* only to be regarded as a forerunner, his serious development as a composer of Masses began with the *St. Cecilia Mass,* which was obviously meant to demonstrate his capabilities in a newly recovered domain of work and which was to some extent based on styles he adopted (from such composers as Hasse). It is a fine demonstration of his competence, but a lesser one of his personal capacity. With regard to the latter, the *Great Organ Mass* is certainly much more of a token of future development; here we may rightly talk of a style that is personal rather than "official." The two light-textured and smaller Masses from the 1770s, the *St. Nicolai Mass* and the *Little Organ Mass,* are more relaxed in style; they are full of fine detail, but they do not aim at solving new problems. In the *Mariazeller Mass* Haydn took up again a more "official" line, as in the *St. Cecilia Mass,* also planned for Mariazell. But he was no longer imitating the Cantata Mass model. The plan for the *Mariazeller Mass* is essentially the same Haydn was to use in his late Masses.

In this respect he had arrived at an established tradition. But the very personal style of the *Great Organ Mass* was not absorbed in the style of the *Mariazeller Mass.* When after a fourteen-year interval he returned to the composition of Masses—at a time when the medium of choral music had come to be a real challenge to him—he eventually did merge the style of the grand "official" Mass and of the personal, more intimate Mass style of the *Great Organ Mass.* It has been the privilege of the last generation to get to know and to value Haydn's Masses as one of the finest expressions of his gift of development and expansion.

Notes

1. See *Three Haydn Catalogues, Second Facsimile Edition with a Survey of Haydn's Oeuvre* by Jens Peter Larsen (New York: Pendragon Press, 1979).

14

Beethoven's C-Major Mass
and the Late Masses of Joseph Haydn

This Beethoven colloquium is designed to pose questions of Beethoven research that are related to two aspects in particular: the relation of documentation and performance practice as formulated by the principal heading, and the relation of Beethoven and the Viennese tradition as expressed in the subheading. This second aspect determined the choice of the topic of this paper: the relations between Haydn's late masses and Beethoven's C-Major Mass.

As is well known, the C-Major Mass was commissioned by the younger prince Nikolaus Esterházy when Haydn had become too old to compose further masses. Beethoven literally served as Haydn's successor, and he was expected to continue Haydn's work. The critical remarks, however, that the prince directed at Beethoven after the performance are well known, too: "Well, dear Beethoven, what is it that you have done here?" (*"Aber, lieber Beethoven, was haben Sie denn da wieder gemacht?"*) Beethoven was greatly offended by this remark, and he was never again asked to compose masses for the prince.

It seems appropriate to ask what caused the prince's reaction. What induced him to regard Beethoven's mass not as a successful continuation of the Haydn tradition, but rather as a renunciation of that tradition?

I should like here to insert a few preliminary remarks. In my youth it would not have occurred to anyone seriously to compare Beethoven's and Haydn's masses. Haydn's masses had fallen into disfavor for reasons that cannot be discussed here. A few quotations should be sufficient proof. In Kretzschmar's classic *Führer durch den Konzertsaal* we can read: "It must be the concern of our time to vindicate Haydn the symphonist from underestimation. To get excited, however, about Haydn as a composer of masses may justifiably be left . . . to the blind worshippers of the great master. We must agree . . . with the archbishop of Hohenwarth and praise him because of his offhand banning of the performance

Originally published in German in *Beethoven Kolloquium, 1977, Dokumentation und Aufführungspraxis* (Kassel, 1978), pp. 12–19.

of Haydn's masses at churches of Vienna."[1] Concerning Beethoven's C-Major Mass, on the other hand, he states that despite its "insuperable rival," the *Missa solemnis,* it was an "invincible and remarkable work within the history of the instrumental mass. . . . With regard to details, this mass does not quite fulfill all justified desires, but with regard to the musical spirit of the single movements and to the choice of most of the basic musical ideas it may be called a worthy and magnificent composition."

Paul Bekker in his Beethoven biography of about the same time writes about the C-Major Mass: "There were hardly any works that could serve Beethoven as models for the planning of his work. His knowledge of the literature did hardly exceed the music of the preceding generation. And none of these works could serve him as a model."[2] Bekker does not even mention Haydn. Yet in his discussion of the *Dona nobis* from the *Missa solemnis* he says (somewhat surprisingly): "He designs a broadly conceived musical picture in which the passion of fighting and the longing for peace struggle for command. Beethoven may have been inspired to this poetical, free-shaping of the Dona by the war music from the Agnus Dei of Haydn's *Missa in tempore belli* of 1796."[3]

Today we have a different situation. Brand's book on Haydn's masses,[4] their publication in a critical edition,[5] and the large number of recordings have made it impossible to disregard or to negate the great artistic and historical significance of these works. Especially the six late masses form a self-contained group of exceedingly personal compositions, an apex in the development of Viennese classical music. It is self-evident that Beethoven proceeded from Haydn's masses when he was asked to compose a mass for Prince Esterházy. They were easily accessible. Breitkopf & Härtel had published four of the six late masses in score from 1802 to 1804: the *Missa Sancti Bernardi von Offida* ("Heiligmesse") and the *Missa in tempore belli* ("Paukenmesse"), both of 1796, the *Missa in Augustiis* of 1798 ("Nelsonmesse"), and the *Schöpfungsmesse* of 1801.

Nevertheless, the long-lasting negative attitude toward Haydn's masses still seems to exert a certain aftereffect. Permit me to quote just one example. Charles Rosen's *The Classical Style,* one of the most remarkable recent contributions to the discussion of the classical style, is full of fresh observations and personal judgments. With regard to Haydn's church music, however, he still adheres to some old prejudices. He introduces the works as follows:[6] "Joseph Haydn's masses were already under attack for their unsuitable character during the composer's lifetime. He himself thought his brother Michael's church music superior to his own." A little later he writes: "The discomfort that his religious style caused his contemporaries was ruefully acknowledged by Haydn."[7] Still later he speaks of "Haydn's comparative failure as a composer of liturgical music. . . ." Of the individual masses only the *Missa in tempore belli* is analyzed to a certain extent, and the critical comments prevail. Initially he states: "The masses are, of course, full of admirable details and contain much writing of great power," but then he continues that passages from the Allegro Moderato section of the *Kyrie* "can only have sounded as trivial to Haydn's contemporaries as they do to us today."[8] According to Rosen the cello solo in *Qui tollis* "has great sweetness, but to be accepted as an adequate setting of *Qui tollis peccata mundi* it requires more tolerance than the most emotional religiosity of eighteenth-century painting." He continues: "The most immediate weakness of Haydn's religious style appears naturally enough in the setting of the Nicene Creed." With regard to Beethoven's masses he states a little later:

> It was left to Beethoven to reconcile the liturgical tradition with the classical style, and paradoxically by evading the problem altogether; both his masses are frankly concert pieces, and more effective outside than inside a church. Yet the evasion is compensated by an evocation of ecclesiastical atmosphere attempted in no work of Haydn or Mozart. The care taken to that end is heard at once in the opening measures of the C-Major Mass, op. 86 of 1807.[9]

The remarks on the "discomforting" impression that Haydn's church style left on his contemporaries, or on his consideration of Michael Haydn's church music as being superior to his own works must rest on misunderstanding. Rosen mistakes incidental remarks for serious and generally accepted comments. If Haydn had preferred his brother's style to his own, he would certainly have been able to write in that style too. Of course, he was aware of the difference of his own genius and his brother's respectable talents. And as for the "evocation of ecclesiastical atmosphere" in Beethoven's C-Major Mass it is hardly possible to regard that as a suitable characterization. We shall return to this later.

I considered these introductory remarks necessary, because it still seems to be difficult to eliminate nineteenth-century biases. If we want to form a view on Haydn's late masses and Beethoven's C-Major Mass, we have to free ourselves from the former negative attitude toward Haydn's masses, which unmistakably is still in effect even in Charles Rosen's discussion. At the same time we should perhaps approach Beethoven's mass with yet a more open mind. In most cases discussions of this work are primarily devoted to its character as forerunner of the *Missa solemnis* more than to its position as an individual composition. Perhaps I should ask you to forget for a moment that Beethoven composed another mass after the C-Major Mass. That may help us quite simply to ask: when Beethoven in 1807 took over as successor of Haydn to compose a mass for Prince Esterházy, to what degree did he use Haydn's late masses as starting-point or as a model? And to what extent did he—willingly or unwillingly—give in general the style and character of the mass a new stamp?

Let me commence with some general remarks on Haydn's late masses. Earlier he had composed masses of very diverse characters: short and unpretentious ones, such as the very early *Missa brevis* in F (about 1750) and the *Missa brevis Sancti Joannis de Deo* ("Kleine Orgelmesse," probably about 1775); the large-scale *Missa Cellensis in honorem B.V.M.* (*"Cäcilienmesse,"* 1766), a unique composition in the manner of a cantata mass; two masses in an almost chamberlike style yet of very different characters: the *Missa in honorem B.V.M.* (*"Grosse Orgelmesse,"* about 1770) and the *Missa Sancti Nicolai* (*"Nikolai-messe,"* 1772); and finally the *Missa Cellensis* (*"Mariazeller Messe,"* 1782), which can be regarded as an early precursor of the late masses. It is evident that we cannot speak of a tradition with regard to six masses composed within thirty years. Each mass more or less presents a special case.

With respect to the late masses, however, things are different. The six masses were composed within seven or eight years (approximately one mass a year); a series of works of much the same character, all of them commissioned by the same person, Prince Esterházy, and all performed under almost identical conditions. As is the case with regard to the London symphonies, composed a few years earlier, we cannot speak of a development, of an increasing mastery of the composition. Problems of structure and technique of composition belong to earlier times. The wealth of contrasting expressions within the different movements and periods, and the never-slackening power of invention and conception contribute to the appearance of these masses as a group of brothers and sisters. One cannot mistake their close relationship, although each offspring comes forward with its own distinct individuality.

With regard to the formal layout the similarity of the group more than individual design manifests itself. Apart from some rather small differences there is an overall conception common to all six masses. Similar to the first movements from the late symphonies, the *Kyrie* mostly consists of an introductory Adagio section followed by an Allegro (Moderato) main section. Only two of the masses have a first movement without this subdivision: the *Kyrie* of the *Nelson Mass* (Allegro Moderato), and the one of the *Harmony Mass* (Poco Adagio). The *Gloria* is subdivided into four or five contrasting sections. The first of these is always an introductory Allegro or Vivace; in three instances it is followed by a *Gratias* of a somewhat subdued, intimate character, leading to the *Qui tollis* in a contrasting key, whereas the three other masses take up a different tempo and character only in the *Qui tollis* (Adagio). The *Quoniam* introduces a new Allegro or Vivace section, closing with a fugue or a fuguelike development at *In gloria Dei patris/Amen*. The *Credo* has a similar structure: it starts out with an Allegro (or Vivace), followed by the *Et incarnatus* as an Adagio (or Largo) middle section, *Et resurrexit* again is an Allegro (or Vivace), and the concluding *Et vitam venturi* is a Vivace (or Allegro) section, mostly a fugato. The *Sanctus* is an Adagio (in one case Andante), mostly with a concluding Allegro (*Pleni/ Osanna*). The *Benedictus* is surprisingly varied within the extremes of Andante and Molto Allegro; in two instances it makes use of a new *Osanna*. The *Agnus Dei* always consists of two sections, a slow *Agnus I* (Adagio) followed by a faster *Dona nobis* which partly employs imitation.

As suggested by this short survey the changing contrasting sections may often create the impression of the changing movements of a symphony. The most obvious example of this is perhaps the *Kyrie* of the *Missa in tempore belli*. The Adagio sections suggest a comparison to the respective movements of a symphony or even of a concerto. In the movements with longer texts—*Gloria* and *Credo*—the text inevitably gains an important structural function. With regard to the overall impression, the alternation of purely instrumental ritornellos, choral declamations, soloistic ensembles, and purely soloistic sections (e.g., intonations) are a considerable enrichment of the overall sound image. The quasi symphonic movements are juxtaposed by very characteristic contrapuntal movements. Remarkable examples are the typical closing fugues in the *Gloria* and *Credo* mentioned above, but also some occasional very specific contrapuntal sections, such as the canon at the fifth in parallel octaves at the beginning of the *Credo* of the *Nelson Mass*, or the canonic *Et incarnatus est* from the *Missa Sancti Bernardi*, which is based on a very short secular canon. In a unique manner these masses realize a synthesis of Haydn's roots in the great Austrian baroque traditions and of his symphonic mastery, the price of a lifelong struggle.

If one approaches Beethoven's mass from the perspective of Haydn's late masses—and that was the situation of the listener of 1807 whose position we should try to adopt—it is scarcely possible to trace back the prince's reaction to formal changes of the mass. That is already clear from the simple fact that the listener who is exposed to the music for the first time—as part of the liturgy and without a score—will hardly be able to perform a comparative formal analysis. Another obvious reason is that Beethoven's mass is based mainly on the same formal procedures as the Haydn masses, as far as the series of movements is concerned—and exactly this formal succession is most readily perceived.

I should like to quote from Bekker once more. Concerning the C-Major Mass he says:[10]

Provided that after the first performance on 13 September 1807 in Eisenstadt Prince Esterházy actually expressed the remark "Well, dear Beethoven, what is it that you have done here?" then it proves the perplexing impression that Beethoven's church music left on the listeners accustomed to quite a different sort of music. Surprising was especially the ternary structure of the *Kyrie*, the free, almost dialogue-like juxtaposition of choir and soloists, the ingenious poetical-musical setting of the single sections of the *Gloria* and the *Credo*, the expansion of the *Benedictus* at the expense of the short, solemn and tender *Sanctus*, the almost passionate, grievous *Agnus Dei* with the meaningful reference of the *Dona nobis pacem* to the prayerful theme of the *Kyrie*. All these features which deviate from convention reveal Beethoven's artistic independence in fulfilling his task as composer of the Mass in C.

With regard to the formal aspects of the composition, however, it is hardly justified to speak of "all these features which deviate from convention." The so-called ternary form of the *Kyrie* is found very similar in Haydn's *Missa Cellensis* (*"Mariazeller Messe"*); the only difference is that Haydn in his middle section does not employ a contrasting theme, but a variant of the primary theme—as he often does in his symphonies. A large *Benedictus* after a much shorter *Sanctus* can be found in most of his masses, and the return to music from the *Kyrie* at the end of the *Agnus Dei (Dona nobis pacem)* is very characteristic of the *Missa Sancti Nicolai,* which is among the masses that most likely were known to Beethoven.

The statement of "the ingenious poetical-musical setting of the single sections of the *Gloria* and the *Credo*" on the other hand, signifies a basic feature. When Beethoven offered the mass to Breitkopf & Härtel on June 8, 1808, he emphasized just the special character of his text setting: "I believe in my mass—to have treated the text as has rarely been done." The meaning of this somewhat oracular statement is not quite evident, and different interpretations are possible. However, it may provide the most obvious basis for our attempt to clarify the relation between Beethoven and the style of Haydn's late masses.

As pointed out above, the general outline of the C-Major Mass follows the (traditional) subdivision of the mass movements—especially of the *Gloria* and the *Credo*—in Haydn's late masses. Yet the filling-out of this general frame is very different as with Haydn.

In Haydn's masses each movement (or section of a movement) is as far as possible, treated as a unity. Often a formal unity is found resembling a movement of an instrumental composition, as for instance the mentioned *Kyrie* of the *Missa in tempore belli,* and many other movements. In other cases the uniform impression is achieved by a homogenous rhythmic motion and an unchanging accompaniment. The underlying conception of the respective section or movement aims at a consistent musical impression as the primary experience. Such an experience, of course, presupposes basically a distinct character of the themes, the declamation motives, the instrumental accompaniment, etc. This character again depends very much on the general character of the respective section of the text, but there will not be much room for any concern for a specific characterization of the quickly changing phrases of the text.

In Beethoven's mass the striving for a uniform impression of the movements or the sections is no longer a primary concern; the emphasis on an intensification of the expression of the various textual motives becomes a main objective.

The course of a movement is determined by the constant contrasting of motives, of soloists and choir, and by the steady exchange of modulatory and dynamic deployment. As early as 1815 Amadeus Wendt, a perceptive connoisseur, gave a fine characterization of the impression Beethoven's music left on him:[11]

Many of Beethoven's compositions, for example many of his symphonies and sonatas, one can only comprehend and appreciate as musical fantasies. Here even the most perceptive listener often loses track of the basic musical idea. He finds himself in a wonderful labyrinth where on all sides the eye catches views of exuberant thickets and the rarest blooms, but losing the thread of his homeward journey, the artist's fantasy being in a constant flow, that only rarely grants repose, and an earlier impression is often extinguished by later ones.

It is difficult to decide objectively, how much the decrease of uniformity and the increase of expression of the changing aspects of the text may count as gain or loss. This kind of judgment, however, is not our concern here. I only wish to point out the fundamental similarities and dissimilarities of Haydn's masses and Beethoven's C-major Mass. Let us end this short comparison by raising briefly a couple of additional questions which may similarly only be formulated but not discussed in detail.

1.   Is it possible to regard the contrasting styles of the masses by Haydn and Beethoven as a reflection of the old duality Classicism-Romanticism? Let us disregard all definitions, and let us keep to real contrasts. I cannot agree with Blume who states in his essay on the Classic period in *MGG:*

> There are only approximate definitions, and probably only such are possible, because every definition must consider the "Classic" in its relation to the "Romantic," since both these style concepts are basically one, being but two different refractions of the one concept of shaping. There is no "Classic" style period in the history of music, only a "Classic-Romantic" one, within which those forms that are "classically" determined can at most be characterized as phases.[12]

In proceeding from such a point of view we shall scarcely be able to comprehend the essence of Classical and Romantic music.

In his still-captivating book *Das romantische Beethovenbild,* Arnold Schmitz challenges the tendency of depicting Beethoven as a true Romantic. In his conclusion he states: "The romantic image of Beethoven does not portray the true Beethoven, but the prototype of the romantic artist. It is colored with paint coming from the palette of romantic philosophy, but not matching the historical reality. . . . The romantics are firmly convinced that Beethoven is one of them. They do not realize the deep gap between their own and Beethoven's formal conceptions."[13]

I quote these two opinions just to stress how dangerous it can be to believe in unshakable conceptions. I should like to let rest the question whether one should consider the C-Major Mass as a "romantic" or as a "specifically Beethovenian" composition. Yet it seems evident that the contrast between this mass and the late masses of Haydn, composed only five to ten years earlier is so striking, that they cannot offhand be regarded as belonging together. The general formal conception is related, but the character of expression and the style intention is different. The classical tradition determines the character of Haydn's masses, but not of the Beethoven mass.

2.   To what extent can Haydn's masses or the Beethoven mass be regarded as "true church music"? Again there are many contradictory opinions, but very little objectivity. The traditional disregard of Haydn's masses—dating back to nineteenth-century Cecilianism—on the one hand, and the romantic adoration of Beethoven the "hero" on the other, made it difficult to realize a well-balanced judgment. Neither Haydn's nor Beethoven's mass style may in itself be regarded as "churchly" or "unchurchly." None of them is "operatic." Haydn's style is a late-eighteenth-century style. Beethoven's is marked with strong individuality; maybe it is a little too much adjusted to the artistic ideals of Beethoven and too little for those of the church.

3.   And finally: how does Beethoven's more expressive mass style influence the performance style? Here too, I want to be brief and to limit myself to one aspect only: the dynamics. In Haydn's masses long passages are still governed by unchanging dynamics; tonal contrasting and *sforzato* effects are added, but there is only little in the way of graduated dynamic, *crescendi* and *diminuendi*. (The beginning of the *Missa Sancti Nicolai* is a quite elementary example; the Largo introduction to the *Missa in tempore belli* makes use of contrasting effects in the manner of "Es werde Licht" in *The Creation,* but this is an exception.) In Beethoven's mass as in many of his other works the use of emphasized dynamic transitions is an essential element of the musical effect. The beginning of the mass with its melodic and dynamic intensification in measures 8 and 9 is an obvious example and may immediately have given the audience at the first performance a slight shock.

We have come to the end with our comparison of Haydn's and Beethoven's mass styles, and we may ask a final question: was the reaction of Prince Esterházy reasonable? Or must it be considered an expression of intellectual sluggishness? Did he only want to hear music he was used to? I think it must be admitted that the C-Major Mass as compared to Haydn's masses was so far beyond the classical traditions, that his reaction must be regarded as the quite understandable reaction of a music lover, who for many years had been a faithful devotee of church music. A new tradition did not come into being. A work of quite special character was born that paved the way for an even greater, even more original work. We have only come so far now that we are capable of comparing the masses of Haydn and Beethoven without traditional biases, and of appreciating the originality and greatness of the works of both masters. How precious is the heritage of the Viennese classical tradition!

Notes

1.   Part II, vol. 1 (1916 ed.), p. 201.

2.   P. Bekker, *Beethoven* (1912), p. 374.

3.   Ibid., p. 399.

4. Carl Maria Brand, *Die Messen von Joseph Haydn* (1941).

5. Joseph Haydn, *Kritische Gesamtausgabe/The Complete Works*, Series XXIII, vol. 1 (Boston, Vienna, 1951); *Joseph Haydn Werke*, series XXIII, vol. 2–5 (Munich-Duisburg, 1958–67).

6. Norton Library Edition, p. 366.

7. Ibid., p. 368.

8. Ibid., p. 370.

9. Ibid., p. 373.

10. Op. cit., p. 375.

11. Cited after A. Schmitz, *Das romantische Beethovenbild* (1927), p. 105.

12. Translation from Friedrich Blume, *Classic and Romantic Music* (New York, 1970), p. 9.

13. Op. cit., p. 178f.

15

Haydn's Early Symphonies: The Problem of Dating

Haydn's early symphonies were virtually unknown until the appearance of the first three volumes of Breitkopf & Härtel's (unfinished) "Collected Edition" (1907–8).[1] Pohl had of course written about them in his Haydn biography (1875–82),[2] which for about half a century served as the foundation for any serious study of Haydn's music. But since no editions of these works were available, they remained obscure. Only a small selection of the late symphonies was known by music-lovers in general, as well as by musicians and musicologists.

The three volumes were welcomed, not least as a promise of the realization of the Haydn Edition which had been due for a very long time. It was less clear, however, how one should fit the early symphonies into the traditional picture of the classical symphony. The general concept of a symphony was based on works like the symphonies of Beethoven or Brahms, or perhaps even the late symphonies of Haydn and Mozart. From this point of view the early Haydn symphonies would have to be regarded rather as a somewhat primitive, preliminary stage. Measured by the model of the so-called sonata form of the textbooks, they turned out to be rather unorthodox in various ways, not following the accepted "rules." In many of his symphonies, including some of the later ones, Haydn—to cite only one example—did not introduce a real "second theme"; this was registered as a primitive feature: Haydn had "not yet" found his way to using a second theme, rather than seeing in it a different approach to musical form, a divergent tradition aiming at unity rather than at duality as a basic principle.

As a valuable addition to the edition there was in the first volume a new list of Haydn's symphonies.[3] In this survey Mandyczewski, the general editor, had arranged all the symphonies known to him under Haydn's name into four groups: authentic works, overtures, dubious and spurious symphonies. The list of 104

Reprinted from *Music in the Classic Period: Essays in Honor of Barry S. Brook* (Stuyvesant, N.J.: Pendragon Press, 1985), pp. 117–31.

authentic symphonies has served as a foundation for Haydn research since then. The number of dubious or spurious symphonies has increased rather much; many symphonies regarded as dubious have been given up definitely as works by Haydn, but not a single dubious work has been accepted as an authentic symphony.

The list of authentic symphonies was in principle arranged according to the chronology of the works, though with some reservations, as stated in the preface: "The order of the symphonies in [group] I is arranged chronologically as far as possible. Since according to our present knowledge only 39 of these 104 symphonies—the ones marked Aut.—are still extant in Haydn's original manuscript (and even these not all quite complete), there has been much room left for probability. Placing a work too early was expressly avoided."[4]

Mandyczewski's datings are based on autographs (if available) and otherwise in many cases on entries in the old Breitkopf catalogues[5] or that of the Göttweig music collection.[6] In some instances dates are found which seem to be based on estimates, since they do not refer to any known source. However, it is obvious now that many of the early symphonies are placed wrongly, a matter that we shall discuss a little later.

The chronological arrangement of the works created an impediment to the full understanding of Haydn's early development as a symphony composer. The theory of evolution was still very much in the air, and there was a tendency to interpret the succession of works in Mandyczewski's list as the immediate reflection of a process of ripening, progressing from work to work. A strict acceptance of the Mandyczewski chronology—as, for example, in Kretzschmar's review of the three symphony volumes—[7] must certainly make Haydn's early development seem rather inconsistent, as we can see it more clearly today with an increased knowledge of the chronological problems.

These shortcomings are demonstrated in the first published study of Haydn's early symphonic development, by Bernhard Rywosch.[8] Apart from a short introduction to general problems concerning the structure and character of the symphony, the book consists of a series of reviews or analyses of the individual symphonies, work by work, in the order set out by Mandyczewski's list, as if this were actually the real succession of the works. This adherence without reservation to Mandyczewski's arrangement has been a regrettable handicap to the author.

For my own part, I had written (but not published) a small dissertation on Haydn's early symphonies a few years earlier.[9] Like Rywosch, I had used Mandyczewski's list as a basis without reservations. However, it was less of a handicap for me, since I did not aim at a chronological presentation. My central concern was a classification of the early symphonies, a division into four basic types: the type of symphonies in three movements, originally derived from the Italian opera overture; the type of works deriving from the church sonata or the "parthia," characterized by a slow first movement (not just a slow introduction); the type with elements of the concerto; and finally the four-movement type which came to be the definitive symphony model.

In the course of the 1930s the trend toward a revision of Mandyczewski's chronology slowly began to come about. It appeared first, perhaps, in my analysis of the so-called *Quartbuch,* in connection with my long discussion with Sandberger.[10] I stated as a general fact that the old Breitkopf catalogs would rarely announce a symphony earlier than two years after it was composed. In several cases Mandyczewski had taken the date of a symphony from one of the Breitkopf catalogs and given it as, for example, "before 1764." Although this would point to something like "before or about 1762," it was often (if not usually) interpreted as "about 1764." In two cases—Nos. 65 and 72—a substantial change was suggested.

An important new basis for evaluating the date of composition of a great number of symphonies was found when it could be shown that the so-called *Entwurf-Katalog* was not—as the name might indicate—made as a draft for the well-known catalog of Haydn's works from his late years (1805), but as a personal catalog of works, mostly in Haydn's own hand, started about 1765 and carried on more or less consistently for various groups of works.[11] Though the catalog did not solve all problems, it did provide a lot of evidence.

After the war the trend toward a chronological revision took on greater prominence. In the list of symphonies that appeared in the first published volume of the Haydn Society edition,[12] two classes of dates were given: 1) the date of the earliest known source, and, if this did not indicate the date of composition (as it would in the case of a dated autograph), 2) a conjectural date (or a limited period) of composition according to an evaluation of musical style. Of the 40 symphonies published in the three volumes of early symphonies, 15 or 16 could be dated by autograph (or other means). Of the remaining 24 or 25 symphonies, 22 were assigned an earlier date or period than the traditional one given by Mandyczewski. Landon, in his book about Haydn's symphonies[13] and in his edition of the symphonies,[14] dated about a dozen symphonies still somewhat earlier. The list of symphonies in the Haydn work list in *MGG* (once more by Landon and me)[15] combines and balances the Haydn Society list and Landon's later suggestions. The several indications of a short period (e.g., 1760/63) instead of a year, as well as the many additions of "um" ("about") or a question mark, make it quite clear that this is still to be regarded as a preliminary stage, not a definitive chronological survey. But the message of the changed chronological indications is obvious: a great number of the symphonies were undoubtedly composed earlier than Mandyczewski's list would indicate. As far as the individual work is concerned, this may perhaps seem less important, but we can only arrive at a real understanding of the development in Haydn's early symphonies if we accept the relativity of the traditional listing. However, the Hoboken catalog,[16] of which the first volume appeared at just about the same time as the Haydn article in *MGG,* scarcely touches upon the problem. With few exceptions, it repeats the chronological indications given by Mandyczewski.[17]

A penetrating analysis of the chronological problems within a limited group of later symphonies was made by Sonja Gerlach.[18] Several special features found in the sources were utilized, and they led to convincing conclusions. Though Gerlach's work is valuable for the works in question, it would hardly be possible to carry out a similar investigation for the early symphonies, since the source situation is here quite different.

Unexpectedly a collection of valuable material bearing on the question of chronology of the early symphonies turned up around the time of the Haydn jubilee of 1959: the "Fürnberg copies" from Keszthély. They came to be known through the catalog of the Haydn material in the Széchényi library, which appeared on that occasion.[19] The collection comprises a number of symphonies and chamber works. With one exception all of them seem to be quite early works; only the manuscript K. 1139, an arrangement of the baryton trios 34–39 as ordinary string trios (two violins and basso), cannot be earlier than 1766/67 (the date of composition of these baryton trios).

The copies belong to the former Festetics collection in Keszthély, but the specific feature which had to arrest the attention of Haydn scholars was the stamp of a former owner—"Fürnberg/Obrist Lieut."—on a number of copies. The name Fürnberg, known from the traditional description of the origin of Haydn's first string quartets, might suggest that these were copies that came directly from the composer, and the nature of the works in question—quite early symphonies and chamber works—would seem to confirm this assumption. Although we do not know if Fürnberg actually sponsored performances of symphonies, it seems very likely that he would wish to have not only chamber works, but also symphonies of the young composer whose career he had helped to start. The authenticity of the copies was further evidenced through occasional traces of Haydn's own writing. In time, the collection was apparently taken over by the "Obrist Lieutenant," the son of the original owner, and later by Count Festetics. The fact that—apart from the single manuscript (or manuscript group) K. 1139—all the works must be counted among the very early ones, with no single work known to have been composed later than 1760 or 1761, goes well together with the statement in Haydn's contract of 1761 that he was not allowed to give away copies of his works composed for the prince—like the symphonies—without special permission.

Robbins Landon has recently set forth a new hypothesis about these manuscripts.[20] He suggests that they all belonged originally to Count Morzin, for whom the works were composed, and that they came to the Fürnberg family only after Count Morzin gave up his orchestra. This hypothesis certainly sounds very interesting, but it must be stressed that we have next to nothing that can confirm it. What is handed down to us about Haydn's activities in the service of Count Morzin is, like most of what we know about Haydn's life before he came to the Esterházys, to be found in the early biographies (Griesinger, Dies, Carpani), and their information about those activities is so vague that it is very difficult to get a convincing picture of Haydn's Morzin period. In connection with his hypothesis about the Fürnberg copies as a Morzin collection, Landon maintains that "Haydn composed some nineteen symphonies for Count Morzin," and he assigns to him a "scriptorium," a group of no less than ten "Fürnberg-Morzin Copyists."[21] I believe there is a strong tendency toward exaggerating the proportions here. According to the two basic sources (Griesinger and Dies), Haydn took over his position as Morzin's Kapellmeister in 1759 and had it only until 1760—Griesinger (with surprising precision) even gives the date of 19 March—and if it is true that the orchestra was only playing in Lukavec during the summer, it would seem that Haydn had perhaps only one summer as active Kapellmeister for the count. However, there is much uncertainty involved in these questions; when Haydn married in November 1760, he was still designated Music Director to Count Morzin. It seems likely to me that the Morzin engagement can only account for a part of Haydn's activities during his pre-Eisenstadt years in Vienna, and that we will do better in assuming that Haydn was part of the general Viennese symphonic development around this time, and not writing for one specific patron—as he was going to do shortly afterwards in Eisenstadt/Eszterháza.

The dating of the early symphonies in Landon's great Haydn biography is based on a division of the works into three main groups: 1) the supposed "Fürnberg-Morzin" symphonies, 2) the symphonies of 1761–65, and 3) the symphonies of 1766–75. The symphonies of the first group are all supposed to date back to the years up to 1760–61, this dating being based on their relationship to the Fürnberg collection and on a numbering on the title pages of these copies.[22] Landon regards this numbering as a reflection of the original sequence of works, which may in itself seem doubtful; moreover he puts in optional symphonies in empty spaces in his "system," which may well fit in chronologically, but which tends to diminish the persuasive power of his mixed group. The symphonies of the second group comprise first of all a substantial number of works which can be determined by dated autographs, and a few more which are placed here for other reasons. For the symphonies of the third group there is but a limited number of dated autographs available. The ordering of the Entwurf-Katalog, especially the first two pages, serves as the principal basis for the chronological arrangement of these works. We shall return to this chronological survey shortly.

The latest list of symphonies is part of the very comprehensive and reliable work list by Georg Feder in *The New Grove*.[23] Within its limited space it gives a wealth of information. However, the principles used in assigning dates in the individual genre-by-genre work lists seem to vary to some extent. According to the introduction: "Items are numbered chronologically (as far as possible) within each category." The meaning of the chronological indications is further clarified by means of the following scheme: "1766 = composed 1766; [1766] = year of composition 1766 not documented; –1766 = composed by 1766; –? 1766 = possibly composed by 1766."[24]

If we consider the first group of works, the Masses, we find the two "organ Masses" ("Grosse Orgelmesse" and "Kleine Orgelmesse") as Nos. 5 and 7 with the following chronological indications: "–1774 [?1768–69]" and "–1778 [?ca.1773–77]." The first Mass is placed between two Masses dated 1766 and 1772, that is, using as a guideline the suggested date 1768–69, not the earliest fixed date, 1774. (The second Mass comes between two Masses that date from 1772 and 1782.)

If we look at the list of symphonies, it is different in several ways. There are no numbers in italics, as there are in most of the other groups; the Mandyczewski (Hoboken) numbering is used, which is quite natural, but perhaps it ought to have been stressed that this numbering is only approximately chronological. As far as the dates are concerned, the leading principle here is to give the earliest fixed date. An additional indication of a conjectural date is found in ten "Fürnberg symphonies" (either "–?1760" or "–?1761"), as well as in the symphonies analyzed by Sonja Gerlach, and in a few other instances (Nos. 36, 39, 58, 64, 65, 72). In other cases the dates may differ significantly from the suggested datings in the list mentioned above. To give only one example: Symphony No. 18 was dated "about 1764" in Mandyzcewski's list; in the Haydn Society list it was given as ca. 1760/64, while it was dated ca. 1761/64 in Landon's symphony book and *MGG*, and "about 1764" in Hoboken (following Mandyczewski). In *Haydn: Chronicle and Works*, I, Landon assigns the symphony to around 1759, basing that date on a manuscript in the Fürnberg collection, while Feder gives the date as "–1766" (= "by 1766"), implicitly referring to—though not quoting—Breitkopf's catalog of 1766 as the earliest datable source for this symphony.

These changing chronological indications may perhaps seem rather bewildering to a nonspecialist. But it should be kept in mind that there are two different points of view behind the disparity of dates: 1) the principle of giving a date which is definitely confirmed by a reliable source—even if that date represents not the time of composition but an (indefinite) later date at which the work was reported as known; and 2) that of giving a conjectural date, which, though less definitive, may come closer to the time of composition. A combination of these two different approaches—as anticipated in the list of symphonies in the Haydn Society edition—may perhaps still be the most satisfactory solution.

Obviously, a list of works aiming at establishing absolutely incontestable dates (that is, a date by which time the work was known) can be made with a high degree of objectivity, as demonstrated in Feder's list of symphonies in *The New Grove*. As opposed to this, a list of works that aims at giving the time of composition, either by a fixed date, when fully documented, or through conjecture, must of necessity be less definitive and less objective. But it must be possible to state what is real knowledge and what is conjecture. No doubt, Landon has come a long way in his list of symphonies, and I am in agreement with many of his results and conclusions. However, in some cases his conjectures seem less convincing, and—perhaps the most conspicuous weakness in connection with his stunning achievement—he tends to mix facts and conjectures with a minimum of reservation (or with no reservation at all). I would like, therefore, to end up with a brief comment on what is known and what is conjectured in connection with the dating of Haydn's early symphonies.

When Mandyzcewski arranged his list of symphonies 75 years ago, dated autographs were known for the following works: Nos. 7 (1761), 12–13 (1763), 21–24 (1764), 28–31 (1765), and 35 (1767). After the publication of his list two more dated autographs turned up: Nos. 40 (1763) and 49 (1768). These fourteen symphonies are the only early symphonies that can at this time be dated with absolute certainty. A few more symphonies have been given a definitive date on circumstantial grounds only. This is true for Nos. 6 and 8, "Le matin" and "Le soir," which, based on the autograph date of No. 7, "Le midi," are supposed to date from 1761, though 1761–62 might also be a possibility, at least for No. 8. But that is a purely formal question, and that the three symphonies belong together is not to be doubted. They make a quite special group among the early symphonies. No. 9 is generally referred to as dating from 1762, based on information in the catalog(s) of Alois Fuchs from about 1840. According to Fuchs, the autograph of the symphony belonged to Artaria at that time; however, Pohl already did not know it, and he simply referred to Fuchs. Most likely the date of 1762 is right, but it cannot be regarded as definitive.

The year of the first symphony was for a long time regarded as an unshakable fact, based as it was on Haydn's statement to Griesinger that he had composed his first symphony—the incipit is added by Griesinger—in 1759 for Count Morzin. Yet Landon, referring to a list of symphonies allegedly arranged by Haydn himself about 1800 and divided into four groups (1757–67, 1767–77, 1777–87, and 1787–97), suggested that the beginnings be pushed back to 1757, and he entered the indication "1757–61" for a number of symphonies.[25] Obviously, Haydn's late recollection—which refers to some symphony numbers that we cannot check—cannot be taken as unambiguous evidence. A stronger piece of evidence turned up when an old copy of No. 37 was found with a contemporary dating "1758" on its cover. Although the source, from a Czech collection, is not an authentic one, the date is probably an immediate, contemporary record of acquisition, though it cannot be regarded as definitive.

It was, however, the appearance of the Fürnberg copies, described above, which created the basis for a thorough reevaluation of the question of Haydn's beginnings as a symphony composer. Nevertheless, it must be difficult for a nonspecialist to find out what can be termed definitive knowledge in this respect. So let us try to sum up.

It is a fact that a number of symphonies and quartets now at the Helikon library in Keszthély came into the Festetics collection from the "Obrist Lieutenant Fürnberg," son of the Baron Fürnberg for whom Haydn, according to the reports by Griesinger and Dies, wrote his earliest quartets, now supposed to date back to around 1757. It is furthermore true that a number of these copies show some additions in Haydn's own hand. How early they came into the possession of the Fürnberg family is not known, but Haydn's close contact with Baron Fürnberg might indicate that they came directly from Haydn to Fürnberg, and since Haydn's contract of 1761 with Prince Esterházy forbade him to hand over copies of his works to other people without special permission, it is reasonable to suppose that this direct delivery stopped after his appointment as Esterházy Kapellmeister in 1761. It is also true that there is no single symphony among the "Fürnberg copies" that can safely (or likely) be dated later than that year. For these and other reasons it seems well founded to assign the group of symphonies that belonged to Fürnberg to Haydn's early years, those prior to his engagement as Esterházy Kapellmeister. However, it must be stressed that Landon's interpretation of all these works as part of a former Morzin collection—as a "Fürnberg Morzin legacy"—is only an interesting hypothesis, and that the same is true about his suggested chronological arrangement of the symphonies and his introduction of a Fürnberg-Morzin "scriptorium," a circle of copyists working (supposedly) for the Morzin "Kapelle." We must regard these symphonies as works from Haydn's last years in Vienna, before he started a new career at the Esterházy court. To this group of symphonies belong: Nos. 1, 2, 4, 5, 10, 11, 15, 18, 27, 32, 33, 37, and "A" (Hob. 107), but hardly Nos. 3 and 20 (as suggested by Landon).

To the years 1761–65 (from Haydn's appointment as Esterházy Kapellmeister to his first entries in the "Entwurf-Katalog") belong twelve symphonies, enumerated above, for which dated autographs are still extant. Nos. 6 and 8 are supposed to date from the same time as No. 7 (1761), but, as already hinted at, this is a probable, not a fixed date. No. 9 was probably composed in 1762 is already stated.

In (or about) 1765 Haydn began keeping an account of his compositions. They were registered in the so-called Entwurf-Katalog, which seems originally to have been intended only to give a survey of his works up to that time, but eventually came to be used (more or less) as a current register of his compositions.[26] As a result of this changed plan, some of the groups of works grew much too large for the space allotted to them. They were entered first on the regular staves, then on additional staves besides these, and later on empty staves or added leaves elsewhere in the catalog. Though the list of works is not as systematic as might be desired, careful analysis of it yields a lot of information. However, two points should be stressed: 1) the incipits are normally not dated, and the evidence that they hold for the chronology must be derived from an estimation of the order in which they were entered; 2) even if the order of the entries undoubtedly reflects that of the compositions, for the most part, a certain irregularity is to be found. In some instances works may have been forgotten and then entered later in a "wrong" place; the possibility of a delayed entry must therefore be kept in mind. The opposite case: a premature entry, is of course not possible; the inclusion of a work among others that are generally assumed to date from an earlier period is consequently an important piece of evidence.

The symphonies to be considered here are noted down on the first two pages of the Entwurf-Katalog.[27] After two early works—the scherzando in A (Hob. II:38) and the symphony (Hob. I:27)—a list of symphonies continued on the regular staves comprises the following works: Nos. 29, 31, 28 (all three composed 1765), 35 (1767), 59 (by 1769), 38 (by 1769), 49 (1768), 58 (by 1767/68?), Hob. Ia: 10 (the Overture to "Lo Speziale," 1768), I:26 (by 1770), and 41 (by 1770). The symphonies are given numbers in Haydn's hand: the two early works are marked 20 and 12, the two symphonies 29 and 31 are counted as 40 and 41, and the following nine symphonies as 45 through 53. According to small changes in the notation, the sequence of entries may possibly be as follows: symphonies 29 and 31:1765; symphonies 28, 35, 59, and 38:1767–68; symphonies 49, 58, Hob. Ia: 10 and (I) 26:1768–69, and symphony 41:1769–70. The list of symphonies on the normal staves breaks off here, and two Masses follow: the Mass (missing until quite recently) "Sunt bona mixta malis" and the "Great organ mass," supposedly from 1768–70.

The first continuation of the list of symphonies on added staves on the left side of the page appears at the top of page 2. It comprises three symphonies: 39, 20, and Hob. I:106, with autograph numbers 54–56. The last work, recently acknowledged as an overture, most likely to "Le pescatrici," may date back to 1769–70,[28] but the two symphonies 39 and 20—both, as opposed to the other incipits here, added rather cursorily in pencil notation—are probably to be regarded as later entries, especially the last one.

The list of symphonies then continues on page 1, again on added staves on the left side of the page. From the top of the page the order of symphonies indicated is this: 45, 46, 65, 48, (46 crossed out again, then), 47, 44, 52, 43, and 42. The order of entries is not easy to determine. It might perhaps seem as if Haydn started from below and ended in the upper left-hand corner. The datable symphonies come from a narrow period of time: 1771 (No. 42)–1772 (Nos. 45, 46, 47), and the sequence of works must be taken as substantial evidence for dating the other symphonies from about the same time. Nos. 43 and 44 were both advertised in the Breitkopf catalog for 1772, and given the usual delay, that would point to 1770/71 as the latest date of composition. No. 52, which is to be found in the Breitkopf catalog of 1774, must certainly date from the same time as the two neighboring symphonies, 43 and 44: 1770–71. No. 65, which received so high a number of Mandyczewski's list on the basis of its appearance in a Breitkopf catalog of 1778, must also be supposed to date from about the same time as the surrounding symphonies, none of which is later than 1772. No. 48 ("Maria Theresia") presents a special problem. The symphony has always been regarded as a tribute to the Empress, composed to celebrate her visit to Esterháza in 1773, in which year it was also announced by Breitkopf. It has accordingly been dated from 1772 or 1773. However, a recently found Elssler copy carries the indication "769" (1769) on the title page.[29] It is not an authentic indication, even if the copy must be called authentic, but of course it is an important piece of evidence, though it would hardly be easy to advocate antedating of the symphony for reasons of style.

Counting all the symphonies together—enumerated here as belonging to one of three groups: 1) the early, pre-Esterházy symphonies, 2) the chronologically fixed symphonies from the years 1761–65, and 3) the symphonies of 1765–72 as listed in the Entwurf-Katalog—we have covered all symphonies either known or assumed to belong to the period up to 1772 except the following: Nos. 3, 14, 16, 17, 19, 25, 34, 36, 72, and "B" (I:108). *Termini ante quem* for these works are given by their appearance in the following catalogs: Göttweig—1762 (3), 1764 (14), 1765 ("B"), and 1766 (16); Breitkopf—1766 (17, 19), 1767 (25, 34), 1769 (36), and 1781 (72).

As stated earlier, we do not know any examples of the appearance of a Haydn symphony in one of the Breitkopf catalogs earlier than one or two years after it was composed. Furthermore, the nonappearance of these symphonies in the Entwurf-Katalog argues strongly against their having been composed after 1765. Taking these two factors into consideration, we may narrow down the upper limits even a little more: 3 (1762), 14 (1764), "B" (1765), 16 (1765), 17 and 19 (1764/65), 25, 34, 36, 72 (1765). Since it is not possible to enter here upon a discussion of stylistic analysis as a means of investigating chronology, let me just add as a purely personal conviction that Nos. 3, 14, and 16 probably belong to Haydn's earliest Esterházy years (1761–63), 34, 36, and 72 to the following years (1763–65), while "B," 17, 19, and 25 may date back to either immediately before or just after Haydn's Esterházy engagement in 1761.

I do not think it will ever be possible to arrive at a definitive chronological ordering of Haydn's symphonies with exact time of composition or succession for all works. But there is reason to believe that the survey that can be achieved today comes close enough so as to provide us with a reliable foundation for the study of his symphonic development. For the first of the three groups considered, the symphonies from Haydn's last pre-Esterházy years in Vienna, we can establish a group of thirteen early symphonies (perhaps a few more), composed within three or four years, but neither fixed dates (years) nor a known order of composition with those years. (Landon's grouping must be regarded as hypothesis, not as proven fact.) I still believe that an understanding of Haydn's way to the classical symphony is found primarily through a study of the special types of early symphonies within this period of experimentation, not through any attempt to pin down a fixed line of progression. The second group, far more than the first or third, comprises a great many chronologically fixed works, no fewer than twelve in all, but also includes a number of symphonies that can only be tentatively attributed to this period, and not to a precise year. For the third group, the Entwurf-Katalog helps us establish an approximate, relative chronology, even if exact dates are lacking.

Mandyczewski's list of symphonies at the beginning of this century laid a solid foundation for Haydn research, especially with respect to authenticity, which at that time was undoubtedly the primary problem. His chronological arrangement was less convincing and has to some extent blocked the way to an understanding of Haydn's symphonic development, his early development in particular. I have tried to describe how an amended chronology has developed gradually with the growth of Haydn research since World War II. I have further stressed the difference between the two approaches: the trend to fix an absolutely sure upper limit for a symphony, and the endeavor rather to come as close as possible to the time of composition. The first of these trends undoubtedly permits a higher degree of objectivity. The second approach is more risky. But if we want to arrive at a real insight into Haydn's symphonic development, we shall have to take some risks. We have come closer not only to an objective statement of upper limits, but also to a responsible outlining of actual dates for Haydn's early symphonies. It still remains to be seen how far we will be able to change from an outline to final solutions.

Notes

1. *Joseph Haydns Werke, Erste kritisch durchgesehene Gesamtausgabe,* series 1, Symphonien, vols. I–III (Leipzig [1907–8]).

2. C. F. Pohl, *Joseph Haydn,* I–II (Berlin and Leipzig, 1875–82).

3. Vol. I: iii–viii.

4. "In I ist die Reihenfolge der Symphonien, soweit es möglich war, chronologisch festgesetzt. Da von diesen 104 Symphonien sich, soviel wir bis heute wissen, nur 39—die mit Aut. bezeichneten—in Haydns Handschrift erhalten haben (und auch diese nicht alle vollständig), so hat die Wahrscheinlichkeit manchen Spielraum gehabt. Besonders wurde vermieden, ein Werk zu früh anzusetzen" (*Joseph Haydns Werke,* I: viii).

5. *The Breitkopf Thematic Catalogue. The Six Parts and Sixteen Supplements 1762–1787,* ed. Barry S. Brook (New York, 1966).

6. *Der Göttweiger thematische Katalog von 1830,* ed. Fr. W. Riedel, 2 vols. (Munich and Salzburg, 1979).

7.   Hermann Kretzschmar, "Die Jugendsinfonien Joseph Haydns," *Jahrbuch der Musikbibliothek Peters*, XV (1908): 69–90 (reprinted in *Gesammelte Aufsatze über Musik und anderes* II [Leipzig, 1911]: 401–27).

8.   *Beiträge zur Entwicklung in Joseph Haydns Symphonik 1759–1780* (Turbenthal, 1934).

9.   "Haydns aeldre Symfonier i deres forhold til tidligere symfonisk komposition" (typewritten, 1928).

10. "Haydn und das 'kleine Quartbuch'," *Acta musicologica* VII (1935): 111–23.

11. Larsen, *Die Haydn-Überlieferung* (Copenhagen, 1939; 2d ed., Munich, 1980), part VI, "Der Entwurf-Katalog und die kleineren authentischen Kataloge," pp. 209–50.

12. *Joseph Haydn: Kritische Gesamtausgabe/The Complete Works: Critical Edition*, ed. J. P. Larsen and H. C. Robbins Landon, series I, vol. 9 (Boston, Leipzig, and Vienna, 1950): x–xiii.

13. H. C. Robbins Landon, *The Symphonies of Joseph Haydn* (London, 1955).

14. *Joseph Haydn, Kritische Ausgabe sämtlicher Symphonien/Critical Edition of the Complete Symphonies*, 12 vols, ed. H. C. Robbins Landon (Vienna, 1965–68).

15. "Haydn, Franz Joseph: Werke," *Die Musik in Geschichte und Gegenwart* V (Kassel, 1956): cols. 1886ff.

16. Anthony van Hoboken, *Joseph Haydn: Thematisch-bibliographisches Werkverzeichhnis* I (Mainz, 1957).

17. A synopsis of the lists mentioned here is given in Larsen, "Probleme der chronologischen Ordnung von Haydns Sinfonien," *Festschrift Otto Erich Deutsch zum 80. Geburtstag*, ed. Walter Gerstenberg, Jan LaRue, and Wolfgang Rehm (Kassel, 1963), pp. 90–104.

18. "Die chronologische Ordnung von Haydns Sinfonien zwischen 1774 und 1782," *Haydn-Studien* II (1969): 34–66.

19. *Haydns Werke. in der Musiksammlung der Nationalbibliothek Széchényi in Budapest*, ed. Ferrö Vécsey et al. (1959).

20. *Haydn: Chronicle and Works, (I) Haydn: The Early Years, 1732–1765* (London, 1980), pp. 239–42.

21. Landon, *Haydn: Chronicle and Works*, I, pp. 250–51.

22. Ibid., pp. 240–41.

23. "Haydn, Joseph, works," *The New Grove Dictionary of Music and Musicians* VIII (London, 1980): 360–401 (symphonies, 371–73).

24. Ibid., p. 360.

25. *The Symphonies of Joseph Haydn.*

26. Larsen, *Die Haydn-Überlieferung*, part VI; and *Drei Haydn-Kataloge in Facsimile* (Copenhagen, 1941; rev. ed. as *Three Haydn Catalogues/Drei Haydn Kataloge* [New York, 1979]).

27. See Larsen, *Die Haydn-Überlieferung*, pp. 212–14, 219–21.

28. Gerlach, "Ein Fund zu Haydns verschollener Sinfonie," *Haydn-Studien* III (1973): 44–46.

29. Landon, *Haydn: Chronicle and Works* I: 280–81.

16

Haydn and *Das kleine Quartbuch*

The origins of Haydn's development as a composer of symphonies are veiled to a certain degree. Pohl—whose great merits in Haydn research are certainly not to be belittled—gives up almost completely on this question. In the first volume of his Haydn biography[1] he states: "Haydn forgot to tell us whether there had been any models for his first symphony, and which they were." He then is satisfied with citing a large number of composers who wrote symphonies around 1760, and who for this reason could come into question. Spitta aptly remarks in this regard: "He paves part of the way for the historian, but he does not enter it himself."[2]

The search for Haydn's predecessors that set in more strongly around the turn of the century unfortunately was determined too much by the Mannheim polemic, the aftereffects of which still have not been left entirely behind, just as the problem is far from being resolved despite valuable contributions from various sides. However, so much is certain that the entire development must no longer be regarded as a rectilinear, but as a rather complicated, ramified one. Common features which formerly were considered proof of influence, in many cases turn out to be parallel phenomena manifesting themselves in simultaneous, but maybe entirely separate, lines of development.

Therefore it affects neither Stamitz's nor Haydn's significance in the least, to state that stylistically there is almost no relation between these two masters. Except for isolated passages in the very first symphonies that might point toward some influence—for example, the beginning of the first symphony—Haydn goes in entirely different directions than Stamitz in regard to all crucial points. Riemann himself stressed this with respect to the "manners."[3] Heuß, in his excellent essay "Über die Dynamik der Mannheimer Schule,"[4] emphasizes "that since such [i.e., Mannheim] crescendos are rarely found in Haydn, he apparently turned against this method of composition." More recent research (Sondheimer, Schökel, Tutenberg) points out the differences in other areas, especially the

Originally published in German in *Acta musicologica* (1935), pp. 111–23.

formal differences in the overall shape of the symphony (Tutenberg's four form types),[5] and of the individual movement, in particular the first movement (the problem of the "secondary theme").

In light of these statements, it created a sensation when Sandberger (in his recent essay, "Zu Haydns Repertoir in Eisenstadt und Esterhaz"[6]) presents as fact that Haydn not only knew Stamitz's compositions very well, but also preferred them to those of Wagenseil, and that even in his mature years he used Stamitz as a source.

The highly respected old master of Haydn research draws these most interesting conclusions from a catalog in the princely Esterházy Archive in Budapest, which he describes as "a two-volume thematic catalog in quarto—compiled and written by Elßler and arranged according to keys—of the symphonies, divertimenti, etc., that were performed by the court orchestra under Haydn's direction."[7]

Unfortunately, we are not told where this information about the provenance and purpose of the catalog is obtained. The catalog itself provides no clues; moreover, obvious features seem to suggest that it hardly can have originated close to Haydn. Since this question is of great importance to Haydn research—which, of course, would very much like to know exactly what instrumental music was at hand in Eisenstadt—I will dwell on the catalog a little further.[8]

It consists of two volumes in small quarto format,[9] one of which lists only symphonies while the other is devoted to chamber music. Thus even in format this "*kleine Quartbuch*" (as Pohl calls it) differs from the princely inventories in folio (from the years 1759, 1806, and 1858). In addition, all these volumes in folio bear titles designating them as catalogs of the princely music collection, whereas the *Quartbuch* has no heading at all. Moreover, it did not belong to this collection from the beginning, but entered the princely library along with the books and the music purchased by the prince from Haydn's estate. This becomes evident from an inventory (1858) in which it is listed as a "Thematic catalog of different compositions of different masters. 2 volumes," with the explicit note: "From Haydn's *"Kunst und Musikalien"* [!], and also from the *Nachlaßverzeichnis* "Inventory and evaluation of the *Kunstsachen* left behind by Herr Joseph Haydn, Doctor of Music, who died on May 31, 1809 in Gumpendorf, . . ."[10] in which it is listed under the same title as no. 570. Traces of Haydn's personal dealings with the catalog are found in form of autograph entries at the beginning of both volumes. In the symphony volume it says: "Herein contained are 61 symphonies and two divertimenti by Jos. Haydn," and in the chamber music volume similarly: "94 pieces are marked here by Jos. Haydn." It is very remarkable, however, that Haydn in his revision of the symphony volume had to cross out quite a number of themes designated "Haydn" but that had not originated from him. No less than fourteen works (eleven by

Michael Haydn, one by Holzbauer, and two unknown to me) were eliminated, and were not counted among the "61 symphonies and two divertimenti." This definitely contradicts the assumption that this is an Eisenstadt repertory catalog, for in Eisenstadt the compositions of Michael and Joseph Haydn would certainly have been distinguishable from each other.

The contents of these two volumes consist of about 300 themes from symphonies by 26 composers—the anonymous theme C48 turns out to be a chamber work by Asplmayr (C53 in the second volume of the *Quartbuch*)—and about 450 themes from chamber works by 28 composers. In each volume the themes are arranged according to key, and then according to composer within each key. The sequence of composers is approximately determined by number of themes: those represented by more works (the more famous, more popular composers?) take precedence over those with fewer works. This arrangement is not quite consistent, but the following order approximates that of the symphony volume: Haydn (63 themes + 14 that he rejected), Vanhal (50), Ordoñez (19), Ditters (22), Bach (18, of which 13 are by Johann Christian Bach; it is not clear which Bach composed the other 5), Gaßmann (10), (van) Maldere (33), [T?] Hu(e)ber (12), Pichl (6), Bartta (6), Wagenseil (5); less consistent are the following: Holzbauer (4), Hofmann (4), Schlöger (2), Krottendorfer (2), Schmid (2), Ziegler (2), Stamitz (13, of which 4 are by Johann Stamitz, 6 are by Carl Stamitz, 2 are of uncertain authorship, and 1 is by Pichl[?]), Gossec (6); and finally, with 1 theme each: Albrechtsberger, Piccini, Kymerling, Zimmermann, Michael Haydn (who, however, is the author of 11 of the works attributed solely to "Haydn", as mentioned above), Fils, and Abel. In the chamber music volume the arrangement is even less consistent and also a little more complicated, for within the individual keys the quartets usually appear first, followed by the other forms—almost exclusively trios. Nevertheless, the following approximate order can be recognized: Haydn (95, he himself states 94), Vanhal (71, two of which are listed twice), Ordoñez (27), Ditters (23, with two works listed twice), Bach (10; of these 6 are by J.C., 2 are by C.P.E. Bach, and 2 are of uncertain authorship), Klopp (6), Kyffmer (10), Hofmann (6), Boccherini (12), Aumon (4), Wagenseil (25), Gaßmann (13), Venatorino [Mysliweczek] (25), Schmid (24), Abel (11), Paradeiser (19), Buccelli (10), Stamitz (22, 8 of these are by Johann, 6 are by Carl Stamitz, and 8 are of unknown origin),[11] Kram(m)er [Wilhelm Cramer], (6), Mozart (6), Zimmermann (6), Stadt (12), and finally, with 2 works each: Ziegler, and Fils, and with 1 each: Graun, Schlöger, Asplmayr, and Wutky.

This survey of the contents clearly reveals that here we are facing a markedly Austrian repertory. Of the 300 works of the symphony volume there are only 70 by foreign composers; the remaining approximately 230 compositions are by Austrian (or Czech) composers. In the chamber music volume, we count about 110 foreign and 340 native works. Thus in all, more than three quarters of the contents is Austrian.[12]

Compared to other catalogs of the time—for example, the Breitkopf cata-logs—the *Quartbuch* has an extremely local character. Whereas many of the more famous—especially Italian—contemporary composers are not represented at all, in both volumes we come across quite a number of lesser figures whose names remained almost or entirely unknown abroad. If we are faced here with Haydn's repertory, then we must conclude that there were no symphonies in Eisenstadt by composers such as, for example, Hasse, Jomelli, and Galuppi. However, this cannot be right! We know for sure that before and around 1760 Prince Paul Anton had purchased a great many works of these and other Italian composers, as is evident in the inventory first completed in 1759, but added to until 1761, mentioned by Pohl only in passing.[13]

This catalog is divided (very characteristically!) into four main groups: *Musique vocale italienne, Musique instrumentale italienne, Musique vocale françoise,* and *Musique instrumentale françoise.* Each of these groups is again subdivided into different subgroups. In the second group we find as class V *"Sinfonies à plusieurs instruments."* For the sake of comparison with the above list, let me cite the contents of this class. The order of names is the following (one symphony each if no number is provided): Cocchi, Gravina Nap., Hasse, Martino [Sammartini], Auletta di Napoli, Buranello [Galuppi], Giomelli, Peretz, Gluck (*Innocenza giustificata*), Peretz, Chiesa, Stamitz, Piccino, Manna, Tamm, 1 *sans nom,* Hasse, Hasse, Logroscino Nap., Cocchi, 1 *sans nom,* Vitolo, Siless, Maranzini, Gluck, Adolfati, (the following entries were made by Haydn's predecessor Werner!) Hasse, 6 Ziegler, Holzbauer, Pugnani, Bokh, 1 *Senza nome,* Valentini, Rinaldo di Cap., Wagenseil, Jomelli, Wagenseil, Cal-derara [*sic*], Prota, Galuppi, Growina, Wagenseil, Hasse, Hasse, Perez, Orsler, Martino, Ruggero, Pugnani, Galuppi, Stamitz, Sciroli, Jomelli, Ordoñez, Hasse, Perez, Maggiore, Conforti, 1 *Senza nome,* Traetti, Galuppi, Maijo, Wagenseil, Sciroli, 1 *Senza nome,* Wagenseil, 4 *Senza nome,* 6 Pugnani, 6 van Maldere, Scharlattj, Hasse (*Alcide*), 10 Ditters, *L'arbre enchanté,* Haydn, Hasse, Jommelli, Scarlatti (*Issipile*), Traetta (*Armida*). Giuseppe Scarlatti's *Issi-pile* is entered in 1761; the preceding works back up to Hasse's *Alcide* in 1760.

It appears from this list that Haydn actually found a large international repertory in Eisenstadt. Here the situation is exactly the reverse of that discussed earlier: of the works listed only about one-quarter are of Austrian, and about three-quarters are of foreign (Italian!) origin. Compared to that the *Quartbuch,* if regarded as an Esterházy catalog, would manifest an almost too strange change of repertory; in addition to the great number of new names this would be shown in the fact that almost two-thirds of the works present around 1760—among them symphonies by Gluck, Hasse, Jomelli, Galuppi, etc.—were not taken into con-sideration when the *Quartbuch* was compiled.

If we take into account all these facts (the difference in outer appearance and layout between the authentic Esterházy catalogs and the *Quartbuch,* the way in which the book entered the collection, the great difference as to contents between the *Quartbuch* and the catalog of 1759, and finally Haydn's subsequent deletion of the "Haydn" symphonies that were not his work), then the assumption that the *Quartbuch* was a Haydn catalog ("Elßler's repertory catalog") must be considered rather unlikely.[14] However, if this is not the case, then we must regard the *Quartbuch* as a catalog of a foreign collection that somehow came into Haydn's possession. A basis for this assumption which might also serve as a clue for further investigation can perhaps be found in a note in the chamber music volume.

On the last leaf of this volume there is a short list: "Missing A. nos. 27, 28, 29, 35, C. nos. 17, 51, (etc.)." Further down, a pencilled entry follows: "Lilienfeld 6 of Schmid, 6 Abel, 6 Vanhal with the flute and basso," as well as a list of the mentioned eighteen works: "A. nos. 5, 20, 22. B. nos. 7, 23 (etc.)." This note probably refers to the convent of Lilienfeld (Lower Austria), and it seems reasonable to understand from it that the music mentioned had been either sold or loaned to the convent. The two possibilities would again allow two interpretations of the catalog: as a sales catalog of a music dealer (similar to the printed Breitkopf catalogs), or as a listing of a private collection, perhaps that of another monastery. This latter assumption might find support in the occurrence of names such as Aumon, Kymerling, and Paradeiser (priests of St. Florian and Melk). However, this assumption, of course, remains hypothetical.[15]

If, for the present, we must leave the question of the provenance of the catalog unanswered, we can determine the date of its compilation with some certainty. This becomes rather evident from a survey of the chronology of the works in it. In this respect the series of Haydn symphonies is of a special significance, as the *Quartbuch* contains all those that, according to Mandyczewski,[16] date from before 1775—i.e., up to and including no. 60—except nos. 4, 6–8, 20, 33, 50, 51, and 53, in addition to nos. 65 and 72. The four symphonies from the year 1774 handed down to us in autograph (nos. 54–57), and the symphony no. 60, which was performed in Vienna in January 1776 (and therefore was composed in 1775 at the latest), are listed in the catalog. The symphony no. 61 (composed 1776) as well as all the demonstrably later symphonies are missing. We may well consider this if not as proof, as at least a strong argument in favor of the assumption that the catalog originated, or was completed, shortly after 1775.[17]

Of the quartets, the first 36 (except nos. 13–18) are entered. However, here we find the quartet in E-flat major (brought to new honors by Marion M. Scott) instead of the one in B-flat which currently passes for no. 5. The two sets of op. 17 (1771) and op. 20 (1772) are still included, whereas the following op. 33 (1781) and the later works are missing. Further chamber works by Haydn include—besides a series of early string trios—22 trios for baryton, viola, and bass, those that are the nos. 2, 3, 18, 26, 27, 29–31, 44, 45, 64, 65, 83–87,

94–96, 123, and 124 according to the *Haydn-Verzeichnis*.[18] Whereas the nos. 2–96 stem from the years before 1770, nos. 123 and 124 probably date from the time of 1772 to 1775, which again points toward the dating "about 1775."

Here we must mention a special feature with regard to the order of the themes. Whereas usually within each key the themes of Haydn's compositions are placed first, several times one or two supplementary themes are found at the end of a key. Similar additions are found in the cases of some other more prominent composers. These supplements do not just seem to signify works that had been forgotten or omitted; rather one gets the impression that here we face small addenda which register works that had been added during or soon after the compilation of the main catalog. Thus of Haydn's works this alleged appendix lists—besides the early no. 11—the symphonies nos. 48, 52, 54–57, and 60. Since nos. 50, 51, and 53 are missing in the catalog, and since nos. 49, 58, and 59 certainly date back to the time before 1770, these numbers (with the exception of no. 11) embody just the symphonies composed last (1772–75) of the Haydn symphonies contained in the catalog. In the chamber music volume we do not find a similar separation with regard to Haydn's works. This may be due to the fact that the listed works, with the possible exception of the two last compositions for baryton, all belong to the time before 1772.[19]

If we investigate the chronology of works by other composers listed in the *Quartbuch,* we arrive at quite similar results. The printed Breitkopf catalogs from 1762–87 serve as the major source of such investigations. It must only be noted that they usually list the works no sooner than two to three years after their time of composition. This is true of the offered manuscript copies, but is even more certain for the prints that were advertised via Leipzig by publishers from Paris, Amsterdam, Lyon, etc. In Haydn's case this can be established easily by means of the symphonies that exist in dated autographs. Thus we find the symphonies nos. 22, 23, 24, 28, 29, 30, 31, 35, 42, 45, 47, 49, 54, 55, 56, 57, 61, 63, and 73 in the Breitkopf catalogs with a 3, 9, 5, 3, 4, 8, 14(!), 5, 2, 4, 1, 2, 5, 2, 2, 4, 2, 3, 5, and 1 year delay, respectively. Only quite exceptionally may we presume that a symphony had been composed less than two years prior to its citation in the Breitkopf catalog. Regarding the great number of Haydn symphonies that in Mandyczewski's list are dated according to the Breitkopf catalog, we must presume that, for example, "before 1772" must not be interpreted as "about 1772," but rather as "about 1770," if not earlier.[20] When we take into account how much Haydn's works alone were in demand by the early 1770s, we may certainly assume that these observations are generally valid with regard to the works of lesser known composers as well.

Next to Haydn the best-represented composer in the *Quartbuch* is Vanhal. We find forty of his symphonies in the main body of the catalog and ten in the supplement. Twenty-six of the forty symphonies appear in the Breitkopf catalog until 1775, six in later catalogs, and eight are missing altogether. Of the supplementary symphonies, only one is cited prior to 1775 (1771), and eight are cited after 1775 (1 in 1776/1777, 4 in 1778, and 3 in 1779/1780), whereas one is missing. The thirty-seven chamber works of Vanhal that appear both in the *Quartbuch* and in the Breitkopf catalogs are distributed thus: 9 in 1771, 12 in 1773, 4 in 1774, 5 in 1776/1777, 6 in 1778, and 1 in 1779/1780. The six works (trios) cited in the catalog of 1778 (a Paris print) belong to the supplement. The divertimento of 1779/1780 probably stems from an earlier period. Of Ordoñez's symphonies in the *Quartbuch* there are only two in the Breitkopf catalogs (1766 and 1775). His chamber music is represented only by the six quartets "op. 1," printed in Lyon (Breitkopf, 1778); they belong to the supplement of the *Quartbuch*. The nineteen symphonies of Dittersdorf which appear in both sources[21] are distributed as follows: before 1772: 16; 1773, 1775, and 1776/1777, one symphony each. All of his chamber works in the *Quartbuch* stem from the time before 1775—as far as can be stated. Thirteen symphonies of J. C. Bach were composed (according to Breitkopf and Tutenberg[22]) back in the 1760s. The six quartets (op. VIII—Breitkopf, 1772) were composed before 1767 according to Schökel.[23] Of a few less often represented masters, only those works that are common to both sources (*Quartbuch* and Breitkopf catalogs) shall be cited: Bartta: 4 symphonies (2 in 1774, 2 in 1776/1777); Boccherini: 6 trios and 6 quartets (1768); Wilhelm Cramer: 6 trios (1769); Gossec: 6 symphonies (1769); Mysliweczek: 6 quintets (1768); Pichl: 5 symphonies (1769–75); Giuseppe Schmidt: 6 trios—attributed to Asplmayr the following year in a Paris print!—and 9 quartets (1773); Carl Stamitz: 6 symphonies (1773) and 5 quartets (1775); Huber and Zimmermann: one symphony each (1775); and finally we find in the *Quartbuch* the 6 quartets K. 168–73, composed 1773 by the young Mozart. In addition, there are the compositions by Johann Stamitz (d.1757), Filtz (d.1760), Schlöger (d.1766), van Maldere (d.1768), Gaßmann (d.1774), Paradeiser (d.1775), and Wagenseil (d.1777), that without further investigation can be dated before (or about) 1775.

The *Quartbuch* undoubtedly is a valuable example of an Austrian music collection from about 1775. For even though it gives no direct evidence of Haydn's repertory, we may justifiably assume that to a large degree it followed the same road. In addition, this catalog, together with a few others from the same time—e.g., the Sarasin catalog in Basel, and the old Göttweig catalog (with many dates!)—forms a welcome supplement to the Breitkopf catalogs with regard to the bibliography of early classical instrumental music. Many of the themes included are rarely (if at all) found elsewhere. With respect to the frequent mix-up of authors of works from this transitional period, the catalog may render a good service in many instances, even though neither here nor in the related catalogs can absolute infallibility be expected. Finally, the Haydn bibliography must be especially concerned with this catalog because Haydn controlled the contents of the symphony volume. We shall examine this question in greater depth. Before proceeding to this, let us just make some final remarks concerning the topic of Haydn and Mannheim.

From the fact that in the *Quartbuch* Stamitz's name appears thirty-five times, whereas Wagenseil turns up only thirty times, Sandberger concludes: "That Stamitz surpassed even Wagenseil in Haydn's favor sets us thinking, and leads to imperative conclusions." Even if we might claim the catalog as representative of Haydn's taste, we could not adhere to this superficial conclusion. For only twelve works by Johann Stamitz are found in the catalog; there are just as many by Carl Stamitz, and ten are still unidentified. It must be stressed that the G-major theme no. 62 in the chamber music volume, cited by Sandberger as a symphony by (Johann) Stamitz and as a model for Haydn's *Impériale* symphony (no. 53), actually belongs to a quartet by *Carl* Stamitz (as can be verified in at least four different prints). Whether or not Haydn knew the quartet in question must be left undecided. In any case, it appears rather risky to cite this isolated case of a similarity of themes—be it accidental or not—as primary evidence of Haydn's "ties to the Mannheim school." Rather risky, too, appears the attempt to infer "relations between Haydn and the Mannheim school" from the remark, *"Composto per il Elettore Palatino,"* on a late print of an early composition by Haydn. For even if this dedication had originated by Haydn himself at the time of the composition (which cannot be established without further confirmation), it may well be regarded as a purely commercial affair. A possible attempt to gain the favor of the elector by a dedication certainly does not imply relations to the Mannheim orchestra. Finally one can scarcely conclude from the presence of isolated works by Mannheim masters—an overture by Cannabich, and one symphony each by Holzbauer and Carl Stamitz—in the inventory of 1806 that these works "were still performed at the time of Hummel," but only that they were still available in the music archive.

If we compare the Haydn symphonies in the *Quartbuch* with Mandyczewski's list, certain differences come to light. The absence of some of the larger symphonies—such as the three program symphonies (nos. 6–8), but especially the symphonies nos. 50, 51, and 53, which were composed shortly before the catalog was finished—would be as strange for an Esterházy catalog as it would be explicable for a foreign catalog. As for the program symphonies, one might argue that they must not necessarily be considered as symphonies. In the Breitkopf catalogs and elsewhere, *Le matin* (no. 6) is designated as divertimento, and *Le soir* (no. 8) as concertino; and actually, these concertolike symphonies seem to some extent not to fit into the symphony series. Haydn himself, however, acknowledged them as symphonies in the Elßler catalog.

Of the fifty-three symphonies that are common to the *Quartbuch* and to Mandyczewski's list of the undoubtedly authentic symphonies, fifty-two are also found in Elßler's *Haydn-Verzeichnis*. These symphonies therefore have been confirmed twice by Haydn, and their authenticity is beyond question. One of these fifty-three symphonies, however, no. 25, is not listed in Elßler's catalog. Pohl mentions this, and refers instead to the *Quartbuch*,[24] whereas Mandyczewski hints at "a final possibility, though not a probability, that it might not be by Haydn." This symphony is attributed to Haydn in an early Paris print, in two citations in the Breitkopf catalog of 1767, as well as in old manuscript copies in Göttweig, Regensburg, and Zittau, and is (to my knowledge) not attributed to a different composer in any other collection. Also, in spite of its slightly unusual form, it is fairly close in style to the undoubtedly authentic early compositions of Haydn. Thus, its inclusion in the complete edition can certainly be justified, though it appears to be too primitive to have been composed at the time to which it is attributed ("about 1765").[25]

Besides these fifty-three symphonies we find in the *Quartbuch* another eight symphonies, counted among his works by Haydn himself, that either do not occur in the list in the complete edition at all, or are listed among the group of spurious works. Nevertheless, it would be irresponsible to conclude from this that the number of authentic symphonies must be increased by eight. Two of these works can be found in the *Entwurfkatalog* and in the *Haydn-Verzeichnis* as "Divertimento a 9ve" (*Haydn-Verzeichnis* 17 and 20). (Two other divertimenti [*H.V.* 2 and 9], placed as nos. 1 and 2 of the G-major symphonies, were marked by Haydn himself with the addition "Divertimento" both at the respective themes, and at the beginning of the volume ["61 symphonies and 2 divertimenti"].) A third work that does not appear in the cited sources is called "parthia" in the Göttweig catalog, and subsequently by Pohl (Mfr. XI, 40926), a designation that seems to be correct. The B-flat major symphony, on the other hand, that appears in the *Quartbuch* as no. 3, and in the *Haydn-Verzeichnis* as no. 7, could have been admitted into the first group of Mandyczewski's list. The reason for this lack of admission appears to be that Pohl, following a Zittau source, called the work "Parthia" (Mfr. XI, 40930).

Whereas for these four works the question of designation was the major problem, the question of authenticity is the most important with regard to the last four symphonies. Three of them appear in Mandyczewski's list of the spurious symphonies, namely III, 11 (Michael Haydn); III, 16 (J. Schmidt); and III, 27 (Michael Haydn), whereas the fourth one is listed in Perger's catalog of Michael Haydn's works[26] as no. 36. However, that does not resolve the question with absolute certainty. Perger himself stresses that the identification in several cases may be rather uncertain, especially if there is only a single, casual copy as source.[27] Mandyczewski tacitly based his list of spurious works on the principle that a symphony circulating under Haydn's name, but not listed in Elßler's *Haydn–Verzeichnis* must be considered spurious, if only one attribution to another composer can be found. His main sources for the identification of other authors were the Breitkopf catalog and Perger's Michael Haydn catalog mentioned above. He refers to the authority of Pohl in only one instance (III, 28); in all others, he cites Breitkopf or Perger. Since none of these sources may be considered infallible, and since we cannot entirely disregard the possibility that some—even though not many—symphonies are forgotten in the *Haydn-Verzeichnis,* the possibility must be considered that a few symphonies designated as spurious by Mandyczewski might nevertheless be authentic. However, this undoubtedly would be an exception, for in general a work of another composer is much more easily attributed to Haydn than vice versa.

In any case, it is not permissible to regard Haydn's inclusion of these four symphonies in the total number as an irrefutable proof of his authorship. According to the extant sources, one of these symphonies (III, 27) absolutely must be regarded as a work of Michael Haydn. A former owner of the now missing autograph even gives us the date of the composition. Another symphony (Perger 36) exists—according to Perger—only in a single copy in Kremsmünster. But it is also listed in the Göttweig catalog under Michael Haydn's name. Since the symphony is not found under Joseph Haydn's name—the *Quartbuch* only states "Haydn"!—we are probably again facing a small slip of Haydn's memory. Regarding the remaining two symphonies, a decision based on contemporary attributions is scarcely possible. Number III, 11 (Perger 37) is, according to Perger, known under Michael Haydn's name only in a single copy in Kremsmünster. Number III, 16 is listed as a work of J. Schmidt in Breitkopf 1774. In both cases, however, confusion cannot absolutely be ruled out. Here (to adapt Mandyczewski's saying in a slightly altered version) we are facing "a final possibility, even if not a likelihood, that these two symphonies might be by Joseph Haydn."

In spite of the authentic notation, "Herein contained are 61 symphonies . . . by Jos. Haydn," we only may acknowledge the undeleted symphonies as authentic with the reservation that Haydn's authorship must be strongly questioned if there is no other contemporary corroboration, or even if there are attributions to other composers in different sources. Of course, we must consider the deleted symphonies as unconditionally spurious. This is not unimportant, since quite a number of these works are otherwise expressly designated as works of Joseph Haydn (e.g., nos. 27, 35, and 36 of the symphonies designated "spurious" by Mandyczewski, as well as some symphonies not listed by him). An aid confirming and supplementing Mandyczewski's indications is furthermore given by the themes of works by other composers in the *Quartbuch.* Here we find additional evidence of Vanhal's authorship of III, 8, 18, and 30 (III, 12 has already been dealt with above), of Dittersdorf's authorship of III, 29, and of Michael Haydn's authorship of III, 13 (the only symphony expressly designated "M. Haydn" in the *Quartbuch*). Of works from Mandyczewski's last group the *Quartbuch* lists IV, 1 under Kymerling, and IV, 34 under Gaßmann who is listed as composer of the symphony in Göttweig as well (1766). The *Quartbuch* also registers the true authors of quite a number of more-than-dubious "Haydn" symphonies that occasionally appear under his name, and that are not taken into consideration by Mandyczewski. A typical example is the B-flat major symphony—published a short time ago as a work by Haydn—that can be found under the Vanhal symphonies in the *Quartbuch*. The correctness of this information is proven by two citations in the Breitkopf catalogs (1772 [ms.], and 1774 [Paris, "op. XVI"]), and by contemporary copies in Regensburg and in the Esterházy archive.

There may be different opinions concerning the origin of the *Quartbuch* and related matters. However, there can be no doubt about its value as a source both for the bibliography of early classical instrumental music and for future research concerning the early history of classical instrumental music. Professor Sandberger's excellent instincts in immediately recognizing the significance of the catalog and bringing it to the attention of the public must be greatly appreciated.[28]

Notes

1. C. F. Pohl, *Joseph Haydn* I (Berlin, 1875): 280.

2. "Zur Musik" (Berlin, 1892): 167.

3. *Denkmäler der Tonkunst in Bayern* VII, 2: XXIV. See also Gál, "Die Stileigentümlichkeiten des jungen Beethoven" *Studien zur Musikwissenschaft* IV: 62.

4. *Riemann-Festschrift* (Leipzig, 1909): 449.

5. *Die Sinfonik Joh. Chr. Bachs* (Wolfenbüttel-Berlin, 1928): 46ff.; pp. 175ff. deal with Haydn.

6. *Jahrbuch der Musikbibliothek Peters 1933,* ed. Kurt Taut (Leipzig, 1934): 35ff.

7. This very valuable catalog—not only with regard to Haydn research, but to the bibliography of the pre- and early classical instrumental music altogether—was known to Pohl, as is revealed by his manuscript notes and in a citation in his Haydn biography (I: 291). However, he apparently did not attach particular importance to it, and his successor Mandyczewski (who was able to make use of Pohl's notes) does not mention the catalog. For this reason it has remained almost entirely unknown until today.

8. These investigations would not have been possible without the kind permission of His Highness Prince Paul Esterházy, who allowed me to study in the princely archive several times. I should like to express my sincere gratitude for this permission and for the excellent help of the princely archivist, Dr. J. Harich. My studies were also facilitated by Dr. Hedwig Kraus, Director of the library of the Gesellschaft der Musikfreunde, Vienna, who allowed me to use the notes of Pohl and Mandyczewski. In addition, valuable support was rendered by Mr. Carl Brand (Berlin) and Dr. Victor Luithlen (Vienna).

9. Ref. 161/2; earlier ref.: No. 2, fol. 184.

10. Pohl-Botstiber: *Joseph Haydn* III (Leipzig, 1927): 278; copy in Pohl's collections.

11. The identification of the B-flat major theme no. 34 as a trio of Carl Stamitz is based on the kind information of Mr. P. Gradenwitz.

12. Some of the non-Austrians temporarily had contact with Vienna. According to Gerber (old dictionary) van Maldere visited Vienna in 1758 (c.f. R. Haas, *Gluck und Durazzo im Burgthea-ter* [Vienna, 1925]: 114) Carl Stamitz appeared there twice as Viola virtuoso 1772–74 (C. F. Pohl, *Denkschrift aus Anlaß des hundertjährigen Bestehens der Tonkünstler-Societät* [Vienna, 1871]: 57). Whether Kyffner is J. J. P. Küffner from Regensburg (1713–86, born in Nuremberg), or his son Joseph (?) K., who (according to Schilling) was born in 1758, and who (according to Gerber) had played the harpsichord at Prince von Palm at Vienna until 1785, and later was active in Paris and London, cannot be decided. Probability speaks for the father, if the given date of birth of the son is correct (which, however, is far from certain). The younger Joseph K. (1776–1856) from Würzburg can not be considered at all, and his father Wilhelm K. (d.1798) can hardly come into question. By the way, the Küffner biographies of the standard encyclopedias supply a rather confused picture. One cannot even recognize whether they are three or four people! Schilling in his major work turned the two Josephs into one person, whereas the supplement gives us an authentic biography of the younger. Gathy maintains this confusion, whereas Gaßner in his excerpt from Schilling adheres to the supplement. Fétis turns the son from Regensburg and the father from Würzburg into one Wilhelm-Joseph, makes him having been born in Kalmüntz near Regensburg in 1738 and having been active in Würzburg as well as in Vienna, Paris, and London. This seems to be no happy fusion, but still it has been developed further by Mendel-Reißmann. Finally Lipowski—followed by Mendel-Reißmann—mentions a Father Liberatus Kuffner, who is unknown elsewhere. Eitner eludes the problem in concealing the information supplied by Gerber concerning the Küffner who was active in Vienna, Paris, and London.

13. I: 212.

14. As far as I can see Elßler does not come into question as the compiler of the catalog. In any case, the handwriting exhibits very characteristic deviations in comparison to attested documents by Elßler. In addition, Elßler started his activities as copyist as late as ca. 1790, and the repertory of the *Quartbuch,* as we shall soon see, concludes about the year 1775!

15. The possibility that Haydn had personal contacts with Lilienfeld—by which Sandberger's assumption could attain welcome corroboration—probably does not come into question. In response to my inquiry (July 1933) the Reverend Prior kindly gave me the following information: "Nothing is known here of music by Haydn which might have come to the convent in the way mentioned."

16. *Joseph Haydns Werke,* series 1, vol. I: ivff.

17. The appearance of the two symphonies 65 and 72 does not change this statement since 65 (Mandyczewski: "before 1778") was undoubtedly written before 1775, maybe as early as 1770–72, and 72 ("before 1781") certainly originated even earlier, probably about 1765. The entry of these two symphonies into the list of the complete edition followed the information from the Breitkopf catalog that only establish a *terminus ante quem.*

18. This selection does not come into question as a catalog of the Baryton trios in the possession of Esterházy. It is well known that Prince Nikolaus valued and cultivated these compositions that he himself had suggested. And these exact works were certainly extant completely, partly bound in volumes of twenty-four pieces, as we can derive from the so-called *Entwurfkatalog.* On the other hand, there are smaller or larger collections of Haydn string trios in different foreign libraries, which turn out to be arrangements of baryton trios. A few of these works in the arrangement for string trio can be found at Kremsmünster. W. Oliver Strunk described similar, more extensive collections, now in the Library of Congress, in his valuable essay on the baryton trios (*Musical Quarterly* 18 [1932]: 216ff.).

19. Otherwise, it must be stressed that the layers hinted at are not reflected in the writing style. For this reason one could assume—quite hypothetically—that we are dealing with a copy, not with an original catalog.

20. This statement in general does not imply a criticism, since Mandyczewski expressly stated his intent not to render a too-early date for any symphony. The very interesting, though very difficult problem of the chronology of Haydn's symphonies shall not be pursued further here.

21. See also the thematic catalog in Krebs, *Dittersdorfiana* (Berlin, 1900): 55ff.

22. Op. cit. By the way, it is not quite understandable why Tutenberg devoted so little attention to the Breitkopf catalog—the citation on p. 201 is neither correct, nor complete, since in many instances they corroborate (e.g., nos. 10, 22, 23, 25–27, 34, 36, 48, and 60), and only occasionally antedate his chronological statements.

23. *Joh. Chr. Bach und die Instrumentalmusik seiner Zeit,* (Wolfenbüttel, 1926): 78.

24. I:291.

25. Kretzschmar (*Gesammelte Aufsätze* II [Leipzig, 1911]: 416) regards this and the—undoubtedly authentic—no. 10 musically "too empty to pass for Haydn." No. 25 "in several stylistic traits . . . directly points to Dittersdorf." However, one can hardly claim this symphony to be by Dittersdorf. Krebs does not even cite it in his thematic catalog.

26. *Denkmäler der Tonkunst in Österreich* XIV, 2: xvff.

27. A few examples that also may serve as supplements are: Perger 39 (= Jos. Haydn III, 12) is not by Michael Haydn but by Vanhal. The theme can be found in the *Quartbuch* and in Breitkopf 1768; copies of this symphony in the Esterházy archive, and in the court library in Berlin. Perger 50 according to Breitkopf 1766 is by Wagenseil; one copy is in Göttweig, where the symphony is listed twice (1761 and 1765) in the catalog, each time under Wagenseil. The two divertimenti, Perger 113 and 114, are by Joseph, not Michael, Haydn.

28. The discussion between Sandberger and me, which followed this article, is found in *Acta musicologica* (1935–37). For a reexamination of *Das kleine Quartbuch* see my article, "Evidence or Guesswork, The *Quartbuch* Revisited," *Acta musicologica* (1977), 86ff.

17

The Haydn Tradition

Introduction

A basic condition for scholarly work of any kind is that it must be possible to make a clear distinction between the fixed knowledge from which it proceeds and the area of uncertainty that needs clarification. If it cannot advance from an established foundation of knowledge, then its first aim must be the creation of such a foundation.

In Haydn research, a foundation in the form of a list of works generally accepted as authentic does not exist. In spite of extensive and valuable preliminary work from different contributors, it has not been possible so far to achieve a critical thematic catalog of Haydn's works, and the complete edition that was initiated so late has until now covered only a very limited part of Haydn's production. Haydn research—which has not been carried on with any real consistency—has shed some light only on certain periods and areas. And the vagueness with respect to the clearing-up of problems within other areas of Haydn's output gave rise to a general uncertainty that has even increased considerably during recent years. A short historical retrospective is needed to make the present situation of Haydn research fully understandable.

The "complete" editions of the keyboard sonatas, keyboard trios, and *Lieder* (Breitkopf & Härtel), and of the quartets (Pleyel) that appeared about 1800, authorized by Haydn himself, established a long-lasting foundation for an investigation of these genres. An authorized survey of other groups of works existed in the form of the thematic catalog that was initiated by Haydn and compiled by his copyist Elssler in 1805. This *Haydn Verzeichnis* (hereafter referred to as *HV*) was never published, but its enumeration of works was already reported by Haydn's early biographers around 1810 and later was reprinted many times. Rather early, attention was called to the fact that the *HV* could not be regarded as a complete

This essay is drawn from *Die Haydn-Überlieferung* (Copenhagen, 1939) from which it has been excerpted and translated into English. Subsequent references to *Die Haydn-Überlieferung* are to the original edition.

catalog and that at several points more information was needed. However, a real investigation of this problem did not come about. Valuable material for an investigation of the problem was contributed by the catalogs of Gerber (compiled as early as about 1803, but published only in the second volume of his *Neues Lexikon*) and Fuchs (written around 1840–50), but both catalogs remained without much influence for a long time, the first one because it was not a thematic catalog, and the second one because it remained unpublished and practically unknown. Thus the "complete" editions and the *HV* formed the traditional basis for the discussion of Haydn's works until well into the second half of the nineteenth century.

A new basis for Haydn research was created only in 1867, when Carl Ferdinand Pohl, at the request of Jahn, undertook the writing of a rather extensive Haydn biography. The first volume appeared in 1875, the second in 1882, and the third and final volume was only completed in 1927 by H. Botstiber, who made use of the materials left behind by Pohl. Pohl did not go much beyond the traditional foundation, but part of his preliminary work was an extensive thematic catalog (more than one thousand manuscript leaves) that was meant to serve not only as a main source of the biography, but also as the basis of a printed thematic catalog that he never finished. In the manuscript catalog he entered not only the works contained in the authorized editions and in the *HV* but also some compositions confirmed as authentic in other ways, as well as a large number of compositions existing somewhere under Haydn's name, but lacking authentic corroboration.

This expansion of the mass of alleged or authentic Haydn works was bound to lead to an attempt at demarcation. Either the number of the works regarded as authentic had to be more or less enlarged, or it would have to be established or at least made plausible that many of the works attributed to Haydn were not to be regarded as authentic. Pohl himself did not undertake such a demarcation; probably because he planned to leave that to the projected catalog. In the biography he—quite legitimately—almost exclusively counted on the unquestionably authentic works, both in the text and in the thematic list of the works of the Esterházy years (1766–90) which supplements the second volume and which is often referred to for want of a larger thematic catalog. It appears from several comments in the manuscript catalog and in the book that Pohl rejected a larger number of the works lacking authentic corroboration. But beyond this we can tell little more about Pohl's opinion concerning this problem, probably because he had not really arrived at one.

Thus it was ultimately left to Mandyczewski to expose quite clearly the problem caused by the many spurious works, and to work out a classification. He did this in a catalog of the symphonies published in the first volume of the complete edition (1907). Primarily based on Pohl's materials, Mandyczewski lists 194 symphonies and overtures distributed among four categories: 1) symphonies by Joseph Haydn (104 nos.), 2) overtures by Joseph Haydn (16 nos.), 3) symphonies falsely ascribed to Joseph Haydn (38 nos.), and 4) symphonies of uncertain authorship (36 nos.).

There is only a small difference between the total numberings of Pohl and Mandyczewski, and they are in almost full agreement with regard to the sorting out of the authentic works for the purpose of the biography and the complete edition, respectively, because both of them are based on the *HV*. However, by entering the nonauthentic symphonies into the "official" list of the complete edition, and by his attempt at a division of these works into spurious and dubious ones, Mandyczewski, as opposed to Pohl, exposed the problems of the Haydn tradition quite openly and on a large scale.[1] Mandyczewski's separation of dubious and spurious symphonies is characterized here as an attempt—in contrast to his classification of the authentic symphonies, which rests on a solid basis—because only the works listed in Perger's catalog (*DTÖ* XIV, 2) as symphonies by Michael Haydn and the works advertised in the old Breitkopf catalogs as works by other composers have actually been attributed to these masters without further investigation. Neither an extensive gathering of the sources needed for an examination of this kind, nor a clarification of critical principles is to be found here.

In his three volumes of keyboard sonatas within the complete edition (1921–22), Päsler went even further than Mandyczewski. Beyond the traditional thirty-four keyboard sonatas and five sonatas for violin—contained in the *Oeuvres complettes*—he included thirteen (mostly early) sonatas in the edition itself, not only in the thematic index. Of these fifty-two sonatas, twenty-nine were not listed in the *HV,* whereas only one of the 104 symphonies of Mandyczewski's first category was absent from the *HV.* The authenticity of the sonatas not included in the *Oeuvres complettes,* however, could be proved, partly by means of authentic records from Haydn's late years and partly by means of supposedly authentic copies from the early years, which made the inclusion of all these works in the complete edition appear justified.

From this development the following situation resulted: to the works acknowledged by Haydn—through authorized editions and the *HV*—and those accepted as authentic by Pohl in his biography were added a great number of compositions handed down under Haydn's name. These included several demonstrably authentic ones, some others that were probably authentic and in any case were included in the complete edition (Päsler), and still others categorized as dubious or as frankly spurious (Mandyczewski). It cannot come as a surprise that this development led to general doubt about the entire Haydn tradition. The incompleteness of the *HV,* evident from the comparison of the piano sonatas listed here with those in Päsler's edition, seemed to suggest a general incompleteness of the *HV* due to its dependence on the weakened memory of the elderly Haydn. It could be agreed that it was possible to establish quite a large number of works as undoubtedly authentic with the help of this and some further sources; otherwise it would seem justified to attach little importance to a lack of authentic corroboration of alleged Haydn works due to the supposed general incompleteness of the *HV*. Thus the development increasingly led to a disintegration of the traditional foundations of Haydn research.

The questions concerning the Haydn tradition became particularly urgent in late 1932 when the senior master of Haydn research, Adolf Sandberger, made a sharp attack on Mandyczewski's symphony catalog, first in a Munich radio lecture, and repeated later in various places. The gist of Sandberger's statement can be found in a quotation from a report which in its main features corresponds with other press reports.[2]

> Sandberger has worked systematically since 1892, and he has arrived at the result that Mandyczewski does not know or acknowledge at least seventy-eight symphonies. A number of those regarded as dubious or spurious by him are incontestably and demonstrably authentic, and the authenticity can in part be evidenced by Haydn's own testimony. The list in the complete edition that has caused so much damage must, therefore, disappear, the sooner the better. In the series of the alleged first forty symphonies as they are presented in the first three volumes, dozens of works are missing, and must be inserted.

By virtue of Sandberger's established authority, this attack not only reduced the general confidence in Mandyczewski's list, but generally contributed essentially to the disintegration of the fixed foundations of Haydn research, although no proofs were presented concerning the alleged invalidity of Mandyczewski's list. As proof of the authenticity of his "newly discovered" symphonies, Sandberger—in the course of later polemics—once cited the use of a variation theme that—even if shaped differently—occurs in Haydn too, in addition to the "nature" [*Artung*], the "substance" [*substantiellen Gehalt*] of the works, and the success of "convincing performances for an international audience." Obviously he considers critical examination and intuitive understanding of the musical style as a satisfactory basis for decisions concerning questions of authenticity. Works whose authenticity is not verified by reliable external evidence but are merely supposed to be authentic because of their "nature" are given the same status as undoubtedly authentic compositions.

The ultimate consequence of this development was recognized by H. Gál, who in 1938 published a symphony that he had "rediscovered" a year earlier, based on an old print with Joseph Haydn's name, although the work—except for the finale which was borrowed from a symphony by Joseph Haydn—exists in Michael Haydn's original autograph. This could already have been derived from Perger's catalog (1907), and it had been pointed out by several Haydn specialists before the publication of the symphony. Gál, however, preferred to disregard the evidence of the authentic source and to stick to his assumption that the symphony was a work by Joseph Haydn—an assumption that actually would imply a forgery by Michael.[3] In order to prove his conception, Gál referred to a thematic parallel to a string quartet by Haydn and to different general stylistic features. Evidently he holds to the concept that the results of an examination of style must be placed not only next to, but even above the evidence of signed autographs.

The development described above, the forsaking of a foundation of research based on first-rate sources in order to acknowledge works whose claims to authenticity rest on some sort of stylistic investigation, necessarily raises two questions: 1) Does the stylistic test of authenticity actually offer so much certainty that its results must count as equal or even superior to the evidence of authentic sources? and 2) Should it not be possible—if we go beyond the *HV* and the late authorized editions, back to the early authentic sources (autographs, copies, prints, catalogs)—to find criteria for an evaluation of the questions of the Haydn tradition that may eliminate the present insecurity? For it should not be ignored that the uncertainty that has produced this trend did not arise because the problem proved insolvable, but simply because a solution was never attempted.

We shall comment briefly on the first of the two questions raised above. An extensive discussion of the problems of investigating authenticity would exceed the scope of these considerations. A few virtually self-evident general statements may suffice to characterize the relative significance of source criticism and style analysis in the process of testing authenticity.

1. Each examination of authenticity must proceed from a foundation of solid evidence. Style analysis alone can never give evidence for judging authenticity; this can be achieved only by style *comparison*. The comparison must be based on undoubtedly authentic material, and this can only be obtained from source evidence. Style comparison can consequently only be put to work when a relevant foundation has been established by means of source evidence. The larger the foundation, the more secure becomes the style comparison.

2. The source investigation proceeds from quite simple and clear criteria—confirmation by the author himself or by known, reliable persons; tracing back of a source to the more or less close surroundings of the composer—and it leads to a simple division of the works contained in the sources into the following categories: authentic works, works with a well-established tradition, dubious works, presumably spurious works, and provably spurious works. In the first and last categories we can count on full security, but in the second and fourth only on probability. A decision concerning the works of the third category—which, however, cannot be clearly set apart from the two neighboring categories—is not possible on the basis of the source tradition.

The style investigation, on the other hand, must start out with a more or less arbitrary choice of criteria that serve as the basis of the style analysis, and it has no fixed standard for evaluating the significance of the relevant stylistic features. A definite rejection will be possible quite often—as in the case of obvious anachronisms. But there are scarcely any decisive *positive* style criteria. Parallel thematic phrases may just as well represent the conscious or unconscious imitation of another composer's ideas as a repetition of a composer's own ideas. The identity of the composer will sooner be revealed by less characteristic and less prominent "idioms" of style that are not imitated easily. Even if a work seems closely related to undoubtedly authentic works, we can at most state—regardless of any subjective conviction—that the proposed composer in question may well be the author but not that the work *must* be by him.

3.   Determining the reliability of external sources is mostly entirely an objective act of observation, even though occasionally—for example, with the examination of handwriting—there may be room for subjective decisions. But it is hardly possible to imagine a style investigation of an entirely objective character, not only because, as pointed out above, there can be no objective standard for evaluating the different stylistic criteria, but also because it is very difficult to keep the examination based on scholarly knowledge absolutely free of subjective elements. Such elements, strengthened by the pleasure of discovering new artistic values, may lead to hasty and intuitive conclusions, which on principle obstruct the objectivity of a subsequent investigation of details. A determination of authenticity on stylistic evidence alone—when documentary evidence is lacking—therefore does not at all imply, as occasionally is maintained, that "the music itself decides." Between the music and the decision allegedly made by it comes a third element: the individuality of the observer. The result of the examination of the music will be determined by the subjective qualifications of the observer, by his critical abilities, and by his more or less thorough knowledge of the stylistic complexities in question.

Even if we may leave out existing, less successful results of stylistic authenticity investigations, expecting more convincing results in the future from a systematic development of stylistic examination, a simple, basic consideration points out the relativity of its results. *Only* source examination is able to establish an entirely reliable research foundation by sorting out the definitely authentic works. The works with a well-established—but not authentic—tradition will in many cases stand out as "probably authentic" by virtue of undoubted stylistic relations to authentic works. In other cases these will be rejected as stylistically doubtful. If the source examination does not offer any evidence for determining authenticity, the stylistic investigation may well allow a rough classification, such as a distinction of the compositions that must be rejected entirely, those that may perhaps come into question, and those that are clearly related to provably authentic works. Because of the general character of style investigation, however, the authenticity of the works confirmed only in this way cannot be regarded as established, or even as almost established. Above all, it must be stressed that their use as a basis for further determinations will add a fundamental uncertainty to the entire succeeding investigation.

We are left with only one possibility: to establish a solid basis for Haydn research by an extensive examination of the source tradition. The investigation must aim at the clearest possible delimitation of works with an authentic tradition, of works with a well-established tradition, and of works confirmed only by uncertain sources. Further we must take a stand with regard to the assumed general incompleteness of the *HV* by compiling a control list of early sources that may enable us to complement the information of this catalog. The authentic works and those with a well-established tradition of authenticity must be listed as completely as possible. In such areas of Haydn's oeuvre where complete or approximate certainty cannot be achieved, we must attempt to derive clues from the nature of a work's tradition in order to evaluate the problems of the work category in question.

The investigation of the Haydn tradition is the subject of this study. Not without serious hesitation did I venture to clarify these problems, which were, so to speak, pressed upon me against my will. In order to gain a broadened foundation for studies on Haydn's early symphonies—my (unpublished) master's thesis on this topic dated back to 1928—I had collected material for studying the works of his predecessors, as well as those early Haydn compositions that may have served as the "pioneering forms" of the symphonies. In the early 1930s, with this purpose in mind, I visited the three collections that are particularly valuable with regard to Haydn research: the Esterházy Archive in Budapest, the Gesellschaft der Musikfreunde in Vienna, and the Staatsbibliothek in Berlin, as well as some other, mainly German, collections. Even questions of the musical text and of the chronology of the symphonies had to be taken up more thoroughly. I deliberately left the problem of authenticity aside. Initially, I found Mandyczewski's list of authentic symphonies a thoroughly reliable basis for research, for it was needed to clarify the problems of the authentic symphonies before trying to include the dubious ones in the investigation. Also, I shrank from the very comprehensive task of an authenticity investigation which would require more time and expense than I could devote to it if my main project were not to recede into the background.

However, after the publication of Sandberger's attack on Mandyczewski's list of symphonies, I could no longer maintain this position. It now seemed indispensable to me to take a stand concerning the authenticity problem in the symphonies; and during a three-month study trip in the summer of 1934—devoted largely also to critical textual work—I added to my material concerning the symphony problems by checking the relevant holdings of some additional collections in Germany, Italy, Switzerland, France, and Belgium. After examining all the material of Haydn symphonies from some thirty collections, I had to state as a general result that though there are actually quite a number of symphonies allegedly by Haydn—even more than those listed by Mandyczewski—not a single symphony beyond those 104 listed as authentic by Mandyczewski has thus far been proven authentic. Moreover, the majority by far of the allegedly nonauthentic Haydn symphonies appear doubtful on stylistic grounds. This problem was also touched upon in the course of a polemic with Sandberger, which began with other

questions (in *Acta musicologica* and the *Zeitschrift für Musik,* 1935–37). However-
er, the few remarks that had to suffice on that occasion probably did not contribute
much to a clarification of this matter beyond the circle of Haydn specialists. Thus
gradually an urge arose to devote a more extensive investigation to the questions of
the Haydn tradition, to promote the reestablishment of a solid foundation for
Haydn research. For this purpose I had to supplement my material in various ways,
although from the beginning I planned to restrict my examination primarily to the
problems of the symphonies and other instrumental music, but to refrain from an
extensive investigation of the bulk of authentic and nonauthentic vocal compositions.

My examination of the *Entwurf-Katalog* and the Kees catalog, and of their
significance as sources of Elssler's catalog *(HV),* was mostly complete as early as
1934, and I had also done much work on the problems of the copies. During further
travels, 1935–37, I thoroughly studied the autographs in the three main collections
mentioned above. I also checked the entire Haydn holdings of the Esterházy
archive—mostly from the Haydn estate—and I made a comprehensive survey of
the many old copies of early, largely unpublished instrumental works from the two
extensive Haydn collections in Berlin and Vienna (Ges. d. Mfr.), as well as from
some smaller collections, especially from the Austrian monastic music archives
well known for their holdings of music sources. Special difficulties were related to
the problems of the countless prints; a close study of only the material of the
outstanding Hoboken Collection might take several years. I had to content myself
with an attempt at circumscribing the area of authentic prints as well as with some
statements concerning the chronology of the prints. Some printed sources—catalogs of libraries and antiquarians—were useful in this respect. It was a great help,
particularly with regard to work on the vocal compositions, which were covered
much less by my own material, that I could use the papers from the estates of Pohl
and Mandyczewski—especially Pohl's thematic catalog, which around that time
again turned up in the archive of the Gesellschaft der Musikfreunde. In that way
the incomplete bibliographic information in Pohl's biography could be complemented to a great extent.

Regardless of all my efforts, only an incomplete compilation of sources was
possible. However, various circumstances seem to confirm the supposition that
the sources introduced here enable an almost complete survey of works with an
authentic or well-established tradition. Nevertheless, it will undoubtedly be possible to add to these works, too, to some degree, and I shall appreciate any
information referring to this. I have tried to make up for the lack of completeness
of this study by attempting the utmost clarity in the classification of sources, and I
hope by this also to have paved the way for a future thematic catalog. I have
attempted to rectify the many incorrect statements that have come my way, not in
order to criticize my predecessors, but for the sake of clarity. Unfortunately, I
cannot believe that I myself have avoided introducing new sources of error. The

scattered materials mostly had to be inspected on the spot, which made the later rechecking of the collected notes very difficult, in spite of the kind support of helpful colleagues. . . .

The *Entwurf-Katalog*

For the establishment of the body of undoubtedly authentic works, a few work-lists made or checked by Haydn himself are of particular importance. Besides some smaller, nonthematic compilations, such as the diary notes about works composed in England,[4] we have to deal primarily with the so-called *Entwurf-Katalog (EK)*, now in the Staatsbibliothek Berlin (Mus. ms. 607), together with the *Katalog Kees* (Regensburg, Fürstliche Thurn und Taxisiche Bibliothek, *Joseph Haydn 85*), as well as the so-called *Haydn-Verzeichnis (HV)* written by Johann Elssler in 1805, the original manuscript of which can be found in the Esterházy Archive at Budapest. Different copies of this exist in Leipzig (Breitkopf & Härtel, also written by Elssler) and in Vienna (library of the Gesellschaft der Musikfreunde). The so-called *Quartbuch* also must be counted among the catalogs controlled by Haydn, even though it does not represent a specifically Haydn catalog.

Of the two main catalogs only the *HV* was taken duly into consideration from the beginning. The *EK*, on the other hand, was given remarkably little attention, although it is closely linked with the *HV* and, moreover, was for the most part written by Haydn himself.

The genesis and further particulars of this catalog are rather in the dark. Pohl refers to the catalog several times,[5] without ever entering into a description of it. Mandyczewski, strangely enough, does not cite it among his sources for the thematic list of the symphonies.[6] However, we find it cited in Päsler's preface to the complete edition of the keyboard sonatas.[7] Altmann, in his congress lecture, *"Über thematische Kataloge,"*[8] states that "the Preussische Staatsbibliothek keeps in the original the thematic catalog that Josef Haydn has set up. When he started it requires further investigation." Finally we find the catalog listed as no. 1 in Lachmann's catalog: *"Die Haydn-Autographen der Staatsbibliothek zu Berlin."*[9]

A description or examination of the catalog is given by none of these authors. Only Päsler discusses it as the *"Entwurf-Katalog* written by Haydn and Radnitzky,"[10] a statement that was shown above to be wrong. Pohl, in a manuscript survey of his sources, refers to it as "Dehn's catalog," and this is further corroborated by a remark in a symphony catalog compiled by F. Wüllner on the basis of Zulehner's list of Haydn's symphonies, which is also part of Pohl's materials. Wüllner designates the *HV* as catalog A, and "the original catalog that I compiled from the copy that Jahn had made in 1851 from an autograph in Dehn's possession," he calls catalog B. A close inspection of this catalog B proves it to be the *Entwurf-Katalog*. We can thus trace the catalog in Berlin back to Dehn, but it is open to question how it found its way into the world from Haydn, who still possessed it in 1805 when it served as a primary source of the *HV*; it is neither mentioned in the catalog of Haydn's library and music collection, written by Elssler (1807), nor in the list of Haydn's estate.[11] Of course it may be conjectured that Elssler, after having used it as a source for the *HV*, put it aside as used up and, so to speak, worthless material, and then forgot about it. Whatever happened, the question is of little importance to us here. Yet it is not only the fate of the manuscript in later years that is hidden from us. Tradition is also silent about its origin. Unlike the *HV*, the *EK* has no explanatory title. We are actually forced to derive everything from the manuscript itself. Fortunately, however, it is possible, after the first somewhat discouraging view of the disorder and diversity of the manuscript, to arrive at a distinction between the different layers and groups which allows us rather exactly to determine the development of the catalog in its principal features, as the following analysis will show.

The *Entwurf-Katalog* consists of seventeen leaves, the first two in oblong format, ca. 36 x 26 cm, trimmed a little, and the others in upright format, ca. 23 x 36.5 cm. The thick paper of the two oblong sheets contains a fragment of a watermark, the lower half of a garland (?) with the letters W O L F F G. The paper of the first twelve of the upright-folio sheets—which is a little thinner—alternately bears as watermarks the stags nos. 1 and 2,[12] and the letters J G S, whereas the much heavier paper of the last three sheets shows the stag watermark no. 12 and the letters J G W. Since the oblong sheets, as will be explained below, actually constitute the part of the catalog that originated last, we may designate the three different sections C, A, and B. A numbering can be found in A, with the page numbers 1, 3, 5, etc. on the front pages of its leaves. The second leaf of B bears the number 2; C, on the other hand, has no numbers at all. For practical reasons we shall number the pages in A, B, and C with the serial numbers 1–34.

The catalog was written by three (four?) different hands; in the manuscript they are distributed as follows. The first theme on page 1 is written by Elssler senior; everything else on this page and on page 2, by Haydn. Pages 3–4 include the first themes on page 5 and again are in Elssler's handwriting; the remainder of page 5 and pages 6–12 entirely stem from Haydn. On pages 13–14 follow again a series of themes entered by Elssler senior; on page 13 Haydn later added supplementary themes. Pages 15–24 have only entries by Haydn. On the first page of section B, page 25, and in four themes on page 26, a handwriting appears that presumably, but not necessarily, is again that of Elssler senior,[13] yet from a somewhat later time and written down a little sketchily. The remainder of page 26 and pages 27–30 are again wholly by Haydn. Section C presents on page 31 and in two themes on page 32 a new copyist, whom we shall designate as the Kees copyist for reasons to be explained later.[14] Haydn himself added tempo indications to his thematic entries. The remainder of C features a continuation and a supplement, all in Haydn's hand.

The appearance of the writing styles in the catalog is accordingly rather mixed. Yet even more diverse is the picture we gain from an examination of the contents of the *EK*, that is, from a compilation of the works listed by themes and by titles. We will start out with a brief, summarizing survey (table 2). With the distinction "right" or "left" we designate here the thematic entries that appear on the right on the original staves (often with an additional title also on the left), and the indications of works added later on newly inscribed staves on the left in part A of the catalog. The symphonies are quoted according to the complete edition (GA); the other works, according to the *HV* if not stated otherwise. A ÷ indicates that the work is cited without theme. The numbers printed in smaller type signify that the work was later crossed out.

The arrangement of works in the catalog shows an alternation of separate sections (pp. 1–2, symphonies; pp. 3–5, ensemble divertimenti [including quartets]; pp. 13–14, string trios; p. 19, concertos; pp. 20–23, keyboard compositions; pp. 25–28 and 31–34, symphonies), with a random mixing of themes (p. 2, symphonies; church music, quartets; p. 18, church music, operas, baryton pieces). Particular problems with this conception are the baryton compositions, especially the trios, which are found—according to the numbering that was, in the main, already entered into the *EK* and definitely established later in the *HV*—dispersed on the following pages: 7, 8, 15, 16, 11, 10, 16, 15, 16, 11, 12, 24, 8, 6, 9, 24, 12, 17, 7, 11, 17, 24, and 17.

There can be but *one* explanation for this strange grouping of the baryton trios: the great majority of these compositions did not yet exist at the time of the first version of the catalog. Such an increase of works of this type was not foreseen. Very soon space could only be found for the quickly multiplying favorite works of Prince Nikolaus, which were entered in every available spot: on empty staves on the right side as well as on supplementary staves left in the wide margin, and finally also replacing planned themes of vocal compositions (the titles of which remained beside them).[15] This statement immediately leads to the question of the genesis of the catalog. But before we take up this problem, we must try to find out whether the succession of leaves is the original one, or if the disorder may possibly be partly explained by a rearrangement of the sheets. That such a rearrangement *alone* cannot account for the confused order of the themes is already evident from the succession of the baryton trios noted above.

Let it first be established that the internal order of the three sections A, B, and C is entirely irrelevant to the understanding of the catalog; for these three parts clearly stand out from each other, and the disorder described above is only related to the main part. The leaves of this part, comprising pages 1–24, are connected with each other in that pages 1–2 belong with pages 23–24, 3–4 with 21–22, etc. A rearrangement of pages will consequently in each case not only affect two, but four pages. And since the pages 20–23 form a coherent succession, the order of the pages 1–6 and 19–24 is established beforehand. The middle section of this part does not present a similarly consistent succession of works in the current order of

Table 2. Arrangement of the *Entwurf-Katalog*

Page	Left	Right
1	Sff. GA 45, 46, 65, 48, 46, 47, 44, 52, 43, 42	Scherzando A (Pohl I, p.318 Nr. 6), Sff. GA 27, 29, 31, 28, 35, 59, 38, 49, 58
2	Sff. 39, 20, IV. 16, Cantilena pro adventu (A 2/4), Cant pro adv. a due (÷)—Qu.20,23,24	Sff. II. 10, (I.)26, 41, Mass 2, 3, Cant. pro adv. (D 6/8), Divert. a 5 (HV 5), Qu. 22, 19, 21
3		Divert. (mst.) 9, 17, 20, QU. 3, 4, 2, Div. 6, Qu. 9, 1, 10
4		Div. 11, 2, Qu. 11, Div. 10, 16, 12, Qu. 12, Div. 13, 3, 14
5	Qu. 35, 36, 32, 33, 34, 31	Div. 15, Qu. 7, 9, Div. 1, 8, Div. 7, 4 Bar. 62, 63
6	Qu. 26, 25, 28, 30, 27, 29	Bar. 64–72, Conc. p.2 Bar.
7	[Solo p. il Bar. =] Son. p. il Bar. c. Vc. 7–8; Bar. 110, 111, 108, 107, 105, 106, 109, 112	Bar. 1–10
8		Bar. 11–12, 12 Bar. Cass. Stück [only 1 Thema]. Div. p. il Bar. Solo (Duette) 1–4, 4 Responsoria de Venerabili (only) 1 Thema), Bar. 62, 63
9	Bar. 91, 90, 88, 92, 82, 83, 84, 85, 86, 87, 93	Bar. 73–81, 89, 94
10		[Duetto 1–5 =] Mehrst. Bar. Cass. 17, Duetto 4, 1, 5, 6; Mehrst. Bar. Cass. 15, Bar. 26, V. Conc. 3, Bar. Conc. 2, 1
11	Bar. 114 [= Mehrst. Bar. Cass. 6], Mehrst. Bar. Cass. 8, 12, 7, 10 9, 11	Bar. 25, 37–45
12	Son. p. il Bar. c. Vc. 1–5	Bar. 97, 46, 47, Vc. Conc. 3, Bar. 48, 49–53
13	Str. Tr. 21—V. Solo with acc. of a and Va. 1–6	Str. Tr. 1–10, 11
14		Str. Tr. 12–20, Trio p. il Corno (÷)

17 Bar. 121, 120, 119, 118, 117, 116, 115, 125, 111

Opera, *Acide, La Marchesta Nap., La Vedova, Il dottore, Il Scanarello* Coro 1mo—quinto [NB! Only the theme from *Acide* was entered; it was later replaced by the theme from the following works]: Bar. 98, 99, 82, II, Bar. 100–104

18 Salve Reg. (E)—Salve Reg. (g) Many opera titles without themes

Mass 1, Stabat Mater, "La canterina," "Applauso," "Lo speziale," "Le pescatrici," Bar. 29, Bar. Son. 12, Bar. 19 Off. "Non nobis"

19 Vc. Conc. 3

V. conc. 1, 2, Cb. Conc. Horn Conc. Vc. Conc. 1, Fl. Conc., Org. (Cemb.) Conc., Cemb. Conc. 1

20 Cemb. Conc. 3; 6 Keyb. Son. 774 (÷), 6 Keyb. Son. 776 (÷)

Cemb. Div. [with and without Acc.]1, Cemb. Conc. 2, Cemb. Div. 2–4

21 Cemb. Div. 8

Hymn *de venerabili* 1–4, Te Deum [÷, substituted by]: Cemb. Div. (Son.) 25, 5–7, 23

22 Cemb. Conc. 3

Cemb. Div. (Son.) 24, 9–12

23 Cemb. Div. 14

Cemb. Div. 13, 15–18

24 Bar. 124, "126," 96, 94, 95, 123

Bar. 54, Mehrst. Bar. Div. 13, 16, Bar. 55–61

25 Sff. GA 64, 42, 51, 55, 43, 54, 56, 57, 68, 9

26 Sff. GA 61, 66, 39, 69, 67, 71, 63, 75, 53

27 "These following are missing": Sff. GA 27, 12, 72, 34(II), 60, II.1, 70, 62, 74

28 Sff. GA 73, II.13, 78, 77, 76, 81

29 Trio (Son. p. il Cemb. e V. e Vc.) Nr. 9 [according to numbering given on p. 306 of *Die Haydn Überlieferung*]

30 Deutsche Lieder at Artaria's / 2 parts for each of 6 songs (÷), 12 English . . . in England/ translated into German (÷), 2 duets with keyboard only by the poet Badini from England/ Sacred Lied with keyboard only/ *Dir nahe ich mich,* funeral Lied/ *Hier sein Grab,* English Song/ *She never told her love* (÷), Spirit Song, *Hark! what I tell to thee* (÷)

31 Sff. GA 83, 87, *Die 7 Worte* (÷). Sf 4, 37, 58, II.4, 89, 88, 91

32 Sff. 90, 92/99, 101, 97, 94, 95, 96, 100 /[right]: II.3

33 Sff. 102, 103, Sf. conc. B ("op. 84"), 104, 94, 93, Bar. 64, Sf. 18 (And.), 2, 17; [right]: 34 (All.), 73

34 Sff. 19, 15, 32, 3, II.5, 36, 59, 54 (All.), 33, 27

pages. A view on the baryton trios, however, reveals that by interchanging pages 9–10 with pages 15–16—that is, by turning around this sheet—we will achieve a much clearer order of succession for the beginning of this list. The immediate succession of page 16 and page 11 is especially obvious! In this way we achieve, on pages 7–8, 15–16, and 11–12, an almost unbroken series of the first fifty-three baryton trios—only no. 26 is lacking. Since pages 9–10 fit between 14 and 17 quite as well—or quite as badly—as between 8 and 11, there can be no objection to this exchange. This single change, however, decides the order of leaves in this part of the catalog, and in the following we will proceed from the resulting order of pages: 1–8, 15–16, 11–14, 9–10, 17–24. As mentioned before, similar problems do not arise with respect to sections B and C, since their contents are clear and coherent.

The significance of the baryton trios for determining the time of origin of the catalog can now be stated more precisely. After the entering of the first fifty-three trios, the first six successive pages 7–8, 15–16, 11–12 were filled up (except for a few empty spaces). It was not possible to continue on the next page because that was occupied already by the string trios. And so we find the following trios, 54–61, only on the last—until then blank—page of the original catalog, page 24. However, the trios entered on pages 11–12 already exceeded the space originally provided for these works, for under the title of the first trio at the top of page 11 we find an older entry: "*Menuetti*—(?)" with three (two?) "*item*s" following at the next three staves. From this we gain a valuable basis for the establishment of the chronology. For the last of these works, trio 53, was already composed in 1767 according to the still extant autograph (Esterházy Archive, Mus. Ms. I, 48). And if the trios composed up to 1767 already exceeded the limits of the catalog, then it must have been compiled in 1767 at the least, but probably a little earlier. There is even reason to assume that only the first twelve trios belonged to the original disposition, for they are immediately followed (p. 8) by some baryton pieces of a different kind and by a vocal composition, and only on the next page (15) do we find the continuation, trios 13–22. This may well point to the years 1765–66: in 1765 Prince Nikolaus complained of having seen "as yet very few" baryton pieces,[16] but in 1766 no. 24 already existed.[17]

However, the baryton trios are not the only works that may contribute to the dating of the catalog. It is revealing to look at the very first group in the catalog, the symphonies. The themes noted on the original staves on the right on pages 1–2 specify the following symphonies: GA 27, 29, 31, 28, 35, 59, 38, 49, 58, 26, and 41. Of these the nos. 29, 31, and 28 date back to 1765, 35 to 1767, and 49 to 1768, as we know from dated autographs. Nos. 27 and 38 are quoted in the Breitkopf catalog of 1769, no. 59 is registered in Göttweig and Kremsmünster 1769, no. 41 in Göttweig 1771, and quoted in Breitkopf 1772, no. 26 is found in Göttweig 1772, and in Breitkopf 1775, and no. 58 in Göttweig 1775. Since for stylistic reasons the two last-mentioned symphonies must necessarily be dated before

1770—the direct adaptation of the minuet from baryton trio 52 (1767) may point to 1767–68 with regard to GA 58—all these works, maybe except for GA 41 composed around 1770—must date from the 1760s. Already GA 42 from 1771 and the symphonies of 1772 (45–47) were placed to the left as supplements. As in the case of the baryton trios, we are apparently facing different stages in the entering of the symphonies, too. Based on the writing style, one might tend to conjecture an incision between 31 and 28, 38 and 49, and maybe also between 26 and 41. This would lead to an assumption of 1765, 1767–68, and 1768–70 as chronological stations in this list, an assumption that may be supported by a comparison of the handwriting with autographs of some of the works in question.

A third major group may also be questioned in this connection—the keyboard sonatas or, as they are still called throughout in the *EK*, the *Divertimenti per il Cembalo*. Of the divertimenti entered on pages 20–23—one for four hands, three with other instruments, fourteen *per il Cembalo Solo*—eight are known only from this source.[18] The sonata GA 3, the beginning of which coincides with that of the baryton trio 37,[19] composed in 1766–67, is otherwise devoid of any external chronological specifications, and so is GA 4;[20] GA 6 is advertised in Breitkopf 1766; of the three larger sonatas GA 19, 45, and 46, that are included into the *Oeuvres complettes* like the sonata mentioned last, the first two were composed in 1767 and 1766, respectively, as shown by their autographs; although no. 46 was published together with 45 as late as ca. 1789, it belongs stylistically with the two others, and should not be dated later than around 1770. Besides these, the A-major variations appear as the last theme of this series, announced in 1771 in Breitkopf's catalog, and as an insertion on page 21 on the left GA 14, advertised in 1767. This again leads us to the time about 1770, or perhaps still around 1767. Here, however, it must be stated in accordance with our observations concerning the baryton trios that the entry of the D-major sonata, GA 19, composed as early as in 1767 (p. 21 above), only became possible by the abandonment of the original plan. For page 21 had from the beginning been reserved by Haydn himself for the *"Hymnus de venerabili"* 1–4 and for the early *"Te Deum laudamus,"* as noted next to the upper five staves. For this part of the catalog, too, we accordingly arrive at a time of origin a little *before* 1767, or, more broadly, *around* 1767.

These datings of the earliest entries, based on available dates of some of the works in question, are very well in accordance with the evidence of the watermarks. In part A the two stags 1 and 2 are found together with the letters I G S, that is, the earliest watermarks of the Esterházy papers known to us, that we find in dated autographs from the time 1762–68.

We have established the *period of the first version of the catalog* as *ca. 1765,* and we shall attempt to outline the main features of its development. Our first question must concern the original version of the catalog. Obviously the following sections were planned: 1) symphonies (pp. 1ff.), 2) divertimenti for several instruments (four or more—pp. 3ff.), 3) baryton compositions (pp. 7ff.), 4) minuets (pp. 11ff.), 5) string trios (pp. 13ff.), 6) operas and secular choruses (cantatas—pp. 17ff.), 7) concertos for different instruments (pp. 19ff.), and 8) hymns, Te Deum (pp. 21ff.). In the making of this original version Elssler senior assisted in entering, besides the first symphony theme, the bulk of the divertimenti for several instruments and of the string trios. His activities are, however, limited to this; after ca. 1765 there are no traces of his handwriting in the catalog. The later development is determined by the expansion and revision of the catalog that took place around 1767–68. As already stated, this revision involved minuets that disappeared in favor of the great number of baryton trios, and the hymns had to give way to the keyboard compositions that obviously were not planned for in the first disposition. But at that point there was already too little space for the baryton trios. The new trios first filled up some empty pages intended for other works; however, as early as around 1770, it became necessary to look in the wide margin on the left for free space, not only for further trios, but also for symphonies, quartets, masses, and other works. For the symphonies this space did not suffice, and some further leaves, section B, were added in the mid-1770s in order to record a number of new symphonies. Section C, on the other hand, must not be regarded simply as an extension of the original catalog, but as an independent catalog fragment, as shall be pointed out below. We shall consequently disregard this section for now and restrict ourselves to sections A and B of the catalog as we proceed to a closer examination of the individual genres.

Symphonies

As already stated, the symphonies listed on the right on pages 1 and 2 are from the years 1765–70. Strangely enough, there is not a single symphony in this list provably composed before 1765, although we know of quite a number of early symphonies that can be attributed to the years before 1765 either by the autograph—for example four symphonies of 1764 (GA 21–24)—or by a dated copy—like four symphonies dated 1762 according to the Göttweig catalog. That might lead to the assumption that the catalog was only intended for works composed after 1765, perhaps supplementing an older catalog. But this assumption is refuted by the presence of earlier works of other genres in the catalog. It must certainly be assumed that a great number of the divertimenti for several instruments and of the string trios date back to the 1750s and early 1760s. Breitkopf announced eight divertimenti and six string trios as early as 1763. The date of origin of the opera *Acide* and of the four Italian comedies (*EK*, p. 17) certainly is 1762, and that of the organ concerto in C major (*EK*, p. 19 *"Per il clavicembalo"*) is 1756. Since it is hard to believe that the symphonies were registered differently, it seems reasonable to suppose that the list of symphonies is incomplete, and that a section containing the earlier symphonies may be lost. This assumption is supported by further observations. As the first theme on page 1 we find—before GA 27—the A-major scherzando with the note *"Synfonia Ex A"* in Elssler's handwriting. Yet everything else in this section is written by Haydn himself. A comparison with the other entries by Elssler, the ensemble divertimenti and the string trios, suggests that the lonely theme at the top of page 1—moreover the only one of six related scherzandi—and similar to the theme on page 5 is not to be seen as a beginning but rather as a continuation. And still one more point: all symphony themes recorded on the right of pages 1–2 and the three on the left of page 2 were numbered by Haydn himself; and this numbering does not start out with no. 1, but proceeds in the following manner: no. 20 [*Scherz.* A], no. 12 [symphony GA 27], no. 40 [GA 29], no. 41 [GA 31], 45–56 [GA 28, 35, 59, 38, 49, 58, II. 10, (I.) 26, 41, 39, 20, and IV. 16].[21]

It is not possible to say when this presumed beginning written by Elssler may have disappeared. Probably it was still in existence when the cited completions on page 27 were inserted—apparently already in the 1770s—for it does not make sense to regard these few works as supplements of the still-extant part of the list. If the beginning of the catalog—one or perhaps even two leaves—had disappeared, then it must be concluded that the end of the catalog has been reduced correspondingly, but we have no knowledge of its possible contents. Whatever the facts of the case may be, pages 1 and 24 bear distinct marks of having served as covers for a long time.

A continuation of the symphonies on the left of page 2 can be found on the left margin of page 1. This continuation contains the symphonies GA 42–48, 52, and 65. Of these, 42 was composed in 1771, 45–47 in 1772; 43–44 can be found in Breitkopf 1772, and 48 [Mandyczewski: 1772] was performed in 1773 on occasion of the visit of the Empress Maria Theresia in Eisenstadt. Number 52 was announced in Breitkopf 1774, and 65 in 1778. For these two symphonies the quotation here is important evidence that they, together with the other symphonies listed on the left side, originated around 1772. The symphony GA 50 (1773) is not found in the *EK;* all the symphonies that provably were composed in 1774 appear only in the following continuation.

This continuation starts on page 25, on the first page of the added section B, the watermark of which—stag 12—indicates a year of origin around 1775. The themes on pages 25–26 (entered by Elssler [?]) denote the symphonies GA 64, 42, 51, 43, 55, 54, 56, 57, 68, 9, 61, 66, 39, and 33. Numbers 42, 43, and 39 repeat earlier quotations; 9 and 33 stem from the early years (both listed in Breitkopf 1767; 9 according to A. Fuchs documented for 1762 by an autograph); 54–57 were composed in 1774, and 61 in 1776; 51 was announced in Breitkopf 1774, 64 in 1778, and 66 and 68 in 1780. To this series probably also belong the first two of the subsequent themes written by Haydn: GA 69 and 67. The last of these two symphonies, together with GA 68 and 66 (entered already by Elssler), constitute Hummel's opus 15, published (according to Gerber) in 1779, whereas the first one was registered in the same year at Göttweig. These themes may well have been noted down around 1777–79. The themes subsequently entered by Haydn obviously represent at least two (or three) later layers. The six themes on pages 26 and 28 (GA 71, 63, 75, 53, 73, and II.13), as well as the three at the bottom of page 27 (GA 70, 62, and 74), probably belong to the early 1780s; the remaining themes on page 27—"these following are missing"—perhaps still belong to the 1770s; and the last four themes on page 28 (GA 78, 77, 76, and 81) probably can be dated to 1784. The first movement of 63, in any case, already existed in 1777, but it may well be that the completion of this symphony took place later. According to Gerber it was published in 1779–80 as Le Duc's opp. 29–30, together with 71 and 75, with which it is also associated here, as well as with nos. 70, 62, and 74 (page 27). It was also published as Hummel's op. XVIII (*libro* 1–3, 1781–82). Number 53 is dated 1774 in the GA, based on a rather vague account of a London performance; in any case, it was advertised in 1780 by Breitkopf. Number 73 and II.13 date back to 1781 (?) and 1779, as mentioned before.[22] For GA 76–78 based on Torricella's print, we have established the date of ca. 1783, whereas 81 presumably originated as late as in 1784. Since only this symphony, and not the two symphonies GA 79 and 80 sent to Forster along with it the same year, is listed in the *EK*, it seems reasonable to assume that only this one was finished, and that consequently the entry occurred exactly in 1784. Of the supplementary themes on page 27 we have already discussed GA 27, 12, and 34. These are followed by GA 72, 60, and II.1. Number 72 undoubtedly belongs to the 1760s; 60 originated in 1775. Number II.1 is one of the "*6 Sinfonie*" (overtures) published by Artaria in 1782, but nevertheless almost certainly dates back—like the other works from this series—to an earlier time. The slow movement exists in autograph; it is written on Esterházy paper, its watermark (stag 8 and I G W) indicating the period of 1769–73, a time corresponding very well to the musical character of the movement.

In summarizing we can state that the list of symphonies in the *Entwurf-Katalog* was presumably made in the years 1765–84. During this time Haydn added to the catalog at certain intervals. Judging by content and writing style we may assume the following approximate dates for his entries: 1765, 1767–68, 1768–70, 1772–74, 1777–79, 1781–82, and 1784. Besides a small number of earlier works, his list of symphonies contains all of the symphonies registered by Mandyczewski under the numbers 26–78 and 81, with the exception of 30, 32, 36, 37, 40, and 50. Of the latter, only no. 50 undoubtedly originated after 1765 (autograph 1773), whereas 40 and 30 were composed in 1763 and 1765, respectively, 32 and 37 probably before, and 36 around 1765.

Divertimenti

The divertimenti listed on pages 3–5 comprise a selection of works for different ensembles. The scoring is specified by Elssler only with some of the quartets.

However, his indications were largely supplemented by Haydn's adding of the number of parts. To the first three divertimenti on page 3 (*HV* 9, 17, and 20) is added the postscript *"a nove ("9ve,")Stromenti"*; the designation of the quartets (3, 4, 2, "0," 9, and 1) was corrected from *"Cassatio"* to *"Divertimento"*; and the last two (which had not been specified by Elssler as *"a 4tro,"* as had the other four and the subsequent one [quartet no. 10]) were characterized as *"a Sei Stromenti"*—in accordance with the edition of de la Chevardière ("Op. 3")—and as *"a quatro."* Furthermore, on page 4 the following additions by Haydn are found: (div. 11): *"a Sei,"* (div. 2): *"a cinque,"* (qu. 11): *"a Sei"*—as in the case of quartet 9 in accordance with the early Paris print—(div. 10): *"a Sei,"* (qu. 12): *"a quatro."* The remaining works on the page in question were not considered by Haydn on this occasion; but Elssler gives some clues concerning the instrumentation, noting *"Feld-Part"* next to the theme of div. 16; *"Feld-Parthie"* and *"Corno Inglese"* next to the theme of div. 12; and *"clarinetto"* next to the theme of div. 14. On page 5 Haydn designates the quartets 7 and 8 entered by himself as *"Divertimento a quatro,"* the div. *HV* 1 as *"Divertimento a cinque,"* and div. 8 as *"Divertimento a Sei con 2 flauti."* They are followed by two *"Feld Parthie,"* the first one *"Ex A"* not being cited thematically; the second one is div. 7. The last work of this group follows, div. 4, designated as *"Divertimento a cinque cioe 2 clarinetti 1 fagotto e 2 Corni."* Of the later pencil notes only the first at the top of page 3 (div. 9)—*"gehen die Hörn ab"* [?] ("the horns are missing")—seems to stem from Haydn, whereas the addition (qu. "0"): *"ein nicht gestochenes quart."* ("an unprinted quartet"), cited by Pohl[23] and M. Scott[24] and the remark *"als quartett"* ("as quartet") next to quartet 9 and 11 (see above), which seems to refer to the compilation of the *HV*, may have been written later by Elssler junior.

The divertimenti listed here—we shall discuss the quartets separately below—are probably only partly still extant. Nos. 3, 4, 10, and 12–14 have not turned up as yet. Dates can be established in the following cases: div. 9, Gw. 1764; div. 20; Gw 1763; div. 11, Br. 1767; div. 2; Br. 1765; div. 16; Aut. 1760; div. 15; Melk 1765; div. 1; Br. 1768; div. 8; Aut. 1767; div. 7; Melk 1765.

Probably all of these works existed as early as 1765 and were entered around this time. The two works indicated by the last theme written by Elssler (div. 15) and the next to the last written by Haydn (div. 7), were known in 1765; and Haydn's handwriting almost certainly points to ca. 1765 as the date of the entering of the intermediary themes. The very last theme of this series, div. 4, may possibly have been inserted a little later, but certainly still in the 1760s, before the two baryton themes at the bottom. There is no further continuation of this section. The six eight-part divertimenti published in 1781 as op. XXXI, of which at least nos. 2–6 were originally baryton pieces, are only indirectly represented by a reference to the original version on top of page 10: *"6 Divertimenti a 8 Stromenti per il Bariton."*

Quartets

It is very characteristic of the period of the first version of the catalog that the string trios received their own heading, but the quartets did not. We find the two first series interspersed with the divertimenti. The only one missing is no. 6, and instead of the later no. 5 (B-flat major) we find the one in E-flat major that originally belonged to the set,[25] and that we will call number "0" for our purposes here. Nos. 7 and 8 were added by Haydn not much later, probably still in 1765; the other themes are in Elssler's hand. The third series (nos. 13–18), however, is missing completely in the *Entwurf-Katalog*, as well as in the Breitkopf catalogs, in the *Quartbuch*, and in Göttweig.

Quartet no. 43, which Pohl (following Sauzay) counts among the early quartets (II, 44)—Schnerich (p. 183) mentions 1760 as the year of composition without identifying his source—was composed as late as 1785 according to the autograph in Berlin, and consequently it is not cited here. Quartets nos. 19–24 (op. 9) may well have been entered at the bottom of page 2 about the same time as the symphonies in the upper right, that is, towards the end of the 1760s. The entire page makes a rather uniform impression; the writing style still indicates the 1760s. There is no exact dating of these quartets. In any case, they were known in 1769 (Breitkopf catalog). Since only three staves were left unused, three quartets had to be entered in the left margin. However, the entire set was registered at the same time.

This entry marks the quartet as an independent genre, separate from the divertimento genre. However, there was no more space for a new genre; the two following sets, op. 17 (comp. 1771) and op. 20 (comp. 1772), that is *HV* 25–30 and 31–36, had to be entered into the left margin on pages 5 and 6. The entries probably occurred—within a short period—in the early 1770s. They end the series of quartets. Those composed after the ten-year interval are not to be found in the catalog.

String Trios

The string trios listed on pages 13–14 form a particularly uniform group. Except for the two themes inserted by Haydn at the left top and at the right bottom of page 13, everything was written by Elssler. The last six themes are numbered 14–19, not including Haydn's supplementary themes on page 13. These six themes refer to the trios cited in Breitkopf 1766 and may well be identical with the ones announced already in 1763 without themes, whereas nos. 1–4, 8, 10, and 12 appear in Breitkopf 1767; 15 was listed in Göttweig as early as 1762. That all of these are early works is also evidenced by stylistic considerations, as stressed already by Gerber, who introduced his section D, *"Trios für Bogen und Blasinstrumente,"* with the following words: "What we have of his work in this genre seems mostly to belong to the decade of 1760. Thus what was published after 1775 appears to belong entirely to the arrangements *[arrangirtes Wesen].*[26] The early closing of this list also becomes evident from Haydn's immediately following entry: *"Trio per il corno di caccia"* (citation of clef and meter, but no theme), certainly dating from the 1760s. This trio—apparently the only one of its kind—was composed in 1767, according to Pohl.[27] A continuation of this group is nonexistent except for the two supplementary themes already mentioned, which were entered presumably about 1770 at the latest. Already in the 1760s this genre was dying out, even though the Breitkopf catalogs of the 1770s still continually advertise written and published trios of various authors.

String Duos

On the left of page 13, next to the string trios, we find six duos for violin and viola added later and originally designated as *"Solo per il Violino"* only, but later supplied with the new heading: *"6 Violin Solo mit Begleitung einer Viola."* Haydn's handwriting indicates the (mid?) 1770s as time of inscription, which is in accordance with Pohl's information:[28] 1776 "appeared as [manuscript] copy." Breitkopf's catalog of the year 1776–77, probably the source of Pohl's information, lists only the first and the last pieces, in F and C. It may well also be that Gerber's remark[29] ("No. 1 in F and No. 2 in C I have already known since 1769 as original solos") refers to these two pieces, even though they are cited by him as violin duos. An old copy in the library of the Gesellschaft der Musikfreunde (IX, 32003) has all six duos in this version. I do not know the source of Gerber's dating. In a printed edition these six pieces were published by Artaria as op. 77 in late 1800 or early 1801, and three of them, furthermore, by André as op. 93 in 1800, according to Gerber.[30] There are no further string duos in the *Entwurf-Katalog*—except for the baryton compositions.

Baryton Trios

The chronological problem of these works is much less complicated than it is in any other larger group of works. The baryton trios were composed within a rather short time span in a rather great quantity. They followed each other so closely that it was possible to retain an approximately consistent numbering, at least until no. 94, as we can see from the extant autographs, which besides the—sometimes missing—year of composition bear the number of the respective piece. In addition, all of them were intended for princely use and, according to a princely rebuke of 1765,[31] were to be sent to Prince Nikolaus "cleanly and purely copied," a fact that must have had some significance with regard to the retention of the order. The number of the baryton trios preserved in autograph is relatively small but sufficient, in view of the given numerical order, to generally establish the chronological arrangement.[32] The following autographs are dated: 24 (1766), 42 (1767), 53 (1767), 79 (1769), and 105 (1772). An indirect dating of Trio 109 can be derived from the watermark—stag 9 and I G W—indicating the years 1769–73. In addition, the conclusion of the fourth set of 24 Trios, nos. 73–96, can be determined by a small receipt, reading as follows:[33]

> Specification / what I spent for His Highness for four books of Italian music paper in order to write the last 24 trios. Each book costs 21 Xr [Kreutzer], amounting to / 1 fl. [Gulden] 24 Xr / These 1 f. 24 Xr. were correctly paid to me by the Rentambt / on the 22 Xbr. [December] 1771 / Josephus Haydn mprio.

Thus the completion of this set, judged by Pohl as "approximately towards the end of 1770," probably did not occur until 1771. The number of baryton trios was indicated as "still very few" in 1765; but in the following years it grew as follows: 1766—24; 1767—53; 1769—79; 1771—96; 1772—105, reaching 109 by 1773. Of the other trios, numbered HV 110–25, some appear also to have originated ca. 1771–73, as we shall see, and the remaining ones, as Pohl assumes, by ca. 1775. The last dated baryton (ensemble) pieces are from this year, and around the same time the two baryton virtuosos, Lidl and Franz, were dismissed from the princely service.[34]

As mentioned above the distribution of the baryton trios in the catalog became very irregular due to the great increase of the number of these works. The first fifty-three could still be entered in an almost regular succession—even though at the expense of a planned series of minuets. With no. 54, however, the problem of lack of space became rather burdensome. The series continues with nos. 54–61 on page 24, and nos. 62–63 at the bottom of page 8. Here obviously a short break occurred, for in continuing Haydn overlooked the two last works and started over again with no. 62. Nos. 62–72 are found in immediate succession on pages 5–6. When he realized the double entries, he crossed out again the last-entered nos. 62–63. The next continuation on page 9 includes nos. 73–94, that is, all the trios from the above-mentioned fourth book still extant, except for the last two (nos. 95 and 96). The twenty-two themes of these trios fill in the entire page. The two missing themes follow on the left of page 24, together with other supplementary themes. However, before we enter into a discussion of the following themes we must briefly describe the different numberings of the baryton trios within the catalog.

The trios discussed until now mostly show triple numbering throughout: 1) to the left of the theme, a continuous series of numbers; 2) below the theme, a series corresponding to the previous one with a # before each number; and 3) above the theme a number and a volume number (for example "No. 1 in the 2nd book"), counting from nos. 1 to 24 in each volume, with a + preceding each number. These numberings give the list of trios a more uniform appearance and makes its piecemeal origins less visible. The order of the numberings can be derived from their outer appearance.

The primary series is the one beside the themes. Like those, it did not originate all at once, but in different stages. It seems justified to imagine a division like this: 1–9, 10–12, 13–20, 21–31, 32–63 (p. 8), 62 (p. 5)–72, 73–92 (?). The connection between the entries of the themes and the numberings offers certain problems, for the series of numbers did not arbitrarily result from the entering of the themes into the catalog, but—judging by the extant autographs and authentic copies—was fixed in advance and determined from the actual chronological sequence. We can infer from the beginning of our list (p. 7) that the numbering on the left obviously served to establish a survey of the works that was to be completed with themes—exactly as we may observe with regard to other groups in the catalog. Possibly the themes were entered a little later. The next entries (10–12 and 13–20) show a closer connection between theme and number. The entering of two themes (18–19) into one line did not cause any confusion, but was taken into consideration by the sequence of numbers. In the following, however, there is a certain divergence between the succession of themes and of numbers. A consistent sequence of numbers was disarranged in that first the trios 34–36 were entered instead of nos. 23–25; 23 came instead of 26; 24 was added on the left between 36 and 23 and in addition was inserted together with 25 in the now-free space of 34 and 35, but again crossed out later; the omitted no. 29 was entered next to 30 on one staff, but also a second time together with 19 on page 18 and again crossed out; the missing no. 26 was finally inserted on page 10. By these interchanges and inaccuracies the themes on page 11 were displaced, and all the numbers on the page subsequently had to be corrected. The last number, 43, was written twice, and the numbering on page 12—taking no notice of that—continued from 44 to 53, whereas on page 11 the theme of the forty-fifth trio already appeared. Thus two spaces were left open on page 12 in order to reconcile the sequence of numbers and themes again. Into these empty spaces were inserted the later trio 97—without any number—and a cello concerto in C major, and the numbering was crossed out and changed accordingly. The following series of themes, 54–63 and 62–72, are free from errors except for the mentioned double entry of 62 and 63 that has caused no confusion. Page 9 proceeds from no. 73 to 87 undisturbed; but the following numbers, 88–93, were replaced by a new numbering, covering also the formerly unnumbered 94 and nos. 95 and 96 on page 24 that originally were furnished with different numbers.

This numbering, proceeding from no. 1 to no. 96, is the aforementioned one written below the themes with a # before each number. In contrast to the first numbering, this one clearly was entered in a single stretch with its termination at no. 96, pointing towards the time around 1771 when the fourth set of twenty-four trios was finished. In connection with the new numbering, all themes without a tempo indication were furnished with one.

It is clear that the third numbering, indicating series numbers, was written in one stretch up to no. 63 (p. 8—"N. 15 in the 3rd"), and the numbers 64–72 ("N. 16 in the 3rd" up to "24 in the 3rd") apparently shortly after, probably still about 1768–69. However, corresponding numbering of the last twenty-four trios discussed here, 73–96 ("the 1st in the 4th" to the "24th in the 4th"), is quite different, though in itself written all at once and—as especially revealed by numbers 88–96—evidently at the same time as the second numbering (that is, presumably 1771).

Due to this numbering the sequence of the first ninety-six trios must apparently be regarded as definitely fixed. It is found, too, in the *HV,* and its validity is generally confirmed by the extant numbered autographs,[35] the fourth volume with the nos. 73–96 (Esterházy Archive), the approximately contemporaneous copy of the third volume with the nos. 49–72 (Library of Congress, Strunk Ms. A, p. 247), and by the somewhat later copies of the trios 25–96 in the Artaria collection (Berlin Mus. ms. 10037).

The end of this series shows a divergence of the primary entry from the final version. With regard to nos. 88–91 and 92–93 it was limited to a simple rearrangement, whereas 95 was displaced entirely and 96 was even omitted. Of a series of six themes, originally numbered 95–100—on the left of page 24—these two were the first and the second. Instead of nos. 95–100, these six trios in the final version received the following numbers: 95, *HV* 124; 96, not in the *HV,* henceforth referred to as "126"; 97, *HV* 96; 98, *HV* 94 (already listed on page 9, therefore crossed out here); 99, *HV* 95; 100, *HV* 123. As a continuation follow the themes on the right of page 17, referred to by the nos. 101–8, which are *HV* 98, 99, 82 (second movement!), and 100–104; then nos. 109–14 on the left of page 7, which are *HV* 110, 111, 108, 107, 105, and 106. At the bottom of page 7 follow two themes without numbers, which are *HV* 109 and 112, and finally, as the last entry of this kind on the left of page 17, also without numbers, *HV* 121–15 (that is, in reverse order), 125, and 111. Thus together with the isolated themes of trios 97, at the top of page 12, and 114, on the left of page 11, all 125 baryton trios are listed, except for 113 and 122, which are not found in the *EK.*

The themes discussed here were entered on several occasions, obviously corresponding to their time of composition. Therefore it seems reasonable to assume that trios 123 and 124 originated contemporaneously with 94–96, that is, in 1771 at the latest. Trio "126," not entered into the *HV,* is found together with a number of baryton trios, arranged as string trios, in Kremsmünster (H120, 13), formerly in the possession of a Ph. Razesberger, and for this reason may well be considered a true baryton trio in addition to the 125 from the *HV.* That the trios counted as 95–100 on page 24—the aforementioned "126," *HV* 94–96 and

123–124—belong together, is further stressed by the themes indicating baryton trios in the *Quartbuch,* citing besides some earlier works[36] the two sets 83–87 and the aforementioned *EK* "95–100," as well as by the mentioned string trios in Razesberger's possession in Kremsmünster, which only comprise the mentioned two sets except for *HV* 96.

For the later trios the actual difference between primary and final numbering is not essential. The themes on the right of page 17, *EK* 101–2 and 104–8, are in accordance with the sequence in the *HV* of 98–104, only displaced a little because the themes *EK* 95, 96, 100, and 103 are skipped in the *HV*. *EK* 109–14, page 7 on the left, list the trios *HV* 105–11 (109 is skipped), yet in a rather different order; the unnumbered series, *HV* 121–15 on p. 17, simply reverses the order of the themes. The listing and numbering of the themes *EK* 109–14 correspond to *HV* 105–8 and 110–11, suggesting that all these trios came into existence approximately at the same time as the dated *HV* 105, that is, ca. 1772. All the themes clearly show Haydn's handwriting from the 1770s. That Haydn himself—and not Elssler junior who wrote the list in the *HV*—supplied the final numbering of the late baryton trios becomes evident from the earlier mentioned copies of the trios 73, 97, 101, 106, 107, 111, 113, 114, 117, and 120,[37] for which Haydn from early on had used the numbers known from the *HV*, only exchanging 97 and 117. Apparently, a fifth book of trios never came about, even though a sufficient number of works was available. Certainly, there would have been a reference to such a book.

Other Baryton Compositions

It is not possible to check these compositions, the greater part of which presumably is lost. We mainly depend on the *Entwurf-Katalog* and the *Haydn-Verzeichnis* as the only evidence of the existence of such works. As already mentioned, the series of baryton trios in the *EK* was interrupted after no. 12 (p. 8) by other baryton compositions. At the first of these themes we read: "*12 Cassatiostücke von dem Pariton*" (?); these one-movement bagatelles[38] are still preserved in the Esterházy Archive.[39] They are followed in the *EK* by "*Divertimento 1mo Per il Pariton Solo,*" "*2do,*" "*3zo,*" "*Sol(o),*" "*4to,*" later given the numbers 8–11 and called "duets for the baryton" (in the handwriting of Haydn's old age!). However, they were not listed in the *HV* as duos but as *Cassationsstücke* nos. 2–5. Judging by their location in the catalog—between the twelfth and thirteenth trios—they must be counted among the earliest compositions for baryton, which is corroborated by the sometimes markedly Baroque themes.

A new series of baryton compositions is found on page 10, consisting of five duos, one divertimento for two barytons and two horns, and two baryton concertos, followed by a concerto for two barytons on page 6. Judging by the handwriting these themes were also entered in the late 1760s, approximately at the same time as trios 64–72 (the two concertos on page 10 a little later?). These themes, too, in part bear distinctly Baroque features. Only the piece in G major, designated as *"Duetto 2do" (HV* duet 4) is still preserved in the Esterházy Archive (XI, 47). There it is in a copy by Elssler senior, as are the twelve short trios.

An isolated theme for a baryton solo piece is found on page 18. The *"Divertimento per il Pariton Solo"* was entered between the supplementary—later cancelled—trio themes 29 and 19, and like these it was certainly entered before 1770. In the *HV* it is listed under the *"Sonaten per il Pariton col Violoncello"* and so are the two *"Solo p. il Bariton"* (p. 7) and the five *"Sonata per il Bariton col Violoncello"* (p. 12) that were apparently entered in the *EK* as late as in the mid-1770s on the left side as supplements. Haydn himself apparently intended to unite the baryton solos or duos (Bar. and Vc) listed in the *HV* under three headings—*Duetten, Sonaten, Cassationstücke*—as becomes evident from a later continuous numbering in the *EK* (marked with a * in order to facilitate the orientation). He counts the duos on page 10 as 1–5, the two solos on page 7 as 6–7, the duos on page 8 as 8–11, and the sonatas on page 12 as 12–16.

A last group of baryton compositions is the ensemble divertimenti or cassations. The divertimento for two barytons and two horns has already been mentioned. Two other works of the same kind are listed on the main staves on the right of page 24: the two *"Divertimenti"*—later changed into *"Quintetto 1mo, 2do,—per il Pariton con due corni, Viola e Basso."* They interrupt the list of the trios between nos. 54 and 56 and obviously were entered at about the same time as these works, that is, about 1767–68. The last entry of baryton compositions in the *EK* is the six *"Div. a 8te Stromenti"* (p. 11). They cannot have been added before 1775, since two of them can be assigned to this year by their autographs. They are also referred to by the note at the top of page 10: *"NB 6 Divertimenti a 8 Stromenti per il Bariton."*

Concertos for Different Instruments

The original layout on page 19 comprises the following: violin concertos *HV* 1 and 2, double bass concerto, horn concerto, cello concerto 1, flute concerto, organ concerto—listed as *"Per il clavicembalo"*—and cembalo concerto no. 1. All these supposedly date back to before or around 1765. The organ concerto was composed in 1756, the horn concerto in 1762. The two violin concertos are found in the Breitkopf catalogs of 1769 and 1770, respectively, the cembalo concerto in the catalog of 1767. The cello and the flute concerto were not advertised until 1780 by Breitkopf, and the double bass concerto not at all; yet as with the other themes, these, too, clearly suggest early works of a Baroque character. Some further themes of keyboard works, entered a little later, comprise, besides four accompanied keyboard divertimenti, the concerto no. 2, cited by Breitkopf in 1771. The G-major concerto *HV* 3 is found as a supplement on the left of page 20 (crossed out again) and on page 22, probably entered before or around 1770. Finally, also apparently before or around 1770, the violin concerto *HV* 3 was inserted immediately before the two baryton concertos on page 10, and the cello concerto *HV* 3 (Br. 1780) on an empty staff on page 12, as well as a second time next to the first cello concerto on page 19. Further, at the top of page 20, we find the following indication: *"Concerto p Violino e Cembalo. In F. e ancora altri Due Concerti p l'organo in C."* The first of these pieces is identical with the F-major concerto that Breitkopf had announced in 1766, and that was published a short time ago.[40] One of the two mentioned organ concertos in C may well be the C-major concerto also announced in the Breitkopf catalog of 1766, which stylistically is very close to the organ (cembalo) concerto existing in autograph (1756).

Keyboard Works

The series of divertimenti on pages 20–23 has already been discussed above;[41] to this nothing needs to be added here since the list of the keyboard sonatas, as opposed to the other main groups, was not expanded any further except for the general references to the two collections of the 1770s: *"6 gedruckte Sonaten v. 1774"* and *"6 Sonaten von Anno 1776"* (p. 20). The late addition *"Hartl im 1ten Cahier"* to the sonatas GA 45 (p. 21) and 46 (p. 22), referring to the first volume of the *"Oeuvres complettes"* (1800), will be discussed below. Only one piano trio, the one composed in 1785 in A, no. 9, slipped into the catalog, in part B (p. 29). Judging by the handwriting this is a later entry (about 1800), as is the list of songs on the following page. The source was probably the autograph that was part of Haydn's collection.

Sacred Vocal Works

The original layout left only a little space for works of this kind. Only four hymns *de venerabili* and one *Te Deum* were to be listed on page 21. When they were supplanted by the keyboard works, they received only a note on page 8: *"Quatuor responsoria de Venerabili."* Above this is entered *"Missa"* and next to it *"Lauda Syon"* (together with a theme). Apparently Haydn later became a little uncertain as to the numbering of these works. The *"Missa"* he gave the number 2, the *"Lauda Syon"* a 1, the responses a 2, later 3, until he crossed out all these numbers, again entering *"4 Responsoria de Venerabili"* (late handwriting).

Masses were not scheduled at all in the original plan. The very early F-major mass—the rediscovery of which in late years gave joy to Haydn—had presumably slipped his mind around that time, and if not, he would scarcely have attached any importance to its inclusion. The first masses in the catalog are found on page 2 following the symphonies entered around 1768–70. The first one is an unknown D-minor mass *"Missa sunt bona mixta malis"* on a traditional, imitative vocal theme; the words *"Kyrie eleison"* were added later. The second one is the "Great Organ Mass" in E-flat, composed in 1766 (?) and here designated as *"Missa in Emol in honor B.V.M"* These two masses are followed by a *"Cantilena pro adventu"* that was supplemented by two similar works on the left.

A second small group of themes of vocal church music is found at the top of page 18, otherwise mainly reserved for operas. On the right there are the themes of a C-major mass designated as *"Missa Cellensis"* and of the famous *Stabat Mater*. Actually, however—Carl Brand kindly called my attention to this—we are not facing the *"Mariazeller Messe" (Missa Cellensis)* but the *"Cäcilienmesse."* It was dated 1781 by Pohl because of the time of publication of the printed parts. Yet there is some reason to assume that this mass existed by 1773 at the latest. The *Stabat Mater* was registered at Göttweig in November 1773. Thus the year 1773 might serve as a *terminus ante quem* for both works. The first of the two neighboring Salve Reginas in E was composed in 1756, the second in G minor in 1771. At the very bottom an *"Offertorio im Stile a Capella"*: *"Non nobis Domine"* is inserted. According to Pohl-Botstiber[42] this piece is to be dated as late as 1799. The writing style of the entry in the *EK*, however, points towards a substantially earlier time, probably as early as the 1770s.

The main list of masses in the *EK* is found on page 15, as an addition next to the baryton trios 13–22. Apparently the three themes of the "Great Organ Mass," the "Nicolai Mass," and the "Little Organ Mass" *(Missa brevis)* originate in the 1770s. The "Great Organ Mass" was mistakenly quoted a second time here and was consequently crossed out again. It was first named *"Missa St. Nicolai"* and then corrected to *"Missa St. Josephi."* Of the three masses, the "Great Organ Mass" dates from 1766 (?) and the "Nicolai Mass" from 1772. The "Little Organ Mass" was extant in 1778 in Göttweig; the watermark of its undated autograph is also found in a manuscript of the year 1777. The fact that for the theme not the bass part of the first measure, but of the third measure is cited, gave rise to a double entry in the *HV*.

As a continuation of this group of themes a small list of masses without themes is found further down on the same page. First there is the early *"Missa brevis in F a due Soprani,"* followed by the *"Missa in tempore belli"* (*"Paukenmesse"*), the *"Missa Sti Of(f)idi"* (*"Heiligmesse"*) (both of 1796), the *"Missa in Angustiis"* (*"Nelsonmesse"*) (1798), and finally an obviously early mass *"Missa Rorate coeli desuper in G"* (with theme, *HV* 5). The *"Theresienmesse"* (1799) and the two last masses, on the other hand, are missing. Thus we may regard 1798–99 as date of these last entries.

Operas and Secular Choruses

The entire page 17 was planned for works of this kind from the beginning. On the left we find the title indications: *"Opera Acide," "Comedia la Marchesa Nespola," "la Vedova," "Il dottore," "Il Scanarello," "Core Primo," "2do," "3zo," "4to," "quinto,"* and in addition at the top of page 18: *"Coro 6to."* At a later time, probably along with the filling out of the empty staves with baryton trios themes,[43] the three unspecified titles of comedies were supplied with the epithet *"Comedia"* and the first three choruses with the text incipits *"Vivan gl'illustri sposi et," "Al tuo arrivo felice,"* and *"Dei clementi."* Still later the following explanations were added: 1) *"als sich der Fürst Anton vermählte,"* 2) *"bey (?) Zurückkunft des Fürst Nicolaus von Paris,"* and 3) *"bey wider genesung des Frürst Nico. Estr."* With regard to the first two of these three choruses, this addition fixes the time of origin. The wedding of Prince Anton took place in 1762, and the return of Prince Nikolaus in 1764. Also the pastoral *"Acide"* and the comedies fall into the year 1762.

Of the vocal compositions listed here, only the first one, *"Acide,"* was fixed thematically (beginning of the symphony), whereas the staves next to the other works—cited by title or text incipit—temporarily remained empty. When the baryton trios exceeded their boundaries more and more, this page, too, had to be turned to for space. First, themes of the baryton trios were entered into the empty staves on the right, later into supplementary staves on the left between the titles and text references as well. This arrangement induced Pohl—following Elssler!—to consider the respective, long since forgotten choruses as compositions based on the listed baryton pieces, alleged favorite compositions of the Prince.[44] Being forced to date them later than the latter, he relates the first chorus to Prince Anton's *second* marriage (1785) and the second to the return of Prince Nikolaus from a later trip (1781). The entire layout of the catalog and the writing style of this page (17) clearly reveal that the choruses were entered *before* the baryton trios, even though the text incipits may have been inserted at the same time as the trios and the explanations still later. To postdate these choruses to the 1780s is for this reason, out of the question, and the supposed relation between them and the baryton trios appears to consist only in their inscription on the same page of the *Entwurf-Katalog.* Elssler's *Haydn-Verzeichnis* repeats the two trio themes—*HV* 116 and 115—as choruses (nos. 1 and 2) without text references. But Elssler certainly had no other source for them other than the *EK.*

Page 18 offers perhaps the most disorderly picture in the entire catalog. The first entries on this page must have been the citation of *"Acide"*—which had already been cited on page 17 and was therefore crossed out again—and the registration of the three major works, *"Opera la Canterina"* (1766), *"Applauso,"*[45] and *"Opera lo Speziale"* (both 1768), followed by *"Opera le pescatrici"* (1770) probably shortly after. All four of these works are accompanied by themes on the right side on the ordinary staves. The following staves, however, were filled with complementary baryton themes. Before the first expansion of the catalog followed seemingly the aforementioned church compositions *"Missa Cellensis"* (*"Cäcilienmesse"*) and *Stabat Mater*, filling in the two empty staves before the four mentioned works. All later entries of operas are without themes. Here, three expansions can be distinguished. The first, probably carried out in the late 1770s (about 1777?), comprises the following works: *"Opera l'incontro improviso"* (1775), *"Oratorio il Ritorno di Tobia"* (1774–75), *"Opera l'infedeltà delusa"* (1773), *"Opera il mondo della luna"* (1777), and at the top right the three puppet operas *"Opera comique Philemon und Baucis"* (1773), *"Opera comique Didone abbandonata"* (1777), and *"Opera comique Vom abgebrannten Haus (?)."* In the 1780s a continuation occurred with *"la fedeltà premiata"* (1780), *"Armida"* (1783), and *"Orlando Palatino"* (1782). Finally, in the 1790s, the neatly written titles at the bottom were added: *"Opera Seria. Acide und Galathea a 4tro Voci. Poesia v,"* *"l'isola disabitata"* (1779) *"Opera la Vera Costanza"* (1777), *"l'infedeltà fedele"* (probably a lapse resulting from the two titles *"l'infedeltà delusa"* and *"la fedeltà premiata"*), and *"Orfeo in England cp. Act, Badini"* (1791).

Lieder

The last group of works are some of Haydn's lieder on page 30, the last of the three sheets added about 1775, in the uniform handwriting of his old age. The first citation, *"Deutsche Lieder bey Artaria 2 Heft jedes zu 6 Lieder,"* is not quite correct, for the first two lied collections (1781, 1784) comprise twelve lieder each. We shall return to Haydn's numbering of the lieder below.[46] The second citation, *"12 englische—in England / ins deutsche übersetzt,"* gives us a *terminus post quem* of the entry, since the German editions of these lieder were published by Artaria in 1794 and 1798. Still one more title indication follows without a theme: *"2 Duetten bloss mit Klavier v. Poet Badini aus England."* Whether these duets on texts of the author of Haydn's opera *"Orfeo,"* composed in London, must be looked for among the nonspecified vocal compositions—"different songs," "2 Songs," *"Maccone* [?—Gries: *"Gesänge"*] for Gallini"—in the catalog of the works that originated in London;[47] or whether they are identical with the two duets discussed above,[48] may be open to question. They are succeeded by two German lieder, GA 17 and 24, both with themes, and by two English ones, GA 34 and 38, both without themes. Three of these four lieder were already contained in the printed editions mentioned above. They were, nevertheless, listed separately here, apparently because some copies of them were at that time part of Haydn's collection, but are now lost.[49] Only the last of these four lieder, "Spirit Song / Hark! what I tell to thee" (GA 38), was still unpublished at the time of its entry into the *Entwurf-Katalog* (published in 1804).

We have come to an end with our analysis of the two parts A and B of the *Entwurf-Katalog*. Only the four sheets of C, characterized above as an independent fragment of a catalog, remain. Unlike A and B, this section comprises exclusively symphonies, twelve of them in the handwriting of the "Kees copyist," all the others by Haydn himself. The themes written by the former at the same time include two of the Paris symphonies, GA 83 and 87 (both 1785), the *"7 Worte Christi"* (1785), three early works, GA 4, 37, and 58, the overture II, 4 (published around 1786),[50] and the symphonies GA 88–92 (ca. 1787–89). The continuation of this list, which cannot have been written before 1789, occurred only after the travels to London, maybe at the same time as the masses and lieder around 1799, as the handwriting might suggest. Except for the overture II.3 (inserted later), all themes were apparently written by Haydn at about the same time. The contents of his additions consist of the London symphonies—he forgot GA 98, but listed 94 twice and also the *Sinfonia concertante* B-flat major (1792)—and of quite a number of earlier symphonies. Next to GA 18 (with citation of the slow movement that originally was the first movement), 2, and 17 he expressly states: *"von drey alt Sinfonien."*

It might seem obvious to regard this series of symphonies as a direct continuation and completion of the earlier lists of symphonies within the catalog. But this assumption cannot be maintained. The themes written by the Kees copyist lead to a different conclusion, with numbers that run from 81 to 92 and that have no connection either with the numbered themes of pages 1–2 or with the unnumbered ones on pages 25–28. Rather, these must refer to a missing beginning which is made up of eighty symphonies. Moreover, Haydn's supplements cite a number of themes already contained in the earlier fragments (GA 34, 73, [II, 5], 59, 54, 33, 27) obviously serving as supplements in connection with a different source. We shall pursue this question immediately.

Continuing the series of numbers that stopped at 92, Haydn gave his themes the numbers 93–121. This numbering was, however, corrected and changed a couple of times. The supplementary themes received the numbers 93–107, and the London symphonies (including the *Sinfonia concertante* B-flat and the overture II, 3 [1794]) were given the numbers 108–21. The last change of numbers occurred when the theme II, 3 was entered—*"NB zu einer englischen Opera 1994 [sic]"*—certainly only around 1805. The final summation is the statement *"Hier sind in allem 121 Sinfonien."*

The significance of the *Entwurf-Katalog* can now be determined more precisely on the basis of the preceding investigations. *The Entwurf-Katalog was established by Haydn with some help from Elssler senior around 1765 as a running catalog of his own compositions, and was continued until around 1777 with shorter or longer intervals; after this period it was supplemented only occasionally—in the early 1780s and late 1790s—and only at certain points.* The works composed before 1765—string trios, divertimenti, concertos, symphonies, keyboard works, vocal church compositions—are listed in the catalog rather incompletely, as may be established without much doubt. Nevertheless, the authentic corroboration of the works presented here must be seen as an invaluable contribution to the examination of authenticity, owing to the almost entire lack of authentic manuscripts and prints from this early period. In the years after 1765 two major groups of works in particular—the symphonies and the compositions for baryton—were registered rather frequently and apparently very completely. The symphonies were registered until ca. 1784, and the baryton compositions into the 1770s. The quartets that were first scattered among the divertimenti were supplemented by separate entries of the two collections of 1771 and 1772. However, the keyboard sonatas not entered before ca. 1767 were expanded only by a short reference to the two sets of six sonatas of the years 1774 (1773) and 1776. The vocal church and chamber music was—after the first entries about 1765—added about the same time in 1768–70, about 1777, and 1798–99, the masses, etc. were added around 1773, and the operas in the mid-1780s. The lieder were taken into consideration only at a late entry (after 1798).

In comparing the individual groups it becomes evident that larger expansions of the catalog, which was set up ca. 1765 and partly rearranged in 1767, seem to have been carried out around 1768–70 and ca. 1777. And, in this respect, it is natural to remember that Haydn's house was burned in 1768 and 1776. That may reasonably have given rise to a new inspection and to an appropriate completion of the catalog for the purpose of recording the partly lost compositions, which—if needed—were to be procured again from other collections. Whatever may be the case, *the Entwurf-Katalog must be considered the major source for the examination of authenticity for the time from ca. 1765 to ca. 1777.* As far as can be established it lists the works of these years—first of all symphonies, quartets, baryton compositions, operas, and church music—almost completely. The approximately fifty symphonies, eighteen quartets, fourteen keyboard sonatas, about 160 baryton compositions, a round dozen of operas, etc., and a similar number of masses and other music for the church found in the *EK* stand as opposed to only a very few works in the cited categories—such as the symphony GA 50 and the keyboard sonata GA 20—that were undoubtedly composed in these years but not entered into the catalog. These may not be the only works from the period in question forgotten in the catalog; nevertheless, it seems justified to regard the listing of the works from these years as very satisfactory.

During Haydn's later years the *Entwurf-Katalog* was continued only very sparingly; probably this had much to do with the emergence of the authentic prints. We have already established that the works being published from ca. 1780 on—especially the instrumental music—were largely published in authentic prints. The importance of the catalog was correspondingly reduced; apart from the entries of three operas and some symphonies in the first half of the 1780s, no further additions were made from the late 1770s to the late 1790s. The last partial additions to the catalog may well have been caused by Breitkopf's invitation to Haydn to participate in the edition of the *"Oeuvres complettes,"*[51] and thus may have taken place in the summer of 1799. These later, more retrospective additions are of little importance compared to the significance of the entries of the earlier years. They only update the lists of the symphonies, operas, and masses, and attempt a rough summary of the solo lieder. Very extensive groups of works, on the other hand, and not least the printed chamber music, are disregarded. This final expansion of the catalog may help contribute to the solution of different special problems; however, it cannot be taken for even an approximately complete survey of Haydn's compositions from the 1780s and 1790s. For this period the *Entwurf-Katalog* is clearly a less important source than the authentic manuscripts and prints.

Conclusion

As evidenced by our examination, the *Haydn-Verzeichnis* of 1805 can be regarded as the primary source of the Haydn tradition only to a very limited extent. However, it deserves special credit for having established, even if in too limited a way, a compilation of authentic works that helped to prevent Haydn research from losing its way in a chaos of authentic and nonauthentic copies and prints. That Haydn could not have compiled the catalog himself must become evident from a glance at his mental constitution in those years. Härtel's statement that the inventory could be traced back mainly to some Breitkopf catalogs supervised by Haydn a few years before must also be rejected. However, a large number of earlier sources—primarily the *Entwurf-Katalog,* authentic prints of Breitkopf, Pleyel, Artaria, and others, as well as autographs and authentic copies in Haydn's possession—can be shown to have served as models for the different groups of the *HV.* In many cases that enables an authentic corroboration of the respective works, dating back to their time of origin, and, furthermore, a better understanding of the rather inconsistent composition of the *HV.* Through the use of some further authentic and "good" sources it became possible with a certain approximation to establish the degree of completeness of the more important categories of the *HV.*

Among those works fully accounted for—according to the available sources—must be counted certain groups of vocal compositions: masses, oratorios, operas, and three- and four-part songs. Of course, no investigation, however extensive and thorough, can make certain that no authentic work from these genres beyond the fourteen masses, three (four) oratorios, thirteen operas, and thirteen three- and four-part songs will ever be found. The completeness of the listing of these works is further supported by the fact that—except for the last group, the contents of which can be stated exactly from the autograph, authentic print, and Griesinger's correspondence with Härtel—we are dealing with works for performance in a grand style with many performers. Such works do not risk being forgotten very soon. Also the actual tradition confirms the assumption that these groups are not to be complemented. Of the rather few operas and oratorios and of the greater number of masses that appear under Haydn's name without being included in the *HV*, until now not a single one can be proven as authentic or even as probably authentic. Finally, it should not be ignored that the lists of masses and operas in the *EK*—which served as a source for the *HV*—were added to several times during the 1770s and 1790s, the last time as late as ca. 1799.

Among the fairly complete lists of works must be counted those of the symphonies, compositions for baryton (trios and other works), string quartets, and canons. Even if a few provably authentic works have been forgotten in these categories, it would be quite wrong to let some small, obvious gaps induce the assumption of a general incompleteness of these respective lists. Contrary to certain groups that will be mentioned (and which must be considered incomplete because the works in certain categories—especially the early composi- tions—were given slight if any consideration as sources for the *HV*), these groups were compiled with special care. Those gaps already mentioned within the enumeration must therefore be regarded not as examples of "systematic" basic defects in the sources, but simply as evidence of human imperfection in the creators of these sources and, consequently, as general, "accidental," inaccura- cies. The reliability of the inventory of the symphonies can be proven by a great number of authentic and "good" sources from all of the approximately thirty years during which Haydn's symphonies were composed. This is not the retro- spection of the old man of seventy-three years of age, but the generally excellent- ly assembled listings of the thirty- to fifty-year-old Haydn, of the musicians in monasteries avid for symphonies, and of the Haydn specialist von Kees. Further- more, the symphonies still available in authentic manuscripts and prints lead to a confirmation—or perhaps almost to a proof—of the approximate completeness of this survey. The baryton compositions were probably all composed in the time ca. 1765–75 and their listing in the *EK* is therefore especially complete. The complete collection of the canons could be registered in the *HV* according to the manuscripts from Haydn's possession.

Only with regard to the string quartets must a certain reservation be stated, since the list of these works—compiled by Pleyel and approved by Haydn—may have taken into consideration only the quartets in print and not the unpublished ones. Here is actually a systematic limitation to the listing, though probably not an important one, because only very few (authentic) Haydn quartets seem to have remained unpublished. The compilation of the available alleged Haydn quartets not in this list resulted only in a very small number of quartets that may be regarded as well documented; also the order of the *EK*—which lists the quartets (all of them also cited by Pleyel) together with the divertimenti, but lists the string trios separately—seems to indicate that still quartets were not numerous around 1765. After that time, however, certainly no new Haydn quartets remained unpublished. Thus the list of quartets in the *HV*—and those listed by Pleyel—may also, regardless of the evident limitation, be considered approximately complete or, concerning the later works (after ca. 1765), quite complete.

A different situation is encountered as far as the ensemble divertimenti, string trios, keyboard concertos, and keyboard divertimenti (with or without accompaniment) are concerned. None of these groups can be considered adequately registered through the compilation of the respective work lists in the *HV*. With regard to the keyboard works, the insufficiency of the list in the *HV* is partly caused by the fact that the last three volumes of the *"Oeuvres complettes"* had not been considered; but even in disregarding this easily filled gap, we must certainly still regard the inventory of keyboard works as far from complete. Only the group of the late piano trios (15d) as well as the group of sonatas for piano and violin (15b, comprising only one number) may thus be regarded as complete. Of the keyboard sonatas and the accompanied divertimenti, on the other hand, many authentic or well-documented works are absent, almost all of which date back to the time before the *EK* or even before Haydn's appointment in Eisenstadt. Also the lists of keyboard concertos and of string trios, and—to a lesser degree—of ensemble divertimenti certainly need extensive completions. The incompleteness of these listings is again almost exclusively the result of the fact that they mainly deal with early works that had been given away and forgotten by Haydn a long time before the *EK,* almost the only source of the *HV* for such compositions, was initiated.

Some further lists of works, like the concertos, the smaller church compositions, choruses, and cantatas, the "operettas" (puppet operas, etc.), as well as the arrangements of Scottish folk songs, may likewise hardly be regarded as complete; however, for practical reasons we did not attempt to check or complete these groups. In this connection the solo cantatas and arias must be mentioned, too; they are represented in the *HV* only by *Arianna,* which was included in the *"Oeuvres complettes,"* and hence also found among the lieder in the *HV.* Also to be added is quite a number of inserted arias, etc., preserved in autographs. The lieder themselves are listed in the *HV* almost in full, as far as they exist in printed editions. The existence of unpublished lieder, however, occasioned more or less by chance, must be regarded as an ever-present possibility. The volume of lieder in the complete edition did not give the final answer to this problem, even though it contains the entire stock of the lieder published by Haydn himself, and thus undoubtedly the bulk of Haydn's lieder.

Regarding the just-mentioned groups, the incompleteness of the listing in the *HV* depends only to a certain degree on the neglect of early works. The special character of these listings has to do with the fact that they consist of many works that must be characterized as occasional compositions (religious and secular choral works, arias, and lieder), since they were not intended for regular princely musical performances or for the publishers but instead owe their origin to changing occasions and stimuli. It is obvious that works of this kind can easily fall into oblivion—especially if we are talking of smaller, less important works—if they are not registered rather quickly by the steady continuation of a catalog. That Haydn did not want to have larger works of this kind composed for a single client (only to be buried and forgotten) but wished to utilize such occasional works for further purposes can be seen in the case of the Wallerstein symphonies.

The rather haphazard registration of smaller works of this kind appears in a few other listings of the *HV* that can hardly be called work groups, since each actually lists only a few related works or just one series of works. To these belongs the evidently incomplete list of marches, containing only two works—probably composed in England—as well as those of the flute trios and of the duos for violin and viola, both of which can be regarded as typical representatives of compositional genres that Haydn probably tried out only occasionally, following some outside impetus.[52]

Finally three groups must be mentioned that have been neglected entirely: the rather substantial series of dances, the pieces for a musical clock, and the lira concertos and *notturni*. The first two groups were perhaps excluded on purpose as "occasional music" in the truest sense of the word. But it is surprising that the lira compositions were not cited, even though they were intended for a group of instruments beyond the usual musical practice. For Haydn later arranged several of these pieces for a "normal" chamber ensemble, and some of these arrangements were in part present in his own collection. Nevertheless, these occasional compositions outside the normal groups remained unrecorded.

We have collected and analyzed a great number of sources, serving either directly as sources for the *HV,* or as material for an examination and completion of its lists of works. Based on our investigations, we may confidently state that the idea of general uncertainty of the Haydn tradition is wrong. Of course a definitive, unambiguous list of works is just as unattainable in the case of Haydn as it is in the case of Bach or Mozart. There will always remain the possibility of discovering hitherto unknown works, or of eventually receiving a confirmation of the authenticity of some dubious work. However, even if we keep this possibility open, we may consider quite a number of the work groups described above as registered with full or approximate certainty. The actual elements that have caused the assumption of a general uncertainty can be traced back to two main categories: the early works (until ca. 1765) and the occasional compositions. The most complete survey possible of the last-named works is to be expected from the coming Haydn catalog. The determination, publication, and examination of the early compositions belongs among the most urgent tasks of Haydn research. As for the central groups of works from Haydn's middle and later years, however, a solid research foundation exists, even if scholarly investigations and publications are still in an early stage. The source foundation of these works has been decisively changed through our examinations. Instead of depending on the memory of the aged Haydn, we may trace them to early authentic sources or sources from Haydn's immediate surroundings. Thus we gain primarily an important, direct confirmation of a great number of single works; at the same time we obtained an indirect one with regard to the validity of the work groups, since the theory of the general unreliability of the *HV*, owing to Haydn's age, could be rejected.

Haydn research must proceed, not from the chaos of alleged Haydn works of unknown provenance but from this firm tradition, based on an established source foundation.

Notes

1. In his thematic catalog of Haydn's symphonies in the second volume of the Brussels Conservatory Library (1902), Wotquenne included a small group of *"Oeuvres douteuses"* (15 entries) that were also considered by Mandyczewski. Wotquenne's classification, however, is void of any major significance because his main list contains an even larger number of dubious or provably spurious works.

2. Willy Krienitz, "78 neue Haydn-Symphonien," *Allgemeine Musik Zeitung* 60 (1932/33): 153.

3. Gál's hypothesis that Michael Haydn had only copied a work by his brother fails, owing to the explicit confirmation of the autography: *"di me Michele Haydn m.p."*

4. See Larsen, *Haydn-Überlieferung,* p. 249.

5. Pohl I, *Vorwort:* viii, 231, 256; II: 38, etc.

6. GA, series 1, vol. 1: iii.

7. GA series 14, vol. 1: 14.

8. *Beethoven—Zentenarfeier* 1927: 282.

9. *Zeitschrift für Musikwissenschaft* XIV(1932): 289.

10. Cf. W. Oliver Strunk, "Haydn's Divertimenti for Baryton, Viola, and Bass," *The Musical Quarterly* XVIII(1932): 216.

11. Cf. Larsen, *Haydn-Überlieferung,* p. 24f.

12. Ibid., p. 163ff.

13. If in this section we cite Elssler we always mean Elssler senior unless otherwise noted.

14. See Larsen, *Haydn-Überlieferung*, p. 243ff.

15. Ibid., p. 236f.

16. Pohl I: 248.

17. Strunk, op. cit, p. 222.

18. Päsler, *Vorwort*, p. xivf.

19. Ibid., p. xx.

20. The two Salieri minuets (1772) that are loosely attached to it can hardly be related to it; the sonata must date back to before 1770, as is seen immediately if it is compared to the C-minor sonata composed in 1771, or to the six sonatas of 1773!

21. This numbering obviously did not arise from a later summarizing but, judging from the writing style, was entered together with the themes, at least from no. 40 on. It must be given some attention, since it might give evidence of the number of symphonies composed before 1765 but not listed here. The number of symphonies composed up to ca. 1770—that is up to and including GA 41—should accordingly amount to fifty-six. However, it would be wrong to conclude that we shall have to count on fifteen unknown symphonies from this period. To the forty-one symphonies must be added GA 49, 58, and 59, as well as the overture II, 10 and the lost symphony IV,16. Furthermore, we may well conclude from the entering of the scherzando in A, the last of the six advertised by Breitkopf in 1765, that these six works—not listed otherwise in the *EK*—were included in the number fifty-six. Presumably also quartet no. 5, available as a symphony in Göttweig among the *"Symphoniae et Parthiae,"* not among the *"Cassatio, Divertimento et Quadro,"* and in the *Quartbuch* in the volume of symphonies, must be included. That would raise the number of symphonies from forty-one to fifty-four, and correspondingly reduce the number of early symphonies not entered into the catalog to just two. However, the possibility will still remain that some of the first forty-one symphonies, listed in the GA, are missing, and in their place there might be unknown works. The remark on page 27 of the catalog might seem to indicate this: "these following are missing." Of the first forty numbers of the GA, however, this supplement contains only three, GA 27, 12, and 34 (Allegro), and in addition, on pages 25–26, GA 9 and 33. Since 27 is actually not missing, and since 34 was most likely entered into the main list with the slow movement (as the real first movement)—a double entry of exactly this symphony is found in the *HV* (nos. 17 and 91)—, we would obtain space for only three or four more symphonies. Yet it can scarcely be ignored that these five or six (supposed) empty spaces might actually be reserved (wholly or partly) for well-known works, only with different titles (divertimenti). Thus from the present numbering at most the *possibility* of a very small number of unknown symphonies from before 1770 can be deducted.

22. Cf. Larsen, *Haydn-Überlieferung*, pp. 51 and 109f.

23. Pohl I: 342.

24. See the Marion M. Scott edition (Oxford University Press, 1931), p. 5.

25. See the Scott edition.

26. *Neues Lexikon* II: 579. The *"arrangirte Wesen"* that he is talking about means, of course above all, the many arrangements of baryton trios by which Haydn—or others—attempted to make these works useful for ordinary string instruments. See also Strunk, op.cit.

27. See Larsen, *Haydn-Überlieferung*, p. 46.

28. Pohl II: 78.

29. *Neues Lexikon* II: 580:"E.Duo's und Solo's für Bogeninstrumente."

30. Gerber mentions op. 93 as a set of arranged works, but according to Pohl's thematic catalog, it actually comprised nos. 1, 4, and 6, of the present duets. Gerber further lists as violin duets the printed editions op. 46, Paris—according to the Katalog 1932, no. 712, this edition was not published until ca. 1800 (based on the no. 1556 of the plates), in spite of the low opus number—and op. 58, André (1791): '*VI dieselben.*" Whether these two prints are early editions of the same works is open to question.

31. Pohl I: 243.

32. See also Pohl I: 255; Strunk, p. 222; Larsen, *Haydn-Überlieferung*, p. 51.

33. Esterházy Archive, kindly made available to me by the princely archivist, Dr. J. Harich. The trios themselves in the handwriting of Elssler, senior, are in the same collection in three beautiful, full leather volumes. The bindings can also be dated by a receipt (February 3, 1772).

34. The anecdote of the princely participation in a performance of a composition by Anton Kraft who had entered the orchestra in 1778 (Pohl I: 256, and I: 252f.) seems to contradict Pohl's assumption that Prince Nikolaus ceased to play around 1775.

35. The two trios, *HV* 41–42 (Berlin), however, are designated as nos. 40 and 41.

36. Cf. *Acta musicologica* VII(1935): 117.

37. Larsen, *Haydn-Überlieferung*, p. 60, 63.

38. Cf. Pohl I, p. 254.

39. XI, 46, according to the inventory of the year 1858.

40. Published by Helmut Schultz in the *Musikwissenschaftler Verlag* (Leipzig, Vienna).

41. See Larsen, *Haydn-Überlieferung*, p. 217f.

42. Pohl-Botstiber, p. 149.

43. Cf. Larsen, *Haydn-Überlieferung*, p. 214f.

44. Pohl I: 254; II: 191, 214; Strunk, p. 244–45 (quoted after Pohl).

45. The latter remark concerning this work: "*bey Gelegenheit einer Prälaten Wahl zu Kremsmünster war schon die Rede,*" has already been mentioned. Cf. Larsen, *Haydn-Überlieferung*, p. 79f.

46. Ibid., p. 307f.

47. Ibid., p. 249.

48. Ibid., p. 109 and 144.

49. GA 34 is included, together with GA 31 and 33 (all three published in Haydn's second volume of English songs) as nos. 28–30 of manuscript music in Elssler's catalog of Haydn's library; in the *Nachlassverzeichnis* all three are united by the number 501. GA 17 and 24 follow as nos. 33 and 34 in Elssler's catalog and, together with no. 38 in this catalog—GA 42 with a different text: "*Von allen sterblichen auf Erden*" (cf. Esterházy Archive X, 60)—as no. 502 of the *Nachlassverzeichnis*.

50. Larsen, *Haydn-Überlieferung*, p. 110.

51. Ibid., p. 138f.

52. Here the traditional story shall be called to mind, according to which, Haydn is supposed to have answered Romberg's question as to why he never had written a quintet: "Because no one ever commissioned one from me!" (Pohl-Botstiber, p. 314.)

Viennese Classical Style

18

Some Observations on the Development and Characteristics of Viennese Classical Instrumental Music

A general survey of our days' musicological work in different fields would unveil a rather uneven distribution of activities. It is a well-known fact that Renaissance and Baroque music research is flourishing whereas research in music from the Classical and the Romantic Era is advancing more slowly. There may be various reasons for this state of affairs, but no doubt one major difficulty in studying Classical music is related to the historical situation of this music: it is neither close enough to us to enable a direct approach, nor far enough from us to be met without a certain amount of prejudice. It is part of our musical life to such an extent that it might seem as if its language would present no problems. However, music has changed, sonorities have changed, and listeners' and scholars' minds have changed so much that we must try to get behind some layers of covering paint if we want to come close to the original picture. These changes have happened gradually, while the performance tradition of the music in question has been unbroken—unlike what has happened to the music of Bach, Buxtehude, or Ockeghem. For this reason it may be difficult to imagine how much we will have to adjust ourselves, if we want to judge the problems in Classical music just as unbiased as we try to do in the case of Bach, Buxtehude, or Ockeghem. What makes it especially difficult to arrive at a fairly unbiased judgment, is perhaps the fact that any attempt at forming a tradition of scholarly approach to this music is constantly confronted with the average performers' and listeners' traditional approach, at times causing rather idle discussions about performance style.

Expressed a little differently we may stress the strange fact that the music of Haydn and Mozart, unlike Bach's or Handel's or Palestrina's music, has com-

Reprinted from *Studia musicologica, Academiae scientarium Hungaricae* 9/1 (1967), pp. 115–39.

monly been put up not against the music of their forerunners but of their successors, or in any case of one great successor, Beethoven. An important consequence of this is the use of the same analytical tools, and above all, the widespread generalization of classical form problems as concentrated in one textbook model, the so-called sonata-form. This form, however, was not known by the Vienna Classics themselves, but launched by the theorists like A. B. Marx and others from about 1840.[1] It was deduced from their works, neglecting the essential changes in style from the early Haydn to the late Beethoven, or rather, mainly taking Beethoven as a basis. Its primary purpose was to be used as a model for the training of composers. Nevertheless, this abstract formal pattern came to serve as a never failing instrument in the study of music history, and no doubt it has contributed vitally to obscuring the problems of classical music.

The Bach-renaissance in the second half of the nineteenth century helped to raise the question of a historical approach to Classical music. The confrontation of two worlds, the polyphonic towering of Bach's *Kunst der Fuge* from 1750, and the symphonic masterpieces of Mozart and Haydn from 1785–95, close to each other in time, far from each other in spirit, would stand out like a challenge to music historians: how was it possible to explain what had happened in music between Bach and Haydn–Mozart? Break or continuity? Revolution or evolution?

In an age stamped by an almost religious belief in theories of evolution it would seem reasonable to seek a "missing link" between Bach and Haydn. Of course the sons of Bach were drawn into the discussion. Not in the first place Joh. Christian Bach who was regarded as the black sheep of the family, since he had given up the solid Lutheran church music traditions of his family and "adopted Italian manners to suit the tastes of the fashionable classes."[2] The name of Ph. Em. Bach on the other hand presented itself more naturally, highly estimated by the great Vienna classics as a master of character and influence. It is interesting to see that Hadow in the old *Oxford History of Music* (Vol. V, 1904) devotes a whole chapter to "C.P.E. Bach and the Growth of the Sonata."[3] As suggested already in this chapter-heading, the interest was focused mainly on the development of sonata form, not quite the field where Ph. Em. Bach really influenced the Vienna classics.

Just around 1900 a theory was launched which has exercised a strong and lasting influence. Hugo Riemann, the great German musicologist, found himself convinced that he had finally solved the problem in presenting the Mannheim school and its most conspicuous figure, Johann Stamitz, as the initiators of the Classical style. "Johann Stamitz is the so long sought for predecessor of Haydn."[4] Until then the Mannheim school had been known primarily—and rightly—as influential in the field of orchestral technique, not as a school of composers. Riemann was right in calling the attention to Stamitz as an interesting personality in the music before Haydn, but not in making him a composer of crucial importance. The so-called Mannheim style was filled up with elements of Italian origin, but Riemann and his school would go as far as to point out that Joh. Chr. Bach "helped the style which was initiated by the Mannheim composers to become popular in Italy" (!) The Mannheim composers had close contacts with one important place not too far from their own residence: Paris. However, Barry Brook in his recent brilliant study on the French symphony in the second part of the eighteenth century emphasizes rightly that this was a question of mutual influence. Against Riemann's leading idea it must particularly be stressed that there is no real connection between the Mannheim style and the style of the great Viennese composers.[5]

Riemann's Mannheim theory has had a long-lasting effect of confusing the picture of the transition from Baroque to Classical style. Here, as in various other cases, his real merit was to raise the problem, and to bring it closer to a solution rather through the opposition he aroused than through his own theories. Much of the discussions, which took place in prefaces to "Denkmäler"-volumes[6] and in various periodicals, was unfavorably stamped by prejudice and polemics on both sides. Of lasting importance, however, was an article, appearing after the discussion was over, Wilhelm Fischer's "Zur Entwicklungsgeschichte des Wiener klassischen Stils."[7] In this article Fischer may be said to have laid the foundation to a new approach to these problems. He did not try to analyze eighteenth-century music with standards taken over from nineteenth-century textbooks. His leading idea was to throw light on the development in question through a consistent contrasting of stylistic idioms in Baroque and Classical music. Most important was his establishing of two fundamentally opposed types of melody: "Fortspinnungstypus" and "Liedtypus," the first one, the "spinning out"-type, a more freely developed asymmetrical sort of melody, the second one the well-known "symmetrical" 2–4–8-bar-melody.

Fischer's article appeared just at the beginning of World War I, and this may be why it was not given the deserved attention. After the war, problems concerning the development of the Classical style were taken up by various scholars and from different angles. Valuable contributions to the establishing of a more solid basis for studying these problems were given among others by R. Sondheimer,[8] F. Tutenberg,[9] F. Blume,[10] H. Eimert,[11] and K. Westphal.[12] To these may be added some remarkable more general works by H. Mersmann,[13] E. Bücken,[14] and—particularly—R. von Tobel.[15]

Though of course several valuable contributions to the study of Classical music have appeared in later years, the important change in the aspects and approach to the problems of Classical music, which took place in the 1920s and 1930s, may seem to have influenced the general understanding of these problems less than one might have expected. After World War II one special problem in connection with Classical music has been focused upon: the problem of evidence, of authenticity and chronology, in connection with a widespread investigation of sources.[16] Certain happenings, especially regarding Haydn's music, had called for a widening of source foundations already in the 1930s, and the growing activities in the field of Collected editions in the 1950s stressed the need of studies of that type. A few remarks about the nature and importance of this kind of study should be put in here, before we enter into a discussion of problems of style and form.

The need of a thorough source-critical foundation for studies in Classical music made itself felt rather late. Apart from what such a foundation means to the editing of scholarly music editions, it is the work on problems of authenticity which most clearly has to depend on it. More than any other problem of this kind it was the question of a list of Haydn's symphonies which made this clear, and which gave rise to substantial investigations. Odd as it may seem, it turned out that out of nearly 300 symphonies ascribed to Haydn only a few more than 100 may be considered authentic. This is certainly a unique case, but problems of a similar kind are to be found in many other contemporary composers. The same symphony may be found in one collection under the name of (J. Chr.) Bach, in another collection as by (Leop.) Hoffmann and in a third collection as a composition by Holzbauer.

The question of chronology may in some cases present only small problems. This may be true, if the composer in question has consistently dated his compositions and the manuscripts are still extant or if he has managed to keep account of his activities as a composer in a separate catalog. But in very many cases we have not got such first-hand information. As far as printed editions are concerned, the dating presents problems not to be found in editions of our time. If opus numbers are used, they are the publisher's, not the composer's choice, and the same composition may occur under quite different numbers, and of course without printing year. Fortunately we have got some very good bibliographical publications in later years, helping us to date prints from the Classical period.[17] Still more complicated is the dating of the thousands of undated contemporary copies, in which also the problem of authenticity is especially prominent. The growing knowledge of watermarks may help to clear up these problems, which have been too much neglected in the well-known thematic catalog.[18] The evaluation of sources, and the establishing of a chronological basis are of primary importance, not only in regard to the biography and work list of a single composer, but also to check whether supposed relations between two composers or between two single works can find any documentary evidence. Too much supposed "influence" from one composer to another is still based on pure guesswork, or on the assumption that all music known today to a music scholar—through modern publications of "Denkmäler" and the like—was also known to a musician in the eighteenth century. We shall have to clarify the local traditions, to find out whether a work supposed to have been used more or less as a model by another composer was actually composed early enough for that and may likely have been known to this second composer, or whether it is merely a question of more casual likeness. There is still very much work to be done in this field.[19]

Much has been written about changing styles in eighteenth-century music. Parallels have been drawn to styles in other arts, like architecture, painting, or literature. In some cases these parallels are certainly justified. In others they must be regarded as inadequate or even misleading. These designations are such as "Baroque," "Rococo," "Preclassic," "Classic," "Style galant," "Sturm und Drang," "Empfindsamkeit," and even more. No doubt it is possible to find music, which would more or less seem to justify the use of each of these names for a specific phase or a group of works. But they have been employed much more than that. They have served as a sort of label for numerous works which have no connection with the real idea of the style in question. And they have helped to set up schemes of development which have more to do with the borrowed literary or other style concepts than with the musical development itself. There is reason to believe that we might come closer to an understanding of what really happened, if we could for some time forget about these labels and what they stand for, and limit ourselves to the study of the music.

Of the names mentioned the first one, "Baroque," may well be said to come closest to covering a general approach, characterizing music from the period just before 1750 ("late Baroque") in much the same way as, e.g., contemporary architecture, sculpture, and more. It may be questioned to what extent the chronological limits in these various fields go together, and of course there are different traditions in music, literature, and painting, regardless of similarities, but all in all the use of "Baroque" as a musical term does not involve any real problems of interpretation.

This, however, is not true to the same degree for the designation "Classical era" in music. Even if we put aside completely the problems which might arise out of the more general sense of the word,[20] we may find the term somewhat indistinct. From one point of view the parallel to the "Neo-Classicism" of Winckelmann might be stressed, but this would leave Gluck almost alone as a central figure in musical Classicism. From another point of view it is possible to arrive at an interpretation of the "Classical era" as being most distinctively represented by Beethoven, Cherubini, and Spontini.[21] There should be little doubt, however, that the two names to be put into the front rank as *the* representatives of the "Classical era" in music must be Haydn and Mozart, but the qualities in their music which one might stress as decisive characteristics have little to do with either Gluck or the Beethoven-Cherubini-Spontini epoch, and at the same time they seem to have much less in common with the "Classical" tendencies in art and architecture of their time than have Gluck or Cherubini. This seems to indicate that the use of the term "Classical era" in the field of music cannot be paralleled to the application of the same word to other fields of art just as simply as in the case of the term "Baroque."

Still more indefinite are the relations between music and such terms of style as "Rococo," "Sturm und Drang," "Style galant," etc. What is called "Rococo" at one time, is termed "Style galant" at other times, and "Sturm und Drang," "Crise romantique," "Empfindsamkeit," or "Expressive style" are used as changing characterizations without any clear distinction. Even in their original meaning these terms do not designate styles of such general character as "Baroque" or "Classical era." They stand for more limited concepts, more or less restricted to certain areas or social classes, some local development, or literary fashion. In relation to music the term "Style galant" ("galanter Stil") is used to describe music which is no longer Baroque, but may have very little to do with a positive characterization of a courtly "Style galant." *Empfindsamkeit* is the German expression which is supposed to correspond to the word "sentimental" in eighteenth-century sense, but the specific North German *Empfindsamkeit* is far from the "sentimentality" of Laurence Sterne, and on the whole in its proper concept it is scarcely capable of covering as wide a field as is often attributed to it. *Sturm und Drang* is a German literary fashion in the 1770s; nevertheless the word is used generally to explain changes in Haydn's music, composed in a Hungarian residence in the late 1760s.

These few references might suffice to stress the need of caution in applying too directly these designations in matters of music. But even if we could define the meaning of these expressions better, we should hardly be able to tell how far-reaching effects they had. Were they so widespread that they could not fail to impress any musician and make him change his aspects of music, consciously or unconsciously? Or are we too willing to believe that what is accepted by us as main currents in the eighteenth century was also known and accepted by everybody at that time? Let it be stressed again how much it is needed to find out about the development in Classical music without inducing ourselves to presuppose literary or other impulses from outside whenever we find signs of a changing approach in music.

If we try to follow the course of instrumental music in the second half of the eighteenth century, we shall find that there is a great difference between the various local developments. (It is only looking back from a later stage we can make ourselves believe that every composer, each in his place, aimed at developing the sonata form to come as close as possible to the future textbook ideals of the nineteenth century.) Neither were there international music festivals, nor radio concerts and gramophone recordings, and music was distributed largely through written copies; though printed editions were appearing, the importance of the local tradition was very much stronger than today. This is expressed in a typical way in a music magazine from about 1790, where, in an article about the orchestra of Prince Oettingen-Wallerstein, it is stated that "this orchestra is primarily focused (*eingespielt*) on four composers', Haydn, Rosetti, Beeke and Reicha."[22] The local tradition was of course largely formed by the leading personalities among the musicians, but changes in musical life were dependent on conditions from outside. The death of a king or prince, wars, financial troubles might put an end to a flowering music tradition.

It is not surprising, therefore, to find that the various local developments are not following the same rhythm. When trying to survey the development leading to the Viennese Classical style, we should not pretend that it may be regarded as a pattern for all contemporary music. Of course similar currents may be found in other local developments. But it was only this "school" which won universal fame until our days. It is reasonable to suppose that the happy succession of a series of composers like Haydn, Mozart, Beethoven, Schubert (plus numerous poetae minores) has something to do with a specific music tradition.[23]

The main phases in the development leading to the Classical style have been set up in various ways by different authors.[24] The following scheme is suggested here as a basis for further comment: 1) Late Baroque, until about 1740; 2) Midcentury style, ca. 1740–70; 3) Classical style, ca. 1770–1800; 4) Early Romanticism, from about 1800. These datings, of course only approximate ones, are based on the following facts. In 1740, just at the time when Haydn came to Vienna as a choirboy of St. Stephan's, the Emperor Karl VI died, and his two leading musicians, Caldara and Fux, died 1736 and 1741, respectively. A great tradition had come to an end, and Austria had to go through a period of wars and a decline in cultural activities. The time limit "ca. 1740" marks the end of the absolute reign of Baroque music in Austria, but not the beginning of a new era of real distinction. The fixing of the next date, ca. 1770, is not based on any similarly prominent event, but only on happenings in music. Around 1770 Haydn composed the three quartet series, Op. 9, 17 and 20, which, together with a number of important symphonies, stand out as a landmark in the creation of the Haydn–Mozart Classical style. Though Haydn was at that time living in a remote princely residence, not in imperial Vienna, these works immediately found their way to European music centers, and, perhaps more important, to Mozart, whom they inspired to two equally prominent symphonies. The last date given here, ca. 1800, or perhaps more correctly ca. 1802–3, at the same time marks the end of Haydn's activities (*Harmoniemesse;* unfinished last quartet) and the breaking through of Beethoven's mature style (3rd Symphony, "Eroica"; piano sonatas Op. 31).

The first of the four phases named here, the late Baroque, is, as stressed above, the period of Fux and Caldara, not of Bach and Handel. Compared to the music of Bach, which was scarcely known in Vienna until the 1770s, but which is often used as the basis for a discussion of the relations between Classical style and Baroque style,[25] the Viennese Baroque music is by birth and nature more Italian and more vocal. The leading forms of instrumental music are Church sonata (Caldara), Overture (Fux, Muffat), and Sinfonia, with some traces of concerto traditions. Complicated structures like those in Bach's great fugues or

Example 3

Sinfonia

Antonio Caldara

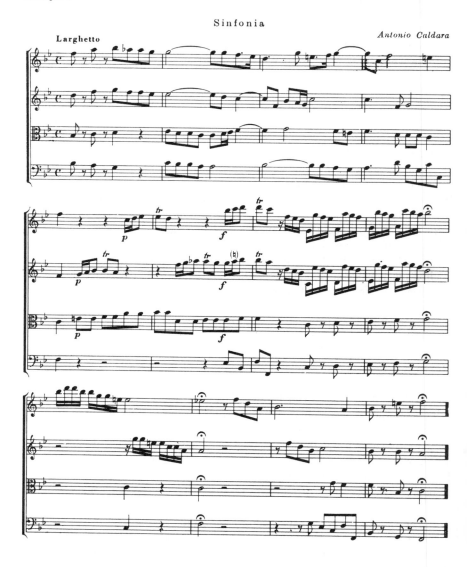

Example 3, cont.

Sonata

Wagenseil

Brandenburg concertos are not to be found in instrumental works, but rather in vocal church compositions by Fux and Caldara.

The second of our four phases, the period between ca. 1740 and ca. 1770, is characterized by a decline in music of a more pretentious nature and an increased interest in lighter and easier music, to suit the taste and abilities of dilettanti. The balance between music of the first kind, music for *Kenner,* and music of the second kind, music for *Liebhaber,* is changed to a considerable degree. What this means to the musical texture, may be seen from two musical examples, the first one (example 3) the introductory movement from one of a series of Sinfonies à 4 by Caldara, to be found in various music collections in Vienna, the second one (example 4) the first period ("exposition") of Sonata IV in Wagenseil's "Sonates en Trios," published as "Oeuvre Premier" by Le Clerc in Paris, presumably about 1755.

A comparison of these two twelve-bar periods reveals a number of important differences. As far as melody is concerned the Caldara example at once shows a continued development through bars 1–4/5, whereas the Wagenseil example shows the breaking up of the melodic line into a number of short fragments. A similar contrast is found in regard to harmonic construction. Our first example presents a development based on a continued harmonic tension, but in our second example the harmonic tension is lost in short intervals through repeated cadencing. A third basic difference is in the contrast between polyphonic and homophonic approach. In the Caldara symphony the old polyphonic tradition, mainly as represented by the specific Trio tradition, is easily recognizable. But in the Wagenseil sonata the "modern" homophonically stamped texture is the predominant feature, significantly symbolized through the many instances of accompaniments in parallel thirds. One point more should be stressed: the much more varied melodic invention in our first example as against the tendency in our second one towards a somewhat monotonous melody structure, composed of rather stereotyped melodic figures.

Those features—the breaking up of the melody into short fragments, the lack of harmonic tension, the homophonic texture, and the use of stereotyped melodic formulas—are typical characteristics of much music from this period, often described as "galant style," or else "preclassical style," but which is here termed "midcentury style" to avoid introducing possible misleading designations. As far as the term "preclassical" is concerned, it might be argued that this is in itself a neutral expression, meaning the music which came before "Classical" music. This understanding is certainly defendable, but a tendency will easily come up to interpret "preclassical" as meaning a style which merges into Classical music, and though this is one possibility, it is not a general pattern.

We may even go so far as to regard the breaking through of Classical music around 1770 to some extent as a return to Baroque traditions in opposition to the style just preceding it. A development of a similar kind, a change of approach in a younger generation, which prefers to look back to the ideas and ways of expression of their grandfathers, opposing the parental traditions, is well known in life, and rather common in art too. The result will normally be a synthesis, sometimes more, and sometimes less successful.

In example 4, the beginning of Haydn's quartet Op. 17 Nr. 4 in C, composed in 1771, a number of single features, pointing to the new approach, is

Example 4

Divertimento a quattro

Moderato

J. Haydn

Example 4, cont.

shown, and the changed general impression makes itself felt immediately. But this new approach, this changed impression is unmistakably related to Baroque traditions.

In all those details, discussed in connection with our two first music examples, where important stylistic differences appear, Haydn tends to be on the side of the Baroque. From the first bar, one is struck by the very strong consistency of the melodic development. The same is true of the harmonic expansion, which is out of an other world than the short phrase-cadencing in the Wagenseil Trio. As for the question of polyphonic-homophonic texture, our example is perhaps less characteristic; other quotations might give a stronger impression of how much just the trend to polyphony comes to the fore in the quartets from these years. Finally Haydn's mastery of original melodic invention and, not least, of varying again and again the same motive, putting it into ever new light, can scarcely be fully illustrated either in this short example, but here again he is pronouncedly on the Baroque side.

In spite of all traces of Baroque tradition, it is, however, obvious that this is not a relapse into an old style. It is a new style, but with strong impulses from the grand Baroque tradition. These traits comprise melodic and harmonic development and tension, but in the melodic invention the traces of a synthesis between old and new traditions are obvious, and this is true for the harmonically conceived texture throughout. A further characteristic feature in the music from this phase in the development of Classical style is a strong rhythmic impulse which is again immediately sensed as related to Baroque rhythm.

In Haydn's symphonies, quartets, and piano sonatas from these years we find such a remarkable special character that it is understandable that an explanation has been sought for in terms like *Sturm und Drang* period or *Crise romantique*.[26] But neither do we find traces of a crisis in Haydn's life nor would it be easy to explain a development starting shortly after 1765 and extending until ca. 1772 in such a way. (When this theory was launched, it was partly based on wrong chronology.) What happened was most likely that Haydn at last got tired of the worn-out style of midcentury music, and realized how much more expansive force was to be found in the traditions of Baroque music. In the resulting synthesis of old and new style, other features were drawn into the process such as the C. P. E. Bach influence, stressed by Haydn himself, and a stronger sense of expressive characterization resulting from his increasing activities as an opera composer. This extremely interesting forming of a new style may be viewed against the special Vienna conditions: a strong Baroque tradition followed by a rather weak transition period in which no prominent new style was formed. The way was open for a new style without much competition from leading composers of the interim generation. Furthermore, though the music had changed in several respects it had not developed such decisive new features as would make a synthesis of old and new style impossible. It is interesting to note that this development would scarcely be possible if music in Vienna had developed along the same lines as in Mannheim. What Leopold Mozart called "das vermanierierte Mannheimer goût" could hardly have given way to a synthesis of this kind. The fact that the Vienna composers were much more conservative may be regarded as an essential condition for the birth of the Vienna Classical style.

The development of a specific Classical style based on Vienna music traditions was so far primarily the work of Haydn. Mozart's way to the Classical style, and his contribution to its forming, was completely different. In the years 1762–73, from when he was six till he was seventeen, he spent almost seven out of eleven years travelling to all important places in Europe, absorbing all sorts of music, most willingly Italian and operatic music. He spent most of one year (1768) in Vienna but did not contribute to the forming of any new traditions then. During a visit to Vienna in the autumn of 1773 he seems to have met Haydn's new style, and during the following months he contributes to this "new wave" with six quartets, composed still in Vienna, and two remarkable symphonies, composed after his return to Salzburg.

After this most remarkable establishing of a new style, the surprising thing was that neither Haydn nor Mozart tried to expand it further. It is impossible that they should not have been aware of its possibilities of further development. The only reasonable explanation seems to be that they were going too far. Even if they themselves had sensed the need of a new music tradition, their listeners, at the same time being their patrons, may not have agreed. Most likely they were both forced to moderate their expansion and accommodate their artistic activities to please the taste of their audience better. Haydn gave up composing new quartets for about ten years, and Mozart a little longer still. Mozart also finished writing symphonies for a long time, replacing them with Divertimenti, Serenades and Violin Concertos, and Haydn wrote symphonies in an easier style, more up to the taste of his princely audience.

The full ripening of the style, inaugurated by Haydn around 1770, was not arrived at until Mozart freed himself from the Salzburg bondage, and settled down in Vienna in 1781. Here the final synthesis was carried out, the melting together of the Vienna "new style" from about 1770 and the more internationally stamped mature style of Mozart. It is a rather common belief that in these last ten years of Mozart's life there was a close friendship and almost a sort of teamwork between him and Haydn. This seems to be very far from what really happened. We know that they met some evenings on the occasion of quartet-playing in 1785 (perhaps already in 1784), and we know that Haydn went with Mozart to one or two rehearsals of *Così fan tutte* in 1789. But apart from Haydn's casual visits to Vienna during winter in the 1780s, of which we have very little real knowledge, they seem to have lived in Vienna at the same time only a few months in the autumn of 1790, after Haydn left Eisenstadt, and before he went to London.[27] The mutual influencing in these years is manifest, though certainly to a changing degree, and most conspicuous in some special forms, above all in the string quartet. A renewed stressing of Baroque tendencies is caused by v. Swieten's drawing Mozart into his performances of Handel and Bach, and a little later through Haydn's impressions of English Handel performances. A touch of an ideal popularization of music is met with in Mozart's late "musical," *The Magic Flute,* in Haydn's London symphonies, and in his two famous oratorios, dating from the turn of the century, *The Creation* and *The Seasons.*

The Classical style, as found in Haydn's and Mozart's instrumental music from the beginning of the 1780s and onwards, stands out clearly against midcentury style, but also against the style of Beethoven and his followers. The traditional summarizing of these two styles as Classical-Romantic music may be explained through the coherence between them, the one growing out of the other, and through the fact that they have much in common as far as only forms are concerned. But as far as the essentials of musical style are concerned it is not a question of one, but of two worlds, though this is often too much overlooked in performance as well as in analyzing. It is not possible to give an adequate description of the Haydn-Mozart style without a clear conception of what separates these two styles.

Behind the difference of style is a basic difference in general approach, which again has to do with changing conditions in social and musical life. The "Classical era" is the time in which the idea of music "for connoisseurs and amateurs" (*für Kenner und Liebhaber*) is exercising a very strong influence. Scarcely at any other time in European history of music is there such an unmistakable endeavor to write music which is at the same time enjoyable to both parts. Perhaps more than in most other places this is true of Classical Vienna, where an interesting feature in musical life is the playing together of musicians and amateurs, in chamber music performances, or in "mixed" orchestras like the one playing in v. Kees's private concerts.[28] The development of instrumental music in the hands of Beethoven gives evidence of a quite different general approach, conditioned by changing social and performance traditions. The composer's aim is no longer to suit his listeners' taste, but to express himself, or even to come close to a sort of preaching or moralizing through music ("*Alle Menschen werden Brüder*"). The collaboration between professional artists and amateurs is losing ground, partly owing to the increased technical difficulties in much music, which tend to cutting off the amateurs in ensemble, as in chamber music performances. New and important figures in nineteenth-century music life are the great prima donna soloists (Liszt, Paganini) and the star conductor ruling the symphony performance in the way of a dictator, not in the spirit of ensemble music. The concert-goers are reduced to passive listeners. The ensemble spirit is overwintering in the music practicing of the choral societies, basing their existence mainly on the performance of Baroque and Classical choral works. The need for some sort of music to be played in private houses by amateurs is covered to a great extent by a wealth of commercialized piano arrangements and variations on popular melodies.

The balanced musical community met with in Vienna in the specific Haydn-Mozart period is reflected in the Classical style. It is just balanced in the most positive sense of the word. Compared to midcentury style it may seem modern, individualistic, Romantic. From the point of view of Romantic music it may be found anything but that. It is not to be regarded primarily as a means of self-expression. It is music for music's sake and for the listener's sake. The ambition of the composer is to write good music and—for that matter—successful music.[29] It may be music of a more festive or of a more serious character. The one is not more legitimate than the other. When in 1788 Mozart composed three splendid symphonies, very different in mood, each of them would certainly express one side of Mozart's musical thought and feeling. Only a lack of understanding of the "Classical" spirit could cause the narrowed conception of Mozart's personal expression as revealed only in one of these, the symphony in G.

The difference between the two styles of music, discussed here, may be demonstrated easily through music examples, showing melody types, harmonic structure, rhythmic character, and more. It is, however, still more conspicuous in such general features as sonorities, dynamics, and basic motion, which are more suggested than really expressed by means of musical notation.[30] The change of function in these fundamental elements is one of the decisive features in the development from Classical style to Romantic style, and may be summarized rather simply like this: serving originally as supporting pillars in the general musical construction they develop into flexible means of expression, capable of carrying the individual self-expression of the Romantic composer to a peak.

The basic motion, in Baroque music the principal element, in Classical music still of primary importance, is submitted to changes in two respects. Firstly the change in general approach to the choice of time values. The exaggeration of tempo contrasts tend to dissolving the remnants of any tactus-sensation, individualizing the feeling of tempo to such a degree as to call for tempo indications of a more individualized character (as compared to the Baroque "Tempo giusto" or "Tempo ordinario"), or even metronome indications. Secondly the introduction of rubato traditions (in the nineteenth-, not the eighteenth-century meaning of the word). Again a quite central quality in Baroque music, the unchanged, "motoric" motion, is still valid to a high degree for classical music,[31] but in Beethoven a rubato performance must be required in a rather early stage.

The influence of changing sonorities is demonstrated clearly in piano music, but above all in orchestral music. Though rather large orchestras were used in some leading music centers (Paris, London) in the late eighteenth century, the average orchestra was small, compared to later standards. The increased number of orchestral players is one important feature in the development of nineteenth-century orchestral sound, but other innovations are still more remarkable. New—i.e., new in symphonic style, though known before in other connection—are instruments like trombones or double bassoon and others. Another feature is the conscious use of sound qualities (in traditional instruments) not exploited before, like high tones in cello playing or deep tones in the clarinetto. But above all it is the altered balance between the various groups of instruments which causes a decisive change in orchestral sonorities. The number of woodwind players is raised, and the brass group comes to the fore. All this taken together means an increase in massiveness and powerful effects on one side, and a much-widened scale of instrumental colors and contrasting on the other side. The art of instrumentation or orchestration becomes a central discipline of primary importance. But it should not be forgotten that this is an art quite different from the Classical style in music. The balance of design and color has given way to a cultivation of color as a primary creative impulse, color for color's sake.

What is said here about instrumentation, is true in much the same meaning for the use of dynamics in Classical and Romantic music. The Baroque tradition of dynamics in orchestral, or rather ensemble music, was concentrated mainly on two forms of dynamic underlining, the unbroken dynamic unity and the contrasting dynamics found in the concerto. Besides this a certain amount of "expressive dynamics"—the singer's or violinist's private performance dynamics—has been traditional. In Classical music the two basic forms of orchestral dynamics are modified and supplemented by a third, the "graduated dynamics," as it might be called (*Übergangs-Dynamik* in German). Symbols of this new type of dynamics are the signs of crescendo and diminuendo, coming up in the course of the second half of the eighteenth century. The importance of this widened conception of dynamics is above all an increased flexibility of the dynamic shaping. In the balanced Classical style this flexibility is a very characteristic feature.

The turn to Romantic feeling is characterized by a much stronger, more conscious use of dynamic effect. Effect dynamics of this kind were foreshadowed by the Mannheim orchestral style—indebted in its turn to Italian traditions—but in the Mannheim music the tendency of "modern" dynamics had no counterpart in music itself; the result was a rather idle effect, pointing to future development, but without any real influence in its own time. The realization of "modern" dynamics happened in Beethoven's music soon after 1800. His third symphony may well be called the first powerful manifestation, but it is still more directly perceptible in works like his overtures *Coriolan* and *Leonore Nr. 3*. Here we have arrived at a stage where, similar to what happened in regard to orchestration, the Classical balance is broken, giving way to a singular dynamic effect as the primary creative impulse.

It has been the aim of this comparison to stress the basic difference between Classical and Romantic instrumental tradition, because they have been too much considered as one tradition only. It is not the question of a comparison for the sake of an appraisal, but only to help clarify the nature of Classical style as expressed in the music of Mozart and Haydn. Classical style in music should be conceived as a rather short brilliant synthesis, not a primary step to a greater and more powerful development. It is a style which may perhaps be called unique in its complete interior balance. Many elements of this style are capable of further expansion, increased expression, power, tension, but it is obvious that any specific gain in effect involves a loss, a decrease in balance.

This interior balance, which may be called the true nature of Classical style in instrumental music, is reflected in all essential features of Classical music: in the going together of professionals and amateurs, of *Kenner und Liebhaber,* in the equal importance of formal and expressive features, the synthesis of homophonic and polyphonic approach, in the consummation of about 200 years' development of "functional" harmony and tonality, in the striving for clarity, the balancing of design and color, the combination of fixed and graduated dynamics, and still a number of other features.

We have left to the end some further considerations of problems of form, some of which, as stressed above, played a considerable role in the discussion of the origins of Classical music fifty to sixty years ago, and do so still in many presentations of this phase in music history. Since the symphony in its Classical form had four movements, Allegro, Slow movement, Menuetto, and Allegro or Presto, and the Neapolitan symphony from the first part of the eighteenth century, supposed to be the basis for the development of the Classical symphony, had only three, Allegro, Slow movement, Presto, it was taken for granted that the problem of cyclical development was limited to the insertion of the menuetto as a third movement. Johann Stamitz, who actually used the four movement form with some consistency, was credited with this "innovation." We must regard this, however, as a pronounced oversimplification of the problem. A development of this kind is only one of several possibilities, because the symphony did not simply grow out of one preceding form, but it was the result of a synthesis of various Baroque forms.

As easily demonstrated, the first period in Haydn's symphonic development is marked by experiments with the cyclical form. Three movement-symphony, Overture, Church sonata, Divertimento, and Concerto can be traced as forerunners, which influenced the development. Of his string quartets the first twelve numbers are with slight exceptions based on the five-movement divertimento form, Allegro–Menuetto–Andante (or the like)–Menuetto–Presto. The change-over to a four-movement form consequently means a reduction, which may cause the first or second minuet to drop out, in the first case resulting in the common four-movement form, in the second case in the form with minuet in the second, slow movement in the third place, a form which may actually be found in rather late quartets, long after its complete disappearance from the symphony. As far as Mozart's symphonies are concerned it is obvious that he does not make much fuss about this problem. As opposed to Haydn, who settles for the common four-movement form in the 1760s, Mozart goes on composing alternately three- and four-movement symphonies until his latest works in this genre (with three movements still in the *Prague* symphony 1786).

It should furthermore be noted that even in the first named case, a four-movement form growing out of a three-movement form, it may be questioned which movement represents the addition. As suggested already by Botstiber[32] and carried out further by Sondheimer[33] and Tutenberg[34] it seems more reasonable to regard the Finale as the real addition, since in most cases the last movement in the early three-movement form was more or less a minuet or a Tempo di Menuetto. In fact, one of the most interesting features in the development of the Classical symphony is just the extended endeavor to form a finale corresponding to its function within this stage of development of the symphony.

Of all the different forms in which single movements of the Classical symphony or sonata are cast, by far the most attention has been directed to the so-called sonata form, which is nearly always used in the first movement, very much in the finales, and several times in the slow movements. The discrepancy between a general textbook description and the actual diversity of forms of this kind found in Mozart and Haydn has already been stressed. Again an obvious oversimplification is demonstrated, and at the same time an anachronistic tendency is at work, measuring these forms with a standard pattern from later times.

Two major partialities may be named here: the belief in a basic dualism as a principal feature, or even an absolute necessity, and the general view of themes as the primary and proper substance of the form, and the rest of the music as secondary material.[35] Obviously these axioms are deduced from nineteenth-century traditions. They may well find support also in some late eighteenth-century music, but they are not able to cover the various types of sonata form to be found in the Classical era. The claimed principle of duality is not valid in the sense given to it in nineteenth-century textbooks; a contrasting theme in the dominant is not enough to support this claim. And the concentration of interest in themes, as standing out from "bridge passages and other subsidiary material" makes it difficult or impossible to grasp what is really going on specifically in a great many typical Haydn compositions.

It is essential here to note a basic difference between Haydn and Mozart in regard to construction and development of themes in a sonata-form pattern. (Let it be stressed, that the following observations do not intend to set up new textbook patterns, but to point out certain typical—though of course not exclusive—formal features.) It has to do partly with differences in artistic personality, partly with the contrast between their ways of development. As mentioned above, Haydn's mature style was based on a renewed absorption of Baroque traditions; Mozart's, on the other hand, on the assimilation of a great many impulses from midcentury music from various European music centers, but above all from Italy and from the opera. In accordance with this, Haydn has a strong predilection for stressing the wholeness and unity in a movement through the use of a limited thematic material, which is developed and varied again and again. And his themes tend to using a construction which favors a decomposing into motives to be developed in the course of the piece in a manner often reminding of Baroque traditions. Mozart, on the other hand, is much more inclined to presenting a number of themes or themelike passages succeeding each other in well-planned contrast and variety. His themes are mostly beautiful melodies in their own rights, not complex motive constructions to be used in the same way as in Haydn.

A remarkable difference between Haydn and Mozart, connected with the difference in the nature of thematic forming just mentioned, is found in the molding of the first part of the sonata form, the exposition. The exposition is normally divided up into two or more sections, separated from each other by pauses, cadences, change of motion and thematic material, dynamics, and more. In many cases, especially in Mozart, the cadencing in connection with the change of tonality from tonic to dominant will be so much stressed that a decisive cut is felt here. This enables the dividing up of the exposition into a first section and a second section, but mostly without any feeling of a dualistic construction in nineteenth-century sense, more often with one or several further themes which tend to stressing the variety, not a "dramatic" duality.

A typical construction of the exposition, still more inconsistent with nineteenth-century sonata form ideas, is found very often in Haydn, and to some extent also in Mozart. Here the exposition is not divided up in two but in three sections, which might be termed "Opening group," "expansion," and "closing group." This three-section structure is mostly underlined through "tectonic" pauses after full cadences, in typical cases either on tonic and dominant or on dominant and double dominant or the like. The second section, following the first full cadence, does not as a rule bring a "secondary theme." It may have no real theme at all, but only a combination of motives in a spinning-out-like manner, or it may very often (also in late works as e.g., symphony nr. 104,

"Salomon") open with a variant of the principal theme. A new theme is often seen at the beginning of the third section, but though it may sometimes come close to a traditional secondary theme in expression, it will have quite a different effect, owing to the changed structure. In the textbook sonata form there is supposed to be a basic (structural) contrast between the principal and the secondary subject. This contrast should be behind the forming of the exposition, and it may be carried further within the development section. But in the three-section exposition, the inner tension does not arise out of a contrasting of themes. The development character of the second section often carries the exposition to a culmination just midways between the actual themes, and the theme which may appear at the beginning of the third section is no essential component, like a secondary theme in the traditional sense, but rather a more prominent cadential theme. In a formal construction of this type, therefore, the interpretation of themes as primary, "bridge-passages," and others as secondary material, may be very misleading. The themes may serve as starting impulse and as cadence stressing respectively, and the free development, following the opening group, is not a sort of bridge between the essential structural features, primary and secondary theme, but a very important feature itself.

Behind the variations in sonata form construction some historical development may also be traced. As one side of this development the mutual influencing of piano sonata, chamber music, and symphony traditions may be named. A strong influence from the concerto is an important feature, and this is also true for the development section.[36] The more the formal expansion is based on the development of material from one opening theme or motive group only, not on the dualism in two contrasting themes, the more concerto traditions will generally be sensed.

It has been the aim of these general remarks on form and style in Classical instrumental music to stress the importance of a more consistent historical approach, viewing the problems of Classical style in the light of the actual development of this style, not from a bird's-eye view of a later development. In consequence of this approach we had to question or to oppose certain rather widespread traditional views and statements, some of which have been made untenable long ago but are still going strong in many textbooks on music history.

This is true in the first place for the understanding of the development of Classical music as a sort of inter-European common evolution. It is certainly more defendable to view it as a number of principally local traditions with a varying degree of interrelations. As far as the Vienna tradition is concerned, it should be regarded not simply as an evolution, but to some extent as a return to the spirit of Baroque music, and finally as a unique synthesis of Baroque and midcentury elements, made possible through the bringing together of Haydn's and Mozart's individual styles.

It is also true for the understanding of the so-called sonata form as one (late) pattern, founded on thematic duality. We have tried to suggest how much more varied a picture is found in the actual Classical forms, and that even in Haydn and Mozart alone basically different sonata forms are met with, which again are conditioned by a different personal background and development, as well as by contrasting procedures regarding thematic construction and development. The tendency of viewing the historical development of Classical instrumental forms more or less from the point of view of an abstract sonata idea should be abandoned since it can never do justice to the various stages of development.

Finally we have tried to stress the importance of a deliberate discrimination not only between Baroque and Classical, but also between Classical and Romantic music. Though closely connected in regard to purely formal development they are two different worlds. No discussion of the ambiguous concept of Classical music can veil the fact of a quite specific art, materializing in the short space of time from ca. 1770–1800 in Vienna through the genius of Haydn and Mozart.

Notes

1. Cf. J.P. Larsen, "Sonatenform-Probleme," in: *Festschrift Friedrich Blume* (1963), and reprinted in translation in this volume.

2. Parry, *The Art of Music* (1894), p. 224.

3. Vol. V, chapter VII: 183–205.

4. "Johann Stamitz ist der so lange gesuchte Vorgänger Haydns," in: *Denkmäler der Tonkunst in Bayern* III(1902): foreword. Similar quotations may be found in many later books and articles by Riemann and his students.

5. J. P. Larsen, "Zur Bedeutung der 'Mannheimer Schule,'" in: *Festschrift Karl Gustav Fellerer* (1962), p. 303ff, and reprinted in translation in this volume.

6. *Denkmäler der Tonkunst in Bayern* VII/2 (1906) and VIII/2 (1907), and *Denkmäler der Tonkunst in Oesterreich* XV/2 (1908) and XIX/2 (1912).

7. *Studien zur Musikwissenschaft* III (1915): 24ff.

8. "Die formale Entwicklung der vorklassischen Sinfonie," in: *Archiv für Musikwissenschaft* (1922); *Die Theorie der Sinfonie* (1925); a long series of preclassical symphonies, edited by Sondheimer (Edition Bernoulli), cannot be regarded as scholarly editions, and many of his later writings are badly prejudiced and marked by an unfortunate tendency of "model"-hunting.

9. *Die Sinfonik Johann Christian Bachs* (1928), particularly the introductory account of the various symphony types, which was also published separately as "Die Durchführungsfrage in der vorneuklassischen Sinfonie," in: *Zeitschrift für Musikwissenschaft* (1926/27): 90.

10. "Fortspinnung und Entwicklung," in: *Jahrbuch der Musikbibliothek Peters für 1929* (1930); Blume used the term "Fortspinnung" in a different sense from W. Fischer or rather he used "Entwicklung" to cover nearly the same as Fischer's "Fortspinnung"; in scholarly works of later years the term is generally used in Fischer's sense.

11. *Musikalische Formstrukturen im 17. und 18. Jahrhundert; Versuch einer Formbeschreibung* (1932).

12. *Der Begriff der musikalischen Form in der Wiener Klassik* (1935).

13. *Angewandte Musikästhetik* (1926).

14. *Geist und Form im musikalischen Kunstwerk* (1929).

15. *Die Formenwelt der klassischen Instrumentalmusik* (1935).

16. See also Mendel, "Evidence and Explanation," in: *Report of the Eighth Congress of the International Musicological Society, New York 1961* (1962), pp. 3ff.

17. Deutsch, *Music Publishers Numbers* (1946), rev. ed. in German, 1961); C. Johansson, *French Music Publishers Catalogues of the Second Half of the Eighteenth Century* (1–2, 1955); Al. Weinmann's series of carefully edited catalogs of music editions by Artaria and other Viennese publishers (1956, seq.).

18. Cf. J. LaRue, "Watermarks and Musicology," in: *Acta musicologica* (1961): 120ff.

19. See also J. LaRue, "Significant and Coincidental Resemblances between Classical Themes," in: *JAMS* XIV(1961): 224ff.

20. See also the very clear discussion of this aspect in F. Blume's article "Klassik," in *MGG*.

21. Bücken, *Geist und Form*, p. 88.

22. *Musikalische Real-Zeitung* 13/8 (1788): 52.

23. Barry Brook tends to explain the fame of the Viennese school, as compared to the French symphonists of the same period, partly through the fact that "until our day the musical taste has been so much formed and influenced by the style and technique of Germanic cultures." (La Symphonie Française dans la seconde moitié du XVIIIe siècle, 1962). Hans Engel, on the other hand, stresses that only the music of Haydn and Mozart, not the period as a whole, may rightly be termed "classical." "Haydn, Mozart und die Klassik," in: *Mozart-Jahrbuch 1960* (1961), p. 74f.; "Sources of the Classical Idiom," in: *Report of the Eighth Congress of the I.M.S., New York 1961*, vol. I(1961): 285. See also the same report, vol. II: 135ff. for a report of the discussion.

24. See, e.g., Fischer's classification in Adler's *Handbuch der Musikgeschichte* (2d. ed., 1930, II: 795): I. Preclassical transitional period (until about 1760); II. Early-classical (ca. 1760–80); III. "High-classical" period (ca. 1780–1810); and IV. Early Romanticism (ca. 1810–28).

25. Even Fischer in his *Zur Entwicklungsgeschichte des Wiener klassischen Stils* (1915) starts with Bach, but in his article on Instrumental Music 1750–1828 in Adler's *Handbuch der Musikgeschichte* (1924), he introduces a sinfonia by Fr. Conti (1721) as representing Baroque instrumental tradition.

26. Wyzewa started this in an article in *Revue des deux mondes* in June 1909 (p. 735), and it has been reproduced in countless books and articles since then.

27. J. P. Larsen, "Haydn und Mozart," in: *Oesterreichische Musikzeitschrift*, "Haydn-Sondernummer" (1959), p. 32ff, and reprinted in translation in this volume.

28. Cf. J. P. Larsen, *Die Haydn-Überlieferung*, p. 243ff.; H. C. Robbins Landon, *The Symphonies of Joseph Haydn*, p. 36ff.

29. See e.g. Mozart's nice description of the first performance of his Paris symphony in a letter of July 3, 1778.

30. Today's mechanical reproduction through records and tapes has at last made it possible to hand down a reproduction to posterity. Mechanical clocks from the time of Haydn and Mozart have

been found which may give some idea of time values, but not of sonorities and dynamics. Descriptions like those relating to the Mannheim orchestral performance (Schubert, Burney) do not give any real information, but only personal, comparative judgments.

31.   See, e.g., Mozart's remarks on piano playing in his letter of October 24, 1777.

32.   *Geschichte der Ouverture* (1913), p. 75.

33.   *Die Theorie der Sinfonie* (1925), p. 36 *et seq.*

34.   *Die Sinfonik Johann Christian Bachs* (1928), p. 55.

35.   See, e.g., *Grove's Dictionary,* 5th ed. (1954), VII: 886ff. (Sonata): "Nevertheless, the principle of duality in the material, however subtly extended, is indispensable to sonata form, and movements from which it is absent are better classified by another name even if superficially presenting certain of its appearances. . . . A normal exposition comprises first and second subject-groups in their contrasted keys, often complicated by bridge passages and other subsidiary material."

36.   See also Tutenberg, *Die Sinfonik Johann Christian Bachs.*

19

Towards an Understanding of the Development of the Viennese Classical Style

When I began studying musicology—or music history as we used to say at that time—I was rather soon captured by the problems concerning Haydn and his position in eighteenth-century music development. This was partly due to the fact that I liked Haydn's music, but partly also to a rather pronounced feeling that there would be problems enough to work on in the field of Haydn research. I can say truthfully that my expectations were fulfilled. During the last thirty to forty years so much progress has been made in Haydn research that it may seem almost unbelievable to us who remember how it was in the 1920s, when Pohl's Haydn biography, dating back to 1875–82, was still the standard reference book. Nevertheless, there is still much work to be done, fortunately.

I would like on this occasion to comment on one special problem which has perhaps been less favored by new research than many other questions: the problem concerning the development of the music tradition which is commonly called the Viennese Classical Style. In the forming of this tradition Haydn and Mozart both played a decisive role, but their ways of doing it were widely different. That has to do with differences in their personalities, in their education and development, and in their contact and association with music in Vienna.

Mozart, always open to new impressions, had spent seven years travelling to all possible European music centers before he was eighteen. He had a truly international background, but even though he spent a whole year in Vienna when he was about twelve years old, and later received important impressions from Haydn's music, he did not really associate himself with music in Vienna until the ten last years of his life, 1781–91.

Haydn, on the other hand, by nature much more slow-growing than Mozart, spent twenty important years of his youth in Vienna, from the age of eight until

Reprinted from *Report of the Eleventh Congress of the IMS, Copenhagen 1972*, 1 (1974), pp. 23–32.

he was nearly thirty, practicing and studying church music and theater music, concert music, and music for popular entertainment. Apart from a short engagement in Bohemia, he was active for the following thirty years in Eisenstadt and Esterház, to a great extent left to his own inspiration, but still in some contact with music life in Vienna. He had nothing like the international background of Mozart. His background was music made or played in Vienna or under his own supervision in Eisenstadt/Esterház. He certainly had occasion to experience music by Italian composers like Galuppi, Sammartini, Porpora, and others, or by German composers like Hasse or Ph. Em. Bach, but primarily he grew out of the specific music traditions in Vienna around 1750. I shall try to say a little about these traditions, as far as we are able to trace them, but before I do that I would like to make a few remarks about some specific conditions and complications with which the scholar in this field has to cope.

First of all there is bound to be a strange dualism in our approach to this music. We are dealing with music and with cultural conditions 200 years old and it should not be necessary to stress that to study this music as it developed in the eighteenth century must involve a certain historical understanding and approach. On the other hand, we have to do with music which has more or less been part of European music culture in an unbroken tradition since it was made. Bach's music had to be called to new life in the nineteenth century. Nobody would claim that there was an unbroken Bach tradition since 1750, but Haydn's and Mozart's music—or part of it—was played during all this time. To most people it would certainly sound as a bad joke if you were to tell them that we ought to hear Mozart's music as some sort of "historical music." Of course I don't mean to say that! But if we, as musicologists, are going to study the development in eighteenth-century music, we will certainly have to face the problems from the point of view of a musicologist, not just a concert-goer. It is part of the musicologist's job to know the music well, and to know about its background, about performance practice and much more. But the real problem, the *conditio sine qua non,* if you are going to study what happened in music 200 years ago, is how to forget your twentieth-century prejudices and as far as possible adjust your perception of the development in music to a contemporaneous approach. I am convinced that insufficient understanding of this principal claim has led to a lot of wrong conclusions about eighteenth-century music.

An aberrant historical approach is involved also in another problem concerning the understanding of this music: the use of textbooks on music theory as media for research in music history. Though there are certainly textbooks on musical forms of a more broad-minded conception, there are incontestably still many which carry on a tradition from the nineteenth century. They put up models for teaching composition said to be based on the Viennese Classical tradition, but certainly guided primarily by the standards of Beethoven, not of Haydn or Mozart. When these textbook models—most famous of them the so-called sonata form—are used as a basis for studying the development of musical forms in the eighteenth century, we arrive at some sort of "inverted historical perspective," which has been a prominent feature in much of the literature about these problems. Instead of following the development of a form from one stage to the next, the author will confront the form in question with the textbook-model of the same form and state that it has "not yet" developed this or that specific formal idiom. One might almost talk about a "not yet-approach" as a typical way of analysis. Even if there are similarities in form, the use of these post-Classical patterns as standards measures for analyzing pre-Classical music must be regarded as irrelevant.

One problem more I would like to underline is not related specifically to our question, or even to musicology in particular, but to present-day academic traditions in general. For generations scholarly qualifications have been given most credit in the general concept of a professor, but just now it would seem as if teaching qualifications are given at least as much attention. One consequence of this may be that a professor will have less time for research than before, but maybe there is another greater risk: he may have to adjust to the teacher's, more than to the scholar's approach. The scholar is seeking for information, the teacher has to give information. And since he cannot possibly be an expert in all fields and all periods, he will have to rely a great deal on textbooks. Not only the students, but even their teachers, may be getting too fond of answers and less inclined to leave questions open. We may end up with a perfect textbook knowledge, which can be checked by a computer, putting "right" or "wrong" to the answers we are able to give.

Now let me stress at once that I certainly don't mean to blame the textbooks for giving answers which are more or less unacceptable to the specialist. We are dealing with a period which you might call one of the black spots on the music history map. It would be very unfair to reproach the textbook authors for not having solved the problems which are only beginning to be focused upon by the researchers. What I want to emphasize is the advantage, or even the necessity, of putting all your textbook knowledge to trial if you want to contribute to the clarification of the problems we are dealing with here. You will certainly find out afterwards that a great deal of the textbook knowledge was valid, but you will not be able to tell which part of it was reliable until you have put it to trial. Too much of our supposed knowledge is actually ready to be replaced by more valid information. I shall try to put up against each other the traditional knowledge, as reflected more or less in the textbooks, and the research problems which still have to be solved, the way I see them. I will divide my comments into three groups: 1) the composers and their works; 2) problems of style and expression; 3) problems of form and formation. A few introductory remarks about the research which has been built up around the problem of the pre-Classical development may perhaps be put in first.

Until about 1900 this problem had scarcely been taken seriously into consideration. If touched upon at all, music history writers would not do much more than take a guess at some names of composers who might possibly be regarded as forerunners of Haydn and Mozart. But in 1902 Hugo Riemann had the courage to tell the musicological world that he had solved the problem: "Johann Stamitz is the so long sought for predecessor of Haydn." Since Stamitz was virtually unknown to everybody, and since it would seem that he was very little known in Vienna in the eighteenth century, and apparently never mentioned by either Haydn or Mozart, Riemann's statement was bound to meet with rather strong scepticism from various sides. Of course it was a challenge to Vienna, and Guido Adler and his assistants, above all Wilh. Fischer, published two volumes of "Wiener Vorklassiker" and Fischer wrote his fine article "Zur Entwicklungsgeschichte des Wiener klassischen Stils" (1915), until now perhaps the one publication which most directly traces the development in question on purely musical lines.

World War I put an end to further discussions. After the war some articles appeared, notably by Rob. Sondheimer, who also edited a long series of works by pre-Classical composers, but unfortunately much too freely arranged. Various books and papers could be named dealing with Haydn, with Joh. Chr. Bach and others, but the problem of Haydn's forerunners was not really taken up again. By and by, Riemann's idea about Stamitz and the Mannheim School gained ground, mainly, I think, because it filled a gap, not because it was ever shown that Stamitz had actually influenced the Viennese tradition.

After World War II problems concerning pre-Classical and early Classical music have come more to the fore. I think we must rightly credit American colleagues for having worked most deliberately on these problems, most remarkably Jan LaRue with his "Union Catalogue of Eighteenth-Century Symphonies," Barry Brook with his monumental study of the French symphonists and his facsimile edition of the Breitkopf catalog, and Bathia Churgin with her dissertation and edition of Sammartini's symphonies, but several other scholars could also be named. Among Viennese contributions Herbert Vogg's dissertation on Tuma and Warren Kirkendale's well-known book on "Fuge und Fugato in der Kammermusik des Rokoko und der Klassik" deserve special mention. Czech scholars have given us valuable editions in the fine series "Musica Antiqua Bohemica" and several valuable articles as well.

To sum up: serious work on pre-Classical music development has been carried out more systematically in later years than before. Yet common knowledge about this development is still to a large extent determined by information and views dating back to the beginning of this century.

The first of the three questions we are going to comment on concerns the composers and their works. How much knowledge about Viennese composers working around 1750–60 do we get from the average textbook? Most likely you will hear very little about them. If any names are given they will probably be the composers represented in the two volumes of "Wiener Vorklassiker," which appeared just before World War I: Reutter, Wagenseil, Monn—or the two Monns, Georg Matthias and Joh. Christoph—Schlöger, and Starzer. Perhaps you may add names like Gassmann, Hoffmann, Dittersdorf, Ordoñez, and Vanhal, but they are contemporaries rather than forerunners of Haydn.

Are these names the right ones and the only ones to be quoted now as in 1908, when they were introduced to be put up against Stamitz and the other Mannheim composers? I think they all deserve a place in the list of forerunners of Haydn, but the list ought to have other names added to these few. In his Haydn biography Pohl already quotes a reference from 1766 in which a correspondent from Vienna in Hiller's "Wöchentliche Nachrichten" mentions—besides Haydn—the following composers of symphonies: Leop. and Anton Hofmann, Franz Tuma, Georg Osler, Karl Ditters, Karl von Ordonitz, Jos. Ziegler, and Joh. Christoph Mann. And some other names should certainly be put in too, like Aspelmayr, Birck, Bonno, and Holzbauer. But some of these names are unknown to all, or nearly all textbooks and music dictionaries. Aspelmayr is actually in *MGG*, but he is there said to be the composer of only three symphonies, though more than thirty symphonies by him have survived. Birck is not entered at all; neither is Schlöger, but that does not mean that they were unknown in their own time, or at least unknown outside Vienna. You will find in Breitkopf's thematic catalog from 1762 4 symphonies by Birck, 5 by Leop. Hofmann, 3 × 6 by Wagenseil, 2 × 6 by Holzbauer, and 4 trios by Kohaut, 22 by Orsler, 29 by Wagenseil, 2 by Birck, 2 by Holzbauer, and 1 by Reutter. Maybe somebody might wonder why I am counting Holzbauer among the Viennese composers, since he is mostly regarded as a member of the Mannheim School; actually he was a Viennese and did not leave for Germany until he was around forty. Many of his symphonies, or even most of them, would seem to be early works belonging to the Viennese tradition. But even if we leave Holzbauer out, the 1762 Breitkopf catalogue lists 126 symphonies, trios and quadros by Viennese composers, and only 16 by Mannheim composers. In the catalog 1766, the corresponding figures are 101 and 40, and in the catalog 1767, 75 and 34. I am quoting these figures because it is a rather common belief that the Mannheim composers were known all over Europe, whereas their Viennese contemporaries were only local names. According to the Breitkopf catalogs this is an untenable assumption. The Paris publishers, too, were aware of the Viennese forerunners and contemporaries of Haydn. In their catalogs from about the same time we find, besides Haydn, Aspelmayr, Dittersdorf, Gassmann, Hofmann, Ordoñez, Vanhal, and Wagenseil. Of course, quite a number of less prominent Viennese composers might be named too, but let us leave these out of the picture. I just wanted to stress that the list of pre-Classical Viennese composers to which attention should be paid is far from complete in the general presentation of this period.

Turning from the list of composers to the lists of their works, we will have to face still more serious problems. Three problems may be regarded as especially prominent: the problems of completeness, of authenticity, and of chronology. I have already touched on the problem of completeness in connection with Aspelmayr, but in all of these composers it is present because their works have been distributed in surprisingly many different collections. It has to do also with the fact that we are dealing mostly with written copies, not with printed editions. Jan LaRue has put all researchers in this field in his debt through his work on the aforementioned "Union Catalogue of Eighteenth Century Symphonies." The work carried out in connection with RISM may help us too.

The problem of completeness is not a question of right or wrong, but of accomplishing a virtually never-ending task. The authenticity problem, which follows as the next step, is different. Though the difficulty of a never-ending registration may affect it too to some degree, the specific problem involved is, in fact, a question of right or wrong: is this a composition by A or by B, both of whom are, in different sources, indicated as the composer? This problem of 2 or 3, or even up to 5 or 6 different indications of author is well-known, especially from the symphonies of Haydn, but it is present in other contemporary composers too. Let me name one special problem which, as far as I can see, has not really been taken up, the problem of the two Monns (or Manns). In his thematic catalog Wilh. Fischer assigns all the symphonies to G. Math. Monn, though in the sources many of them are only said to be by Monn (without initials), and the above-mentioned report from 1766 expressly names Joh. Chr. Mann as a symphony composer. Quite apart from that there is the symphony in E flat published in the first volume of "Wiener Vorklassiker." This is so completely different from any of the other Monn symphonies that it would have to be regarded as very doubtful anyway. Actually it has turned out to be one of the Pokorny symphonies disguised under other names in the Thurn und Taxis-collection in Regensburg. Another example from our field is the symphony in D in Kremsmünster, where the title page has "di Hoffmann vel Holzbauer."

The problem of chronology is of course much more complicated than the authenticity problem—firstly, because it has to do with nearly all the works, except the very few dated autographs, and secondly, because it is not a simple question of yes or no, but of an evaluation of dating within a period of twenty, thirty, or maybe forty years. Of course, we have some basic qualities to judge by like dimensions and form of the individual movements, instrumentation, harmony, and more. We will normally be able to tell with some confidence whether it is an early, middle or late symphony within its author's production, provided, of course, that we know something about his development. But we cannot get really close to an exact date of composition on stylistic grounds alone. The many chronological corrections carried out in the later editions of Köchel-Einstein, may make this clear. You may ask whether it is necessary to have such exact information about chronology. Of course, it is not necessary to know in detail all dates of all works by all the composers in question, but if you want to focus on the central problem, how the way was paved for the Classical tradition, then you have to narrow down your field of vision to the music composed before 1760. B. Churgin has shown that Sammartini was composing symphonies as early as in the 1730s. In Vienna we have a small symphony by Monn dated 1740, and opera symphonies by Wagenseil from the mid-forties. But when was the real outburst of symphonic activities in Vienna? If all the symphonies ascribed to Georg Mathias Monn, who died in 1750, are really his, then the Viennese symphony was already progressing well in the 1740s. In any case it must have been expanding in the 1750s through Wagenseil and others. Various catalogs (like, e.g., the Göttweiger catalog and the Egk catalog of the Olmütz repertoire) give evidence about the situation just before 1760. There is still much work to be done to clear up how things developed in Vienna between 1740 and 1760, the years Haydn spent in Vienna before he began his activities as music director and composer for Prince Esterházy.

There is, however, still one serious hurdle we have to face: the difficulty of getting together a reasonable collection of relevant scores. The number of published works is small, and of those published in scholarly reliable editions still smaller. It is quite impossible to try to work on these problems without including a great number of unpublished works in eighteenth-century copies. But as everybody knows who has worked in this field, unlike opera and church music, which is normally handed down in scores, almost all ensemble music for instruments is only available in parts. Of course, there are similar problems in fifteenth- or sixteenth-century music, but I don't think they are of quite the same dimensions. Let me name only one example: Wagenseil, without any doubt one of the most important forerunners of the Vienna Classical composers. He has composed something near a hundred symphonies, but if you want to study them you will find only two published in the Austrian Denkmäler, and two or three in practical editions. Of the two symphonies in the Denkmäler volume, furthermore, one is an early opera overture (1746), and one an early trio symphony (supposedly from the 1750s); neither is a normal concert symphony.

In his Ljubljana lecture, Blume stressed the need for editions of some of the less famous composers instead of the reedition of the great masters in the new collected editions. I fully agree with his statement that we need some sort of edition of works outside the repertory of collected editions, only I don't think they should replace but rather complement these. The lack of editions of this kind is responsible for two serious drawbacks: 1) Nobody will be able to give a satisfactory survey of the development in ensemble music around 1750, especially in the symphony, until it is possible to have a far wider selection of available scores; 2) We will not be able to take full advantage of monographs on single composers or forms so long as the material on which they are based is practically unavailable to the users of such a book. The addition of a great number of facsimile pages and of six symphonies in score is one of the remarkable features of Barry Brook's monograph on the French symphonies and adds considerably to its usefulness.

I have discussed the problem of organizing some sort of "Score-bank" with a few colleagues especially interested in eighteenth-century problems. I don't think it would be necessary, or feasible, to aim at publications proper, but rather at a distribution of copies—Xerox copies or offset printing according to practical considerations—to a circle of leading libraries, maybe twenty, maybe 100 or 200. That would enable any scholar to get the produced scores either directly or through normal exchange channels. Of course, there are a number of problems involved, like making catalogs, purchasing microfilms, singling out the works to be scored and copied, making the scores and "editing" the works, having the "printing" done and the copies distributed to the subscribers. No doubt a center for the whole thing would have to be established, but I think a distribution of work might be arranged. And of course some money must be found and the right people to work on the project. I would regard the realization of such a project as perhaps the most valuable contribution which could be made to research in our field and I think it would be a natural thing for our society to try to organize a small conference to discuss the plan and to help make it work.

We have spent rather much time discussing our first question, concerning the composers and their works. That must seem natural and defensible because this is the basic problem, in which we will have to invest a large part of our efforts just now and for some time to come. It is not possible to give as much time to our two other questions about problems of style and problems of form. But even if we must limit our discussion, I shall try to give a picture of the contrast between what is generally said in the textbooks, and what seems acceptable from a scholarly point of view at our present immature stage of knowledge.

I think most textbooks will tell you about the development around 1750 that after the grand style of the late Baroque (Bach and Handel), a reaction set in, leading eventually to the Viennese Classical style (Haydn and Mozart). For this post-Baroque, pre-Classical style, you may find a variety of expressions, like Rococo, style galant, Empfindsamkeit, Sturm und Drang, or you may hear about a Romantic crisis or about back-to-nature tendencies. All these suggestions have one thing in common: they are rather specific designations of currents in literature and art and have nothing to do with music. They are used as stop-gaps because we do not know the music itself well enough to pin down the development according to musical styles. Of course, parallels may be found between lines of development in music and literature. In both cases there is some sort of reaction against the Baroque and pioneering for the Classical tradition, but the way this is carried out may be very different. Once we have found out about the musical development on its own terms it may be very interesting and informative to compare it to the development in literature and art. But if we go the other way around and take the currents in literature and art as our point of departure, we will most likely introduce aspects and evaluations which are only partly or not at all valid for the development in music.

The music writers in the seventeenth and eighteenth centuries had a much-quoted confrontation of three "styles": church style, chamber style, and theater style. As the names suggest, these three styles had to do with the place and function of the music in question, but they indicate musical traditions as well. Everybody knows the two types of church sonata and chamber sonata; though not kept strictly separate throughout, they expressed in principle two different traditions, one the offshoot of a vocal tradition with polyphonic features, the other a continuation of dance music with a stressing of rhythmical patterns. Without pretending a full concordance with this three-style pattern, one might express a similar confrontation of stylistic tendencies in the following scheme: constructional style, concerted or playing style, expressive style. The constructional tendency has come to the fore in music at various times. The isorhythmic motet, the fugue, the passacaglia, in our time serial music, stand out as primarily stamped by various constructional tendencies. An expressive approach is met with in much vocal music, specifically in the opera, but in the last two centuries to a great extent in instrumental music of various kinds too. The concerted or playing music spans a wide scale of musical activities and forms, from the more sophisticated professional performance to unpretentious amateur music-making.

In very general terms, the development in music around 1750 may be described through changes in mutual relations among these three tendencies. The late Baroque music, in Vienna the Fux-Caldara tradition, had been characterized by a natural balance among all three elements. But the decline in musical significance after 1740 and the flowering of amateur activities go together with a very pronounced favoring of playing-music and a strong reduction of constructional and expressive elements. The result of this development is the so-called galant music, or, if you want a neutral expression, the "mid-century" style. This is again opposed by the music in the late 1760s and early 1770s, which has been regarded as an exponent of a "Romantic crisis" in Haydn and in his contemporaries, but which may perhaps be seen as a purely (or mainly) musical process in its own right, a renewed interest in expressive and in constructional forming. This brief description is meant only as a suggestion of a possible means of a more directly musical approach to the problem of the stylistic development around 1750. I don't think it is necessary to look for literary inspiration or personal-background motives. A reawakening of the sense of expressiveness and constructionalism in music after years of too-pronounced and too-dominating playing-music may seem a quite natural reaction.

Our last question was about the problems of form. Let me limit myself to some remarks about sonata form, which for generations has been regarded as the end of all formal efforts as far as Classical music is concerned. I have already mentioned the "inverted historical perspective" involved in this approach, and it is scarcely necessary to say much about the textbook description of sonata form; we know it all from numerous presentations. I think I can proceed directly to a questioning of its elements in the light of the actual classical forms.

Our first objection to the traditional sonata form analysis may be the quite general one against the use of a strict model as a "normal" type, making all deviations from this type count as exception, anomalies. Of course, if you limit your description to very general terms you may arrive at a type which is valid—but, on the other hand, is so empty that it doesn't tell you anything of importance. I think we may define the traditional sonata form model as a construction based on two contrasting themes, supplementing and opposing each other, with various connecting material, bridge passages (German: Überleitungen) and others, with a development section and a recapitulation, possibly with a coda at the end. We all know about the scheme of the tonal arrangement, so let us leave that out.

Against the construction as described here, you may raise some serious objections which will turn up as soon as you try to use the traditional model as a point of departure for analyzing early Classical music. I still remember my first shock when I tried, fifty years ago, to analyze Haydn's symphonies and found out that the textbook model did not work. First, there is the question of themes. If you take an old description of symphony and sonata form like the one given by H. Chr. Koch in his well-known "Versuch einer Anleitung zur Composition" from around 1790, you will find that not themes, but periods and incisions are his concern. The stressing of themes as the basic thing in sonata form is one of the features most directly pointing to its orientation towards late- and post-Classical traditions. One more point about themes: as it is known more generally now, a sonata form without a secondary theme in the traditional sense is one of the most characteristic features of many Haydn symphonies, and not as an exception or a primitivism. There is certainly some connection here with Baroque concert traditions, as stressed from time to time in specialized literature, but not very much in textbooks. Another point is the nonthematic developments which are reduced in common terminology to "bridge passages" or any other kind of subsidiary material. Of course, there are passages of this kind, but other nonthematic periods are of primary importance. In short: the fundamental approach to the musical occurrences in the sonata form is so much prejudiced that you will find your way through the forms of the pre-Classical and early Classical music with more confidence if you simply try to find out how the form develops, not how much it is in agreement with the sonata form model.

In the good old days you could find in some books two prefaces—one for the good reader, and one for the bad reader. So let me follow this old tradition and add some remarks for the bad and some for the good listener.

I have made some observations about the problems of the pre-Classical development, and I imagine that they may have impressed some of you as rather exaggerated and too negative. We are all, more or less, relying on textbook knowledge and not quite willing to give it up. I remember some words in a review of a Festschrift in which I had written about the importance of the Mannheim School and directly challenged the textbook knowledge. The reviewer quoted my views and then added, "That could scarcely be true." He did not argue; he only expressed his unwillingness to go against the traditional view. And several times, when I have put a question mark against an established opinion, I have met the answer, "But it is in all the books!" You may regard what I have said as a specialist's view, interesting in itself perhaps, but of no use in the way of general information since it cannot fit into the textbook knowledge and does not present a new, finished textbook knowledge. I can't help it, and I won't blame you for adopting a policy of waiting.

But I hope some of my listeners, especially among the younger generation, may feel that here are some problems to be solved and that you may feel, as I do, that you can only solve these problems if you make a fresh start. I have heard the opinion expressed sometimes that you can only judge the problems of old music if you have an understanding of the problems of the music of today. I think it is the other way round: you can only judge the problems of old music, if you are able to forget about the problems of the music of today. I wish you good luck in a fresh start.

20

On the Importance of the "Mannheim School"

When in the second half of the nineteenth century Darwin's theory of evolution also began to exert a far-reaching influence on the historical branches of the sciences, the idea emerged that the establishment of an evolutionary series of composers that could reflect the development of Classical music was needed. It was easy to place the three names of Haydn–Mozart–Beethoven in an ascending line, but before Haydn something was missing, a link between the late Baroque (Bach) and early Classicism (Haydn). In order to fill this gap C.P.E. Bach was suggested but never really accepted.

Only around the turn of the century was this historical bridge position claimed for a new candidate. In the preface to the first extensive publication of music of the Mannheim composers,[1] Hugo Riemann announced with bold type: "Johann Stamitz is the long sought for predecessor of Haydn." Riemann's uncompromising propaganda for his "discovery" gave rise to a far-flung polemic reaching its peak in the years before 1910. Riemann himself and Guido Adler exchanged arguments concerning the merits of the Mannheim and the early "Viennese school" in the prefaces of volumes of their respective *Denkmäler* series (*DTB* VII, 2 and VIII, 2; *DTÖ* XV, 2), followed by articles in music journals by Heuss, Kamienski, and others.

Various later studies of related topics (Fischer, Sondheimer, Schökel, Tutenberg, Westphal, v. Tobel, and others) contributed to a clarification of these problems. Basically it should first of all be stressed that the development no longer presents itself as simple and schematic as was assumed earlier. The question whether the Mannheim or the early Viennese composers paved the way for Haydn and Mozart has receded into the background to some extent. More recent discussions mostly advocate a more wide-ranging compromise in acknowledging the participation of both the Mannheim, the Viennese, and also of

Originally published in German in *Festschrift Karl Gustav Fellerer zum sechzigsten Geburtstag* (Regensburg, 1962), pp. 303–9.

the Italian and the French composers in this development even though without being more specific. Yet in many instances the influence of old traditions is still in effect and a predominant role as predecessors to the classicists is given to the Mannheim composers. Thus we can read in Moser: "Stamitz was truly a great composer and not least because of his enormous success in Paris he exerted a far-reaching influence on the composers of the younger generation such as Haydn, Mozart, Dittersdorf, Boccherini, Gossec, etc."[2] Wörner states about the Mannheim composers:

> Their merit was the establishment a) of a new style of composition in the realm of symphony and chamber music, b) of a new [style of] orchestral playing. . . . Lasting achievements of the Mannheim composers are:
> 1. the introduction of the minuet as a new movement, the third of the now four-movement symphony;
> 2. the individual shaping of the secondary subject of the first movement;
> 3. the contrapuntal combination of themes together with a subjective expression of the individual parts;
> 4. the preference for special and favorite musical figures, such as *Seufzer* (sigh), *Bebung* (embellishment of the main note by three neighboring notes), *Vogelchen* (little bird: trill with preceding upper second), *fortepiano, Orchesterwalzer* (steam roller: orchestral crescendo of a continuously repeated motive from the lower to the upper range). These manners are partly derived from the Neapolitan buffo opera.[3]

Although this conception does not assign the same importance to the Mannheim composers as Riemann did, it still appears to give a false picture of the development in stating that they exerted a "far-reaching influence" on the Viennese Classicists, and that their symphonies in various ways transmitted "lasting influences." I should like to comment briefly on this question.

In one respect the influence of the Mannheim school must be clearly and generally acknowledged: in the realm of orchestral performance. Their merit as pioneers of a distinct orchestral style was recognized even by their contemporaries, and still in the nineteenth century music historians would call attention to the Mannheim composers on grounds of this merit. It is easily shown that Riemann did not have to "discover" them. For example we can refer to the following statement in Arrey von Dommer's *Handbuch der Musik-Geschichte* (1868):

> From the mid-eighteenth century Germany's high school of orchestral performance was the Mannheim orchestra. From 1753 it was directed by the excellent Kapellmeister Ignaz Holzbauer (1711 to 1783), a proficient and cultured musician. Under him and in particular under the great violinist Johann Stamitz from Teutschbrodt in Bohemia who was Concertmeister of the orchestra around 1756 it was brought to a peak. Under Stamitz and his pupil Christian Cannabich it became the first orchestra in Germany. It served as a model not only with regard to power, precision, and assurance, but also and especially with respect to the fine gradations, colorings, and the nuances of their performance. It appears that here the mediation between loud and soft through the crescendo and diminuendo as regards instrumental music, though not

tried for the first time, was developed much further. The increase and decrease of the tone has certainly been known for centuries as a means of expression. But in orchestral performance it was the echolike alternation of loud and soft, in concertos and solo songs the loud *tutti* of the *ritornellos*, and the soft accompaniment to the solo of the principal voice that had prevailed, even if it cannot be doubted that the mediating grades had been employed as well before even within instrumental music. Therefore, when Burney says (*Travels* II: 74) that "here (in Mannheim) was the birth-place of the *crescendo* and the *diminuendo*" we must interpret this to mean that the use of these mediating tones and gradations was developed and refined here in quite a special way.

(This statement is followed by some remarks concerning the size of the orchestra and the names of the musicians, with reference to Burney, Marpurg, and Schubert.)

Let us, then, acknowledge the merit of the Mannheim musicians—and here of Holzbauer as much as of Stamitz—to have had a decisive impact perhaps on the development of the orchestral performance. But their alleged influence on the form and style of the Classical symphony must be questioned. Of course, there are certain similarities. But, proceeding from Wörner's list, we shall try to pursue the question whether these similarities resulted from direct connections or rather from general tendencies of the time. (Obviously, we will need to limit our remarks to only some suggestions.)

The merits of the Mannheim school regarding the development of the symphony, according to Wörner, refers to the following four elements: 1) The expansion of the symphony into a four-movement cycle by the insertion of the minuet as third movement; 2) "The individual shaping of the secondary subject of the first movement"; 3) "The contrapuntal combination of themes together with a subjective expression of the individual parts"; and 4) The so-called "Mannheim mannerisms" [*Mannheimer Manieren*].

Of these four points the last can be settled first. In a way it must surprise that Wörner regards the "Mannheim mannerisms" as idioms of the Mannheim style of "lasting importance." For actually they were the manifestation of a distinct fashion, of mainly local significance, and moreover (as Wörner correctly states) predominantly of Italian provenance.[5] Only composers of smaller talent, and not those of real importance adopted the specific "Mannheim mannerisms." The fact that the Italian *buffo* style was an essential source of inspiration for Mozart has, of course, nothing to do with Mannheim.

The expanded four-movement form of the symphony by the introduction of the minuet as "new third movement of the symphony," indeed, can be found very often in Stamitz's symphonic oeuvre. Therefore it is quite appropriate to consider this form as characteristic of him. Yet if one wants to regard this form tradition, pointing to a later time, as being of "lasting importance," one has to presume that both Haydn and Mozart were acquainted with his symphonies to the same degree as are the music historians since Riemann. But this certainly was not the case.

They were generally known in Paris, but apparently not much in Vienna. Moreover, one would have to presume that about 1750 only Stamitz, and not his Viennese colleagues (Monn, Wagenseil), experimented with the four-movement form. However, this was not the case, either, for we also have four-movement symphonies by the early Viennese composers. At this time experiments took place everywhere. Stamitz was more talented and more consistent in his experiments than most of his contemporaries, yet this does not make him the only pioneer of the four-movement symphony.

Stamitz did not pave the way for Haydn. This is made entirely clear by Haydn's own development in this area. Neither by imitating Stamitz, nor by merely expanding the three-movement symphony by the introduction of the minuet did Haydn achieve the four-movement form. This becomes evident for several reasons. First, the only symphony of Haydn that reveals some stylistic similarities to Stamitz, his first symphony which traditionally is believed to have been written in Lukavec as early as 1759, consists of three, not four, movements. Second, characteristic of the early Haydn is the five-movement form Allegro–Minuet–Adagio or Andante–Minuet–Presto, found in many divertimenti (including string quartets). The four-movement form can be easily derived from this form by deletion, and not by introduction, of one of the minuets, that is either the second or the first. In the first case the remaining minuet is the second movement of the cycle—as, for example, in many quartets up to his late years, and in the second, similar to Stamitz, it is the third movement, as in some quartets and most of the symphonies. Third, in his symphonies up to about 1765, Haydn employs a great variety of overall structures. In disregarding the borderline cases of the three "program symphonies" nos. 6 to 8, which cannot be considered regular symphonies, one can distinguish the following variants: a) the three-movement symphony with a concluding minuet, *Tempo di Menuetto,* or minuetlike presto in $\frac{3}{8}$, or an occasional gigue- or gavotte-like finale; b) the four-movement symphony with a slow first movement that is followed by an Allegro in the manner of the *sonata da chiesa;* and c) the four-movement symphony with an Andante as second and a minuet as third movement, and with changing types of finales. Furthermore, there are occasional variant forms, presenting insertions of concertante movements, or movements which are reminiscent of the French overture (no. 15), or of suite or variation forms. Only from about 1765, the "normal" four-movement form prevails, although not exclusively. But any attempt to establish a relation to the Mannheim composers here would certainly be a venture. There are really no traces of such an influence, either with regard to form or style. After far-reaching experiments Haydn settled on a form similar to Stamitz's four-movement type, but not in the least in the wake of it.

Stamitz did not serve as a model for Mozart, either. Through several years Mozart changed between the three-movement and four-movement structure, depending on whether he was continuing Italian or Austrian traditions. Unlike

Haydn, he makes use of the three-movement form without minuet even in some later symphonies, such as the C-Major symphony K. 338 from his late Salzburg years (1780), or the *Prague* symphony K. 504 (1786).

Furthermore, hardly tenable is the assumption that the Mannheim school, and probably again Stamitz in the first place, had paved the way for the Viennese classicists by the "individual shaping of the secondary subject." Although one must admit that there are such features in Stamitz's music that might suggest his pioneering with regard to the following development, it seems again out of the question that he may have influenced Mozart and Haydn. Even disregarding the fact that the music of the Mannheim composers was apparently little known in Austria, it must be evident from Mozart's and Haydn's individual developments that they did not follow any prescribed model, but they were coping independently with this problem themselves over many years.

Again Haydn's symphonies are the best example of an entirely different approach to the problem of a "secondary subject." For it is an essential feature of the form of the first movement that Haydn preferred, or which is most characteristic for him, that a secondary subject is not necessary at all. Formal unity rather than the conventional thematic dualism of later times is the most characteristic formal aspect of the first movement of Haydn's symphonies.

In Mozart's symphonies the emphasis on thematic contrast is a much more frequent and characteristic aspect. However, they are not limited to two subjects only, but often employ a variety of thematic formations. Yet again, the shape of the first movements of Mozart's symphonies depends greatly on his alternating connection with Austrian and Italian traditions. At first his early acquaintance with J. C. Bach, later his adoption of Italian traditions and his sense of contrasting themes developed in the operas brought on the development of a complementary character of the secondary subject. But it is not easy to find out where and when Stamitz's influence could be placed.

"The contrapuntal combination of themes together with a subjective expression of the individual parts," according to Wörner, is another special quality of lasting influence of the Mannheim style. True, the "marriage of counterpoint and freedom," as Sandberger called it, was a nucleus in the stylistic synthesis about 1770. Yet it seems neither proven nor provable that a Mannheim influence was involved in the stylistic settlement that plays such an important role in the Viennese music (in a wider sense) of this time. The great contrapuntal traditions of Fux and Caldara could still be felt, and a synthesis of this tradition and the "modern" homophonic traditions of the successors suggested itself. But any attempt to explain this synthesis as having been caused by Mannheim traditions seems entirely devoid of reason.

Let me summarize these remarks on the problem of the "lasting influence" of the Mannheim composers. Without any doubt they have decisively influenced the development of orchestral performance style. Nevertheless, it was only Beethoven and his successors who drew the real conclusions from this influence. Here, as at other stages of music history, we are facing the delayed adoption of a style or an element of style, to which the generation in between could not really find its way.

But it seems more than questionable whether the "Mannheim school," regarded as a school of composers, actually deserves the attention paid to it even by most respectable textbooks of music history. On Haydn's and Mozart's development they had very little, if any, bearing at all. It is beyond doubt that Johann Stamitz was a remarkable figure in a generation of many talented composers (Pergolesi, Jomelli, Gluck, C.P.E. Bach, Wagenseil, etc.), yet by no means was he the pioneer of the Classical style that he usually is supposed to have been. In several respects he anticipated later developments, but the composers which may actually be regarded as his pupils mostly were less influential composers of only local significance. One exception may perhaps be Franz Beck who may be considered more important, but who nevertheless must be counted mainly as a local celebrity.

The line of development from Stamitz to Haydn and Mozart that Riemann wanted to establish would best be dismissed. Although it may seem terribly reactionary, I might stress the validity of Dommer's more than hundred-year-old music history quoted above. Its conception of the Mannheim school seems altogether more appropriate than the conception expressed in most of today's discussions, in which Riemann's over-estimation of the Mannheim composers still lives on. For an adequate discussion of the prehistory of Viennese Classicism we certainly need further source material. At the same time, however, we need to discard traditional, deeply rooted prejudices.

Notes

1. *Denkmäler der Tonkunst in Bayern* 3 (1902).

2. Moser, *Lehrbuch der Musikgeschichte,* 11th ed. (1950), p. 169.

3. Karl-Heinz Wörner, *Geschichte der Musik,* 3rd ed. (1961), p. 307–8.

4. I do not quote these two authors because they adopt an extreme point of view within this discussion, but only because theirs are widely known and accepted textbooks. The division of the influential series *Archive Produktion* of *Deutsche Grammophon Gesellschaft* points in the same direction. The period from 1760–1800 is subsumed under the heading *Mannheim und Wien.* There is a special subheading for *Die Mannheimer,* but none for Haydn.

5. As a curiosity I should like to recall the saying of Riemann's pupil Mennicke, who in his (despite its biases) influential study *Hasse und die Brüder Graun als Symphoniker* (1906) maintains that J. C. Bach "made the style developed by the Mannheim composers known in Italy" (p. 79).

21

Sonata Form Problems

The concept of sonata form belongs to those firmly entrenched concepts that are as much at home in the textbooks of music history as in those of music theory and music pedagogy. Nevertheless, or perhaps in part even because of the nearly universal use of this designation, the contents of the form remain unclear. Or, in other words, the more that clarity seems to prevail, the less does the description of the form often coincide with the actual historical picture of sonata form. This is probably due in large measure to the fact that the theoretical-pedagogical literature has favored the idea of a rigid, typical textbook form, while the historical representation of the form must strive toward a less schematic description that can serve for a larger number of historically observed, diverse forms. Just as the fugue form in Bach's music only rarely corresponds to the scheme of the textbook fugue of the nineteenth century, so also historical research into the music of the Viennese Classical period invites difficulties when it takes textbook sonata form as a starting point.

Along with the conflict between didactically and historically oriented form description, a second factor must be named that severely restricts the validity of the general concept of sonata form: the formal concept in question first arose in the second quarter of the nineteenth century, after Beethoven had altered the basis of form perception so fundamentally that every discussion of pre-Beethovenian music based on these assumptions must almost unavoidably tend to force upon the music a basic nature quite foreign to it. This is apparent above all in the assertion of a fundamental contrast between principal theme and second theme as the central issue in the form. How much effort has been spent in the course of time in trying to find the second theme in a sonata movement, in order to obey the law of thematic dualism, and how much force has been employed in order to change an entirely different formal process into a model for dualistic formal principles![1]

Since the beginning of this century many attempts have been made toward a

Originally published in German in *Festschrift Friedrich Blume* (Kassel: Bärenreiter, 1963), pp. 221–30.

revision of the concept of sonata form, but they do not yet seem to have produced a general reorientation. In some music history textbooks one certainly finds prudent reservations concerning the traditional representation, but one hardly encounters a new formulation of the concept that might do justice to the sonatas and symphonies of Haydn and Mozart just as much as to those of Beethoven. Some indication may be given here of the problems that are bound up with such a reorientation. First, however, a small terminological digression.

As a terminological concept, the designation "sonata form" seems to have been coined by A. B. Marx. In the second volume of his *Lehre von der musikalischen Komposition*[2] he discussed the "ambiguity of the term," the possibility of denoting through this expression either the form of the whole sonata or that of a single movement. Rather hesitantly, he chose the second possibility. With the great dissemination of Marx's book this term became established if only over the course of several decades. In any case, up to the 1860s one finds such designations as "the first form," "the form of the first allegro," the "form of evolution," or "form of free development of musical ideas," "the main form," or "the allegro-form."[3] As a generally accepted designation for the single movement, not for the cycle, the expression "sonata form" prevailed until after the First World War. In the 1920s and 1930s new tendencies emerged. Stimulated by the phenomenological way of thinking (Kurth, Mersmann), some authors refrained from using the term "form" for something already formed, differentiating when necessary "form" from "formation" [*Formung*]; and instead they used expressions like "formation type," or "sonata movement" (Westphal), or "sonata movement type" (von Tobel) for a movement in sonata form. The old problem of "ambiguity" in the term "sonata form" also made itself felt again. In a logically unimpeachable manner "sonata form" was made to serve as a designation for the whole cycle, and the complicated expression "sonata-main-movement-form" [*Sonatenhauptsatzform*] was introduced as a movement designation (Grabner and others).

Even if this terminology might be considered formally correct, the gain still seems questionable to me. The use of "sonata form" as a label for single movements must also certainly be regarded as formally correct—in the sense, however, that it is the form especially characteristic of the sonata, not that it is the form of the sonata itself. In fact, an exact parallel exists in the term "concerto form" not "concerto-main-movement-form" [*Konzerthauptsatzform*]. It is still to be questioned what one should make of the label "sonata form" when used for the sonata cycle, since there is really no sonata form of this sort. For the symphony or the concerto one can speak of such a form. But what should be called sonata form in the same sense, regarding for example, the piano sonatas of Beethoven? In practice, I believe, one would hardly use the term "sonata form" as a designation for the cycle, and in return have to drag along the rather unmusical-sounding "sonata-main-movement-form." For this reason I use the designation sonata form in its customary sense and reserve the expression "sonata cycle" for the description of the entire composition.

The traditional representation of sonata form in the teaching of form and composition involves a series of more or less openly expressed axioms, some of the most prominent of which will be identified here.

1. Sonata form consists fundamentally of three principal parts: exposition, development, and recapitulation; these are further enclosed in two repetition-periods (exposition; development + recapitulation). The substance of the development is on the one hand free modulation, on the other hand thematic-motivic "development," a free working-out generally of exposition material.

2. The actual two-part tonal division of the exposition is reflected in a two-part formal division of approximately this type: 1) principal theme and bridge passage; 2) second theme and (freer) closing group.

3. The two-part division is manifested especially clearly in the previously discussed principle of thematic dualism: the complementary character of the two basic themes (principal theme and second theme)

4. The foundations of the movement are precisely these two themes. Whatever lies outside the thematic parts is generally of secondary importance, as is clearly evident in labels like "bridge passage" or (in German terminology) *Überleitung*.

5. The structure of the thematic parts especially, but also of much of the secondary bridge passages and so forth, is largely reducible to 2–, 4–, and 8–measure groupings.

Through the specialized studies of various scholars, particularly in the years from about 1915–35, a number of questions came up that had to raise doubts about the validity now of one, now of another of these axioms. In the first place, Wilhelm Fischer's often-cited study *"Zur Entwicklungsgeschichte des Wiener klassischen Stils"*[4] should be named here. By his delineation of the two contrasting approaches, "song type" and "spinning-out-type" [*Liedtypus* and *Fortspinnungstypus*], he above all caused a break from the well-known theory (stemming from Riemann especially) of prevailing eight-measure groupings. In the 1920s the form of the symphony movement (until then viewed in the light of sonata form) was recognized as being largely influenced by the form of the Baroque concerto movement.[5] That had to lead to an altered view not only of the general structure of the symphony (or sonata), but also of the relationship between thematic formation and free development, in light of the ritornello-episode contrast.

A fundamental criticism of the traditional view of form came from advocates of a phenomenological approach to music. Prominent here, in the first rank, is Hans Mersmann's *Versuch einer Phänomenologie der Musik.*[6] Against the hitherto "uncontested basis of all form investigations, . . . the derivation of all features from the motive," Mersmann established the duality of motive and line as "elemental principles . . . in reality more like ideas than manifestations," whose incarnation is denoted by the terms "period" and "theme." "By its nature, period is the structural manifestation of line, theme that of motive; however, the forces merge in their appearance into a living unity." Finally, "the basic opposition between period and theme . . . [leads] to the equally contrasting structure of their forms of progression [as is implied] in the terms 'completion' [*Ablauf*] and 'development' [*Entwicklung*].—The problem of all 'completion forms' is a problem of sequence, i.e., of grouping of elements of a periodic nature.—The problem of development-forms is a problem of forces and not of sequence." As a sample of an analysis according to these assumptions Mersmann goes through Haydn's E-flat major sonata, No. 49 (pp. 256 et seq.). Rather disappointingly, he concentrates wholly on the demonstration that the entire form process is to be considered a consequence of forces pitted against each other in the main theme. In Riemann's case one might justifiably object that motivic construction is one-sidedly advanced to the foreground while the large dimensions of the form, the multi-faceted relationships of its parts to each other, are disregarded on the whole. Here, however, the analysis of motivic interrelationship is placed in the center; as a "rule of form" this can in some cases be truly central, but in most instances it must be considered irrelevant.[7]

The remarkable study of Kurt Westphal, *Der Begriff der musikalischen Form in der Wiener Klassik, Versuch einer Grundlegung der Theorie der musikalischen Formung,*[8] concentrates on the problem of classical form. It launches a well-considered critique, especially of the "form analysis of Riemann and his school" (pp. 31ff.), and argues against the idea of the unifying power of "community of substance." "Form then—to stress it once again—is not something that is apprehended through relating perception, rather it becomes immediately perceptible in the process of hearing, as a curve of progression overgrowing the single parts. It is not community of substance, but rather this curve of progression, that transforms the mere coexistence of sections into a unity. If this were not so, every musical entity whose individual periods exhibit no community of substance would necessarily fall apart" (p. 36). The description of "Form as a Totality" (deriving from Gestalt theory), and "Form as Curve of Progression" crowns Westphal's analysis. Another quotation brings us to a more exact definition of the term "curve of progression": "The single sections are, therefore, not form-generating. The real matter is not one about parts and their sequence as such, but about their functional interrelationships. The essence of this interrelationship is the curve of progression" (p. 77).

Observations of a markedly similar character are found in the study by Rudolf von Tobel that appeared in the same year (1935), his *Die Formenwelt der klassischen Instrumentalmusik*, which is probably the most comprehensive treatment of the problems of classical form from an historical point of view. But to a certain extent the study leaves behind the impression of a rather conspicuous separation of the inquiry into two parts: the main part, classical music strictly defined (chapters 1–7), and the final part (chapter 8), a detailed discussion of "dynamics of form" [*Formdynamik*], which itself comprises a third of the book and is concerned almost exclusively with Beethovenian and post-Beethovenian music. In the main section von Tobel starts out describing inherited form designations, with an entirely traditional outline of sonata form (pp. 19–21); however, he gives a rich picture of Classical forms together with a wealth of valuable, essential observations, all of which are far removed from any schematic outline, bearing witness again and again to the author's historical foundation. But with the beginning of the eighth chapter the picture changes. Based on Kurth, the inadequacy of traditional form description is very strongly stressed, and the "dynamic" view of form advances to the foreground along with the mania for bar-form, so characteristic of the period just around 1930. Although observations of this sort obviously are aimed primarily at the music of the nineteenth century, they also appear now to place Classical music in a different light. In connection with an analysis of Bach's music it reads (p. 240): "In quest of a symbolic means of representation for these diversified developments with changing transitions, one naturally has to reject completely the system with letter-symbols used customarily and appropriately for static-architectonic form principles. The dynamic undulations require a pliant, individual manner of tracing, which only is to be found in a curve (contour)." Proceeding from the first couplet of the middle movement from Mozart's D-minor piano concerto, the importance of a double analysis is referred to, "viz., the pursuance of the dynamic progression in addition to a thematic-architectonic analysis"; and, following the insertion of an example, it continues: "This repeated involution of the bar-form progression suggests the character of the natural interplay of ripples. The contention is thereby affirmed, that even Classical music obeys dynamic laws and these represent the general form principle of music [*das urmusikalische Formprinzip*]" (p. 247, cf. also p. 269).

The three last-named scholars uniformly stress the importance of tracking the curve of the "dynamic undulations" [*dynamische Wellen*], the "curve of progression" [*Verlaufskurve*], while they cast off as having little or no significance any analysis aiming at a statement of "the parts and their sequence" [*die Teile und ihre Abfolge*]. Undoubtedly, the emphasis on the importance of functional interrelationship (especially clear in Westphal) has been a necessary corrective to the customary approach to form. Still the question is, how might one best achieve an analysis of this character? Perhaps one comes nearest to the realization of this challenge when one strives for a description of functional interrelationships rather than a formal diagram of contour. In any case, Mersmann's curves hardly seem convincing to me. On the other hand, I hold as essential the conviction that a description—or a graphic outline—of this sort does not, really, render superfluous an analysis of form in the sense of a partition, a survey of formal structure; rather such an analysis must precede it. Apparently, criticism of traditional analysis has led to a somewhat dangerous neglect of the fundamental elucidation of formal structure. Since such analysis has fallen into disrepute, it has not been regarded as necessary to follow up the impulses of historical research toward a genuine new orientation. The following remarks may suggest the potentialities of a revision. I restrict myself here to the problems of the first part of sonata form, the exposition. If I rely predominantly on examples by Haydn rather than by Mozart, it is naturally due to the fact that the textbook sonata with its overemphasis on dualistic form is oriented precisely to a form that is typical for Mozart, so the necessity for a revision is much more readily apparent in a study of Haydn's forms.

The assumption of a fundamental two-part division of the exposition, corresponding to the two-part tonal division, was referred to earlier (p. 271, axiom 2). Even if there are innumerable movements with a tonally indicated two-part division, the notion of monopolization by this form still remains absolutely untenable. Actually, it is not entirely correct to speak of this as a two-part tonal division, since the arrangement more clearly shows a three-part division instead: tonic region—T–D transition—dominant region. But in most cases the dominant region is more extensive than the other two together. Furthermore, we can deduce from the development of the form from the suite to the sonata that an implicit parallelism between tonal and formal divisions cannot be postulated. The tonal development within the second repetition-period will generally move along similar lines regardless of whether this period represents a continuous whole or it is composed of two parts (development, recapitulation).

Typical examples of three-part, rather than two-part, division of the exposition are found in many of Haydn's compositions. I cite in the first place the keyboard Sonata No. 20 in C minor, first movement: main theme, mm. 1–8; elaboration section, mm. 9–26 with a forceful build-up of dominant tension, closing section with epilogue, mm. 26–37. As a second example the first movement of the Symphony No. 82 may be quoted: main theme, mm. 1–20, elaboration section, mm. 21–69, closing section, mm. 70–102. Very similar is the Symphony No. 97, first movement: main theme, mm. 1–26 (the slow introduction is not included), elaboration section, mm. 27–62, closing section, mm. 63–94. In these (and many other) movements the curve of progression is totally different from the textbook type. The main theme (or, the main theme group) is tonally closed, though perhaps with a dominant half-cadence. The elaboration section may proceed from the main theme—Marx's "period with a disintegrating second period" [*Periode mit aufgelöstem Nachsatz*]—or it may not: it is made up more or less in the way of a developmental structure, combining free spinning-out and a succession of changing motives. Tonally it conforms to the section of the exposition customarily designated as "bridge passage" [*Überleitung*] or "transition" [*Vermittlung*]. However, while this section usually comes to an end relatively soon in order to make way for the second theme in the dominant as the second principal formal factor (second after the main theme), the developmental construction—the "elaboration"—itself is actually the second principal factor, not merely a secondary "transition." The formal function of the closing group also differs from that of the textbook type. This type usually includes a second (dispensable) melodic concentration (in addition to the second theme) whose function in the whole movement is not entirely clear. In our three-part exposition type, on the other hand, it appears quite logically as the indication of a long-awaited relaxation, a repose on the dominant after the preceding development of tonal tension. Whether or not—here as in the textbook type—an epilog is appended at the very end has no effect on the general plan of the exposition; however, such an epilog often serves as a point of departure for important parts of the working-out of the following development section.[9] This Haydnesque "closing theme" is quite clearly distinguished from a normal "second theme," since it has a completely unmistakable character of relaxation. Contrary to the "second theme" of a dualistic form, it does not aim at assisting in the creation of formal tension as well.

A second exposition form, typical for Haydn and divergent from the "dualistic" type, has already gained a certain attention, although it has not affected the traditional presentation of these problems in a significant way. Blessinger describes it as follows:[10] "After the bridge passage in his symphonies, in place of the second theme, Haydn often uses the main theme again transposed to the dominant, which then proceeds to new passage-work. Then he often brings in another new, independent idea which, however, does not always have the same sense. In the London Symphony in D major [No. 104] it has a pronounced codalike function. However, in the first movement of the Military Symphony [No. 100] this new idea is manifestly a subsidiary theme. In this case, obviously, the introduction of a closing idea is renounced. This Haydnesque procedure points to early stages of sonata form in an evolutionary, if not in a chronological sense."

The same phenomenon is fully discussed by von Tobel also:[11] "In J. Haydn's masterworks still another tendency of unification culminates—a counterpart to 'thematische Arbeit—, as a reaction against the splitting up [*Aufspaltung*]: the melodic derivation of the second theme from the main theme, and the close interconnection of the exposition-complexes through relatedness of themes. The ways in which Haydn derives his second themes are of an unequalled, fascinating diversity, and they might require a special study." After the bridge passage, generally with "manifold contrasts," "the second section maintains a function similar to that of the beginning of the movement: that of a rather restrained starting-point, of a joint new beginning. The return to the opening section of the movement conforms most naturally to the similarity in purpose, a return which in different works traverses all possibilities from a more general relatedness to an almost straight resumption."

The unification tendency is—as von Tobel stresses but does not pursue further—counterbalanced by a tendency toward variation, which bestows a distinctive stamp on movements of this sort. This has already been pointed out by Blume in connection with the Quartet, Op. 33 No. 3.[12] Similar tendencies are found in the keyboard sonatas, e.g., in No. 24 or No. 38. Among many symphony movements that can serve as examples of the same formal tendencies, I might call attention to the first movement of No. 85 ("La Reine"). The principal theme is presented in this movement no fewer than seven or eight times (mm. 1–11, 20–30, 67–84, 123–33, 141ff., 201–11, 227–44). Contrary to Kretzschmar's contention that the theme is "always [repeated] quite literally with the exception of the tonality," each new statement—with one single exception (the unchanged repetition of mm. 67–84 as 227–44)—means a new variation. This art of variation represents one of the subtlest features of the entire compositional structure.

With the reference to the main theme that appears seven or eight times in ever-new variations, we have inevitably approached another formal problem of the sonata. It was mentioned from the outset how much the validity of the familiar description of sonata form is restricted, first by the character of this structure as a textbook form, and second by its far too one-sided orientation toward post-Beethovenian developments. Yet a third weakness of the traditional description of this form must be stressed here, too. While we find the difference of theme- and period-construction between sonata and symphony very strongly articulated in Koch's *Versuch einer Anleitung zur Composition*,[13] the more recent form description generally tends to equate the two categories. It is overlooked how much the familiar sonata form type derives from the sectional principle [*Reihungsprinzip*] of the keyboard sonata, while the symphonic movement is to a great extent determined by the ritornello principle of the concerto. Indeed, Symphony No. 85 may demonstrate this strikingly. In many instances, the contrast of ritornello and episode, rather than the polarity of main theme and second theme, comes to the fore. Two more features of symphonic structure can also be explained as concerto-derived: the predominance of free development and period structure in the formal design of the exposition, of which the three-part form described earlier represents an especially typical special case (Symphonies Nos. 44, 91; Mozart, *Prague* Symphony K. 504), and the complex, ritornellolike structure of the main theme (Symphonies Nos. 82, 97).

We must forego a further description of special sonata-form problems.

Instead I shall try to give a brief survey of the essential features of sonata form, which takes into account the outlined variations of the form better than the traditional form description characterized earlier. We may again restrict our statements mainly to the problems of the exposition.

1. The tonal development of the exposition can predispose a basic 2- or 3-part division, according to a stronger or weaker emphasis of the tonal transition or the tonal development; either T → (D)D-- ‖ or T/T → (D)D-- ‖ . The symbol (D) means dominant preparation, either as TV, D, or DV.

2. The agents of form construction and of form perception are not primarily the themes, but rather the underlying tonal progression and the changing formal function of the successive periods. The import of the themes can indeed be truly significant, but the formal function is basically the carrier of the themes, not the other way around. This arises particularly from the special case in which a variant of the main theme takes the place and function of a new second theme.

3. The function of a period within the complete course of the exposition can be described by general designations (changing with varying cases) like: opening section, main theme or main theme group; elaboration section or transition group (bridge passage); subsidiary theme, contrasting theme, main theme variant; subordinate theme, second subsidiary theme, motive group; closing theme or closing group; epilog, cadence group, or coda group.

4. A period is generally composed of a larger or smaller number of minor divisions, from the simpler motivic-thematic phrase construction (motive repetition, simple phrase, regular sequence formation, eight-measure period) to the 2- or 3-part period construction, phrase series, or freer development (spinning-out in Fischer's sense), and to the elaborate phrase complex (like ritornello structure), or to figural structure or passagework. A motivic-thematic concentration (theme formation) is often characteristic of the beginning of a main period or group (principal, subsidiary, and closing themes), but it is also possible for other parts of the period structure. On the other hand the beginning of a period without normal ("symmetrical") theme construction (rather put together in ritornello fashion) must be considered an absolutely typical feature of certain forms, especially at the very beginning of a movement. The interrelating of the first two larger periods—tonic group and modulation period—by corresponding beginnings without analogous continuation ("Period with a disintegrating second part") is likewise typical.

5. Within the common framework of a 2- or 3-part tonal division, formal tendencies of highly diverse, even partially contradictory characters can be recognized; as, for example: thematic abundance vs. motivic-thematic compactness; sectional structure vs. developmental form; prevailing homophony vs. texturally free, semipolyphonic part-writing (quartet style); eight-measure groupings vs. asymmetrical spinning-out.

6. The elements essential for the understanding of the structure of a given form can be grouped into two categories, according to their main effect: those that primarily serve the underlining of the division, the structure of the form (structural pause, stressed cadence formation, dynamic change, emphasized motivic contrast, etc.), and those that act (less obviously) as agents of the formal development and the melodic-rhythmic progression (linear development, harmonic rhythm, etc.).[14] For an understanding of the substance of the form both are of fundamental significance: the division of the complete form and the filling-out of the formal framework.

The traditional description of sonata form has canonized a one-sided, established realization of a too-narrowly limited concept of form. If no corresponding clearly defined form has been presented here, it reflects the whole tendency of this small study: the search for a widening of the boundaries both in relation to the tonal form concept itself, and also even more in relation to the highly variable content whose diversity, frequently almost improvisatory in its effect, can hardly be done justice by the traditional sonata form definition.

Notes

1. Cf. F. Blume, "Fortspinnung und Entwicklung," *JbP* 36 (1929): 51–70; 64f. relevant here.

2. I–IV, 1837–47. See vol. II: 497–501: "Die Sonatenform."

3. [*Die erste Form, die Form des ersten Allegro, Form der Evolution, Form der freieren musikalischen Gedankenentwicklung, die Hauptform, die Allegroform*] Cf. J. C. Lobe, *Lehrbuch der musikalischen Komposition* I (Leipzig, 1850): 305 ff.; and B. Widmann, *Formenlehre der Instrumentalmusik nach dem System Schnyder's von Wartensee* (1862), 62.

4. In: *StMw* III (1915).

5. F. Tutenberg, *Die Sinfonik Johann Christian Bachs* (Wolfenbüttel-Berlin, 1928).

6. In: *ZfMw* V (1922/23): 226–69.

7. Unfortunately, the enticing but very dangerous tendency toward the demonstration of extensive "unity of substance" [*Substanzgemeinschaft*] has gained a certain currency. It has been strikingly exaggerated in W. Engelsmanns study, *Beethovens Kompositions-pläne, dargestellt an den Sonaten für Violine und Klavier* (Augsburg, 1931). According to Engelsmann, "each of Bee-

thoven's sonatas, in all its sections, movements, and themes, [is] developed from a single main theme or main motive." More recently H. Engel has attempted to show a tendency toward thematic unity of this type in the pre- and early Classic period in two publications—*Haydn, Mozart und die Klassik* (in *Mozart-Jb.* 10 [1959]: 46–79) and *Die Quellen des klassischen Stils* (in International Musicological Society, Report of the Eighth Congress [New York 1961]: 285–304). "It has not previously been observed that the interrelationship of the first and last movements in the symphony (and the sonata) is extremely frequent and actually belongs to the practice of the pre- and early classic period" (*Mozart-Jb., 71*). "It has been overlooked until now that Mozart and Haydn also use this connection between movements very often" (IMS, Report, 301). Jan LaRue argues against these assertions by Engel in his article, "Significant and Coincidental Resemblance Between Classical Themes (in *JAMS* XIV [1961]: 224–34). He urges rightly that the conscious use of thematic connections of this type is a practice of the nineteenth, not the eighteenth century. In order to demonstrate a relationship, the examples in evidence would unquestionably have to exhibit greater significance. R. Rosenberg, who in his book, *Die Klaviersonaten Ludwig van Beethovens* (1–2, Olten-Lausanne, 1957) displays similar tendencies, admits rather openly that the proof of community of substance of this sort tends very strongly toward the realm of the subjective (p. 6): "The recognition of one and the same motive in various transformations creates a pleasurable aesthetic sensation (obviously not attainable for everyone)."

8. Phil. Diss. Berlin, 1933; Leipzig 1935.

9. Cf. for example the excellent example from Mozart's Sonata in D (K.V. 311), to which Westphal refers, emphasizing the altered functional character of the motive. Op. cit., p. 61f.

10. *Grundzüge der musikalischen Formenlehre* (Stuttgart, 1926), p. 186f.

11. *Op. cit.,* chapter 6, *"Themenverwandtschaft, motivische Beziehungen,"* p. 116ff.

12. *Op. cit.,* pp. 66ff.

13. III (1793): 305f.

14. Cf. J. LaRue, *A System of Symbols for Formal Analysis,* in *JAMS* X (1957): 25–28.

22

Traditional Prejudices
in Connection with Viennese Classical Music

If we would try briefly to indicate the idea, the purpose of scholarly work, including our own field, musicology, we might perhaps express it as follows: We must on the one hand endeavor to collect and bring together all relevant facts, all the needed "knowledge," and on the other hand, we must never cease to put our alleged "knowledge" to tests, again and again, and, when needed, to correct it.

Up to a certain point it is possible to combine these two in principle opposing tendencies, though in many cases one of them clearly takes precedence over the other. Within the different fields of research there is an alternation of periods of new, independent research leading to new or revised conceptions, and periods in which research comes to a standstill because it has been passing on traditional "knowledge" for too long.

Such a renewal of an area of research can be stimulated by a new approach in a special, limited field that necessarily entails further consequences. An obvious example is the situation of Bach research today: here the thorough investigation of sources and of the problems of chronology in many respects established a basis for a renewal of all Bach research.

However, with regard to the music of Viennese Classicism, the situation is quite different. Although here, too, source studies, especially those concerning Haydn's works, opened up new possibilities, a fundamental renewal of research of Viennese Classical music did not occur. We still live largely on the re-search-capital of previous generations. It is, I believe, a widespread assumption that in this field there are only a few problems left, and that there remains little to be done by us today. But nothing could miss the mark more completely. Neither the overall historical view, nor the common conception of the essence and nature of the respective musical forms can stand up to a closer examination. In my opinion, after having been actively involved in the research of the Viennese

Originally published in German in *Symbolae historiae musicae. Hellmut Federhofer zum 60 Geburtstag* (Mainz, 1971), pp. 194–203.

Classical music for about forty years, we have arrived at a stage that necessitates a thorough reorientation in order to advance any further. We have gathered a sum of "facts" that willingly pass from one textbook of music history to the next. But if one goes to the bottom of these "facts," it turns out that much of our general knowledge must be regarded as a sort of "textbook wisdom," that has little or no bearing on the development and the nature of the music in question.

May I try a little experiment? I could imagine a survey of music history that reads the following:

"So-called Viennese Classicism comprises the years from ca. 1750 to 1828 (that is, from Bach's to Schubert's deaths). After a pre- or early Classical period in which the music is characterized by several different currents and influences (*Empfindsamkeit,* Storm and Stress, new-Classicism, etc.) the final breakthrough of the Classical style occurs about 1781 (with Haydn's *Russian* quartets). During the 1780s this style reaches its first maturity due to the close friendship and the mutual influence of Haydn and Mozart. Viennese Classicism reaches its consummation in Beethoven, who at the same time paves the way for a transition to the style of the nineteenth century.

Among the instrumental forms, the symphony comes into the front rank. Haydn and Mozart adopt and further develop the form which the Mannheim composers, by the insertion of a minuet as third movement, had expanded into a four-movement cycle. Its first movement, determined by the so-called sonata form, is made up of three sections: exposition, development, and recapitulation. The exposition establishes two themes, the primary and the secondary subject, whose interplay determines the overall structure. The thematic sections are separated by connecting transition sections, etc."

Let this suffice. And now I should like to ask: How would you react to a presentation of this kind? Would you regard it as a reasonable compilation of the major facts within a limited framework? Or would you think that this or that detail was after all not quite correct? Or would you have more serious doubts about the entire presentation? In my opinion this short passage comes very close to what is found, or could be found in most textbooks. Nevertheless, almost every sentence contains some distortion of the truth, or at least some expression that all too easily might lead to a misunderstanding. However, this kind of a presentation must meet our disapproval not only for its great number of dubious details, but also and even more for its cliché-like character. It is quite evident that this kind of presentation relies entirely on textbook traditions and not on first-hand investigations or even on a reevaluation of traditional conceptions. Everyone who has seriously tried to enter into the problems of Viennese Classicism, and who is used to scrutinizing the traditional presentation and to not letting pass even deeply rooted "facts" without close examination, will consider a short survey similar to the one quoted above as completely misleading.

My advocacy of a new orientation for research within this area might lead to the assumption that I was pleading for the employment of new and advanced methods, such as the use of electronic devices or popular structural analysis. I do not believe, however, that these methods will bring about the necessary renewal. In many branches of the sciences the almost revolutionary use of electronic devices plays an important role in the accumulation of knowledge; and without any doubt there are areas within musicology that can benefit from these devices as well. But, as stated above, the major problem of the investigation of Viennese Classicism is not the accumulation of knowledge, but a penetrating re-examination of those conceptions and methods of research that, on the whole, have tacitly been accepted and passed on for generations—and in this regard electronic devices are of no help whatsoever. And since structural analyses depend in principle on the assumption that the single parts of a composition are profoundly related to each other by a common basic material such as a theme, etc., this process has validity only with regard to compositions that are based on such conceptions. In applying this method to compositions that are not determined by such conceptions, we again become victims of a prejudice, although not of a traditional one. There are many examples that document the fact that the employment of such methods of analysis all too often can lead to a violation of the material.

The possibilities for a renewal of research devoted to Viennese Classicism are—as I see it—not to be found in a mere "modernization" of the methods, but in a thorough criticism of the traditional conceptions and, last but not least, in the reorientation that would develop from this criticism. First of all, we must try to relinquish a perspective that in many respects will depend on nineteenth-century conceptions. We must take the music of the Viennese Classicists—for example, the music of Bach or Josquin de Près—as something existing in its own right; and we must disengage ourselves from a retrospective viewing of these works based on our knowledge of later developments.

I should like to divide my critical remarks concerning the traditional conceptions and prejudices regarding Viennese Classicism into three sections: 1) general problems—the character and delimitation of Viennese Classicism; 2) problems of frame-structure, work-complex, and movement; and 3) problems of filling the frame—thematic and motivic structure, tonal plan, forces of linear progression, etc. (As a precaution I should like to add that I am of course fully aware of the fact that problems of the framing structure and of the filling of the frame cannot be regarded separately, but that "form" and "content" are but two sides of the same matter. Nevertheless, I shall disregard these problems within this limited discussion. Let me, furthermore, stress that my considerations are primarily concerned with the instrumental style of Viennese Classicism, which can certainly be considered a prominent representative of the Classical style-conception, and which also exerted a far-reaching influence on the style of opera and church music.)

General Problems

I shall not discuss the problem of "classic" in general on this occasion. So much has already been written about that problem. However, already here we meet one of the traditional prejudices. It is generally assumed that the stylistic development within music necessarily takes a course approximately parallel to the stylistic development of literature, painting, etc. Therefore one seeks for definitions concerning Classicism in music that stress this parallelism. However, must one take this parallelism for granted? Undoubtedly obvious parallels can be demonstrated within different style periods. Yet if we wish to find in music some representative of the Classical style in the sense of the general cultural development of that time, we should study Gluck, who could never be considered a typical representative of Viennese Classicism. Therefore I should like to suggest the reverse procedure: let us accept Haydn and Mozart as the central—and maybe the only entirely representative—exponents of Viennese Classicism, and let us try to derive from their music guiding principles that must be regarded as characteristic for Viennese Classicism in general. The question whether and to what degree other composers may be considered typical Viennese Classicists will be resolved with the establishment of these guiding principles.

When Haydn and Mozart are mentioned together, it is quite natural, for without any doubt these two together are the virtual embodiment of Viennese Classicism. But on the other hand, this standing combination entails the danger of an overestimation of the common features in their stylistic development. Thus we can read in a special study:[1] "For a decade there was close contact and mutual influence between Haydn and Mozart (similar to that of Schiller and Goethe in Weimar)." The pure facts, however, give a different picture. We only can state for certain that Haydn and Mozart occasionally played string quartets together in 1785 (perhaps as early as 1784), and that a couple of times Haydn joined the rehearsals of *Così fan tutte* at Mozart's invitation in 1789/90. Every other attempt to construct a permanent relationship between them is, in my opinion, rather unsubstantiated—apart from the well-known evidence of their mutual esteem as demonstrated in Mozart's dedication of his quartets to Haydn and in Haydn's letter to Roth in Prague referring to Mozart as an opera composer. None of these documents, however, gives any account of the alleged "close contact" over the period of a decade. Therefore we may certainly include this assumption among the typical, deeply rooted prejudices.

We decided to define Viennese Classicism as the music of Haydn and Mozart, or better to define the Viennese Classical style as the style gaining maturity in Haydn's and Mozart's instrumental compositions. That immediately induces the problem of delimitation in time, and again the question of how it came into being and when it came to an end—regardless of the fact that its aftermath is so evident that it is tempting to go on speaking of a Viennese Classical style well into the nineteenth century.

Any view of such a stylistic development depends very much on the approach of the viewer, whether he aims at a demonstration of connections or of contrasts. And here, I think, we face still another important prejudice. Attempts to explain the development of the Viennese Classical style started at a time that, to a large degree, was determined by evolutionary theories. Basic conceptions of the formation of Viennese Classicism are rooted in these theories, though this is seldom much noticed.

First there is the question of the foundations. From the nineteenth century on, when one realized the difference between the late Baroque style of Bach and Handel, and the style of Haydn and Mozart, efforts were made to find the "missing link" according to the theories of evolution. This is evident in Riemann's announcement of his "discovery" of Johann Stamitz: "Johann Stamitz is the predecessor of Haydn who has been sought for such a long time."[2] Riemann's unreserved attribution of the primacy as founder of the Viennese Classical style to Stamitz has certainly been abandoned. But then one thought to have solved the problem by distributing the role of the "predecessor" among different composers or "schools" in addition to the Mannheim school: the early Viennese composers, the Italians, the "Berlin school," etc. As far as I can see, however, we are not dealing with a smaller or larger group of predecessors, but above all with a reaction rather than with an evolution. It is obvious that Haydn and Mozart adopted elements of musical style from their immediate precursors. Yet one must beware of attempts to uncover ties to music that most likely was unknown to Haydn and Mozart. For it is a widespread prejudice to tacitly presume that they knew everything we now know through studies and editions from the nineteenth and twentieth centuries. The decisive factor in the development of Viennese Classical style is, I think, not the use of certain musical means of expression, but the *style conception* that manifests itself in Haydn's and Mozart's music. I shall not discuss this idea in great length, but will restrict myself to a few observations.

Following the end of the great Austrian Baroque style around 1740, a pronounced reaction came about in Vienna as in other leading musical cities of the time. Whereas formerly—I regret I have to generalize—the universal trend was to strong pathos, large-scale forms, and first-rate professional performances of singers and instrumentalists, now a predominance of easygoing, small-scale music came about, a music that could be generally understood by dilettantes and which was even adjusted to their performing capabilities. This style is often called the "galant" style. However, this expression seems to be rather misleading, since it has little or no relation to what is called "galant art" in general (e.g., Watteau or Boucher). During the years around 1740–70, this rather empty music is widely marking the image of Viennese music; and if we wish to form a real idea of the rise of the Viennese Classical style, we need to proceed from the notion of a reaction to this style, of a revival of the trend toward great music, and not of an evolutionary process.[3]

Up to now one has conceived the stylistic development around 1750 as a direct turning from Baroque music to Classical music. In order to give a plausible reason for this turning, one resorts to the notion of a crisis. For many years attempts have been made to establish a "Romantic crisis" with regard to Haydn's music around 1770; and at the Ljubljana Congress of the International Musicological Society (1967) the years from 1740 to 1760 were discussed as "years of crisis." I believe the matter is much clearer and simpler. Rather than as a direct transition from Baroque to Classicism, the development should be conceived as a two-fold progress: 1) the reaction (around 1740) against the Baroque style, which had prevailed for so long, in the form of an "intermediate style" (the so-called "galant" style); and then 2) the reaction (about 1765–70) against this style, which is especially noticeable in Haydn's music. He did not go through a "Romantic crisis," but he simply realized his artistic will to overcome the intermediate style, to a great extent resorting to the style conception and in part to the stylistic means of Baroque music. The task we are confronted with, if at long last we wish to reach a historically convincing conception of the development of Viennese Classicism, must consist in sorting out the threads meeting in this music. The sequence Baroque—preclassicism—Classicism should definitely be replaced by the sequence Baroque—intermediate style—Classicism. I must emphasize again that in this brief presentation continued generalization has been unavoidable. Therefore these considerations should be regarded as suggestions, as a starting point, rather than as a clear-cut formula.

I have dealt with the problem of the Mannheim school at some length in an earlier paper.[4] Let me summarize it like this: there is no doubt about its significance with regard to the development of dynamics within symphonic music, but it exerted almost no influence on the stylistic development of Viennese Classicism.

The other end of the Haydn-Mozart period is marked by Beethoven, and much can be said in favor of regarding his music as a continuation of Viennese Classicism. Yet it is again the stylistic intention that from early on leads Beethoven's music in a different direction despite the similarities of musical expression. One need only think of works such as the *Eroica* symphony or the *Coriolan* overture, in which from the beginning a different expressive intention asserts itself. Briefly summarized and generalized: it is the individualization of expression that comes to the fore in Beethoven's music, combined with a thorough change in stylistic and expressive means and leading to a dynamic infusion of the music in a wider sense.

The Viennese Classical music, as it asserts itself in Haydn's and Mozart's music, is largely determined by the spirit of the musical art of ensemble playing, by the principle of a musical community. In Beethoven's music the concentration on individual expression—embodied by the composer, the conductor, the virtuoso—comes to the fore rather early. This is the spiritual background, the effects of which can be felt in the dynamic infusion of the music. We will, therefore, obtain a clearer—and more real—picture of Viennese Classicism if we regard Beethoven's music as a special case, as a Post-classical phase. About this it is possible to agree in principle. The next step, however, leads to the difficult problem of sticking to the consequences of this decision. And indeed, here we face another serious prejudice. Even though we realize that Haydn and Mozart's music follows rules different from Beethoven's music, we measure it largely with the standards of Beethoven's and post-Beethoven music, because the conceptions related to these simply have become a second nature to us. It is a major problem of a "renewed" description of Viennese Classical music that we must free ourselves from conceptions determined by Beethoven not only in theory, but also quite realistically in practice. Only then shall we be able to comprehend Viennese Classicism thoroughly and without bias. We shall return to this later.

I should like to call attention to still another fundamental observation. In the eighteenth century, like today, there were different categories of music with more or less individual traditions with regard to place of performance and audience, as well as performance practice and compositional genres. As everyone knows, we have special traditions today also (as, for example, in the case of jazz, electronic music, entertainment music, and so-called classical music). However, what we call classical music today not only comprises what was called Classical music fifty years ago, but also a multitude of different categories of music which in many respects might be divided up according to individual traditions, only linked together by the fact that they are considered "serious" music. In lumping together the different categories and in establishing this music as separate from categories such as entertainment music, etc., one necessarily covers up the original division of this music into rather divergent categories.

Regarding the eighteenth century, we often meet the characteristic subdivision of music into three categories: church, chamber, and theater music. Each of them has its own traditions regarding place of performance (as reflected by the designations), forms and the style of composition, and style of performance.

In a certain, if not entirely decisive connection with this, one also could subdivide the music of this time into three other categories corresponding to their respective characters, such as constructive, "playful," and expressive music. Again I want to stress that I am talking about tendencies and not about strict laws. Bach's *Art of Fugue,* of course, is an example of constructive music, whereas the Baroque concerto largely is defined by its playful tendencies, notwithstanding the grandiose constructive conception of works such as the *Brandenburg Concertos.* The tendency toward a stronger emphasis on the expressive character of course, prevails in operatic music. The music between Baroque and

Classicism is characterized by a nearly total cessation of the constructive element and a strong reduction of the expressive one, whereas only a rather primitive playfulness is retained. The style change about 1765/70, however, restores the trends that had been discarded shortly before: the string quartet includes fugal writing, the symphonies are characterized by the use of distant keys—not least, even minor keys—and manifest a new interest in more expressive music. Thus instrumental music adopts a tendency that in earlier times almost exclusively was peculiar to opera. Last but not least, this change also involves a renewal of the playfulness, *nota bene,* not in the manner of the music of the intermediate period, but in the manner of the Baroque concerto. We must return to this statement later.

Problems of Frame-Structure: Formation of Work-Complex and Movement

Of these problems we can check off the problems of the cycle most easily, because they were actually solved a long time ago, even if a general awareness of this fact cannot be assumed. Within the polemic concerning the role of the Mannheim or the Viennese preclassicists as predecessors of the Classical composers, which took place at the beginning of this century, it was played as a trump card that Stamitz was a pioneer in expanding the symphonic cycle into four movements by the insertion of the minuet as third movement. From the Viennese camp, on the other hand, one picked out a symphony by Monn, dated 1740; a work expanded by a little minuet into four movements.

This discussion, however, was actually quite in vain. We know that Mozart retained the possibility of a three-movement cycle up to his late years (the *Prague* symphony). And it is quite characteristic that Haydn, in his only symphony that clearly reveals Stamitz's influence, the very first one (No. 1), written in Stamitz's native country, has only three movements, whereas the four-movement symphony No. 3, composed shortly after the first one, is clearly determined by Viennese Baroque traditions. Yet we have an even stronger evidence against the evolutionary conception of a simple progression from the three-movement Italian operatic symphony to the four-movement classical symphony in Stamitz's symphonic oeuvre, which should then have been adopted by the Viennese Classicists. For Haydn's typical early instrumental form was the five-movement cycle comprising two minutes which can be found in his early divertimenti, including the string quartets. The four-movement cycle can be achieved by omitting either the first or the second minuet, resulting either in the ordinary four-movement form, or in the cycle with the minuet in the second and the slow movement in the third position. The latter form can be found up to his rather late string quartets. The inconsistency in this respect within Haydn's and Mozart's symphonies and quartets was not understood, because one employed a form that only became normative in the nineteenth century as a general standard for Haydn and Mozart as well.

With regard to the problems of the single movement, the problems of sonata form predominate. The designation "sonata form" as a term from the theory of musical form and of analysis came up much later than the form itself, and for this reason the conception of it was determined wholly by the ideas of postclassical time. This involved not only a limitation of the term, which thus became rather unsuitable for the analysis of music from the Classical period, but also—as a consequence of the retrospective consideration—the monopolization of a certain typical variant of a formal concept, that was originally much more flexible. The so-called sonata form as it was described in textbooks became a model normalized for teaching purposes; and despite the fact that it must be considered as unsuitable for research into the history of form, it nevertheless has been used extensively. Maybe the schematic application of this model may be regarded as the most substantial prejudice in connection with studies in Viennese Classical music. I have dwelled on these problems at some length in my essay *Sonatenform-Probleme*[5] and here I restrict myself to a brief summary.

Of course, the rough overall structure of the form, comprising the three sections exposition, development, and recapitulation, and based on the well-known tonal pattern, is standard with only few exceptions. Yet as soon as we are to examine the further subdivisions of this form, we must fall short in the application of the customary formal conception as a fixed model. The mass of formal misinterpretations resulting from obstinate attempts to make every structure which must pass for a sonata form correspond to the accepted basic scheme is enormous. First of all, it is the assumption of the principle of thematic dualism that leads to fictitious interpretations. In the Classical period of Haydn and Mozart the essential element is in many instances the emphasis on unity by an absolutely dominant principal subject; and contrasting secondary subjects—if they occur—have a much less important position, as foreseen in the theoretical model. But after all, it remains questionable to what degree the thematic conception may be regarded as a determining factor for the movement-structure. From Beethoven on, it became customary to consider the themes as the absolutely essential factor, and everything in between—the so-called transitional sections, the cadences, etc.—as secondary elements. Yet with regard to Haydn, and to Mozart as well, the "playful" forces (in the sense of the Baroque concerto, as stated above) are often of equal or even greater importance than the theme, which, similar to a ritornello theme in the Baroque concerto, marks the beginnings of the periods but does not detach itself from the remainder. A good example is found in Haydn's Symphony no. 45, the *Farewell* symphony. In trying to apply the traditional model of primary subject, transition, secondary subject, etc., one strives in vain and does violence to the form. Two elements determine the form, or perhaps better, the experience of the form: the almost uniform flowing motion embodying the playfulness, and the striking motivic concentration, so to speak, the technique of motivic metamorphosis that also serves as a unifying tendency, yet on the constructive level. Without realizing the special character of forming in this movement, if starting out only from the traditional sonata-form concept, one is not going to understand, but to misunderstand its peculiar musical personality.

There are many other examples of movements where the interpretation, if solely based on the traditional model, must remain quite superficial, or even will be entirely misleading, but we must be contented here with this one example. In our remarks concerning formal problems of the movement in relation to the thematic structure, we have approached already the third section of our group: the problems of filling the formal frame. That was necessary because the traditional conception of sonata form is unsolvably tied to the notion of the thematic structure. Finally I should like to point out some further instances of the formal structure, which have attracted less attention than the question of thematic progression, although they frequently are of considerable importance for the formal shaping as well as for the experience of the form as a whole.

Problems of Filling the Frame (Problems of the Form as a Whole)

In the preceding reflections I have called into question the significance of the themes as determinants of form, because this form conception must be regarded as expressing aspects of the nineteenth, not of the eighteenth century. In search for formal descriptions in the literature of the late eighteenth century, such as H. Chr. Koch's *Kompositionslehre* (1782–93), one finds that authors are talking about "incisions" *(Einschnitte)* and "paragraphs" *(Abschnitte)*, i.e., about the periodic structure, rather than about themes *(Hauptsätze)*. In the eighteenth century the conception of form more or less regarded the grammatical structure—the concept of sentences and periods—as authoritative, and adopted designations similar to those found in the realm of grammar. With regard to the form as a whole, therefore, the changing formation of the periods remains as essential as the thematic structure, and in many cases perhaps even more so. If we wish to characterize the periods and to distinguish among them, we are confronted with elements of form other than the themes, which independently of these or hand in hand with them determine the form. One of these elements is the so-called harmonic rhythm, i.e., the variable sequence of chord changes within the harmonic progression, which has been investigated primarily by American scholars. The contrast of *"Liedformung"* and *"Fortspinnungsformung"* must also be mentioned in this connection, and it would deserve a thorough investigation of its effect on Classical form. However, I want by means of two examples from Mozart's symphonies to briefly point out two other formal features which are related to each other to some degree: the planning of tonal—not the harmonic—development on the one hand and, connected with this, the leading of the bass line (so to speak, the "bass contour"), which is often an explicit reflection of the tonal progression. Anybody wishing to experience the period development of a movement may consciously or subconsciously find his way to feeling these elements as a starting-point, as the foundation of the formal development.

Let us first look at the opening movement of Mozart's *Linz* symphony (K.425) as an example of tonal planning. (I shall disregard the slow introduction, but retain the measure numbers which result from including it.)

Within the tonal plan we can easily realize the following basic principles: a) tonal unity (in form of a closed circle, an expanded or repeated cadence, a pedal point, etc.); b) trend of transition from the momentary to a new leading tonality; c) free modulation without a definite direction; d) clear development toward a new tonic confirmed by a cadence; e) direct tonal contrasting; and f) cadencelike conclusion. In using these letters as symbols we can represent the exposition of the respective movement by the following formula: mm.20–46: a) / 47–53: b) / 54–57: a) / 57–66: c) / 66–71: d) / 71–87: e) / 87–119: f) / 119–22: b).

As an example of the significance of the bass contour I should like to refer to the first movement of Mozart's *Haffner* symphony (K.385). The following prominent shapes of the bass line can be stressed. (The letters again serve as symbols): pedal point: p; stepwise falling or rising bass line: fl/rs; oscillation of dominant and tonic: d/t; cadential formulas: c; secondary, uncharacteristic bass line: x. Using these symbols we arrive at the following survey of the respective movement: mm.1–13: fl–p–c; 13–29: fl; 29–35: c; 35–41: rs + c; 41–48: fl; 48–58: p (+ c); 59–66: d/t + c; 66–74: p + c; 74–80: rs; 80–88: c; 88–94: p.

With these two Mozart examples I only wanted to demonstrate the necessity to get rid of the one-sided thematic analysis if we want to comprehend the essence of Viennese Classical music. Of course, there are many further elements which are important for the overall effect and for the conception of a movement as a whole: categories of tempo and meter, variations of the development of the motion, shaping of the periods of expansion, tendencies to bring contrasting or unity to the fore, etc. There are starting-points enough that have not yet been explored seriously. We must part with the prejudice that we can get our work done using only the textbooks of musical analysis as tools, and we must be determined to approach our tasks as music historians.

Notes

1. Hans Engel, "Haydn, Mozart und die Klassik," *Mozart Jahrbuch 1959* (Salzburg, 1960): 46ff.

2. *Denkmäler der Tonkunst in Bayern* 3 (1902): preface.

3. "Some Observations on the Development and Characteristics of Vienna Classical Instrumental Music," *Studia Musicologica* 9 (1967): 115ff. Also reprinted in this volume.

4. "Zur Bedeutung der 'Mannheimer Schule,' *Festschrift Karl Gustave Fellerer* (1962): 303ff. Also reprinted in this volume.

5. *Festschrift Friedrich Blume* (Kassel, 1963): 221ff. Also reprinted in this volume.

23

Period Style—Generation Style

On the one hand, the term "style" is so widely known, of such general usage, that it should not require any definition. But on the other hand, it is so commodious and multifarious that it is advantageous to specify from case to case the particular aspect of style problems one will discuss. Let us take, in order to demonstrate this briefly, the definition out of a small dictionary. Here it reads:

> Style (Latin for "slate pencil"), characteristic way of expression, especially in the shaping of an artwork; 1) as style of a period (or of a particular area) determined by a common feeling of form, worldview, and the materials used (e.g., Gothic style, Rhenish style); 2) as the individual trait of the artist (e.g., Rubens's style or Wagner's style); also in a more general sense: way of conducting one's life (lifestyle).[1]

Already from this short definition arises the ambiguity of the term. The basic idea, however, remains the same in spite of the many different manifestations: one wants to cover a multiplicity of separate facts with a clear, simple, and unmistakable formula. And here we face two contrasting risks of derailment: devoting too much consideration to the variety of phenomena will be detrimental to the preciseness of the term; too clear-cut a definition, on the other hand, will lead to either a violation of the facts, or to formulating the style concept so generally so that the term more or less becomes meaningless. A special danger is the transplantation of stylistic expressions from one art form to another. All too easily one takes for granted a similarity of the manifestations of style without the necessary reservations. This becomes particularly apparent with regard to the term "period style" with which we are primarily concerned here.

Only during our century has the discussion of music history in.terms of musical style become predominant. As late as about 1900 the two periods that we usually call Baroque and Classic are divided up into three volumes of the old *Oxford History of Music* under the following headings: "The Music of the Seventeenth Century," "The Era of Bach and Handel," "The Viennese Period." And

Originally published in German in the *Händel-Jahrbuch, 1971*, pp. 25–33.

about ten years later they are divided between two volumes of Riemann's *Handbuch der Musikgeschichte:* "The Age of Thorough Bass," and "The Music of the Eighteenth and Nineteenth Centuries"—again the subdivision is based on time periods rather than on style periods. However, that these two great music histories are not organized according to musical style concepts does not imply that they are unaware of research in style. On the contrary, Riemann in particular often resorts to a purely style historical presentation. But the breakthrough of style investigation as a central focus of musicology only took place about that time. It is quite curious that it asserted itself in two or three publications appearing simultaneously in 1911: *Der Stil in der Musik* of the Viennese *ordinarius* Guido Adler, *Style in Musical Art* of the former Oxford professor Hubert Parry, and the *Histoire de la langue musicale* of the Paris professor Maurice Emmanuel. Adler's *Methode der Musikgeschichte,* published in 1919, belongs in this connection, too. Style investigation, the new gospel of musicology, became the leading trend of a large number of special studies after World War I—initially rather too much at the expense of the general historical foundation of musicology. In the subsequent music histories by Adler, Bücken, Lang, Wörner, etc., the subdivision according to style periods predominates. Terms such as "Baroque," "Classic," and "Romantic" replace headings such as "Music of the Seventeenth and Eighteenth Centuries" or "Music of the Age of Thorough Bass." Of course, it can be questioned in each case whether this means an actual or rather a formal new orientation, for actually terms such as "Music of the Age of Thorough Bass" and "Music of the Baroque" cover almost exactly the same period. If one wants to conceive these designations not only in a chronological sense—"Music in the Age of Baroque"—but rather in a substantial sense—"Baroque Music"—, one has to cope with another problem. Is it really possible to use a single stylistic term for such a long period as the Baroque—1600 to about 1750—, or can one arrive at relevant designations only by a further division of this period, for example according to Bukofzer into early, middle, and late Baroque?

A later contribution to the problems of style periods was Blume's extensive series of articles "Barock," "Klassik," and "Renaissance," published first in *MGG,*[2] and later with a few supplementary remarks in his collection of essays *Syntagma musicologicum.*[3] In the essay on Baroque music (1949/1950), Blume emphasized strongly the relation of the musical Baroque style to the Baroque style in general. He does not ignore, however, that a stylistic term transplanted from the other arts has certain disadvantages compared with an expression based on purely musical considerations:

> In music history some ambiguity will of necessity continue to cling to all extraneous terminologies applied to its styles, whereas all terminologies formed from intrinsically musical criteria, while they may be more pregnant, must isolate music from its inherent relationship to other spiritual activities. All future music historiography will be faced with the choice of either

setting up purely musical style-categories labelled in purely musical terms that do indeed stand unequivocally for specific musical matters but remain dissociated from the intellectual ambience and origin of these styles and intelligible only to the professional musician, or using to characterize its own style-periods and style-forms terms that are at the same time applicable in other fields and familiar to the nonmusician also, even though because of this they suffer from a certain ambiguity. But since in the last analysis every categorization of spiritual phenomena is a belated abstraction from the versatile fullness of real life, such ambiguity can be accepted into the bargain if it helps overcome the isolation of music within its own technical history and makes this art comprehensible as a product of the impelling spiritual forces of its time.[4]

A more differentiated conception of the Baroque is expressed in Blume's "Begriff und Grenzen des Barock in der Musik," published in 1961. It concludes with the following observation:

> Only when from C.P.E. Bach, Gluck, and the early Haydn one looks back on the Baroque does the massive and majestic unity of this epoch disclose itself, a unity despite all contradictions. It is as if one wanders through the mountains: one can see jags, precipices, peaks, gulches, falls, and alpine pastures, and it all seems to form a chaos. Only when one moves into the distance, however, does the region appear as a "mountain block," as a self-contained unity that is demarcated against mountain blocks. In this sense the Baroque forms a magnificent unity within the history of music. There is no reason to conceal its internal contradictions.[5]

When the *MGG* article "Barock" was reprinted in *Syntagma Musicologicum*, Blume added a few remarks in the epilog that once more point out the problems in connection with the establishment of a Baroque style of music.

> The conception of the fundamental unity of the musical Baroque that I aimed at in my presentation has remained unshaken by more recent literature. A certain change of my own conception as formulated in my essay "Begriff und Grenzen des musikalischen Barock," likewise does not place this unity in question, even though it emphasizes the inner contradictions and the counteractive currents within the period more strongly than the above discussion.[6]

I have quoted Blume's reflections at some length because they confirm my earlier remarks concerning the dangers inherent in fixing the limits of a style period by means of a central, practical example. On the one hand, one observes a variety without sufficient unity, a "chaos"; and on the other hand from the distance one perceives a connected, uniform "mountain block," the unity of which, however, must be called more or less illusory. However, maybe Blume's comparison does not quite hold true. For all the cultural tendencies and developments that we subsume under the collective designation "Baroque" are, after all, determined by cultural, social, and artistic ideas and traditions, which together determine the specific "Baroque" properties; whereas the mountain block only from the distance can be perceived as unity, falling into disparate parts at close view.

Speaking of "ideas and traditions," I would like to emphasize an essential distinction between these two terms. Ideas are abstract, unreal; traditions are material, real. Speaking of Baroque music we should neither think exclusively of the music from the Baroque period, nor of music which possibly embodies a general idea of the Baroque, but rather of a music which is part of, or arose from musical Baroque traditions. Not the abstract idea of a Baroque music, but the living tradition of this music should decide the conception of a musical Baroque style. Perhaps the uncertainty of the definition of the term, which to some extent becomes manifest in Blume's changing conceptions, has something to do with the proceeding from an abstract idea rather than from real traditions.

The problems of definition that we have discussed here in connection with Baroque music are found similarly in other style periods. They become especially evident with respect to the "Classic." If we proceed from the idea of the "Classical" as embodied by architecture, sculpture, etc., we must regard Gluck as a main representative of Classicism. Nevertheless, the great tradition of Classical music now as before is determined by Mozart and Haydn. The idea remains in the background—but the music does not care!

Even more diverse is the image of the period between the Baroque and Classicism, around 1750. Here we are facing two predominant musical traditions: a conservative one continuing Baroque stylistic traditions, and a "modern" one preferring a simplification—even an oversimplification—of the musical style as a reaction to the long-lasting predominance of the Baroque style. The reaction to this preclassical style leads, about 1770, to the Classical synthesis. For the transitional stages within the development Baroque—Preclassicism—Classicism one often resorted to terms from the realm of literature or art history, such as "galant style," "storm and stress," or *"Empfindsamkeit."* These designations, however, have little or no relation to contemporary musical tendencies. To achieve progress in this area of understanding we must liberate ourselves from the abstract literary ideas and undertake a more extensive study of the purely musical traditions.

For this reason, let us conclude by picking out from some of the prominent features in the forming of musical style concepts the basic criteria, especially those, having important meaning for judging the stylistic development in the eighteenth century.

The definition from the dictionary quoted at the beginning of this discussion gave an example of the term "style" both as the style of a period and as the style of a certain area. Does the conception of a local style, then, contain the danger of overemphasis on abstract ideas, or are we dealing with a realistic criterion which entails no danger?

Again we return to the conception of "tradition." For local stylistic traditions have existed for a long time in the development of European music history. Early on, Gregorian chant recognized a Roman, Ambrosian, Gallican, and

Mozarabic tradition, and later a Germanic and a Frankish tradition. An example from the sixteenth century is the Roman tradition embodied by Palestrina, and the contrasting Venetian tradition embodied by Gabrieli. In the seventeenth and the eighteenth centuries we encounter the Italian and the French operatic tradition, and the North German and the South German organ traditions, etc.

These local traditions in most cases are very real, and for the most part it should not be difficult to establish relevant features of style. Nevertheless, here, too, objectivity may be endangered. The stylistic investigation can stick to features which are not essential, or it can regard elements as being determined by local traditions that actually belong to the common tradition of the time. A particular danger, however, is at hand if an investigation is also more or less determined by some sort of local patriotism. This can be national prejudice, or bias in favor of a certain "school," and more. The Mannheim-Viennese controversy at the beginning of this century may be regarded as an instructive example. Thus one can apparently state here too that the danger increases the more the discussion is determined by fixed ideas (national style, "school" of composers). Proceeding from given local traditions and refraining from a basic integration into an extramusical complex of ideas is a better way.

With regard to the eighteenth century itself one application of the term "style" in particular is known: the division of music into three "styles"—church, chamber, and theater style. Of course, this division is quite a realistic distinction, too, starting out from the function of music more than from the music itself. Nevertheless, it is strange to say that in this case of an actual contemporary stylistic division we tend deliberately to neglect it. The present-day tendency to lump together Handel's operatic and oratorio styles is an example that does not need further comment.

We must return once more to the term "period style" which in the preceding discussion was dealt with only with regard to the more abstract subdivision according to general cultural periods. However, there is quite an objective and realistic division according to time periods that we have not mentioned: the division according to generations. It may be questioned whether a composer represents the stylistic tradition of the Baroque, or whether he already is on a different course, yet his chronological dates, as far as they are known, are objective data which do not depend on our interpretation.

The composers born about the same time more or less have an essential feature in common: they all proceed from the same stage within the development of musical style. It must not be overlooked, however, that the common foundations are complete only in connection with a common area of activity. The three important composers, C.P.E. Bach, Gluck, and Jomelli, born in the same year (1714), spent their youths in quite different musical realms. Nevertheless, a central aspect of their artistic development is that they all had to cope with the late Baroque tradition that they grew up with, and either had to overcome it, or had to shape it anew. The same is true with respect to Wagenseil, J. Stamitz, and G.M. Monn, who are of approximately the same age as well.

It might seem as if the subdivision according to generations were an entirely objective procedure without any risk of going wrong. But here, too, tendencies to establish an abstract system have occurred. Alfred Lorenz in his book *Musikgeschichte im Rhythmus der Generationen* (1928), discussed the problem of the successive generations within the course of music history at some length.

Lorenz is not content with an investigation of the problem of generations itself, but he also outlines an entire system of the course of European music history according to generations. In relation to studies by O. Lorenz, W. Pinder, and others he suggests a regular succession of three times three generations within each period of three hundred years. Moreover, he correlates this succession to an alternation between the principles of homophony and polyphony. Here we again face an abstract system that may be stimulating to some extent, but cannot be derived from actual developments without violation of the facts. That should not, of course, keep us from investigating the effect of the relations and differences between the generations free of the trend to abstraction.

One year after Lorenz's book, Ernst Bücken in his now little-known study "Geist und Form im musikalischen Kunstwerk" extensively discussed the problem of the generations on a more objective basis. In the course of a short summary of the attempts "to determine the periods of music history according to aspects of the cultural history," he also dwells upon Graf Keyserling's "law of the rotation of the styles." He places it next to the conception of the periodic supersession, of effect and countereffect, of action and reaction of the style periods, which had been formulated by Rudolf Louis. Bücken concludes: "The generation is different from and more than the mere addition of its limbs. It is one of the major laws of the orderly course of the entire music history. It is one of the major future tasks of research to illuminate the linkage of the generations with regard not only to their more narrow music historical aspects, but also to the broader socio-cultural dimension."[7]

We have considered the problem of a collective—not of an individual—style under manifold aspects, especially with respect to its temporal and local relations. On both levels we encounter the danger that abstract—extramusical—ideas can permeate the argument, resulting in a misleading of the purely musical style conception. That is true with regard to the much-used external epoch designations, such as "Baroque," and "Classic," and to the more specific ones, such as "storm and stress," and "galant style." Another danger is that the legitimate emphasis on the significance of a local tradition may turn into the uncritical overemphasis of a national or local "school." As long as musicology has not arrived at an explanation of the lines of development within eighteenth-century music on purely musical terms, it is advisable to be very cautious in applying stylistic terms of the general cultural history. Rather than proceeding from terms such as "Baroque" and "Classicism"—to which it is possible to return to later—we should gain a survey of all the many local traditions, based on extensive source study. Just as important is the endeavor to establish the chronology of the compositions. When we arrive so far that we can give a convincing account of the contributions of successive generations, then we will have a better understanding of the course of European music history. And then we can afford the luxury to ask whether we can justly consider the musical development under the aspect of the currently used epoch designations, and whether this may help us to gain a deeper insight into the music.

Notes

1. *Knaurs Konversations-Lexikon* (Berlin, 1934), col. 1627.

2. Friedrich Blume, "Barock," *MGG* 1: col. 1275–1338; "Klassik," *MGG* 7: col. 1027–90; "Renaissance," *MGG* 9: col. 224–91.

3. Friedrich Blume, *Syntagma musicologicum*, ed. M. Ruhnke (Kassel, 1963), pp. 67–123, 123–186, 10–66.

4. Ibid., p. 79; English translation in *Renaissance and Baroque* (New York, 1967), p. 101.

5. Friedrich Blume, "Begriff und Grenzen des Barock in der Musik," *Syntagma musicologicum*, pp. 209–17.

6. Ibid., p. 889.

7. Ernst Bücken, "Geist und Form im musikalischen Kunstwerk," *Handbuch der Musikwissenschaft* (Potsdam, 1929), p. 80f.

24

The Style Change in Austrian Music between the Baroque and Viennese Classicism

Why a congress solely devoted to the young Haydn? Is this not an artificial, a too narrow scope? This might be an obvious question for anyone not familiar with the problems of Haydn research. However, for the small circle of Haydn specialists gathered together here the subject of our conference needs no justification. We all know that it concerns questions of a musical development that should have been thoroughly investigated long ago, but which actually conceals so many unsolved problems that a satisfactory scholarly clarification of this development is still lacking.

We shall need to examine two closely related questions: 1) as music historians we must attempt to realize clearly what was going on about 1750 in terms of music, and what is actually meant by the expression "style change"; and 2) as musicians and listeners we must ask: how do we approach this music so as to be able to experience and perform it best?

These two basic questions will be the primary concern of our discussion. Here, at the beginning of our meeting I shall turn primarily to the first question, which must be considered the starting point for what follows. Talking about the style change between the Baroque and Classical periods, I shall have to immediately express some reservations.

First, as hinted at before, we have only an insufficient basis for a description of this change, since its clarification is the general purpose of our meeting. Therefore you should not expect me to deliver, so to speak, a "complete" picture. I should like to suggest some main lines within this development. First of all, however, I shall try to clarify the foundations upon which we are building. Many of the "facts" stated by textbooks, and even by special studies, must be considered questionable. It is about time to get rid of a great number of fictitious ideas

Originally published in German in *Der junge Haydn: Internationale Arbeitstagung des Instituts für Aufführungspraxis* (Graz, 1970), pp. 18–29.

if we wish to present an account of this style change in harmony with past and future special studies.

Second, in using the terms "Baroque" and "Classicism" we are approaching a particular problem that might give rise to extensive discussions: the problem of the conception of musical periods.

This problem has been discussed already twice this month at separate meetings: the Beethoven symposium in Vienna, and a colloquium during the Halle *Händelfest*. I do not want now to deal with the problems related to the use of these terms in music history (such as major or minor correspondences of stylistic terms in the realm of music, of literature, and of the art of painting, or the problems of the chronological delimitation of these two periods). Here, "Baroque" and "Classicism" refer to, respectively, the period of Fux and Caldara up to about 1740, and the period of Haydn and Mozart, in its mature stage from about 1770 on. What unfolded in between these two periods—separating, connecting, reconciling—shall be the focus of our discussion.

In order to classify this period shortly before and after the mid-century, in relation to the one before and the other after it, various nonmusical concepts have been employed, such as *Rococo, Sturm und Drang, Empfindsamkeit,* and *galant style*. The problem of such a designation is already evident in this grouping. It is quite obvious that none of these rather different terms can serve as an overall designation. It might perhaps be possible to perceive one or another composition as manifestation of one of these categories of expression; but it is more a question here of specific rather than general stylistic trends. These designations cannot seriously be regarded as keys to an understanding of musical developments. Rather, they may burden the musical conception with associations that hinder more than promote an unbiased approach to these problems. It may be better to avoid the use of these borrowed conceptions, and to strive to penetrate into the stylistic development of this interim period on purely musical terms.

Every attempt to come close to an understanding of the stylistic development of the Austrian music ca. 1750 will, from the start, be confronted with two basic difficulties: 1) the quite insufficient survey of musical sources, the greatest part of which must be considered as unknown and unexplored even by specialists; and 2) the lack of a research tradition that would understand and appreciate the music from its own perspective, and not from the perspective of the nineteenth and twentieth centuries.

I should like to introduce my discussion with a few remarks concerning the situation with sources. Everyone who wishes to understand the preconditions of the development of the Viennese Classical style must not ignore Wagenseil, one of the main figures of this period. In her article in *MGG* Helga Scholz-Michelitsch cites "almost 100 symphonies" by Wagenseil.[1] In my own lists of works by Haydn's predecessors compiled over decades, I have noted sixty-eight symphonies and fifty-nine trios, some of the latter of which are also entitled "symphony." But if someone wants to study Wagenseil as symphonist he can draw upon only the two symphonies published in *DTÖ:* an opera symphony from 1746, and a trio symphony, advertised in the Breitkopf catalog in 1762.[2] There is also another symphony published individually. Whoever wishes to go beyond these is forced to make his own scores from old manuscripts or printed parts.

A second example: one of the predecessors and contemporaries of Haydn is Franz Asplmayr born in 1728. Of his extant compositions *MGG* quotes three symphonies and various chamber works. But in Prague alone there are thirty-three symphonies and more than fifty partitas for wind instruments waiting to be scored and to receive scholarly acknowledgment.

Another example from a related area: at the Ljubljana Congress 1967 there was a series of symposia on so-called musical years of crisis throughout the centuries, among them one on "Critical Years in the European Music History 1740 to 1760." One of the participants stressed the significance of the so-called younger Neapolitans and especially that of Vinci. In the following discussion someone else objected that we have too little information about the complicated Italian operatic traditions of the eighteenth century. The first participant replied: "What we need to begin with is a guide to the hundreds of composers of the eighteenth century that we know next to nothing about, and to the thousands of opera scores. . . . I admit to having studied only one opera by Vinci because a copy of the score is in the library that I have access to."[3]

I believe these three examples will suffice to elucidate our musicological situation. For the sake of comparison let us visualize a meeting of literary historians who want to discuss currents of developments within European literature (or even more narrow: within German literature) from about 1750. Without doubt each of the participants would know the entire literature in question, or at least all the major works. Similarly, art historians would be acquainted with many of the works from first-hand viewing and all the others from fine reproductions in specific art history studies. It is hardly possible that anyone would claim the special significance of an artist on the basis of only a single work known to him. In these cases a comprehensive, generally known basis for the discussion would exist, whereas in our situation such a common basis would be a miracle. The situation would be different if we were to discuss the works of Mozart or Bach, or even the thirteenth-century motet. Then one could assume that each participant would know the works to be discussed. In our case, however, we cannot make progress until the dormant material is made accessible. I would consider as the most important precondition for a successful investigation of these problems the establishment of a very large collection of scores so that it would be possible to study and to compare all the symphonies by Wagenseil, Asplmayr, Hoffmann, Ordoñez, Schlöger, Vanhal, and other symphonies from this period at one library. The investigation of the problems of authenticity and especially of chronology must be further pursued hand in hand, and also the question of contacts between the individual composers, of their mutual connections and dependence, and at least of their dependence on the musical traditions of their locality and their time. Many loosely conceived contacts between composers of this period doubtlessly can be traced back to common stylistic tendencies determined by the times. The possibility of a connection must at least be rendered plausible before we may conclude a mutual influence from purely stylistic similarities.

With these last remarks we have approached the second previously cited problem, the problem of an insufficiently rich research tradition. There are several reasons for the fact that it has not been possible to develop a satisfactory research tradition. One of the most prominent is the just-mentioned primitive source situation. Also decisive is the special historical situation of research in music from about 1750. Understandably, musical research had begun the study of the old masters with an emphasis on the great figures. For the eighteenth century one had focussed on Bach and Handel on the one hand, and on Haydn, Mozart, and the young Beethoven on the other. From Bach one found predecessors such as Buxtehude and Vivaldi, but when one wished to go back before Haydn and Mozart one came upon Bach and Handel who were impossible to be regarded as precursors of Viennese Classicism. Obviously there is no progression here similar to the development from Buxtehude and Vivaldi to Bach. Two very different stylistic realms are confronted. The music-historical presentations of this period from the end of the past century seem to show that the problem of the transition from the Baroque to Classicism (or, as it was conceived then, from Bach to Haydn) could not be successfully solved. It was too readily assumed that this transition was mainly a straight-line development. It was seen actually as a search for the missing link, as we can see from Riemann's proclamation of his great "discovery"—Stamitz and the so-called Mannheim school—in the following manner: "Stamitz is the long-sought-for predecessor of Haydn."[4] He managed at the same time to give an invaluable impulse and to cause a long-lasting derailment of this side of musical research. Riemann's discovery of the Mannheim composers was the starting point of the investigation of the important "intermediate generation" with which we are primarily concerned here, too.

The challenge was taken up rather soon by the Adler school turning to the Viennese preclassical composers.[5] Without the two World Wars with all their material and intellectual consequences the urgent task of investigating this period would certainly have been continued much earlier. In a certain sense it may be felt as if we have to resume this research, which started right before World War I, with a fifty-year delay.

A few remarks on the problem of the Mannheim school may be needed. The innovation that the Mannheim school must mainly be given credit for is the promotion of orchestral performance, in particular the exploitation of dynamic effects. This actually was an Italian innovation that became a prominent feature in the music of the Mannheim composers, and certainly had a marked influence on the steady increase of the dynamic side to the music from Beethoven on. But they should not be regarded as a school of composers. After Stamitz, the only really important composer of this group, their style became clearly mannered. Within this narrow stylistic realm there was scarcely room for further development. Stamitz's innovations that Riemann wished to emphasize especially, such as the introduction of the four-movement symphony with minuet in the third place, and the establishment of a contrasting cantabile secondary theme, could only be regarded as decisively influential on the premise that the development of the classical symphonic style took place as an all-European endeavor based on a general communication. Riemann seems not to have been interested in the question, how much or how little of the Mannheim music was known in Vienna. Yet if one studies the sources of the Viennese preclassical history one must certainly gain the impression that there were very few connections between the Viennese music around 1750 and Mannheim or Paris. What was known in Vienna of Stamitz's music may primarily have dated back to direct connection between Vienna and Bohemia. It may have been brought in by the orchestras of the nobles who had their estates in Bohemia and their *Palais* in Vienna, and also by the great number of Czech musicians who had settled in Vienna.

In Haydn's case, of course, his employment at the estate of Count Morzin in Lukavec in summer 1759 must have given him some opportunity to become acquainted with Czech music. However, if we wish to establish Haydn's musical "roots," we must start with Vienna, where he received the decisive impressions of his youth. In spite of many valuable editions and studies in *DTÖ* and in separate editions, in dissertations, and monographs, nobody seriously could maintain that the problem of the decisive influences on his development has been solved.

In Pohl's classic Haydn biography we can read the rather naive remark: "Haydn forgot to tell us whether there had been models for his first symphony, and which ones they were: we must limit ourselves to listing a number of compositions of that kind cited in contemporary sources."[6] Then he quotes some composers such as Hoffmann, Tuma, Orsler, Ditters, Ordoñez, Ziegler, and Johann Christoph Mann. Yet he is satisfied with mentioning their names, and does not enter into a discussion of their music.

The Mannheim-Vienna controversy finally turned stronger attention to the Viennese preclassical generation. In 1908 a first selection of "Viennese Instrumental Music of the Eighteenth Century" appeared in *DTÖ*, followed by a second selection in 1912.[7] The first of these volumes comprised works by Georg v. Reutter, Wagenseil, George Matthias Monn (including a spurious symphony), Matthäus Schlöger, and Josef Starzer. The second volume was devoted almost exclusively—except for a divertimento by Johann Christoph Mann—to works by Georg Matthias Monn, who thus was featured as the main figure of the Viennese preclassicism. Valuable introductions accompanied these two volumes, wholly or in part based on Viennese dissertations (by Horwitz, Fischer, etc.).[8]

Another edition that may be mentioned in this connection is the edition of Reutter's masses,[9] which was prepared by P. Norbert Hofer for his dissertation of 1915, but which did not appear until 1952. A number of later publications—such as a volume of Dittersdorf's instrumental works (*DTÖ*, vol. 81), or the dissertation on Tuma by Herbert Vogg (1951)—contributed essentially to the broadening of our knowledge of Haydn's surroundings. Nevertheless, special studies aiming directly at a clarification of the evolution of the Viennese classical style, similar to the publications from the first two decades of this century, mentioned above, no longer came about.

My attempts here to outline the musical environment that the young Haydn proceeded from must remain sketchy since only a small part of the music is available in score. I have tried to provide a survey as far as possible within the means of a single scholar. A true investigation of these problems, however, must depend on much more extensive source collections and scorings that hopefully will be available one day.

Haydn's musical surroundings, the musical traditions that he was exposed to during his Viennese years of apprenticeship from the age of eight and for almost twenty years reflect the activities of three generations of composers. At the very beginning we find composers belonging to the late Baroque, born before the turn of the century, such as Fux, Caldara, Conti, and some minor figures (e.g., Porsile, Hintereder, etc.). Composers born in the first two decades of the eighteenth century include Tuma, Reutter, Bonno, Holzbauer, Gluck, Wagenseil, Monn, Birck, and some Italian composers whose music also was part of Haydn's musical surroundings, such as Galuppi and Jomelli. With composers born between 1720 and 1740, such as Schlöger, Starzer, Kohaut, Asplmayr, Gassmann, Leopold Hoffmann, Georg Orsler (junior), Ordoñez, and Vanhal, we come closer to Haydn's own generation.

One might suppose that Haydn had scarcely been part of the Fux-Caldara tradition, since with the death of its two most important representatives and of Emperor Karl VI (1740) the splendid era of Austrian Baroque music was over. But a large number of performance dates (in part from the archive of the Hofkapelle) proves that at least some compositions from the older masters were performed once or twice a year for many years. There is, for example, a symphony by Francesco Conti from the year 1722, published in Botstiber's history of the overture[10] in 1913 and cited by Wilhelm Fischer a couple of times as an example of a "preliminary stage" of the sonata form. Similarly, in an article for the Hungarian *Studia musicologica*[11] I quoted a sonata movement by Caldara as a typical example of the basic Baroque character of the music of this composer who died in 1736. Later I found, however, that the parts of both works were in the possession of the Hofmusikkapelle. The performance dates in these copies reveal that the Conti symphony was performed at least twice in 1748 and in 1749, and six times from 1750 to 1753. The Caldara sonata was played at least once in 1741, twice in 1742, and altogether ten times during the 1740s. Both compositions, therefore, probably belong to the group of works that were part of Haydn's musical surroundings, compositions such as he must have encountered over and over again through his duties as choir boy.

Of the generation of composers who took over the musical heritage after the deaths of Fux and Caldara, just at the time of Haydn's first Viennese impressions, Reutter must have been the first to influence Haydn. It might be rewarding to examine Haydn's relations to Reutter, especially with regard to his church music. Furthermore there are the composers who were active at the courts of Maria Theresia and of the emperor's widow, Elisabeth Christine—Tuma, Bonno, and Wagenseil being the most prominent—as well as Georg Matthias Monn, the less prominent organist at the Karlskirche, and Wenzel Raimund Birck, one of the court organists, who has not as yet been appropriately studied. Of the Italians of this generation whose compositions were also important for the development of Viennese Classicism, Galuppi (especially in the realm of opera), Jomelli, and—in spite of Haydn's occasional rejection—the Milanese G.B. Sammartini stand out.

All these composers must be regarded as Haydn's predecessors by birth, even if some of them in later years were active concurrently with Haydn, and possibly were influenced by him in return. Another group of composers must also be regarded as contemporaries of Haydn since they were born a little earlier or a little later than Haydn. In this group belong composers such as Schlöger, Starzer, Kohaut, Asplmayr, Gassmann, Leopold Hoffmann, Orsler (junior), Michael Haydn, and Vanhal. If and to what degree they may have influenced Haydn and Mozart is difficult to decide, since few of their works are known and easily accessible, and a chronological ordering of dates is mostly lacking. Further research is needed to try to uncover these connections, and to replace this sketchy survey of the sequence of generations around the young Haydn by a presentation based on thorough musical analyses and on a reliable chronological foundation.

If we want to clarify the problems of the style change—or perhaps more correctly, the style changes—in Viennese music around 1750, a grouping of the composers according to generations as attempted above suggests itself as a starting point for further investigations. An investigation, however, of the musical traditions, or again, of the changes of the musical traditions, from the time of Karl VI to the time of Josef II, or from the Fux–Caldara period to the Haydn–Mozart era may lead us to even more complex problems. The expression "musical traditions" is not used in its most comprehensive meaning of all musical activities, but rather is restricted to the traditions of characteristic genres, such as opera and cantata. And again I want to confine myself to sketching the changes of the traditions in the realm of instrumental music toward the end of the century, culminating in the symphony and the string quartet as Classical instrumental forms. Thus we shall disregard the similarly important traditions of mass composition, of opera and oratorio, and attempt to gain a better basis of comparison by the limitation to instrumental music alone.

Let me add still one more restriction. I shall not consider the certainly interesting, special tradition of the Viennese keyboard concerto, even if a rich selection of little-known works exists (e.g., in two volumes from the court music collection in the Österreichische Nationalbibliothek,[12] containing keyboard concertos and divertimenti by Wagenseil, Leopold Hoffmann, and others, or in the Kremsierer collection which contains fifty keyboard concertos by Wagenseil).

In being confined to the instrumental ensemble music we are confronted by a few yet rather different groups of works. To some degree these differences are connected with the Baroque division of music into church, chamber, and theater music. The first group is the group of the many sonatas, mostly trio sonatas, which actually must be regarded as *sonate da chiesa*. From the Hofkapelle there is a great number of such works by Fux, Caldara, and others, and some similar pieces by Tuma and others are at the library of the Gesellschaft der Musikfreunde. These "church sonatas" for the most part consist of only two movements, rather like prelude and fugue, or approximating the French overture. "Sonatas" that are actually two-movement excerpts from multi-movement compositions may be found too, such as the sonata by Caldara[13] mentioned earlier. During the following decades we can still find a great number of such sonatas continuing this tradition partly as true church music, partly as chamber music. Kirkendale gives a full account of this repertory.[14]

The second group of ensemble pieces is rooted in chamber sonata and suite, respectively, and consists in part of stylized dance movements. Here again we have to mention Tuma with a whole series of works entitled "partita" and with different numbers of movements. A great number of such partitas, especially for wind instruments, can be found in Czech libraries, as e.g., the large collection of partitas by Asplmayr in Prague mentioned earlier. Similar works are found by Bonno, Dittersdorf, Dušek, and others. The sequence and number of movements of such works varies. Sometimes we encounter the five-movement type with two minuets, as known from Haydn's early quartets and divertimenti, and I have asked myself at times whether here perhaps a Czech influence might assert itself. This could hint at a not too early dating of the quartets op. 1 and 2.

The third significant category of instrumental ensemble compositions, the symphony, is at the same time the most frequently discussed, and in their great variety, the most misunderstood group of works. This genre proceeded from the three-movement Italian opera symphony which also gave name to it. Focussing on the Italian opera symphony alone, however, does not help us to comprehend the complicated course of development of the Viennese symphony of about and after 1750. This would lead us to mistake the incorporation of the minuet as a fourth movement for an individual development, as did Riemann.

It is only possible to understand the development of the Viennese symphony of about 1750 if it is conceived as the synthesis of a number of individual genres of decisive influence on its formation, such as symphony, concerto, overture, partita and suite, *sonata da chiesa,* and intrada. The question is not when one or the other stylistic feature was introduced, or even "invented." Several lines of development occurred side by side and finally merged into each other. The image of the river that grows and becomes important only by the absorption of other rivers suggests itself.

It is not possible here to enter into details of this very complicated development. But I should like to point out some questions that will have to be answered before we can hope really to understand this development.

When we want to envisage the development leading to Haydn's symphonies, an obvious question suggests itself: when and where in Vienna were pieces composed that must be regarded as true concert symphonies in the new sense of the word? The title "symphony" cannot be regarded as real evidence. There are, for example, pieces by Vivaldi that are called symphonies, but cannot be regarded as symphonies as I have defined them here. Some compositions by Birck once gave me an amusing experience. They were located at the same library in two different copies, one as quartets and one as symphonies. Two excellent specialists had used them; one studied the quartet version, the other the symphonic version. But apparently, they did not notice that they were studying the same works. In many cases it is difficult to decide whether compositions called *"a quattro"* or *"a tre"* are chamber music or orchestral music: symphonies at an early stage.

At what time did one become aware of the symphony as an independent genre of special character? It was probably not least the activities of the Paris publishers from the mid-1750s on that helped the symphony come into fashion in all Europe. But Stamitz, who came to Mannheim in 1745 and who died as early as 1757, may well have learned about the symphony already in his home country before 1745, probably in connection with Italian symphonies. And George Matthias Monn who composed a short four-movement symphony as early as 1740, followed by a number of other symphonies until his death in 1750, is scarcely a completely isolated figure, either. Is his apparently exceptional position a result of his greater originality, or mainly due to the fact that, for once the fact of his early death assures that his symphonies must have been composed before 1750? Wagenseil's opera symphonies can be dated, and therefore we know that he wrote an Italianate symphony for an opera for Venice in 1745,[15] whereas his symphony of 1746, published in *DTÖ*[16] is much more marked by Austrian conservative traditions. It is difficult to state when he started to take up the chamber symphony as an individual genre. Many of his symphonies cannot be chronologically verified before the Breitkopf catalog of 1762. Yet it is likely that they were composed much earlier.

I have differentiated between the Austrian and the Italian tradition. Some might perhaps prefer to speak of the Baroque tradition and the "galant style." I believe, however, that it is more appropriate to conceive this development as a contrast, not between two successive, but between two simultaneous traditions. A similar juxtaposition of styles can be observed in Mozart's compositions of the early 1770s.

Into these Austrian traditions also mingle—besides the symphonic elements—concerto-like features (as for example in Caldara's overture of *Adriano nel Siria* [1732]), as well as elements from an old "Intrada" tradition, as in Reutter's *Servicio di Tavola* (1757)[17] (which in spite of its lacking the title "symphony" has been included among the predecessors of the symphony in *DTÖ*). A particularly characteristic contrast between old Austrian and Italian character is found in the quality of motion. This is reflected not least by the difference between a rather independent, individualized bass line, such as a "walking bass" or the like, and the prevalence of different types of rather stereotyped drum bass. These types of bass are poorly individualized melodically, but in return for that they confer upon the whole setting an impression of rhythmic forward drive that must be regarded as a new stylistic quality.

Where must we place Haydn within this scantily sketched development? At first we must ask again when Haydn started to compose symphonies. From an incidental list of his works sent to him by Breitkopf & Härtel in his late years the nonobligatory date of 1757 crept even into more recent literature of importance. However, I think there is no reason to doubt Haydn's exact indication to Griesinger stating that he had composed his first symphony in Lukavec in 1759. It is likely that he may have composed there one or two further symphonies—and perhaps had some contact with Czech music traditions—and that he composed some more symphonies in Vienna before he moved to Eisenstadt. To these may well belong primarily the ones which today are preserved in Budapest at the Széchenyi library and which stem from the Fürnberg collection.[18] In Eisenstadt he appears rather to have composed concertos first, turning to the regular composition of symphonies only after Prince Nikolaus's succession in 1762. This can be derived from the symphonies from the years 1763 to 1765 that are preserved in autograph.

Haydn's symphonies until about 1770 can be divided into distinct groups according to their form and style. A very characteristic group are the successors of the *sonata da chiesa* with a slow first movement (which does not equal a slow introduction!) and a fast second movement. This group comprises works from the earliest years (symphonies nos. 5 and 11) up to 1768 (No. 49). Another separate group are the three program symphonies nos. 6 to 8 from 1761. They resemble the Baroque *concerto grosso* to such a degree that they must be considered as a hybrid genre and not as regular symphonies. During the entire period though we find *concertante* movements—especially slow movements and trios—which, however, do not affect the overall structure of the respective works.

Apart from these two mentioned groups of symphonies there remain three to four rather different groups of "ordinary" symphonies. There is the distinct group of the three-movement type symphonies which clearly emerged from the opera symphony (nos. 1, 4, 10, etc. up to at latest 1765). Compared to the symphonies mentioned above these may well reveal some Italian features: yet if compared to Mozart's early symphonies they seem to be only a little Italianate. Among the four-movement symphonies there are some with suggestions of divertimento, and others with intrada character (above all the C-major symphonies with trumpets and timpani, such as nos. 20, 32, 38). Yet increasingly the less Italianate four-movement type of symphony (cf. nos. 3, 23, 29, etc.) becomes the main stream which absorbs all the other currents, merging them into an all-embracing synthesis.

Thus Haydn's symphonic production from his early years rather truly reflects those tendencies that we have pointed out as characteristic ones from the time before him. Shortly after 1765, however, a new tendency asserts itself which eventually has given rise to many considerations: Haydn's so-called Romantic crisis or his "Storm-and-Stress" period. What happened in Haydn's music in these years was doubtlessly of the utmost importance, and marks the decisive turning point within the evolution of Viennese Classicism. But I do not think that the cited clichés provide any essential or any correct information at all with regard to Haydn's music, even if they may give rise to some interesting contemplations. From my purely musical point of view this period first of all means the final synthesis of the currents that up to then had proceeded side by side. The following main points should be stressed: 1) After Werner's death (1766) Haydn takes up major church compositions such as the *Missa Sancti Josephi ("Grosse Orgelmesse")*, the *Stabat Mater*, and the *Applausus* (1766, 1767, 1768), which bring about an expansion and deepening of the musical expression; 2) Perhaps in this connection, or perhaps also with Haydn's inclination toward the strict style which may have been aroused by Gassmann's many quartets for the emperor, the following quartets and symphonies are distinguished by the enriching of the part-writing up to the employment of canon and fugue; 3) In some symphonies of this time—very markedly in the g-minor symphony no. 39 (probably 1768–69)—two characteristic features stand out: the new emphasis of transitional, strong tonal contrasts by the choice of a minor key for a symphony, and a new rhythmic quality which may perhaps be described as a moving-up of the rhythmic impulse of the drum bass from the Italianate symphonies into the upper parts, and consequently covering the entire texture; and 4) An extension of the periodic structure through the expanded harmonic foundation and a "modernized" use of Baroque *Fortspinnung* asserts itself more and more.

I have to content myself here with these suggestions, and should only like to try briefly to summarize what I think can be concluded about the style change around 1750. As the first and maybe most important conclusion I should like to stress that this style change was probably much less "dramatic" than is often assumed. There is no sudden shift from, say, Bach's *Art of Fugue* to Haydn's early quartets, but a step-wise process with occasional stronger concentrations. Two essential features can be noticed in particular: the synthesis or the fusion of long-lasting traditions, and the moderate, unconspicuous progression of the development. The early Viennese composers lack the aspect of "sensation" which has been attributed to the Mannheim school. It certainly is possible to sense some stages in this development as reflected in the works of the three generation-groups: the initial prevalence of Baroque traditions, followed by a more relaxed and polished divertimento style, which finally gives way to the breaking through of the Classical style yielded by Haydn's stylistic synthesis about 1770. Yet I believe that this development must be regarded less as a succession than as a coexistence of these stylistic traditions. Even after his synthesis of the styles which soon was adopted by Mozart, Haydn did not deny his roots in the Austrian Baroque throughout his life, just as Mozart did not deny the Italian buffo tradition.

Whenever I travel—coming from the North—via Regensburg and Passau to Austria, I often sense already in Bavaria more the atmosphere of Vienna than that of Hamburg. And similarly I might like to ask whether maybe the distance between a Fux sonata and a Haydn quartet in any way is shorter than the distance between Fux and Bach? This is only meant to stand as a concluding question. To answer this question we shall need the joint efforts of musicians and musicologists rather than just a theoretical investigation of stylistic conceptions that only can be relevant with regard to music if they are derived from musical experience itself. But sometimes I have almost the feeling that musicians today may tend to appropriate musicological "historizing" in the negative sense of the word. We need a mutual control—and a self-control—with regard to our perception of these problems.

Notes

1. *Musik in Geschichte und Gegenwart* 14: col. 71.

2. *Denkmäler der Tonkunst in Oesterreich* XV/2 (1908).

3. *IMS report of the Tenth Congress, Ljubljana 1967* (1970).

4. *Denkmäler der Tonkunst in Bayern* III: foreword.

5. *Denkmäler der Tonkunst in Oesterreich,* XV/ 2 (1908), and XIX/2 (1912).

6. C.F. Pohl, *Joseph Haydn,* vol. 1 (1875): p. 280.

7. See note 5.

8. Allow me to note here in passing that in the 1930s a continuation of these volumes was planned. I had several discussions with Guido Adler about the two volumes that I would edit together with Karl August Rosenthal, which would include above all symphonies of Wagenseil and quartets of Gassmann. World War II thwarted these, as well as so many other, plans.

9. *Denkmäler der Tonkunst in Oesterreich* 88 (1952).

10. H. Botstiber, *Geschichte der Ouverture* (1913), music supplement, p. 250ff.

11. "Some Observations on the Development and Characteristics of Vienna Classical Instrumental Music," *Studia Musicologica* (1967), p. 124f. Also reprinted in this volume.

12. S.m. 3348 and S.m. 11084.

13. W. Kirkendale, *Fuge und Fugato in der Kammermusik des Rokoko und der Klassik* (1966).

14. "Ariodante," Nationalbibliothek Vienna, 18.019.

15. *Denkmäler der Tonkunst in Oesterreich* XV/2: 1ff.

16. Compare in this regard: *Haydns Werke in der Musiksammlung der Nationalbibliothek Széchenyi in Budapest* (1959), p. 103ff.

25

Concerning the Development
of the Austrian Symphonic Tradition
(*circa* 1750–1775)

For about two centuries the symphony has been ranked first among the instrumental genres. Haydn, Mozart, Beethoven, Brahms, Bruckner, and many others
composed symphonies, thereby retaining and continuing an unbroken tradition.
This tradition, however, also established a conception of the nature of the symphony that rather one-sidedly regarded the symphony of the nineteenth century
or, more precisely, Beethoven's and the post-Beethoven symphony, as a point of
departure and a paradigm for any consideration of this genre. In more recent
times, this conception may apply, because every symphony composed after
Beethoven directly or indirectly, on a larger or smaller scale, is indebted to him.
However, for a consideration of the development of the symphony before Beethoven, it cannot be correct to proceed from the post-Beethoven tradition. Nevertheless, this has been common practice. More recently it has been recognized, in
principle, that a less one-sided conception is necessary, that we should not ask: to
what degree do the traditional standards of the post-Beethoven symphony apply
here but rather: which are the norms that apply here? What kind of development
occurs here? In practice, however, the old biases are still largely in effect.

When, at the beginning of this century, the question of the influence of the
so-called Mannheim school as precursors of the Viennese Classical composers
was discussed with much vigor, two specific questions were brought up: 1) the
question of three- or four-movement cycles; and 2) the question of whether a
secondary subject was present. Three movements and the lack of a secondary
subject were criteria of an "archaic" character; a four-movement cycle and a
manifest secondary subject were indications of "innovative tendencies." Today it
should be quite evident that a conception of this kind means an over-simplifica-
tion. Nevertheless, the "common knowledge" of the development of the early

Originally published in German in the *Haydn Yearbook 10* (1978), 72–80.

symphony is to a large extent still determined by such a conception. If we wish to avoid perpetuating these deeply rooted prejudices, we should accept as fact as few of these as possible. We must attempt to make accessible more extensive source material and a more extensive formulation of the question. And we have to proceed from concepts and standards that are relevant to our problem.

At the beginning of our discussion lies the question of the conception of the symphony. If we want to avoid applying the nineteenth-century conception of the symphony to the development of this genre around 1750, then it will be our obligation to specify the standards that we can utilize. Let us try first to name some of the characteristic features of the later symphony that we cannot take for granted with regard to the earlier symphonies. The symphony of the nineteenth century was designed as a major orchestral composition with large-scale movements of individual and contrasting characters of expression. The single movement is composed of widely expanded periods that either are of thematic structure—to a large degree thematic dualism is a prime constructive element—or elaborate motives and themes more freely worked out, especially in the development of sections of sonata or rondo forms. The three sections of the sonata form—exposition, development section, recapitulation (frequently expanded by a coda)—are obligatory, as are the four movements.

The symphony from around and shortly after 1750 was not conceived primarily as an orchestral composition. Even the Mannheim symphonies (which more than any others might appear to be conceived as such) are not really the product of an overall orchestral conception, but rather they are equipped with orchestral effects that understandably stirred up some sensation as a result of their novelty. In general, however, there exists no fundamental difference between symphonic and chamber style with regard to texture and melody. The movements of the early symphony are much shorter and are based on thematic contrast to a lesser degree—often not at all—than are movements of later symphonies. The three sections (exposition, development, recapitulation) mostly are present, yet in place of a proper development often a modulatory middle section is present, and a proper coda does not belong among the usual formal elements. Before discussing the pieces themselves I should like to throw some light on the emergence of the symphony as a central form of music-making about 1750.

Long before 1750 symphonies had been composed as instrumental introductions and interludes in operas and other major works. Here, however, we are concerned with the symphony composed independently as a concert piece or at least used as such. While the establishment of the symphony as an independent instrumental composition certainly took place during the years around 1750, it is not easy to give exact dates for this development. However, a few suggestions can be presented.

Some impetus toward this innovation certainly came from Italy. Out of the long tradition of the opera symphony, a new concert symphony tradition developed in the years up to 1750. G.B. Sammartini seems to be the most outstanding representative of this new tradition. His symphonies are documented as early as in the 1730s; and quite a number of them are still extant from the first half of the 1740s. The flourishing of the tradition of the concert symphony, however, seems to have set in fully only in the 1750s. Here, Paris played a leading role, not only with respect to performances and the great number of French symphonists, but also and especially as a center of music publishing. The French publishers' catalogs from these years, which are so important for musical research, clearly document the degree to which the new symphony (which played no significant role before 1750), appears more and more as a leading musical genre.[1] From Germany are known in particular the thematic sales catalogs of the Leipzig publisher Breitkopf.[2] They started as late as in 1762, yet the 1762 catalog alone contains so many symphonies that a tradition must obviously have been established for quite a while.

When, then, did the new tradition of the concert symphony start to establish itself in Austria? To give an exact answer to this question is not easy, for in general only the operatic symphonies (and not the concert symphonies) are dated. The most prominent representative of the early symphony is Georg Christoph Wagenseil. From him we have an extensive series of symphonies for operas and oratorios (overtures), including works from *I lamenti d'Orfeo* (1740) to *Le cacciatrici amante* (1755) and *Il roveto di Mosè* (1756), as well as a series of symphonies in Paris editions, especially from the years ca. 1755 to 1760. Furthermore, a great number of symphonies are also extant in manuscripts in many libraries, all of which are included in Helga Scholz-Michelitsch's thematic catalog.[3] The first Breitkopf catalog of 1762 already lists eighteen Wagenseil symphonies. It is impossible to arrive at a clear distinction between concert symphonies and opera or oratorio symphonies, for many of the latter appear as independent instrumental compositions at a later time. The same is true with regard to symphonies and trios. In Wagenseil's symphonic style the instrumental, chamber music character prevails, and not the operatic character. A close examination of Wagenseil's symphonies may enable us to gain a clearer conception of the development of the concert symphony in Vienna.

The Mannheim-Vienna controversy at the beginning of the century that led to the publication of the two volumes of the "Viennese preclassics" (*DTÖ* XV, 2 (1908) and XIX, 2 (1915)) brought Georg Matthias Monn to the fore. This was related to the fact that there existed a symphony by him dated 1740, with a minuet as the third movement within a rather primitive four-movement cycle. His early death in 1750 suggested the development of the Viennese symphony as early as in the 1740s. (The fact that Monn, like Stamitz, was born in 1717 gave rise to Riemann's rather nasty remark that he could only be compared to Stamitz with regard to his year of birth!) However, there are actually two Monns: George Matthias Monn and Johann Christian Monn (or Mann). Fischer, in his thematic catalog of both Monns, attributed all the symphonies to G.M. Monn, although barely half of them expressly indicate G.M. Monn or M.G. Monn as composer (the remaining ones are designated "Monn" or "Mann" only). But in a correspondence from Vienna, printed in 1766 in Hiller's *Wöchentliche Nachrichten,* we are told that J.C. Monn, too, composed symphonies. In addition to Haydn, the report refers to Leopold and Anton Hofmann, Franz Tuma, Georg Orsler, Karl Ditters, Carlos Ordoñez, Joseph Ziegler, and Johann Christoph Monn as composers of symphonies. Therefore, a thorough investigation of the symphonies would be desirable with regard to Monn as well. First of all, a distinction between the symphonies of the two Monns is needed, as is a dating of the symphonies, as far as is possible.

Ignaz Holzbauer is also among the composers who must undoubtedly count as founders of the Viennese symphonic tradition. From 1753 on, he was a member of the Mannheim orchestra, and for this reason he is mostly regarded as belonging to the Mannheim school. Up to 1750, however, he was active in his native country, Austria. A large number of presumably rather early symphonies from his hand are still extant. A symphony in d minor (*Gesellschaft der Musikfreunde* IX: 23365) contains dates of performances from 1749 on; the symphony, however, leaves a rather Baroque impression. The symphonies that point to the newly emerging symphonic tradition cannot, according to my provisional statements, be traced further back than about 1760. A large number of these symphonies, which have no stylistic similarity to the Mannheim symphony whatsoever but which can be very well related to the Austrian tradition about 1760, can be found in the music collections and catalogs of Austrian convents such as Göttweig and Kremsmünster. Whether they can be dated back to the years before 1750, the year when Holzbauer left Vienna, may be questioned. It is perhaps more likely that Holzbauer maintained some connections to Vienna, and—commissioned by Austrians—wrote symphonies that had nothing in common with the specific Mannheim traditions. Here again is an interesting challenge: to clarify Holzbauer's position in between two different traditions, and also to try to resolve the chronological problems.

More recently the much younger Carlos Ordoñez, born in 1734, has surprisingly been included among the pioneers of the Viennese symphony. This, however, does not seem quite justified. Together with the above-mentioned composers and some other contemporaries of Haydn like Asplmayr, Hofmann, and Vanhal, he belonged to the milieu but was hardly among the pioneers of the symphonic tradition crowned by Haydn and Mozart, even if he had contributed to the symphonic wave a couple of years before Haydn. Of the slightly older contemporaries of Haydn who may have had some influence on him during his years of apprenticeship in Vienna—besides Wagenseil, Holzbauer, and Monn—composers such as Reutter, Tuma, Birkh, and Schlöger seem to deserve special consideration.

Around 1760 the symphony was clearly becoming established, as we can see from some catalogs of music collections of that time. In 1759 Prince Paul Anton Esterházy in Eisenstadt had a nonthematic catalog compiled. The symphonies are listed under the heading *"Musique Instrumentale Italienne"* and under the subheading *"Sinfonies à plusieures instruments."* The symphonies entered first are mostly by Italian composers with the exception of Hasse and Gluck, but in the sequel we also find names such as Stamitz (two times), Ziegler (6 symphonies), Holzbauer, Wagenseil (5 times), Orsler, Ordoñez, Ditters (10 symphonies), and Haydn. All these entries are from 1759 and 1760. The catalog of the music collection of Count von Egk (who as Prince Bishop of Olmütz reigned from 1758 to 1760) dates from exactly the same time.[4] This catalog starts with a series of symphonies labelled "brought along from Vienna." This first series was entered in 1759 and includes works by Holzbauer (4), Schlöger (6), Körzl (5), Haydn (Symphony No. 1), Wagenseil, Hofmann (2), and Sammartini. A long sequence of symphonies by the local composer Neumann is followed by a new series, dated 1760. Here the Viennese composers are less predominant. Two symphonies are by Hofmann, and another two by (Leopold) Mozart, an additional six by (Le) Roy, and one each by Brivio, Sciroli, and Engelbert. After more symphonies by Neumann follow symphonies by Holzbauer (5), Wagenseil (9), Steffan (2), Ziegler (2), Ordoñez, Stamitz (Steinmetz) (3), Sammartini (6), and others. And finally there is the famous Göttweig catalog, compiled later, but in most cases giving the dates of acquisition. From the years before and around 1760 it lists symphonies by Ditters, Hasse, Haydn (from 1762 on), Michael Haydn, Hofmann, Holzbauer, Körzel, Monn (without initials), Ordoñez (1 symphony as early as 1756), Le Roy, Sonnleitner, Umstatt, Wagenseil (from 1756 on; up to 1761 11 entries), Zechner (1756), and Ziegler (from 1760 on). During the 1760s many additional names and symphonies were added. A special feature of the designation of the works should be mentioned. The heading of the group in question is not simply "symphonies," but *"Symphoniae et Parthiae,"* and the heading of the following is *"Cassatio, Divertimento et Quadro."* Accordingly, symphonies and partitas *(Parthiae)* are entered beside each other. A clear distinction between them is not possible.

Here we face another problem of the symphony that can only be touched upon briefly: its evolution, not from a single genre but from a synthesis of several genres both related to and different from one another.

Let me use a familiar image: the relation of a major river and the smaller tributary streams that it absorbs. If you want to describe, e.g., the Danube, you may of course be content with a description of only the main stream from its source to its estuary in the Black Sea. But shortly before and in Passau,—to mention only one instance—it absorbs two major tributary streams, and from this moment on its water is not only Danube water, but Danube-Isar-Inn water (although nobody would normally describe it that way).

I think the development of the symphony is a similar case. In describing the development of the symphony, it is too one-sided to consider only those works that were expressly designated "symphonies." But there is quite a number of different genres which contributed, more or less, to working out the problems of musical form in a similar fashion as the symphony even though they had different names. Without this pioneering work it would hardly have been possible to turn the new concert-symphony into one of the most important genres of all time within such a short period. This synthesis drew upon many genres: overture, opera symphony, partita or *parthia,* concerto, sonata, trio, etc., each contributing to the birth of the new symphony in many different ways. The symphony did not simply supersede these genres. They were transformed; they merged into the new synthetic form. How that happened can only be intimated here. Three aspects of this change would need special discussion: 1) the cyclic overall structure; 2) the various kinds of period formation; and 3) the different types of musical settings.

As stressed above, earlier research had been contented with the description of the development of the symphony as a simple expansion of the cycle from three into four movements by the addition of a minuet as third movement. This was only possible while it was overlooked that the classical symphony did not simply emerge from the three-movement opera symphony. A survey of the wide field of preclassical pioneering forms exhibits a much more diversified form potential. The traditional *sonata à 3* in most cases shows either the complete four-movement cycle of the *sonata da chiesa* (slow—fast—slow—fast), or an excerpt from it, such as the particularly characteristic two-movement series in the manner of prelude and fugue. This form occurs in many trios by Fux that were still frequently performed in the 1740s during church services. There are also sonatas *à 4* in these forms from about the same time. Another very characteristic genre is the sonatas for strings and winds. These pieces approach the realm of the concerto and even of the opera symphony or introduction, and point directly to the *intrada symphonies* of Haydn's early years. The *Nationalbibliothek* in Vienna holds two C-major sonatas of this kind by Caldara (S.m. 3616 and 1617). Both consist of three movements, but the overall structure is different: Allegro—Largo—Fuga/Allegro versus Allegro—Andante—Allegro da capo. There is further a two-movement sonata of this kind by Birkh (S.m. 3614), also in the key of C major, dated 1738. There are some similar compositions in C major by Reutter in the *Gesellschaft der Musikfreunde,* which although lacking the title "*sonata,*" continue this tradition and directly point forward to the *intrada symphonies:* one is headed "*Intrada*" (XIII 8435), and two others are entitled "*Servizio di Tavola*" (XIII 8093, and XIII 2826, dated 1745 and 1757, respectively. The latter, published in *DTÖ* is available on record.) There are still two C-major symphonies with trumpets *(clarini)* and timpani, one of which (XIII 8577) has a number of performing dates referring to 1744 (?) and 1746–53. (By the way, the *Intrada* and the *Servizio di Tavola* of 1745 were performed again about 1770 in St. Stephan's Cathedral.)

A rather diverse genre is the so-called *Parthia* (or *Partit(t)a*) which continues along the lines of the *sonata da camera*. There is a large number of three-part partitas by Franz Tuma in the *Gesellschaft der Musikfreunde*. They have mostly four or five movements and are clearly reminiscent of the suite. Almost all of them have a minuet with trio. There are series such as Allegro—Sarabande—Minuet/Trio—Allegro or Intrada—Minuet—Sarabande—Minuet/Trio—Capriccio, but also such as Overture/Allegro/Grave/Allegro da capo—Allegro—Minuet—Allegro, reminiscent of the "Overture-Suite." A form similar to the *sonata da chiesa* may occur, too, such as Largo—Vivace—Minuet/Trio—Allegro. From here it is only a small step to some *parthias* that already reflect the movement order of the modern symphony: Allegro-Andante—Minuet/Trio—Allegro. The *parthia* may comprise up to six movements, for example in the following order: Andante—Allegro assai—Largo—Allegro—Andante—Minuet/Trio. A comprehensive collection of seventeen three-part *parthias* by Birkh (IX 31817) is found, too, in the *Gesellschaft der Musikfreunde*. (They are only entitled *"à 3"*, but two of the pieces occur in separate copies, labelled *"parthia."*) These works incorporate traits of the overture-suite with those of ballet or comedy music. Ten of the seventeen *parthias* combine a slow introduction with a fast *fuga* or a *fugato,* in some instances resembling the overture, in others the *sonata da chiesa;* these two movements (or a combination of three to four sections of movements) are followed by a minuet and a finale, or in some cases, by a series of three movements. Furthermore, there is a collection of sixteen quartets by Birkh at the *Nationalbibliothek* in Vienna (S.m. 11732 to 11741), and two collections of symphonies *à 4* (S.m. 3610 and 3611) containing the same set of pieces in addition to another three symphonies. Of these nineteen quartet-symphonies, eight consist of four movements, ten of three, and one of two movements. Again they incorporate traits of the *sonata da chiesa* with those of the *sonata da camera* or *parthia*. There are some three to four movement cycles with fugue movements and others that must be regarded as ordinary three or four movement symphonies. Similarly, there are a number of works by Ignaz Holzbauer that are designated as both quartet and symphony, or at once as symphony and *parthia*. An account of the development of the Viennese classical symphony that disregards this comprehensive list of pioneering works necessarily must fail to give a true picture of the genesis of the symphonic tradition.

In the late 1750s Joseph Haydn rather tardily starts to compose symphonies. Yet in the course of the following years he establishes a symphonic tradition which initially proceeds from the variety of precursory forms outlined above, but which more and more is determined by Haydn's own individuality and originality. Any attempt to describe Haydn's development as a symphony composer will soon meet a well-known problem: the chronology of the works is still to some extent problematic. A dated autograph exists for only twenty-five of the sixty to sixty-five symphonies composed up to about 1775. Another ten to fifteen can be dated approximately on grounds of entries in Haydn's *Entwurfkatalog*, or in relation to other compositions, etc. The remnant of twenty to twenty-five symphonies, however, can often only be dated rather imprecisely, (e.g., "before 1763" or so).

Until recently, it was considered a fact that Haydn composed his first symphony in 1759 for Count Morzin in Lukavec. This assumption was based on Griesinger who, in his Haydn biography, quotes the theme of this alleged earliest symphony (which from Mandyczewski on was considered as No. 1). Nevertheless, in his later years Haydn compiled a list of his symphonies for Breitkopf & Härtel, arranged according to decades, starting with the decade from 1757 to 1767. Since this list was made much later one should not attach too much importance to it. Some years ago, however, a copy of Symphony No. 37 came to light, dated 1757. Even if this dating is not authentic, it was apparently entered early. Therefore it is possible, maybe even likely, that Haydn composed symphonies as early as about 1757. (That he had available the necessary basis for writing symphonies may be inferred from his organ concerto in C major, dated 1756.) It may seem surprising that his symphonies are so sparingly represented in the above-mentioned catalogs from around 1760. The Egk catalog lists only one symphony by Haydn, our no. 1, among the symphonies brought along from Vienna in 1759. The early Esterházy catalog also lists but one symphony (without theme) among the works entered in 1760. The Göttweig catalog does not enter any Haydn symphonies until 1762, but quickly makes up for it during the following years.

New evidence of a not quite negligible activity of Haydn as composer of symphonies before his employment as Esterházy Kapellmeister in 1761 turned up in a collection of manuscripts formerly belonging to a member of the Fürnberg family. This only became known to the scholarly world as late as 1959, when the catalog of the Haydn works at the Széchényi library in Budapest was published. This collection contains a rather large number of the undated early symphonies, and probably no single symphony composed after 1761. It suggests that all these symphonies can be traced back to the pre-Eisenstadt years, regardless of whether one conjectures with Landon that they all had been composed for Count Morzin, or whether one holds to the more general assumption that they were intended partly for Morzin, partly for other Viennese customers during the years of 1757 or 1759 to 1761. (We still do not have any evidence of how long Haydn was actually employed by Count Morzin, nor of the extent of his activities in Lukavec and in Vienna.) Stylistically, all these symphonies certainly point toward an early stage of Haydn's symphonic development.

If one surveys these symphonies (nos. 1, 4, 5, 10, 11, 15, 18, 27, 32, 33, and 37) in addition to a few others which presumably had been composed before or about 1760 (Landon's "A" and "B", as well as nos. 2, 3, 14, 16, 17, 19, 20, 25), Haydn's continuation of the tradition from about 1750 outlined above must seem quite obvious. Though he established the five-movement cycle fast—minuet/trio—slow—minuet/trio—fast as the standard form of his early string quartets, and although he made almost exclusive use of a variable three-movement cycle in his string and baryton trios, he did not proceed from a fixed symphonic type, but rather experimented with a variety of formal possibilities.

In examining the cyclic arrangement of Haydn's early symphonies we can immediately distinguish three groups: the cycle resembling the church sonata (slow—fast—minuet/trio—fast), the three-movement cycle (fast—slow—fast), and the four-movement cycle (fast—slow—minuet/trio—fast). The first group, the "church-sonata symphonies," includes the two symphonies nos. 5 and 11, and the three-movement symphony no. 18 (slow—fast—*Tempo di Menuett*). This continuation of the *sonata da chiesa* does not cease with the earliest works but has an aftermath in symphonies of 1764 (nos. 21, 22) and 1768 (no. 49). Of the three-movement symphonies we can sort out a number of works that emerged from the "chamber symphony" which again was derived from the opera symphony (nos. 1, 4, 10, 17, 19, 27). In one instance we find a successor to the *parthia* (no. 16). In the four-movement symphony the influence of the *parthia* tradition is even more evident (nos. 3, 14, 23, 28). This confrontation of symphony (or *sinfonia*) and *parthia* does not refer to the cyclic arrangement but to style and texture. The symphonies representing the first category are characterized more by an extroverted, playful style, whereas those of the second are more or less determined by an introverted, linear-contrapuntal style and often with a feature like the typical Baroque "walking bass." On the whole, these works are of a more unified character with regard to motion.

Among the four-movement symphonies we must distinguish a special group: the early C-major symphonies which must be regarded as a continuation of the intrada tradition (nos. 20, 32, 33, 37). Here the sound effect is predominant: the reinforcement of the orchestra by trumpets and timpani. This, too, is an old Viennese tradition. If you go through the old *"Wiener Diarium"* in order to gain some information on musical performances in the eighteenth century, you will meet many occasions that were celebrated with a "festive music with trumpets and timpani."

Another special group which must be set apart from Haydn's early—but scarcely the earliest—symphonies are the symphonies that in one way or the other are determined by concert traditions. Presumably they can be traced back to no later than the Esterházy years, starting with the three unique "daytime" symphonies (nos. 6 to 8), and continuing through the symphonies with *concertato* elements, mostly in the slow movement or in the trio, but occasionally in the finale, too (nos. 13, 24, 31, 36).

We will now summarize Haydn's use of these different types of symphony:

Haydn ceased to compose symphonies of the three-movement chamber type very early, maybe even before 1761 when he entered on his employment as *Kapellmeister* at Esterházy. The church sonata symphonies occupied Haydn's interest a little longer, up to 1764 and in one case up to 1768. The intrada symphonies mentioned above must be regarded as very early compositions. However, the aftermath of this group can be felt throughout Haydn's symphonic oeuvre in characteristic and significant C-major symphonies, such as nos. 56, 82 *("L'ours")*, and 97. As far as I can see, the foundation of Haydn's symphonic development—the main stream, to refer to the image used earlier—remains the parthia-symphony which during its further development was undoubtedly also influenced by other forms in addition to those mentioned here.

As stated above I should have liked to include problems of the formation of periods and problems of the musical setting in this discussion of the development of Haydn's symphonic tradition, but time is too short for a satisfactory discussion of these problems too. Let me just briefly outline the views I would take.

Most analyses of eighteenth-century music are still largely determined by conceptions based on textbooks of music theory from the post-Beethoven period. The most independent attempt to be rid of these standards and to derive relevant standards from the music itself appears still to be Wilhelm Fischer's sixty-year-old study "Zur Entwicklungsgeschichte des Wiener klassischen Stils" (1915). Its implications have in my opinion never been fully explored. In order to approach Haydn's formal procedures with regard to period structure, etc. one should not rely on modern textbook conceptions. Also, one should avoid applying theories of form from the eighteenth century without a close examination, for all too often they turn out to be overly speculative. One should, rather, proceed from the formal traditions of the contemporary genres, such as sonata, fugue, parthia, concerto, and sinfonia: the ritornello structure of aria and concerto, the "motto principle" *("Devisenprinzip")* in the aria, *Fortspinnung* in linear-contrapuntal compositions and in the concerto, *Reihung, Fortspinnung,* and expansion and development in suite and sonata movements. I believe we can only arrive at a satisfactory analysis and description of the formal procedures in pre- and early Classical music by a new and decidedly historic orientation within this realm. I have dwelled at some length on the problems of the so-called sonata form in another article,[5] and I may perhaps refer to it.

I have mentioned the problem of musical style and texture in connection with the distinction between symphony and parthia. In order to understand the important change in Haydn's development around 1770—which, unfortunately, still is burdened with the cliché-like label "storm and stress"—, one necessarily must turn to changes related to motion (no. 39) and to the expansion of harmonic possibilities. Much remains to be said concerning the genesis of Haydn's personal style—through the merging of tendencies that accentuate sound (*intrada* tradition), linear-contrapuntal elements (church sonata and *parthia* tradition), and playful characteristics (symphonic style) with elements of concerto traditions, etc.,—and (last but not least) concerning those individual features of Haydn's works that lead to the mature Classical style.

With these considerations I have attempted to point out—and I hope I have to some extent succeeded in doing so in spite of their limitations—how closely the development of the Viennese Classical symphony as initiated by Haydn was related to Austrian traditions. As opposed to Mozart (who was able to base his individual development on an international style by appropriating stimuli from all Europe), Haydn adapted a tradition that was rooted in the Austrian Baroque of Fux and Caldara, and that was developed further by the composers of the intermediary generation about 1750—Wagenseil, the two Monns, Holzbauer, Tuma, Birkh, Schlöger, etc. His genius transformed this tradition into a Viennese Classical tradition of international significance. This deed had been carried out in the years up to ca. 1775. From approximately 1780 on, Haydn and Mozart together brought this Viennese Classical tradition to its consummation.

Notes

1. Jens Peter Larsen, "Der musikalische Stilwandel um 1750 im Spiegel der zeitgenössischen Pariser Verlagskataloge," *Musik und Verlag: Festschrift Karl Vötterle* (Kassel, 1968).

2. *The Breitkopf Thematic Catalogue 1762–1787*, ed. by Barry S. Brook (Dover Publications, 1966).

3. Helga Scholz-Michelitsch, *Das Orchester- und Kammermusikwerk von Georg Christoph Wagenseil* (Vienna, 1972).

4. See Jiří Schnal, *Kapela Olomouckeho Biskupa Leopolda Egka (1758–1760), A její* Repertoár (Acta Muse Moraviae, 1965).

5. Jens Peter Larsen, "Sonatenformprobleme," *Festschrift F. Blume* (Kassel, 1963). Reprinted in translation in this volume.

Index